P9-DCP-332

WOMEN AND SPORTS IN THE UNITED STATES

WOMEN and SPORTS
in the United States

A DOCUMENTARY READER

Jean O'Reilly and Susan K. Cahn, editors

Northeastern University Press
Boston

PUBLISHED BY UNIVERSITY PRESS OF NEW ENGLAND
HANOVER AND LONDON

Northeastern University Press
Published by University Press of New England,
One Court Street, Lebanon, NH 03766
www.upne.com
© 2007 by Northeastern University Press
Printed in the United States of America
5 4 3 2 1

All rights reserved. No part of this book may be reproduced in any form or by any electronic or mechanical means, including storage and retrieval systems, without permission in writing from the publisher, except by a reviewer, who may quote brief passages in a review. Members of educational institutions and organizations wishing to photocopy any of the work for classroom use, or authors and publishers who would like to obtain permission for any of the material in the work, should contact Permissions, University Press of New England, One Court Street, Lebanon, NH 03766.

This book was published with the generous support of the Center for the Study of Sport in Society, Northeastern University.

Library of Congress Cataloging-in-Publication Data
Women and sports in the United States : a documentary reader /
Jean O'Reilly and Susan K. Cahn, editors.
     p.   cm.
Includes index.
ISBN-13: 978–1-55553–671–8 (pbk. : alk. paper)
ISBN-10: 1–55553–671–9 (pbk. : alk. paper)
1. Sports for women—United States.
2. Women athletes—United States.
I. O'Reilly, Jean.
II. Cahn, Susan K.
GV709.18.U6074 2007
796.082—dc22   2006031291

CONTENTS

Part III
Competing Bodies: Physiological, Biological, and Psychological Issues

Part VI
The Feminine Image in Sports and Sports Media

Part VII
Law and Equity: Title IX and Its Aftermath

ACKNOWLEDGMENTS

This book would not have come into being without the assistance of a large number of people and institutions. Our highly capable editor, Phyllis Deutsch, and her staff at the University Press of New England have been tremendously helpful and supportive over the years in which this project took shape, as have the staffs of the Department of English and Homer D. Babbidge Library, University of Connecticut (especially Richard Bleiler). We are grateful for the work of Katrina Sinclair as a research assistant and for the financial help provided by the University at Buffalo's College of Arts and Sciences Subvention Fund. We also want to thank the Center for the Study of Sport in Society at Northeastern University for its sponsorship of the book. Our friends and colleagues—Deborah Gardiner, Nicolaas Geenen, Abigail Gillard, Pamela Grundy, Ian and Natasha Jentle, Donald Levy, John Manning, Patrick McDevitt, Brian and Patricia O'Reilly, Sydney and Terry Plum, Don Sabo, Mary Turco, Jacqueline Wood, and many others—have been most generous in their advice, and this anthology is better for their suggestions.

We offer this book as a gesture of our deepest gratitude to Shane and Barbara O'Reilly, and to Tandy Hamilton, whose mid-life athletic blossoming serves as a reminder of why sports matter in women's lives.

INTRODUCTION

In the 1960s a typical women's intercollegiate basketball game would have occurred on a rare "playday" in which students, ordinarily limited to intramural competitions on their own campus, came together for a single competitive game between schools. Such events took place in a congenial atmosphere in which sports(wo)manship and sociability held equal weight with winning and losing. There were no records kept, set, or broken because statistics did not matter. What mattered was playing the game and extending that opportunity to as many players as possible. The teams played by the old half-court rules and each team's players wore the same color pinnies, garments made of front and back rectangular panels, hung over the shoulders by thin straps and tied into place by additional straps at the sides. Gym teachers coached the teams, spectators were kept to a minimum, and after the game all players met for snacks and refreshments before returning home.

This format of intramural women's sports with the occasional playday developed out of two factors: almost complete disregard for girls and women's sports in the larger male-dominated sports world coupled with a firmly held philosophy among female physical educators that highly competitive sport damaged the few skilled female athletes while neglecting the many, whereas higher participation rates in less competitive events benefited all. As a result, with anomalous exceptions like the quadrennial Olympic Games and fan-crazy Iowa girls' basketball, women's sports operated in most settings, from recreational to school leagues to colleges, entirely under the radar screen of big-time sports.

Today, across the country sold out basketball games at universities like Connecticut, Tennessee, and Stanford attract thousands of spectators to watch teams of nationally and internationally recruited athletes whose four years of college are paid for by athletic scholarships. Team budgets include formerly unthinkable expenditures for air travel, hotels, meals, uniforms, shoes, and salaries for multiple coaches. Moreover, today's budgets consist of not only an expense column but also a revenue column of profits made from ticket sales and television contracts. This spectacular transformation in the funding and prominence of women's sport highlights the personal and physical power of young women coming of age in an era of entitlement, in which the right to play sports and receive resources commensurate with men's sports is rarely disputed.

The sea change in U.S. women's sports in colleges, high schools, and recreational leagues across the nation is often attributed to a single congressional act, Title IX of the Education Amendments of 1972. Title IX makes gender discrimination illegal in any educational institution that receives federal aid, which includes virtually every private and public school in the country. And yet Title IX has not acted as a magic bullet capable of eradicating all personal and institutional bias against women's sports. Nine-year-old Natasha Dennis discovered this when playing a girls' soccer game in Lewisville, Texas, in 1990. When her far superior skills spelled certain defeat for the opposing team, a father on the losing side charged onto the field, accused Natasha of being a boy, and demanded that she and some of her teammates be hauled into a bathroom for a designated parent to verify their sex.[1] To this man and fellow doubters, the very best athletic talent still connotes masculinity. Natasha's story and other instances of suspicion and ridicule suggest the fit between girls and athletic excellence remains an uneasy one.

Underneath the smooth surface of success, persistent accounts of personal discrimination and institutional inequities point to a deeper uncertainty, and even hostility, toward a changing culture in which the principle of gender equity has come to override traditional notions of sport as a privileged realm of male activity and masculine power. For example, during the 1990s, more than twenty years after Title IX's passage, Congress held two sets of hearings to re-examine the validity of Title IX, questioning whether it had caused inadvertent discrimination against male athletes. Subsequently, in his first term, President George W. Bush convened a special presidential panel to revisit Title IX, expressing concern that equality for women was reducing opportunities and damaging the psyches of boys and men. Recent history demonstrates that sport culture consistently sparks debate about femininity and masculinity, the attributes associated with womanhood and manhood in a given time and place. The subtext of these gender struggles is a deeper conflict concerning men's longstanding dominance over women in both sport and the broader society.

The powerful gender connotations of sport are not surprising given the historical roots and development of athletic competition in Western societies. For centuries sport has been not only a site of male recreation and competition but also an arena in which boys and men learn, display, and prove their masculine prowess. In this capacity, the sports world has served as a major proving ground for masculinity, with female athletes often perceived as unwelcome intruders. Consequently, woman seeking to participate have met institutional and ideological roadblocks discouraging their athletic involvement and success at almost every turn. These obstacles have taken many forms, from ignoring women's sport altogether to providing paltry resources and responding to women's athletic pursuits with scorn and denigration. Typically the impediments to female participation were even greater for working-class girls and women and for racial and ethnic minorities. Unable to attend well-funded high schools, enroll in college, or join country clubs, or simply lacking leisure time and money, American women of lower social status faced a double set of barriers to participation in organized sports.

But not always. In some cases, like African-American women in track and field or southern white mill workers playing basketball for popular textile leagues, being a member of an ethnic or regional enclave allowed a positive sporting tradition to flourish unimpeded by professionals and journalists who assailed competitive sports for women. Despite widespread discouragement in the dominant culture, a minority of women from diverse ethnic, racial, and class backgrounds consistently sought out athletic opportunities, taking advantage of school, municipal, and elite amateur and professional sports programs whenever they were available. The history of women's sports is not, therefore, a history of discrimination so extensive as to stifle all interest in competitive athletics, but rather an uneven patchwork of avid female athletic participation set within a broader framework of pervasive discrimination, ranging from explicit prohibitions against female athleticism to implicit discouragement and ridicule, to simple lack of opportunity. The story of the rise of women's sports is thus one of hidden opportunities and breakout performances in a culture of pervasive but gradually lessening discouragement of female athletes. This tension between prohibition and possibility is especially evident if we look at the history of women's sport over the last century.

The tension between male prerogative and female interest in sport sharpened in the early twentieth century as women began to reject the physically confining ideal of the staid, domestic, and pious Victorian lady. In the lead-up to the turn of the century, the introduction of the safety bicycle triggered a profound change in women's attitudes toward physical activity, social etiquette, and fashion. First in Europe and later in the United States, the mass appeal of the bicycle to women stemmed not only from the ease with which one could learn to ride but also from the opportunities it presented for freedom of movement. In 1892, at the advanced age of fifty-three, Frances Willard taught herself how to ride the bicycle; her book on the subject is a celebration of her improved health, tenacity, and general attitude and a clarion call for all women to benefit from this marvelous form of transport. And well they might benefit: in an age in which most middle-class women labored daily under the physical restrictions of heavy skirts and petticoats, tight corsets, elaborate hairdos, and unwieldy hats, the bicycle made physical movement that much faster and easier. Unchaperoned cycling excursions became both possible and popular, as distances difficult to cover on foot could be negotiated quickly and independently on a bicycle. The mass appeal of the bicycle in the 1890s also began to change women's attitudes toward fashion, as more and more women rejected their corsets and cumbersome skirts in favor of the bicycle-friendly "rational outfit" of lightly corseted or uncorseted bodices worn with divided skirts or bloomers made of comparatively lightweight material.

By the 1910s, popular magazines praised a new phenomenon called the modern athletic girl, who loved outdoor sports and play as much as men did. The excitement about this new type of athlete reflected both the growing popularity of sport in American society and a profound shift in gender ideals. Victorians had praised women for their domestic roles as mothers and wives while also emphasizing their purity and frailty. This view faded before the robust image of the turn-of-the-century New Woman, noted for her bold, adventurous spirit and her eagerness to engage in public activities like business, education, politics, and sports. The prominence of modernism was often symbolized through the figure of the physically liberated young woman emancipated by bold new styles of dress, liberal sexual mores, and a heightened interest in sorts. By the 1920s, female tennis players and aquatic champions rivaled movie stars for celebrity status as the popular press and advertisers featured them in stories and photos celebrating modern womanhood.

Girls' and women's sports blossomed through the efforts of recreation leaders and physical educators who believed that athletic activity was an important part of female physical and social development. In urban working-class neighborhoods, service-based groups like the Young Women's Christian Association and the Catholic Youth Organization along with newly formed municipal parks and recreation departments organized sports for girls and women. Young working women also found opportunities in industrial leagues sponsored by businesses interested in promoting goodwill within the workforce and local community. Concurrently, middle-class women seized upon an array of opportunities in high school and college athletic programs, which featured extensive intramural offerings and a growing number of interscholastic basketball, baseball, field hockey and track competitions. The popularity of such endeavors prompted the Amateur Athletic Union (AAU), which governed men's amateur sport, to establish national championships in women's swimming, track and field, and basketball during the 1920s. The capstone of women's new athletic freedom came during the international Olympic Games of the 1920s, during which women competed for medals in skating, swimming and diving, and track and field events.

This enthusiasm for women's sports did not go unchallenged. Critics of women's athletic endeavors viewed sports as an inherently masculine activity. Thus, women could succeed only by sacrificing what was seen as their natural femininity for masculine qualities of body and mind. Opponents also complained that vigorous athletic activity exposed the female body to public view and damaged a woman's reproductive organs, possibly ruining her chances for future motherhood. They warned in addition that aggressively physical competition unleashed physical, sexual, and emotional passions that put girls at risk of bodily injury, sexual impropriety, and nervous collapse.

Such critics succeeded in limiting women's athletic opportunities. First, forced into a defensive posture, female physical educators adopted a philosophy of moderation that sought to stamp out all interscholastic sports. Under this policy, educators also modified the rules of girls' athletic games to reduce physical strain and contain competitive impulses. Finally, anti-competition forces succeeded in banning women from certain athletic events. For example, the International Olympic Committee (IOC) eliminated all long-distance running events for women after 1928 so that no women's race was longer than two hundred meters. It wasn't until 1960 that the IOC restored the 800-meter race, and only in 1984 did the IOC offer the marathon as a women's event. These policies, although not universally adopted, predominated until the 1960s, limiting girls' and women's competitive opportunities and sending a message that "real sport" was an activity suited only to boys and men.

Contending forces for and against women's competitive sport created a complex legacy. Certain athletes, like tennis player Helen Wills and swimmer Eleanor Holm, achieved celebrity status, creating a positive image of liberated, assertive, and alluring new womanhood, whereas the great masses of girls and women found only limited opportunities for athletic competition and were as likely to reap scorn as to earn praise if they pursued athletic excellence or passions. These contradictions persisted in the 1930s and 1940s as the team sports of softball and basketball gained great popularity. A girl who first played softball or basketball on a neighborhood sandlot might then join a team through her local recreation program and, in her late teens or twenties, play for an adult team sponsored by her employer or some other local business. The most skilled women joined semiprofessional teams that competed regionally before traveling to the national championship tournament. However, the axiomatic assumption that sporting ability and success are fundamentally masculine continued to plague the best athletes in team and individual sports.

This mixed reception is best illustrated by two high-profile events in these decades, the 1932 Olympic performance of Babe Didrikson and the establishment of the All-American Girls Professional Baseball League (AAGPBL) in the early 1940s. A working-class girl from Texas, the eighteen-year-old Mildred "Babe" Didrikson took Los Angeles by storm in the 1932 Olympics, winning two gold medals and a silver in track-and-field events. Didrikson's astounding abilities made her an instant national celebrity. Yet appreciation for her prowess went hand in hand with more derisive comments about Didrikson's appearance and personality that labeled her a "man-girl" and "Muscle Moll." Criticism of track athletes as manly women gained enough momentum to affect participation in the sport: track, once almost as popular as tennis and swimming, fell to such a marginal position that by the 1940s and '50s most schools and communities simply stopped offering it to girls.

Softball, by contrast, grew in popularity throughout the Depression and war years. In 1942, enterprising Midwestern businessmen launched a professional women's softball league, which they quickly converted to baseball. The AAGPBL operated for twelve seasons, from 1943 to 1954, thriving in midsized cities like Rockford, Illinois, and South Bend, Indiana. National and local media covered the league, whose players, many in their late teens and early twenties, thrilled at the chance to get paid for playing the game they loved best. Yet the league's male directors never trusted that athletic skill could by itself guarantee large crowds and financial success. They conceived of their product as a dramatic contrast between feminine girls and masculine skill, requiring players to wear pastel-colored skirted uniforms, keep their hair long, and attend preseason charm and beauty classes. Such policies sent a mixed message to players and the public: athletic skills were essentially masculine with femininity existing outside, and in contrast to, sport. Girls and women would always remain a sideshow to the real game of men's baseball.

In a conservative post–World War II climate that emphasized family, marriage, and conventional femininity, the popularity of women's sports suffered further decline. Little League programs restricted to boys sprouted everywhere, crowding out informal sandlot and playground teams that had once opened doors to the determined tomboy who excelled at the sport. In high schools and colleges, women's intramural activities vastly outnumbered more competitive interscholastic and intercollegiate events, while in municipal settings women's recreation programs emphasized activities like "beauty culture" and crafts instead of athletic contests. As the number of playing opportunities declined, girls and women who continued to seek high-level competition faced stereotypes of female athletes as ugly, unnatural, and masculine. Even more damaging were insinuations linking women's sports with lesbianism, also stigmatized as masculine. Such condemnation created powerful disincentives for female athletic involvement.

Yet even amidst the chilly climate of the 1950s and early 1960s, a more sympathetic view began to gain momentum from within and outside the world of sport, nurtured by the first stirrings of a reborn feminist movement. In the field of physical education, a younger generation of professionals pressed conservative leaders to relax their stand against intercollegiate competition. This approach took institutional form in 1966 with the founding of the commission on Intercollegiate Athletics for Women, renamed the Association for Intercollegiate Athletics for Women (AIAW) in 1971, which governed and promoted intercollegiate tournaments and championships for women. This organization became the sole sponsor and chief advocate of women's intercollegiate sports in the 1970s. For younger girls, a more favorable climate developed in the 1960s with the nationwide fitness campaign initiated through John F. Kennedy's Presidential Council on Physical Fitness. Subtle changes in the 1960s opened the door for the dramatic changes of the 1970s and 1980s when a thriving feminist movement took up the cause of gender equity in sports and other realms like education and the workplace where women had long been disadvantaged. Feminists, women's sports advocates, and a fitness industry happy to profit from women's new athleticism combined to alter radically ideas about the female body, encouraging a view of liberation that valued strong, fit, and free bodies capable of casting off the physical restraints that marked women's inferior status in an earlier era. In this metamorphosis, female athletes successfully challenged the belief that sport is masculine in nature, positing instead that athletic play is a human endeavor appropriate for all.

This view gained legal support through Title IX of the Education Amendments of 1972. Outlawing gender discrimination in education in general, the law had an enormous—and unanticipated—impact on sports. At the time of its passage, only a few states supported interscholastic high school girls' sports, the most generous collegiate athletic programs allocated only one to two percent of their budgets to women's sports, and golf offered the only professional opportunity for female athletes. Twenty-five years later, girls and women were receiving approximately one-third of college athletic scholarships and the number of girls in high school interscholastic sports had increased from approximately 300,000 per year in 1972 to 2.4 million in 1977, a rate of increase from one out of every twenty-seven girls to one of every three, compared to a steady participation rate for boys of about one in two. Today, although few schools have reached absolute parity, girls and women constitute about forty percent of college athletes. The National Collegiate Athletic Association (NCAA), which defeated the AIAW in a struggle for the right to govern women's sport in the early 1980s, has made a public commitment to continued improvement in those statistics, with the goal of full equity under the standards set by Title IX.

As with school-based sports, women's standing in professional and Olympic sports has not reached parity by any definition. But the phenomenal changes in both the numbers and skill levels of highly competitive female athletes have permanently altered long-standing patterns of discrimination and the corresponding belief in female athletic inferiority. Changes in elite-level sport have had an impact on every other level of participation. Schoolgirls report that athleticism is a source of popularity, female athletes no longer being tarnished by the tomboy epithet. Parents express a similar attitude, with the vast majority now maintaining that sports are as important for girls as for boys. Municipal and independent youth athletic programs, which are not subject to Title IX, have followed the path of educational institutions and created a host of opportunities for girls in soccer, swimming, softball, and volleyball as well as the chance to compete in formerly all-boys organizations like Little League. Interest levels are equally high among adult women, whether at elite levels of national and international competition or among the much larger number of women who take up sports and fitness activities geared toward improved health or enjoyable leisure.

As women strive for equality in sports, as well as in education and work, they raise a critical question that has both legal and policy implications: what constitutes equity? So far the abolition of sex discrimination has been defined in terms of an equitable but not identical allocation of resources and opportunities. Thus, football teams can continue, with rare exception, to be all male and to outspend by far any women's sport offered at the high school or college level as long as women athletes have roughly equivalent opportunities to play other sports and receive scholarships proportionate to their levels of participation. Yet the exact meanings of *equity* and *equality* remain loosely defined and hotly debated. During his first presidential term George W. Bush appointed a special commission to review the effects of Title IX, and in 2005 he directed the Department of Education to make the standards for equity much easier to attain, allowing schools to fund male sports disproportionately over female once they have demonstrated that, within the school, women are less interested in sports than men. The mechanisms for proof can be as flimsy as voluntary on-line surveys administered to students on a school website. Such an approach to gender equity in sports is based upon the assumption that girls and women continue to be substantially less interested in sports than boys and men, implying that sports will always be an essentially masculine pursuit.

Still other critics have come at the issue from the opposite side, valuing women's sport but asking if girls and women want to follow the same path as male competitive athletics given their history of corruption, violence, and commercialism. Responding to the prevalence of eating disorders and serious injuries in sports like gymnastics and figure skating, to the emphasis on competitive success over participation and pleasure, and to a system that rewards winning at the expense of healthy, cooperative learning and well-rounded physical and emotional development, some advocates of women's sports have begun exploring "partnership" models of sport (sometimes called female sports models) that encourage mutual respect, the building of skills, and shared enjoyment at all levels of ability.

We can expect the struggle over gender equity and the cultural meaning of sports to continue for some time in the courts and on the playing fields. In the meantime, increased sports participation among girls and women will generate an expanded sense of entitlement to the many benefits of sport, such as physical strength, athletic skill, and the pleasure and confidence that sport can bring to body and mind. And the meaning of sport will continue to affect and be affected by the larger culture's definitions of—and conflicts over—womanhood and manhood, power and equality.

Women and Sports in the United States presents a selection of essays and documents designed to help readers explore and understand conflicting interpretations of gender and sport in the past, present, and projected future. With this goal in mind, we have organized the book to assist readers in developing both historical knowledge and analytical insight into contemporary sport and gender relations. By focusing on major themes that have shaped the contours of sport in the past and present, each part explores a central issue—a persistent area of conflict and change—within women's sport, through historical and contemporary readings. Most parts include scholarly essays that provide important information and analytical frameworks, journalistic material by sportswriters, opinion pieces, personal narratives of athletes, and legal or political documents. We chose material to provide a range of coverage, diverse viewpoints, interpretive insight, and for the pleasures and/or challenges we hope it provides. To create a more general chronology of key events and "firsts," we've started off with a timeline of important dates in women's sport history, a reference helpful to readers as they move through the book.

Part I, "Pioneering Women in Sport," introduces some of the most important figures in women's sport history, whose stories also raise some of the key thematic issues that succeeding sections explore in greater detail. The section begins with "Olympic Women: A Struggle for Recognition," which looks at how gender inequalities have plagued the modern Olympic Games and the International Olympic Committee from the outset. Author Jennifer Hargreaves also introduces one of the most important pioneers in women's sports, Babe Didrikson, whose athletic career is explored in more detail in "The World-Beating Viking Girl of Texas." Recognizing the impossibility of providing a truly comprehensive parade of pioneering female athletes, we have chosen the remaining selections to represent a variety of sports, concentrating on women whose achievements sparked great controversy or celebration and, in many cases, who overcame barriers of gender, race, or other forms of exclusion that limited women's athletic participation.

Part II, "Negotiating Masculinity and Femininity: The Female Athlete as Oxymoron," lays out the defining issue of women's sport, the question of what happens when women, by definition the feminine sex, enter the realm of sports, which has been culturally defined as masculine. This is the central paradox of women in sport: if sport is masculine, does the athletic woman become masculine, or less feminine, through her very participation? Alternatively, do the best female athletes succeed for the very reason that they already lack feminine qualities? In other words, is the concept of a woman athlete an oxymoron? The readings in Part II focus on two key issues relating to the assumed masculinity of sport: the challenge sportswomen represent to traditional definitions of masculinity and femininity, and the related challenge they bring to the male position of power and dominance that exists in any patriarchal society.

One of the reasons issues of gender difference and power feature so prominently in debates about sport is that sport itself is strongly linked to ideas of the natural body, the physiological and biological hand that nature deals to women and men. Part III, "Competing Bodies: Physiological, Biological, and Psychological Issues," investigates positive and negative aspects of the female body in athletic competition, examining myths and current scientific knowledge about athletic participation and the body. And because the body and mind are so connected, both in terms of our mind's perception of the body and the mental components of competitive sport, the section also includes essays and documents on psychological aspects of sport. In "Competing Bodies" you will find explorations of sex testing in the Olympics, injuries and illnesses to which the female athlete seems to be vulnerable, disabled athletes' attitudes toward sport and physical fitness, and the sometimes dark psychological side of sports. As with Part II, Part III illustrates how conflicts originating in the sporting world will never be contained there, as they spill directly into larger social issues of power, status, and expectations of women and men in society.

To explore further the relationships between larger social formations and sports, Part IV, "Building Inequality into Sport: Institutionalized Bias," concentrates on how cultural biases are built into sport, how disadvantages and advantages of gender, race, and class are institutionalized in the structure of athletic organizations and the rules of the game. The readings here look at how an athlete's background and economic status can steer her toward some sports and away from others, so that working-class figure skater Tonya Harding and African-American tennis stars Venus and Serena Williams became anomalous elite-level participants in both sports. This section also explores assumptions about how physical ability, gender, and other structural constraints operating outside the world of sport—like family expectations, economic need, or access to education—are intimately related to the opportunity structure of sport. Our culture celebrates sport as a site of equality, where the playing field is level and the best "man" wins. These selections ask how differential access and opportunity skew athletic participation rates, denying many girls and women the chance either to play a sport or to gain the necessary skills for success on a not-so-level playing field.

Part V, "Sexuality and Sport," integrates previous sections' inquiries about the body, emotions, and institutional discrimination through a focused exploration of the complex, sometimes explosive relationship between sexuality and sport. For more than a century, American culture has perceived a strong relationship between sport and sexuality because in both areas the body, physical touch, emotional passion, and pleasure are paramount. These congruities have created controversy about the relationship of women's sports to both heterosexuality and lesbianism. We include historical documents that present the connections between sport and sexuality in wholly negative terms: on the one hand, sport encourages masculine aggression and dominance that might spill over into women's sexuality, causing women to become overly passionate and morally lax; on the other hand, allowing women to play "masculine" sports together might encourage homosexuality. Other readings in this section offer critical perspectives as well as a look at the positive sexual aspects of sports for women. Part V also explores issues that have recently come to the forefront, including sexual harassment in sports and the controversial practice of female athletes posing nude or seminude for magazine stories, advertisements, and calendars.

The issue of how the media cover—or uncover—women athletes points to the great importance of media in shaping how women's sport is represented to, and perceived by, the public. Part VI, "The Feminine Image in Sports and Sports Media," focuses on media coverage and gender representation in sports. Media attention to women's sports is on the rise, though both the coverage and the popularity of women's intercollegiate and professional sports is nowhere near the men's level. Rather than focusing on the amount of coverage women's sports receives, this section primarily explores the characteristics of that coverage, including the different ways in which sportscasters cover men's and women's sports, the "feminization" of sports coverage at the 1996 Atlanta Olympics, the relative newsworthiness of different women's sports, and the hidden messages found in women's sports films of the past twenty-five years. Part VI also takes a look at the opposition many female sports journalists have encountered from colleagues, readers, listeners, and, especially, male athletes.

The final section of this book approaches the negotiation of power relations in sports by looking directly at a law whose stated purpose is gender equity. Part VII, "Law and Equity: Title IX and Its Aftermath," focuses exclusively on Title IX to explore the law's purpose and interpretation, its application and enforcement. How did a law addressed only to education become so transformative for sport, and how do we understand the ongoing political battles over Title IX in Congress, in the courts, and in the everyday operations of interscholastic and intercollegiate sport? This section includes historical documents that range from the passage of Title IX in 1972 to the most recent conflicts over its intent and application. Some selections present information on Title IX's interpretation and impact while others highlight competing views for and against Title IX.

Although most of the conflict highlighted in this part revolves around the idea of equity as it relates to sports participation, budgets, equipment, and facilities, Part VII also indirectly raises another issue of equity in women's sport, equally important but often overlooked: should women follow the path of men's sport, marred by chronically low graduation rates, academic and sexual scandal, and financial corruption? Thinking through the meaning of equality eventually raises the question "equal to what?" Does gender equity mean that women aspire to the same model of sport that men have created? These questions remain unanswered, as do questions about the legal definition of equity, whether women and men are naturally different, and whether femininity and masculinity are meaningful concepts in sport or any other realm of culture. And because the phenomenal growth of women's sports has gone hand in hand with a larger movement for women's liberation, underlying the day-to-day operation of sports is an implicit commitment to the liberating potential of sport for women. Yet even proponents of women's sport disagree over what a truly liberating and equitable system of sport would look like. We hope that this book encourages critical thinking and lively discussion about why sport matters to humans and, in particular, what the experience of sport contributes to the lives of girls and women. Is it worth fighting for? If it is, what do we seek to achieve?

NOTE

1. Gary Libman, "Kicking Up a Storm," *Los Angeles Times* (November 8, 1990), E1, 14, 16.

TIMELINE: 125 YEARS OF U.S. WOMEN IN SPORTS

Compiled by Susan K. Cahn and Jean O'Reilly

The following chronology points to many women who achieved "firsts" in sports, whether they were the first to win a championship, break into a previously all-male event, set a world record, or establish women's leagues or organizations to create new opportunities for female athletes. In a sense, the timetable is one long list of pioneers that reflects the enormity of women's accomplishments over the past 125 years, victories that won more than championships but also opportunities and grudging acceptance in the male-dominated world of sports.

1882   At the YWCA in Boston, the first athletic games for women are held.

1888   The modern "safety" bicycle is invented with a light frame, two equal-sized wheels, and a chain drive.

1888   The Amateur Athletic Union is formed to establish standards and uniformity in amateur sport. During its early years, the AAU serves as a leader in international sport, representing the United States in international sports federations.

1892   Gymnastics instructor Senda Berenson Abbott adapts James Naismith's basketball rules for women and introduces the game to her students at Smith College. Her rules confine each player to one third of the court.

1894   The first ladies' golf tournament is held in Morristown, N.J.

1895   Volleyball is invented in Holyoke, Mass. One hundred years later it is the second largest participation sport in the United States.

1896   At the first modern Olympics in Athens, a woman, Melpomene, barred from the official race, runs the same course as the men, finishing in 4 hours 30 minutes.

1901   Field hockey is introduced to women in the United States by Constance M. K. Applebee, a British physical education teacher.

1904   Lydia Scott Howell wins three gold medals in archery, an unofficial Olympic sport at the St. Louis Games.

1912   Swimming and diving debut at the Stockholm Olympic Games, with fifty-seven women from eleven nations competing in those sports plus tennis.

1914   The American Olympic Committee formally opposes women's athletic competition in the Olympics.

1914   Women's basketball rules change to allow half-court play.

1914   The first national swimming championships are held, with women allowed to register by the Amateur Athletic Union (AAU).

1916   A group of forty women form the Women's International Bowling Congress, which will become the oldest and largest women's sports organization in the world.

1917   Lucy Diggs Slowe wins the singles title at the first American Tennis Association (ATA) national tournament, becoming the first female African-American national champion in any sport.

1917   The American Physical Education Association forms a Committee on Women's Athletics to draft standardized, separate rules for women's collegiate field hockey, swimming, track and field, and soccer.

1918   Eleanora Sears takes up squash, after excelling at polo (and shocking spectators by riding astride), baseball, golf, field hockey, auto racing, swimming, tennis, yachting, and speedboat racing. She demonstrates that women can play men's games and is a prime symbol of women's liberation in sports.

1920   Female swimmers become the first American women to achieve full Olympic status, competing in three free-style events. Ethelda Bleibtrey enters all three and wins three gold medals.

1922   The U.S. Field Hockey Association, the national governing body for field hockey in the United States, is established.

1922   The Fédération Sportive Féminine Internationale, founded in 1921, holds the first of four Women's Olympic Games. It includes eleven track and field events and draws over two thousand fans. Six countries participate, including the United States.

1922   The Amateur Athletic Union (AAU) opens track and field events to women.

1923   Twenty-two percent of U.S. colleges have varsity sports teams for women.

1926   New York City native Gertrude Ederle becomes the first woman to swim the English Channel, beating the best male time by almost two hours. She is nineteen years old.

1926   The Amateur Skating Union holds the first national speed skating championships for women.

1926   The AAU sponsors the first national women's basketball championship, using men's rules.

1927   American Helen Wills wins the singles tennis title at the All-England Club. She goes on to win another seven singles titles and holds the no. 1 world ranking for eight years, not losing a set from 1927–33.

1928   The Summer Olympic Games open five track and field events to women.

1929   Tuskegee Institute in Alabama forms one of the first women's college track teams, offering scholarships to promising women athletes and adding women's events to their Tuskegee relays track meets.

1929   Ora Washington, an African-America woman, wins her first of eight American Tennis Association singles titles. Her record holds until Althea Gibson breaks it with nine titles.

1931   The U.S. Women's Lacrosse Association is founded.

1932   Babe Didrikson wins medals in three events at the Los Angeles Summer Olympic Games. Olympic rules restrict women competitors to three events.

1932   Two African-American women, Louise Stokes and Tidye Pickett, qualify for the Olympic Games in Los Angeles. They are not allowed to compete.

1936   The All-American Red Heads Basketball Team is formed. The Red Heads use men's rules and compete against men's teams. The team tours for more than fifty years, playing only men's teams and winning 85–90 percent of all its games.

1936   Gymnastics for women is added to the Olympic program at the Berlin Games.

1937   Bertha Barkhuff sweeps the first U.S. National Badminton Championship for Women.

1943   Philip K. Wrigley, owner of the Chicago Cubs, establishes the All-American Girls Softball League, the forerunner of the All-American Girls Professional Baseball League (AAGPBL).

1945   Golfer Babe Didrikson Zaharias is named the Associated Press Woman Athlete of the Year. She repeats in 1946 and 1947.

1945   The American Athletic Association of the Deaf (AAAD) is founded.

1948   Alice Coachman becomes the first African-American female gold Olympic medalist, in the high jump.

1948   Patty Berg becomes a founder and the first president of the Ladies' Professional Golf Association.

1949   Marcenia Lyle Alberga (also known as Toni Stone) is the first woman to play a full season in a professional men's baseball league. She plays for the Indianapolis Clowns of the Negro Baseball League.

1952   Women compete in open equestrian events at the Olympics for the first time. An open event allows men and women to compete together.

1953   Maureen "Little Mo" Connolly becomes the first woman to score a Grand Slam, winning all four major world tennis matches (Wimbledon and the U.S., French, and Australian Opens) in a single season. She is sixteen years old.

1954   The Iowa Girls' High School Athletic Union is formed and successfully works to establish a statewide program for girls' sports that equals the program for boys. By 1974 almost 500 Iowa schools have full girls' programs, culminating in a state championship tournament for girls as well as boys.

1957   With her first Wimbledon title and first U.S. championship, Althea Gibson becomes the top-ranked female tennis player in the world.

1959   Women's national championships in kayak and canoe events are established.

1960   Wilma Rudolph becomes the first American woman to win three track and field Olympic gold medals—in the 100-meter dash, the 200-meter dash, and the 400-meter relay.

1962   The National Women's Rowing Association is formed. Ten years later the IOC votes to make women's rowing an official sport in the next Olympiad.

1963   The International Sports Organization for the Disabled is founded.

1965   Donna de Varona, a 1964 Olympic swimmer, becomes the first woman sports broadcaster on national TV. She works for ABC.

1966   Roberta Gibb, competing as a nonregistered runner, becomes the first woman to finish the Boston Marathon. She finishes in the top third, ahead of about 375 men.

1967   K. (Katherine) Switzer registers to run the Boston Marathon, using only her initial because women are still barred from official competition. Race officials try to tear her number from her back during the race.

1968   The Olympic Committee conducts gender tests for the first time in international sports, at the Winter Games in Grenoble, France.

1968   Eunice Kennedy Shriver founds the Special Olympics.

1969   Ruth White is named the national fencing champion, becoming the first African-American woman to win a major U.S. fencing title.

1970   Diana Crump becomes the first woman to ride in the Kentucky Derby.

1971   The Association for Intercollegiate Athletics for Women is formed to govern and promote intercollegiate sports and championship tournaments for women athletes.

1971   Billie Jean King becomes the first female athlete to win more than $100,000 in a single season in any sport.

1971   Women's basketball introduces the five-player, full-court game and the 30-second shot clock.

1972   Congress passes Title IX of the Education Amendments of 1972.

1972   The AAU changes the rules of the Boston Marathon, letting women wear official numbers for the first time.

1973   The U.S. Tennis Association announces that men and women will receive equal prize money at the at the U.S. Open.

1973   Billie Jean King beats Bobby Riggs in the "battle-of-the-sexes" tennis match in Houston in front of more than thirty thousand people and a worldwide TV audience of more than fifty million.

1973   Marion Ladewig is voted the Greatest Woman Bowler of All Time. Ladewig's career from 1949 to 1963 includes eight U.S. Open championships, five World's Invitational championships, and nine Bowler of the Year awards. No other person, man or woman, has won that award so many times.

1974   Little League Baseball admits girls, after losing a lawsuit. Bunny Taylor is the first girl to pitch a no-hitter.

1974   Donna de Varona co-founds the Women's Sports Foundation, serving as the organization's first president from 1979 to 1984.

1975   Marion Bermudez is the first U.S. woman to compete in the formerly all-male Golden Gloves boxing tournament in Mexico City. She wins her first match, against a man. She is twenty-three years old.

1975   The International Women's Professional Softball League forms. The league disbands in 1980 because of financial problems.

1976   Rowing, handball, and basketball become Olympic events for women.

1976   Margaret Murdock's silver three-position rifle victory at the Olympic Games makes her the first markswoman in history to win an Olympic medal. The event is open, with men and women competing against each other.

1977   The Boston Marathon has its first female wheelchair entrant.

1978   In a lawsuit filed by Melissa Ludtke of *Sports Illustrated*, a U.S. District Court judge rules that male and female reporters should have the same access to athletes, even if it means reporters enter locker rooms while athletes are dressing.

1978   The Women's Professional Basketball League (WBL) begins play. The league lasts until 1981.

1978   Nancy Lopez is the first female golfer to be named Rookie of the Year and Player of the Year in the same year, winning nine tournaments and $189,813, a record for any rookie, male or female.

1978   Congress passes the Amateur Sports Act of 1978, which prohibits gender discrimination in amateur sports and requires the United States Olympic Committee (USOC) to encourage and promote amateur athletic activity for individuals with disabilities.

1979   The USOC Handicapped in Sports Committee is formed, chaired by Kathryn Sallade.

1980   A total of 233 women compete in the Winter Olympic Games in Lake Placid. Just 21 had competed there in 1932.

1980   Jockey Julie Krone gets her first professional ride at the Tampa Bay Downs racetrack. She wins the race. At her retirement in 1999, she is the all-time winningest female jockey, with more than three thousand wins.

1981   The Association of Intercollegiate Athletics for Women (AIAW) ceases operations and the National Collegiate Athletic Association (NCAA) takes over college women's sports. The long-term effect of this change is a reduction in the number of women coaches and administrators.

1982   Runner Mary Decker becomes the first woman to win the Jesse Owens Award, which is presented annually to the best U.S. track and field athlete. She is the fastest woman at every distance between 800 and 10,000 meters.

1982   The first Gay Olympics are held in San Francisco to encourage health, community, and sport among lesbians and gays. The quadrennial event changes its name to the Gay Games after the U.S. Olympic Committee files a successful law suit claiming exclusive rights to the term "Olympics."

1984   The U.S. Supreme Court weakens Title IX in *Grove City College v. Bell*, effectively denying the application of Title IX to nonfederally funded subunits of educational institutions such as college departments of physical education and athletics.

1984   Joan Benoit wins the first women's Olympic marathon.

1986   The Women's Professional Volleyball Association (WPVA) is created.

1986   Anita DeFrantz is appointed to the International Olympic Committee. She is only the fifth woman ever named to the 93-member IOC and is both the first African American and the first American woman to serve.

1987   Jackie Joyner-Kersee becomes the first woman athlete to be featured on the cover of *Sports Illustrated* (aside from the swimsuit edition).

1988   Diana Golden is named U.S. Female Skier of the Year. In her career she wins nineteen U.S. National Disabled Championship gold medals, ten World Disabled Championship gold medals, and a gold medal in the 1988 Disabled Giant Slalom at the Calgary Olympics.

1988   Congress enacts the Civil Rights Restoration Act over President Ronald Reagan's veto. It prohibits sexual discrimination throughout educational institutions receiving federal funds, restoring the teeth to Title IX.

1989   Debi Thomas becomes the first African-American woman to win a world championship in figure skating.

1989   Chris Evert becomes the first tennis player, male or female, to reach one thousand wins.

1989   Victoria Bruckner is the first girl to play in the Little League World Series, playing first base, batting cleanup, and pitching in the final game.

1990   Jean Driscoll wins the first of seven straight wheelchair Boston Marathons in a world-record time of 1:43:17. She will set a new world record in each of the next four years.

1991   The U.S. Women's Soccer team wins the first-ever women's world championship, beating Norway. In the same year, the U.S. Women's Rugby team also wins the first ever World Cup competition.

1992   Anita DeFrantz becomes chair of the IOC's Committee on Women and Sports, playing a key role in getting women's soccer and softball added to the 1996 Atlanta Games.

1998   Women's ice hockey debuts as an Olympic sport, with the United States defeating longtime dominant rival Canada for the gold medal.

1999   Babe Didrikson Zaharias is selected by *Sports Illustrated* as the best female athlete of the twentieth century.

1999   The National Association for Girls' and Women's Sports (its most recent name) celebrates its one hundredth anniversary.

2000   The International Olympic Committee votes to discontinue the controversial gender testing that has been in use since 1968. It also adds women's weightlifting as an official Olympic sport.

2000   The Women's United Soccer Association announces the formation of an eight-team professional league.

2000   Sandra Baldwin is elected the first female president of the U.S. Olympic Committee in its 106-year history.

2000   Michelle Akers, thirty-four, is named "Woman Player of the Century" by the Federation Internationale de Football Association (FIFA). Akers, despite suffering from Chronic Fatigue Syndrome, led the U.S. National Team with 105 goals in 153 games during her fifteen-year career.

2000   Grand Slam and Sydney Olympic tennis champion Venus Williams signs the richest endorsement deal ever for a woman in sports, a contract worth $40,000,000 over five years with Reebok.

2002   Bobsled driver Jill Bakken and brakewoman Vonette Flowers make Olympic history with their gold medal run in the first-ever women's bobsled event. Flowers becomes the first African-American athlete ever to win a gold medal at the Winter Olympics.

2002   A seventh grader, twelve-year-old Michelle Wie, qualifies for the LPGA Tour's season-opening tournament. She is the youngest player to qualify for an LPGA event.

2003   Nearly three thousand girls play high school football in various positions like kicker, wide receiver, lineman and linebacker, according to the National Federation of State High School Associations.

2004   Forty-four percent of all Olympic athletes are women. Only five countries send no women athletes to complete in this year's Olympics, compared to twelve countries in Sydney in 2000 and twenty-six countries in Atlanta in 1996.

2005   Tennessee Lady Vols' coach Pat Summitt earns her 880th win, becoming the winningest NCAA basketball coach of all time, passing former North Carolina men's coach Dean Smith for the most victories in NCAA history.

2005   Girls' basketball coach Roderick Jackson sues his Alabama high school after he is fired for complaining about unequal facilities for his team. The Supreme Court rules five to four in favor of whistleblowers who speak out against discrimination in school sports.

SOURCES

History of Women in Sports Timeline. Maintained by the St. Lawrence Branch of the American Association of University Women. http://www.northnet.org/stlawrenceaauw/timeline.htm (accessed January 21, 2006).

R. Vivian Acosta, "Women's Intercollegiate Sport: A Longitudinal Study: 25 Year Update, 1977–1992" (Brooklyn College publication, 2002).

Karen P. DePauw and Susan J. Gavron, *Disability and Sport* (Champaign, Ill.: Human Kinetics Press, 1995).

Carol Oglesby et al., ed., *Encyclopedia of Women and Sport in America* (Phoenix: Oryx Press, 1998).

PART I

Pioneering Women in Sport

Part I takes a closer look at just a few of the hundreds, even thousands of women who have acted as pioneers in particular sports or specific eras. The selections explore what it means to be one of the first women to break down gender barriers, and sometimes additional obstacles of racial or economic discrimination. Given the impossibility of creating even a representative sample of women who succeeded against the odds, we have chosen to present a few of the women who were uniquely important athletes of their time, winning fame (or sometimes infamy) and inspiring others to seek similar achievements.

We begin with Jennifer Hargreave's history of women's involvement in the modern Olympic Games, still the most prestigious and spectacular of all international competitions. After charting the International Olympic Committee's opposition to *any* female participation, she shows how, by creating a popular alternative to the Olympics in the 1920s and '30s, a special Women's Olympics, a group of shrewd European organizers pressured the IOC into opening Olympic events to women rather than allowing a rival group to gain control of women's athletics. After detailing women's early participation in the Games, Hargreaves looks at the persistent opposition (even after their official acceptance) to female competitors, and especially gender equality, in the Olympics. She argues that the competition that matters most is not that which occurs in arenas or on playing fields but rather the struggle for control of sports organizations and resources, which remains the basis of men's dominance of the sports world even as women approach equal rates of participation.

Part I then moves away from the general to the specific through Frances Willard's account of how she learned to ride the bicycle in her fifties. One of the most renowned political organizers of her time, Willard headed the largest single organization of American women in the nineteenth century, the Woman's Christian Temperance Union. Faced with the need to improve her health, Willard describes how learning to ride a simple "machine"—the two-wheeled bicycle—gave her a confidence and joy unlike anything she had ever experienced, linking these feelings to a much wider sense of women's growing physical competence and freedom during that era.

Two generations later, Babe Didrikson took similarly bold strides by achieving success in sports firmly associated with masculine skill and prowess. This "World-Beating Viking Girl from Texas" (a Texan born to Norwegian immigrants) discovered that victory in "masculine" sports brought equal parts condemnation and admiration. Nevertheless, the rough-edged working-class champion stared her critics down, often through a disarmingly sharp wit. She posted remarkable records of athletic achievement throughout her life, first in track and field, then basketball and baseball, and eventually as a founder and dominating presence in the Ladies Professional Golf Association, the first successful professional endeavor of any women's sport.

If Didrikson broke barriers of class and dared to go where few women had gone before, Althea Gibson faced a different set of obstacles in her quest to enter the elite world of tennis, a sport in which privileged white women had long found acceptance. Mary Jo Festle analyzes Gibson's early career as she fought for the necessary invitations from the stodgy United States Lawn Tennis Association to participate in major events. Gibson finally overcame exclusionary policies in the late 1950s to become the first African American to win both Wimbledon and the U.S. Open, paving the way for the popular acceptance of other remarkable black women like sprinter Wilma Rudolph, who won three gold medals at the 1960 Olympics.

J. E. Vader's essay "Pioneers" looks at athletes who achieved similar breakthroughs in sports that generally receive less media attention. Vader tracks the careers of marathoner Roberta Gibb, jockey Diane Crump, and Little Leaguer Maria Pepe who, in 1966, 1969, and 1972, respectively, became the first women to run the Boston Marathon, ride in a pari-mutuel race, and play as a registered girl in Little League Baseball. In telling the stories of these three athletes, Vader simultaneously poses a critical question: how did such pioneering contributions not only radicalize sports but also transform the athletes who battled tremendous sexism in their athletic endeavors?

Few events have had more radical impact, and obvious feminist purpose, than the infamous 1973 tennis "Battle of the Sexes" in which Billie Jean King, young and in her prime, defeated an aging middle-aged pro, Bobby Riggs, who gained more attention for his overt "male chauvinism" than he had ever earned in his earlier career. This short *Los Angeles Times* article, posted the day after the match, gives readers a sense of how a single tennis match served to connect the world of sports to the larger feminist revolution occurring in the 1970s. By contrast, the last selection in Part I addresses the end of soccer phenomenon Mia Hamm's career. Hamm's unprecedented personal achievements and role in gaining women's soccer a vast national and international following seem to author David Zirin to have resulted in an "All–Too Quiet Retirement." Zirin tracks Hamm's career as a shining example of the success of women's sports in the post–Title IX era and the impact individual athletes have in inspiring younger girls to take up soccer, or any other sport, with passion and the knowledge that there will be a place for them in the expanding world of collegiate, professional, and international sports. Zirin comments that the media's lackluster coverage of Hamm's retirement proves that while women have gained a place on the sports bus, to this day they remain backseat riders. His essay raises the provocative question of why, more than three decades after Billie Jean King's seemingly decisive victory in the "Battle of the Sexes," women like Hamm still qualify as pioneers, and underappreciated ones at that.

◀▨▶

OLYMPIC WOMEN

A Struggle for Recognition

Jennifer Hargreaves

Introduction

This chapter looks at the history of the modern Olympic Games, characterized as the most prestigious of all international sports competitions. There is a popular tendency to idealize the Olympics and to ignore that they have always been imbued with extreme expressions of male chauvinism and enduring examples of female subordination. The particular difficulties of Olympic sports for women have tended to be exaggerated examples of problems and complexities intrinsic to women's sports in general.

The International Olympic Committee (IOC) is the central administrative authority for the Games. Since its foundation in 1894, it has been an undemocratic, self-regulating and male-dominated institution. At the start, all members were upper-class Anglo-Saxon men, many of whom had strong aristocratic connections, and for almost a century the IOC remained elite and exclusively male. The founder of the modern Olympics, Baron Pierre de Coubertin, was its major ideologue; he wielded power because he was the sole benefactor of the IOC, as well as its president (Mitchell 1977). Until his death in 1937, de Coubertin was intransigent in his opposition to women's participation in Olympic competition, and made his views known through IOC publications. He claimed that

Excerpted from "Olympic Women: A Struggle for Recognition," *Sporting Females: Critical Issues in the History and Sociology of Women's Sports,* by Jennifer Hargreaves. Copyright © 1994, Routledge. Reproduced by permission of Taylor & Francis Books UK.

'women's sport' was against the 'laws of nature' and 'the most unaes-
thetic sight human eyes could contemplate' (cited in Simri 1979: 12–13).
'The Olympic Games', he declared, 'must be reserved for men', for the
'solemn and periodic exaltation of male athleticism' with 'female applause as reward' (quoted in Gerber 1974: 137–8). Under de Coubertin's
tutelage the IOC resisted the participation of women in Olympic sports.
From the start, the modern Olympics was a context for institutionalized
sexism, severely hindering women's participation. They were a powerful
conservatizing force, making an indelible mark not only on the development of Olympic sports for women, but also on the development of international competitive sports in general. However, the original model of
Olympic sports encapsulated demands for change as well as resistance to
them. The history of the Games starkly demonstrates women's struggles,
failures and successes.

The Early Years

The first modern Olympics, which took place in Greece in 1896, exempli-
fies sport as a bastion of bourgeois male privilege. Women were excluded
from these Games, but there is a story about one *unofficial* female participant—a Greek woman called Melpomene—who 'crashed' the marathon
in protest. Her action symbolizes the efforts of those who have struggled
over the years to overcome male domination of Olympic sports. Although at the first Olympics the members of the IOC unanimously opposed women's participation, there were other men in the Olympic movement, and in the newly formed International Federations of sport, who
supported women in their struggle for Olympic recognition. These men
were involved in the development of women's sports in their respective
countries. The period covering the first few Olympic Games coincides
with the formative years of organized sports for women in the West
[. . .]. It was during this time that national and international organizations for women's sports were formed, and there was a steady growth of
competitions, giving sportswomen increasing visibility and legitimacy.

Ironically, the entry of women into the Olympics occurred as a result
of laissez-faire arrangements in the early years. In 1900, and again in
1904, the IOC (which had the ultimate power to control the Olympics)
rather casually handed over the responsibility for arrangements to the organizing committees of the host cities, Paris and St Louis. Under these conditions women were admitted to the Olympics without the official consent
of the IOC (Mitchell 1977). Then, in a more formalized way, the British
Olympic Association took charge of the 1908 Games in London and allowed women's archery, lawn tennis and figure-skating competitions. But

advances were slow and contested. In 1912, at a time when the International Federations were growing in number and importance, and there was increasing popular support for women's sports, the IOC made the decision to reassert its authority over the Olympic programme. With a characteristically sexist and reactionary stance, it systematically blocked women's progress and could only be persuaded to allow a few 'feminine-appropriate' events to take place outside the official programme. But even when women's events were made official, they were not given equal status with men's competitions until 1924. During the first few Olympic Games only very few women were involved. They came from privileged backgrounds, with adequate time and financial resources to make participation possible. But the 1920s marked a watershed for women's participation when controversy over athletics (which had a more popular base of support and were the major Olympic sports) reached a peak.

Continued Resistance to Athletics

In spite of consistent opposition to women's athletics on the grounds that they were particularly unsuited to the female physique, they were growing in popularity and showing early signs of democratization throughout Europe and in the British Commonwealth and North America. Women were therefore in a position to take militant action. It was in 1917 that a Frenchwoman, Alice Milliatt, representing all female athletes, challenged the IOC's rule which prevented women from competing in the Games. She founded a French women's sports organization through which the demand that women's athletics be put on the Olympic programme of 1920 was made. Although de Coubertin's response was to reiterate his demand that all women's events should be terminated, the majority of members of the IOC voted to allow tennis and swimming competitions. The opposition of the IOC to all female participation was no longer total—some of its members now saw women's sports as part of a more general emancipatory trend, which included the entry of women into spheres of work, education and leisure, previously monopolized by men. However, they were unanimously intransigent about women's athletics. In defiance of IOC policy, a group of women from Europe and America arranged an athletics meeting in Monte Carlo in 1921. The programme included a range of events (60 metres; 250 metres; 800 metres; 300 metres and 800 metres relays; 74 metres hurdles; long jump; high jump; shot put; and javelin) which established the composition of future internationals. For campaigns to be successful, groups must be organized and have leaders and supporters; and strategies must be well thought out to win support and change opinion. The female athletes at Monte Carlo ful-filled these criteria: they consolidated a women's international athletic movement with the creation of the Fédération Sportive Féminine Inter-nationale (FSFI), which became an important pressure group for women's international athletic competition and helped to accelerate de-velopment world-wide. The FSFI organized its own alternative *Women's* Olympics in Paris in 1922. The name was changed to the Women's World Games (because the IOC claimed the exclusive right to use the term 'Olympic'), and continued as a popular festival of women's athlet-ics—in 1926 in Gothenburg in Sweden (when ten countries took part); then in 1930 in Prague in Czechoslovakia (seventeen countries); and a fourth and last time in 1934, in London, England (nineteen countries) (Mitchell 1977; Simri 1979). These competitions were unexpectedly suc-cessful, attracting large numbers of competitors and spectators from western Europe, the Commonwealth and North America, clearly estab-lishing athletic events as growth sports for women on a widespread scale. In the face of hostility from the world's major sporting organiza-tion, women had occupied for themselves an autonomous realm of sport which they could control and develop.

The IOC could no longer ignore the evidence that throughout the West women were participating in athletics in greater numbers every year, and attracting crowds of spectators. By this time it was a prerequisite that there be an already established International Federation, and an organ-ized programme of international competitions, for a new sport to be con-sidered for the Olympic programme. Although the FSFI was firmly estab-lished, and the Women's World Games were expanding, it was only when the all-male International Amateur Athletic Federation (IAAF) agreed to take control of women's events that their status as sports for Olympic competition was acknowledged. Although female athletes were again re-fused permission to compete in the Olympics of 1924, it was no longer a unanimous decision, and the IOC could not ignore the growing contro-versy. The problem of the legitimation of female athletics was, therefore, the subject of their Pedagogic Conference in 1925. Medical evidence, considered to be 'authoritative' and 'scientific', was the key presentation, later published in a paper entitled 'Women's Participation in Athletics'. The arguments laid out in this publication provided the justification for slowing the advance of women's athletics during the following years.

The first part of the report seemed to reflect a positive attitude to the female body and a radical understanding of gender:

There are two main features which have to be examined in facing this most diffi-cult problem, which is daily becoming more difficult. The first is that the male and female are derived from the same parent stock. They have been evolved together, and their methods of life are similar. . . . They have somewhat similar organic systems, the differences in skeleton and muscular formation being minor. The differences in the nervous and the blood systems being still less noticeable. . . . The present adaptation of Womanhood itself to the demands created by the labour market, bring her still closer to Manhood in her habits of life. . . . This feature of the question seems to indicate that the recreations and physical exercises taken by men might be found advantageous for women.

—(Cited in Eliott-Lynn 1925: 111)

But then the orientation of the report changed, focusing on the differences between male and female athletes, the limitations of female biology and, in particular, the potentially harmful effects of athletics on women's reproductive potential:

The second feature is that the basic function of men and women is totally different. Women's function is highly specialized, and when it is brought into play those minor differences which I mentioned a moment ago become strongly pronounced, and the woman becomes a totally different creature from that which she was before her role of motherhood was entered upon. . . . The differences which appear in the nervous, skeletal and muscular systems are all necessary adjuncts of the great work of parturition and anything that might tend to hinder or make this more difficult must be very heavily deprecated. . . . We have therefore before us the problem of finding a suitable mean between those sports which tax the muscular frame and put a strain on it, and which are, of course, wholly unsuitable for the feminine organism, which is more delicate and should conserve its energy for the great work before it, and those recreations which are not sufficiently physically energetic to assist the woman towards the most healthy development she may attain. . . . It seems to me, therefore, that if those sports and games which are suitable for men be modified and reduced so that they cannot in any way injure the woman, and if we can create organizations which will enforce these modified regulations stringently, we will have gone a long way towards achieving our objects.

—(Elliott-Lynn 1925: 111)

This medical report was a reaffirmation of the popular nineteenth-century theory of constitutional overstrain [. . .]. By compounding the social with the biological, the discourse of the report shared the ruling class's moral concern for social progress and national welfare, arguing that female athletics should contribute to a 'workable system of eugenics', comparable to that practised in ancient Sparta. The report supported the idea of 'feminine-appropriate' exercise, urging caution about the type and amount of exercise, particularly for young girls between the ages of 13 and 18 years, claiming that 'it is then that their bodies need a tremendous amount of care and attention' (ibid.: ix, x, 27, 114). Importantly, the report provided the national sports associations, the IAAF and the IOC with a 'scientific' justification for limiting women's participation in track and field athletics during the following years.

Assimilation or Separation?

Ironically, the lure of the Olympics, which had been the major stimulus for the organization of women's athletics, was now the bait for women to surrender control to the IAAF, in exchange for a recommendation that female athletic events be put on the next Olympic programme. In 1926, after extended and difficult negotiations, the IAAF recommended a women's athletics programme which was accepted for the 1928 Games—100 metres; 800 metres; high jump; discus; and 400 metres hurdles. It was no coincidence that women athletes were finally admitted into Olympic competition during the year following de Coubertin's retirement from the presidency of the IOC; nor was it surprising that there were only five events on the women's Olympic programme, instead of the eleven in the Women's World Games. In accepting this offer, the FSFI made a fundamental compromise. It was a decision surrounded by controversy, and in protest at the limited number of events, British women athletes, strongly supported by their male colleagues, boycotted the new track and field programme for women at the 1928 Amsterdam Olympic Games.

The example of athletics illustrates the problems women face when they are assimilated into an association where men have the power to make decisions about female sports. Some of the British female athletes had previously argued for separate development in order to retain control of their own sport:

We strongly object to the mixing up of men and women in the Olympic Games or at any other meeting. If this actually happened it would kill our movement, and we should be absorbed by men as in other countries.
—(Vera Searle, quoted in Lovesey 1980: 66)

Women could more easily insulate themselves from opposition in the separate sphere of their own association; in a mixed association they were rendered weak and vulnerable. The nineteenth-century stereotype of woman as a physically limited creature still provided the focus of controversy. When several of the female athletes collapsed in the 800 metres final at the 1928 Games, the event was immediately removed from the women's athletics programme, and provided the IOC with a 'biological' justification for opposing women's participation. Nevertheless, some members of the FSFI believed they were in a position of strength. Following their Olympic debut, female athletes were admitted to the second Empire Games in London in 1934, which gave their events further legitimation; and by this time the FSFI was a vibrant organization with thirty member countries. Female athletics had become popular spectator events in Europe and North America, and so the FSFI was, ironically, now able to use the threat of withdrawal from the Olympics as a lever in the continuing struggle with the IOC. It also planned to continue its own World Games. But the 1938 Women's World Games never materialized because Austria (the intended host country) was annexed by Nazi Germany and war was threatening. Furthermore, much of the impetus was removed when the FSFI was assured in meetings with the IOC that it would have a full athletics programme in future Olympics—a promise that was never fulfilled. The momentum of the FSFI was suddenly halted and women athletes lost their bargaining power. Although there was a new world record set in every women's event in the 1932 Games, even so there were still only 328 women competing in 1936 in just 4 Olympic sports (athletics, fencing, gymnastics and swimming), whereas 3,638 men competed in 11 Olympic sports and in a far greater number of events than women.

The Olympic debate over women's athletics (and by implication competitive sports in general) was complicated further because the women involved in it were not a homogeneous group. In the USA, a lobby against the 'improper' nature of Olympic sports was gaining momentum, spearheaded by the Women's Division of the American Amateur Athletic Federation. This group was composed of physical educators who held powerful positions in education and female sports. They were knowledgeable about prevailing arguments concerning exercise for women and about progressive educational philosophies—ideas which influenced their hostility to high-level competition. They were vehemently opposed to the exploitation of the athlete and to the increasingly commercialized features of male sports, arguing that such trends should be resisted in women's sports. They therefore wanted control to be in the hands of women, and opposed the decision of the Amateur Athletic Union (AAU) to send a women's track and field team to the Women's World Games, and to the Olympics in 1928, 1932 and 1936. In 1932 they sent a formal protest to the IOC in an attempt to suspend athletic events for women from the Los Angeles Olympic Games, and they planned an alternative festival, including singing, dancing, music, mass sports and games: the focus was to be on 'play for play's sake', in direct contrast to the stress and over-specialization associated with individual sporting accomplishment. They also joined forces with members of the medical profession and representatives of other sports organizations to express their fears that competitive sports would render women incapable of bearing children and would have a masculinizing effect on the female physique (Gerber 1974, 1975; Hult 1989; Kennard 1977).

On the one hand, the leaders of women's physical education in the USA appeared to be ahead of their time; they had a critical appreciation of the potentially harmful affects of top-level sports, and a belief in the philosophy of 'activity for all'. They were actively promoting the idea of 'a sport for every girl and every girl in a sport' (Segrave and Chu 1981).

But it has also been argued that because they considered athletic events to be low-status, associated with black and working-class women, their position embodied mainstream ideas, implicitly supportive of class and ethnic divisions in American society (Leigh 1974). Furthermore, by adopting a separatist stance and reproducing the establishment's version of female biology, these women had minimal influence on the accelerating impetus of international competitive sports and the commercialized and exploitative characteristics of which they were so critical. Nor did their policy reduce in any way the seductive appeal that the Olympics had for most sportswomen; it rather strengthened gender differences and helped to make it easy for the IOC to slow the expansion of women's Olympic sports during subsequent years.

The issue of female participation in the Olympic Games shows clearly the complexities of analysis. The early history of women's Olympic sports is a history of struggle and diversity—power and control were fought over, not just between men and women, but between different groups of women. It illustrates the importance of drawing attention to contradictions and conflicts within the broad history of women's oppression in sports.

Gender Stereotyping

By the 1940s, organized sports for women in Europe, the British Commonwealth and North America were spreading in scale and popularity, and the machinery of national and international competition was in place with the establishment of governing bodies of sport and International Federations. The feats of outstanding female athletes, such as Mildred 'Babe' Didrikson from America and Fanny Blankers-Koen from the Netherlands, had captured the public imagination and done much to dispel the myth of the physically limited female. 'Babe' Didrikson was hailed as the 'greatest female athlete of the twentieth century' for her record-breaking ability in track and field events in the 1930s, and Fanny Blankers-Koen demonstrated that supreme athletic ability is not incompatible with popular images of femininity and motherhood. Between 1938 and 1948, she set seven world records in five different athletic events; won four gold medals at the 1948 London Olympics; and then achieved two additional world records in two different events. She produced these outstanding achievements while having and raising a family—at the 1948 Olympics she was 30 years old and three months pregnant.

Contradiction, however, has been a feature of all phases of the Olympic story for women. At the same time as sporting heroines were providing conspicuous exceptions to traditional images of womanhood, conservative efforts to limit participation to 'feminine-appropriate' sports and events were strengthening. Avery Brundage, who was a powerful member of the IOC and became its president in 1952, articulated this view. For example, after the Berlin Olympics in 1936 he said, 'I am fed up to the ears with women as track and field competitors . . . [their] charms sink to less than zero. As swimmers and divers, girls are beautiful and adroit, as they are ineffective and unpleasing on the track.' And in 1949, he expressed disgust at the vision of 'muscular' women in the new shot-put event, arguing that it should be removed from the Olympic programme: 'I think women's events should be confined to those appropriate for women— swimming, tennis, figure-skating and fencing, but not shot-putting' (cited in Simri 1979). Opposition to women's field events came also from women themselves, and gained momentum in 1966 when members of the IOC, who tried to get the shot-put and discus events removed from the Olympic programme, were supported by the Women's Board of the US Olympic Development Committee, which vehemently claimed that 'Often the feminine self-image is badly mutilated when women perform in these two sports'.

Gender stereotyping has been an integral feature of the development of Olympic sports; it has always been easier for women to gain access to those events that it has been argued are more suited to female biology and less threatening to dominant images of femininity. Arguments based on traditional notions of female ability have been used repeatedly to limit the number of Olympic events for women. For example, the banning of the 800 metres after the 1928 Olympics slowed the development of women's distance running tremendously: it was not reinstated as an Olympic event until 1960, and other longer-distance events came much later. Despite repeated appeals to have the 3,000 metres put on the programme, the IOC refused to include it in the Moscow Olympics because the committee said it was 'a little too strenuous for women' and would adversely affect their metabolism. Yet in view of the growing scientific evidence that women may be better suited than men at endurance events (Dyer 1982), and because women were achieving exceptional results in long-distance running outside the Olympics, the IOC's position was visibly weak. Finally, the IOC capitulated, and included the 3,000 metres, together with the marathon, for the first time in 1984 Olympics. Women have also been systematically blocked from Olympic competition in the longer-distance events of other sports, and in those that emphasize strength, require physical contact, and are potentially dangerous (Boutilier and San Giovanni 1982). Arguments are still made to justify women's exclusion from the triple jump, the pole vault, boxing and weight-lifting, on the grounds that women's reproductive systems are vulnerable to injury in these sports. The evidence that there are no medical reasons intrinsic to women that should prevent them, *any more than men,* from participation, is disregarded (Dyer 1982). The female reproductive organs are firmly positioned and thoroughly protected inside the body cavity and are probably less susceptible to injury than those of men. And women, like men, can wear protective apparatus to cover vulnerable parts—their potential for injury is similar to, not greater than, men's. The ethics of arguments to ban dangerous sports such as boxing are as appropriate to men as they are to women; the reason they are applied only to women is cultural, not biological. The inclusion, for the first time in the 1984 Olympics, of two exclusively female Olympic sports—rhythmic gymnastics and synchronized swimming—may have been greeted as a victory, but it only confirmed gender-based associations.

Continuing Inequalities

It is more difficult than ever before to justify continuing inequalities between men and women in the Olympic programme. By their improved performances in high-level competition, women have themselves done great deal to dispel myths about female biology and sporting potential, and have put pressure on the decision-making bodies of Olympic sports to enlarge the women's programme. Even so, the increase in the number of sports has been minimal over the years, although there has been a steady increase in the number of events. For example, in athletics the 400 metres was introduced in 1964, the 1500 metres in 1972; then, as we have seen, it was more than a decade before the 3,000 metres and the marathon became Olympic events for women in 1984. The decisions to include these events were, without exception, the result of conflict and negotiation. For example, preceding the 1984 Summer Olympics in Los Angeles, eighty-two female athletes from twenty-one different countries, with the assistance of the American Civil Liberties Union, failed in a court case to force the IOC and the IAAF to put the 5,000 metres and the 10,000 metres on the women's Olympic programme. Although the case was lost, it was an aggressive demonstration that sportswomen across the world were prepared to fight, and that the issue of female sports had entered the public agenda. Conflict of this sort acts as a lever for change, and the following year the IOC and the IAAF agreed that the 10,000 metres should be put on the women's programme. The struggle continues over the 5,00 metres, the 3,000 metres steeplechase, the pole vault, the triple jump, the hammer throw, the 20,000 kilometres walk and the 50,000 metres walk.

In spite of advances, there is still a large discrepancy when the numbers of male sports, events and competitors are compared with female ones.

For example, at the 1984 Los Angeles Olympics, there were 168 all-male Olympic events, 73 all-female events and 15 'mixed' events, and

> Men competed in twice as many events as women . . . and comprised seventy-nine percent of all competitors. Attempts appear to have been made to broaden women's participation—of the fourteen new events at Los Angeles, three were for men, ten for women and one was open to both sexes—yet many events continue to exclude women. These include several running events, soccer, hammer, judo, rings, pole vault, weight-lifting, boxing, wrestling and water polo.
> —(Williams, Lawrence and Rowe 1986: 82)

At the 1988 Summer Olympics the imbalance between men's and women's events was reduced somewhat—there were 26 sports and 165 events for men; compared with 22 sports and 83 events for women, but there were still twice as many male as female competitors. At the Winter Olympics in that year, there were 11 sports and 30 events for men, but only 6 sports and 17 events for women. At the Summer Olympics in Barcelona in 1992 women were only 40 per cent of the total number of competitors. New sports for women were judo, canoe slalom and windsurfing, but men's events still outnumbered those for women—there were 28 sports and 171 events for men, in comparison with only 24 sports and 98 events for women. There were 3 sports and 12 events for mixed competition. At the Winter Games in Albertville 29 events were for men, 22 for women, plus 4 mixed demonstration events. [. . .]

The main problem for women now, in their quest for equal opportunities in Olympic participation, is that they lack direct power to make changes because they have minimal representation on decision-making bodies. The National Olympic Committees (NOCs), which are in control of Olympic sports in individual nation-states; the International Federations of Sport (IFs), which have the monopoly of power to propose the introduction of Olympic events, and the IOC itself, which makes the final decision about which sports and events are included in the Olympic programme, are all heavily male-dominated organizations. [. . .]

Male supremacy in the IOC has ensured that, throughout the history of the modern Olympics, men have made decisions about women's participation, and male standards have become generalized standards. However, public awareness of gender issues has inevitably influenced the IOC to make changes, and the female membership of the IOC, however small, should help. An example of the IOC's response to external pressure can be found in the *Olympic Charter*. Whereas the category 'sex' used to be omitted from the clause on discrimination (Hargreaves 1984), it is now included: 'Any form of discrimination with regard to a country or a person on grounds of race, religion, politics, sex, or otherwise is incompatible with belonging to the Olympic Movement' (IOC 1991: 9). [. . .]

The IOC, in common with other powerful, male-dominated institutions, has created patterns of participation and control that are difficult to change. Also in common with other institutions, however, the IOC has not been able to insulate itself entirely from changing attitudes to gender outside its immediate influence.

REFERENCES

Boutilier, M. and San Giovanni, L. (1983), *The Sporting Woman*. Champaign, Ill.: Human Kinetics.

Dyer, K. (1982), *Catching Up the Men: Women in Sport*. London: Junction Books.

Eliott-Lynn, S. (1925), *Athletics for Women and Girls: How to be an Athlete and Why*. London: Robert Scott.

Gerber. E. (1975), 'The Controlled Development of Collegiate Sport for Women, 1929–1936,' in *Journal of Sport History*, Vol. 2, No. 1: 1–28.

Gerber, E. (ed.) (1974), *The American Woman in Sport*. New York: Addison Wesley.

Hargreaves, J. A. (1984), 'Women and the Olympic Phenomenon,' in A. Tomlinson and G. Whannel (eds.), *The Five Ring Circus: Money, Power, and Politics at the Olympic Games*. London: Pluto Press.

Hult, J. (1989), 'Women's Struggle for Governance in US Amateur Athletics,' in *International Review for the Sociology of Sport*, Vol. 24, No. 3: 249–64.

IOC (1991), *Olympic Charter*. Lausanne: IOC.

Kennard, J. (1977), 'The History of Physical Education,' in *Signs: Journal for Women in Culture and Society*, Vol. 2, Pt. 4: 835–42.

Leigh, M. (1974), 'The Evolution of Women's Participation in the Summer Olympic Games, 1900–1948,' PhD dissertation, Ohio State University; quoted in J. Kennard (1977), 'The History of Physical Education,' in *Signs: Journal for Women in Culture and Society*, Vol. 2, Pt. 4: 835–42.

Lovesey, P. (1980), *The Official Centenary of the Amateur Athletic Association*. Enfield: Guinness Superlatives.

Mitchell, S. (1977), 'Women's Participation in the Olympic Games, 1900–1926,' in *Journal of Sport History*, Vol. 4, No. 2: 208–28.

Segrave, J. and Chu, D. (eds.) (1981), *Olympism*. Champaign, Ill.: Human Kinetics.

Simri, U. (1979), *Women at the Olympic Games*. Wingate Monograph Series No. 7, Netanya (Israel): Wingate Institute for Physical Education and Sport.

Williams, C., Lawrence, G., and Rowe, D. (1986), 'Patriarchy, Media and Sport,' in G. Lawrence and D. Rowe (eds.), *Power Play*. Sydney: Hale & Iremonger.

HOW I LEARNED TO RIDE THE BICYCLE

Frances E. Willard

I noticed that the great law which I believe to be potential throughout the universe made no exception here: "According to thy faith be it unto thee" was the only law of success. When I felt sure that I should do my pedaling with judicial accuracy, and did not permit myself to dread the swift motion round a bend; when I formed in my mind the image of a successful ascent of the "Priory Rise"; when I fully purposed in my mind that I should not run into the hedge on the one side or the iron fence on the other, these prophecies were fulfilled with practical certainty. I fell into the habit of varying my experience by placing before myself the image—so germane to the work in which I am engaged—of an inebriate in action with the accompanying mental panorama of reeling to and fro and staggering like a drunken man; but I could never go through this three consecutive times without lurching off the saddle. But when I put before me, as distinctly as my powers of concentration would permit, the image of my mother holding steadily above me a pair of balances, and looking at me with that quizzical expectant glance I knew so well, and saying: "Do it? Of course you'll do it; what else should you do?" I found that it was palpably helpful in enabling me to "sit straight and hold my own" on my uncertain steed. She always maintained, in the long talks we had concerning immortality, that the law I mention was conclusive, and was wont to close out conversations on that subject (in which I held the interrogative position) with some such remark as this: "If Professor—— thinks he is not immortal he probably is not; if I think I am I may be sure I shall be, for is it not written in the law, 'According to thy faith be it unto thee'?" [. . .]

As I have said, I found from the first to last that the process of acquisition exactly coincided with that which had given me everything I possessed of physical, mental, or moral success—that is, skill, knowledge, character. I was learning the bicycle precisely as I learned the a-b-c. When I set myself, as a stint, to mount and descend in regular succession anywhere from twenty to fifty times, it was on the principle that we do a thing more easily the second time than the first, the third time than the second, and so on in a rapidly increasing ratio, until it is done without any conscious effort whatever. This was precisely the way in which my

Excerpted from Frances E. Willard, *A Wheel Within a Wheel: How I Learned to Ride the Bicycle.* 1895. Reprint, Bedford, Mass.: Applewood Books, 1997.

mother trained me to tell the truth, and my music teacher taught me that mastership of the piano keyboard (which I have lost by disuse). Falling from grace may mean falling from a habit formed—how do we know? This opens a boundless field of ethical speculation which I would gladly have followed, but just then the steel steed gave a lurch as if to say, "Tend to your knitting"—the favorite expression of a Rocky Mountain stage driver when tourists taxed him with questions while he was turning round a bend two thousand feet above the valley. [. . .]

If I am asked to explain why I learned the bicycle, I should say I did it as an act of grace, if not of actual religion. The cardinal doctrine laid down by my physician was, "Live out of doors and take congenial exercise;" but from the day when, at sixteen years of age, I was enwrapped in the long skirts that impeded every footstep, I have detested walking and felt with a certain noble disdain that the conventions of life had cut me off from what in the freedom of my prairie home had been one of life's sweetest joys. Driving is not real exercise; it does not renovate the river of blood that flows so sluggishly in the veins of those who from any cause have lost the natural adjustment of brain to brawn. Horseback riding, which does promise vigorous exercise, is expensive. The bicycle, however, meets all the conditions and will ere long come within the reach of all. Therefore, in obedience to the laws of health, I learned to ride. I also wanted to help women to a wider world, for I hold that the more interests women and men can have in common, in thought, word, and deed, the happier will it be for the home. Besides, there was a special value to women in the conquest of the bicycle by a woman in her fifty-third year, and one who had so many comrades in the white-ribbon army of temperance workers that her action would be widely influential. Then there were three minor reasons:

I did it from pure natural love of adventure—a love long hampered and impeded, like a brook that runs underground, but in this enterprise bubbling up again with somewhat of its pristine freshness and taking its merry course as of old.

Second, from a love of acquiring this new implement of power and literally putting it underfoot.

Last, but not least, because a good many people thought I could not do it at my age.

It is needless to say that a bicycling costume was a prerequisite. This consisted of a skirt and blouse of tweed, with belt, rolling collar, and loose cravat, the skirt three inches from the ground; a round straw hat, and walking shoes with gaiters. It was a simple, modest suit, to which no person of common sense could take exception.

As nearly as I can make out, reducing the problem to actual figures, it took me about three months, with an average of fifteen minutes' practice daily, to learn, first, to pedal; second, to turn; third, to dismount; and fourth, to mount independently this most mysterious animal. January 20th will always be a red-letter bicycle day, because although I had already mounted several times with no hand on the rudder, some good friend had always stood by to lend moral support; but summoning all my force, on this day, I mounted and started off alone. From that hour the spell was broken; Gladys was no more a mystery: I had learned all her kinks, had put a bridle in her teeth, and touched her smartly with the whip of victory. Consider, ye who are of a considerable chronology: in about thirteen hundred minutes, or, to put it more mildly, in twenty-two hours, or, to put it most mildly of all, in less than a single day as the almanac reckons time—but practically in two days of actual practice—amid the delightful surroundings of the great outdoors, and inspired by the bird-songs, the color and fragrance of an English posy-garden, in the company of devoted and pleasant comrades, I had made myself master of the most remarkable, ingenious, and inspiring motor ever yet devised upon this planet.

Moral: Go thou and do likewise!

THE WORLD-BEATING VIKING GIRL OF TEXAS

'Twas a lucky day for American athletics when Ole Didrickson and his better half came over the Atlantic from rugged Norway.

Under the Texas sun they prospered and raised seven children. The sixth of these was a slim, wiry lass with the blue fire of sea-king ancestors in her eyes and the actinic alchemy of American sunshine in her system.

The Viking capacity for berserk rage in battle filtered down to the Texas maid as a disposition to attack the most prodigious feats with hot resolve and a soaring confidence in her own power of achievement.

Her name was Mildred, but she had another name—her mother vows it is not a nickname—that made her a rival of one of the most famous and popular Americans of history—Babe Ruth.

Yes, and Babe Didrickson, heroine of the Olympic Games, breaker of records, and winner of championships in an amazing variety of strenuous

From *Literary Digest* 114 (27 August 1932) 26–28. © 1932 Time Inc. Reprinted by permission.

athletic sports, threatens to outdistance the home-run king as a figure of captivating interest to all nations of the world.

"Perhaps," suggests one of her home-town papers, the Dallas *News*, "she supplies the proof that the comparatively recent turn of women to strenuous field sports is developing a new super-physique in womanhood, an unexpected outcome of suffragism which goes in for sports as well as politics, and threatens the old male supremacy even in the mere routine of making a living."

Grantland Rice, after playing golf with her, a novice, and seeing her beat his own score, proclaims her "without any question the athletic phenomenon of all time, man or woman." The Dallas *Journal,* enumerating her home-town's reasons for honoring her, includes these items:

Unofficially has equaled every Olympic record for women.
    Winner single-handed of the National A.A.U. women's track and field meet in Chicago July 16.
    Twice given all-American honors as forward on Golden Cyclone girls' basketball team.
    Holder of the world's record for baseball throw.
    Has approximately 100 medals won in individual competition.

Miss Didrickson herself is quoted:

"I brought back eight first-place medals of gold and two second-place medals of silver, and a bronze medal for fourth place. I made eight world's records in the last month, and I am terribly, terribly happy."

Babe Didrickson broke four world's records in Olympic track and field events. First, the javelin throw. Then two in the 80-meter hurdles—first she smashed the previous world's record, and then in the finals she smashed her own. And her fourth was in the high jump, which, as we shall see, did not end as happily as most of her contests.

Sports authorities hail her as Marvelous Mildred, and "the one-girl track team."

One of the most recent bits of news about her is that she will compete in the women's national golf tourney this fall. During the Olympics she played her eleventh match. She was credited with 82 for eighteen holes, and with drives of 250 yards.

Run with us over the tale of her Olympian feats in the Olympics, where she was, as Westbrook Pegler wrote for Chicago's *Tribune* Press Service, "of all the remarkable characters, the one of whom you undoubtedly will be hearing the most in time to come."

. . .

It was the first full day of competition, but already the thousands upon thousands who jammed Los Angeles's great Olympic Stadium were groggy with the record-breaking spree. The spectators fall silent for a moment.

A leather-lunged announcer broke the hush. The name of Mildred Didrickson reverberated through the bowl.

A tall, powerful, graceful girl stept into the center of things with a confident toss of her bobbed head. She held a javelin in her powerful hand. Babe, of Dallas, was ready for her first Olympic trial.

She took a running start to hurl the long, wooden steel-tipped spear.

Then something happened she hadn't counted on. The javelin "slee-upped," to use the pronunciation with which Mr. Pegler credits her. It "slee-upped" out of her hand. And what a mighty "slee-upp" it was. That javelin just kept "slee-upping" right along, and it didn't come down until it had traveled 143 feet and 4 inches.

The fans broke into a roar, writes Mr. Rice in one of his North American Newspaper Alliance accounts, the moment the javelin "struck and quivered in the green turf. The crowd knew a world record had been shattered without waiting for any announcement." The old record was 132 feet and 7⅞ inches.

The amazing feature of Babe's toss was that it was practically devoid of trajectory. According to Braven Dyer in the Los Angeles *Times,* "it might just as well have traveled ten feet more, but for the fact that she threw the wand much after the manner of a catcher pegging to second base. The heave had absolutely no elevation, and sailed practically in a straight line from the time it left Miss Didrickson's mighty right arm until it dug its way into the green turf of the Olympic Stadium.

Then, look at what Babe did in the eighty-meter hurdle trials.

"I'll smash this one, you see," Babe told her pals, continued Mr. Dyer.

Bang! They were off. Miss Clark of South Africa led. Babe began to run a little faster. When they got to the fifth hurdle, the Texas girl pulled up even with her rival. This wasn't enough for Babe. Not by a long shot. She didn't want to win—she wanted a world record. On she went, clipping the barriers with all the technique of an expert male. She hit the tape with all the fury of a Texas tornado. Her teammate, Miss Schaller, beat Miss Clark for a second. And the time, of course a new world record, 11.8 seconds. The old record was 12.2 second.

"Babe may lower the mark again in the finals. She'll probably be disappointed if she doesn't."

And as a matter of fact, that's just what she did, bringing it down to 11.7 seconds. Mr. Rice describes the whirlwind finish in his copyrighted North American Newspaper Alliance dispatch thus:

She and Miss Hall came over the last hurdle side by side. Miss Hall had come along like a runaway kangaroo at the finish, and as the two struck the clay path together the startled Texan saw she was closer to defeat than she had ever been before. She had to call upon everything she had in those last ten yards to slip in front by less than the span of her hand. But the answer is that she was the winner.

Not even the great Nurmi broke four world records in one Olympic. The Babe came here to run amuck and she is running two amucks.

It is sad to have to record that bad luck now overtook her. Entered in three events, she had set three championships as her goal. She had two of them. And now came the high jump as the final test. Damon Runyon in a copyrighted Universal Service dispatch tells how Babe fought it out with Jean Shiley:

The bar is put at 5 feet 4 inches, and both Jean Shiley and Babe (Whattagal) Didrickson clear it at that height, while the mob yells. Miss Gisolf, of Holland, who set the old world's record at 5 feet 3 1/8 inches, goes out when the bar is at 5 feet 3 inches.

About this time, Jean Shiley hangs up a new world's record in the women's high jump with the bar at 5 feet 5 1/2 inches. Miss Didrickson tries it at the same height, but knocks the bar down. She tackles it again, and this time clears the bar to fall in a heap in the sand patch on the other side.

The bar is raised to 5 feet 5 3/4 inches. Jean Shiley and the redoubtable Babe both miss their first attempts. Miss Shiley stands erect, stretches herself with her hands high above her head, starts a little run from a crouch, but falls again. So does the Texas wonder.

Jean Shiley misses her third and last attempt at the bar at 5 feet 5 3/4 inches, and the crowd groans as Miss Didrickson also knocks the bar off just as it looks as if she may get over successfully. The crowd likes the Texas girl and glories in her athletic feats. Now the pair, tied for first place, are to jump it off, each having one trial at 5 feet 5 3/4 inches.

Miss Shiley makes one of her poorest efforts of the day. Now comes the Texas girl. She clears the bar and is well over when the end of the horizontal drops from its support. It seems she hit it with one foot after she is over. The crowd groans in sympathy.

Now the horizontal bar is lowered half an inch and Miss Shiley goes over nicely, landing standing up. Miss Didrickson also clears it, to land in her usual sprawl.

The officials go into a huddle. It seems someone raises the point that Miss Didrickson does what they call "diving" in going over. The athlete's head is supposed to follow the other sections of the body over the bar.

The official argument is quite lengthy, and finally the decision goes against the Texas wild flower, altho she appears to be having her say to the judges. Miss Shiley is the winner. [But, according to the New York *Times,* Miss Didrickson will share in the record recognition.]

Is there anything in the athletic line that Miss Didrickson can't do? Enraptured sports writers tell of her prowess in running, jumping, hurdling, shot-putting, discus, javelin, baseball, tennis, golf, hockey, boxing, wrestling, riding, polo, billiards, pool, skating, football, fencing, basket-ball, swimming, diving, and shooting.

But Westbrook Pegler detected her one failure—"at a ping-pong table on the veranda of the Brentwood Country Club after eighteen holes of golf. She was too enthusiastic for ping-pong, and couldn't keep the ball on the table." Reading on in this *Chicago Tribune* Press Service account, we find her playing a golf game. Mr. Pegler writes:

She showed up at the course looking much more feminine than she had seemed in her flannel track overalls at the Olympic Stadium, and as the round loafed along, the Babe belting long drives from most of the tees, but dubbing some of her iron shots, her personality became clearer. She hit a long one at the eighteenth, and turned around to say, "Gee, I sure would like to learn to play this game."

Before that, on one of the tees, a dozen players, caddies, including several girls, gathered around to watch the Babe hit. This was only the eleventh time she had played golf, but, as she says, she plays best at any game when she is under pressure. She whaled one. It flew straight from the club more than 200 yards, and they began comparing her with Helen Hicks.

Two years ago, Babe had "never competed in any athletic event." But one day, "in a sporting-goods store, shopping for a pair of gym shoes, she picked up a fifty-pound weight and did tricks with it. This caused talk, and was, she says, the first feat of her athletic career, as it brought her to the attention of one Melvin J. McCombs, the man who employs her. He had been an athlete himself, and now became her coach. Nobody else had anything to do with her athletic development. Several coaches have been admitting responsibility for this, lately, but the Babe disowns them all."

"Melvin J. McCombs was my only coach," she said [according to Mr. Pegler]. "If there is any credit in that, he is entitled to it."

"Can you sew?"

"You think you're foolin"?" the Babe said. "Yes, I can sew. I sewed me a dress with seven box pleats at the front and some more in the back—a sport dress it was—that won the first prize in the Texas State Fair at Austin last year."

"Cook?"

"Cook some," she said. "Like gettin' dinner if I have to, and such cookin'. But I'm better at washin' dishes."

"Did you ever have any doubt of yourself in anything you try?"

"No. I generally know what I can do. I don't seem ever to get tired. Sleepy, but not dog-tired. I sleep more than most people."

It is my purpose to suggest that Babe Didrickson is not the boastful party that she may have seemed to be from some of her isolated remarks about herself which have found their way into print during the Olympic Games. In Chicago, as a single-handed team, she won the women's A.A.U. championship, but when she alludes to that she is not a feminine Joie Ray bragging. You ask to know something about her. Instead of sucking her finger and simpering, she tells you how it is. That's fair.

As for instance, "Do you think you can dive?"

"I know I can dive. I can dive off that high tower. I am going to fancy-dive. I sure love to hit that water."

"Have you a lot of medals?"

"Yes, a lot, but the collection is spoiled now. That silver medal for the high jump spoiled it. All the rest were golds—firsts."

The Babe weighs about 120 pounds, and her athletic state generally resembles that of the good male athletes in all the sports which she has tried. She is lean and flat, with big arms and leg muscles, large hands, and the rather angular jaw which the magazine illustrators have established as the standard for cowboys.

The chin of the Babe's, the thin, set lips, the straight, sharp profile, the sallow sun-tan, undisguised by rouge, regarded in connection with her amazing athletic prowess, at first acquaintance are likely to do her injustice. But the mouth can relax and the eyes can smile, and the greatest girl athlete in the world just now, with a special liking for men's games, is as feminine as hairpins. She is a great competitor, come all of a sudden into prominence, who may yet add to her Olympic championships of the track and field and her sewing championship won at the Texas State Fair a title in the fancy dives and a national golf championship.

It's a mistake to think, however, that Mildred's talents are purely muscular, a mistake against which Muriel Babcock warns us in the Los Angeles *Times*. Take a tip from me, says Miss Babcock, continuing:

The Babe can sew, and cook a mean meal. In the wardrobe that she brought with her from Dallas is a blue crêpe party dress which she made herself.

The week-end before she left Dallas for Chicago tryouts, "Mama" (Mrs. Ole Didrickson of Beaumont) came to town to help Babe get ready.

As Babe told her sister, Mrs. C. F. [Cole?] of Santa Monica:

"Ma thought I'd have to be sewed up and all my clothes mended. But I fooled her. Everything was all ready. We just visited."

◀▮▶

PLAYING NICE

Politics and Apologies in Women's Sports

Mary Jo Festle

On a late August day in 1950, thousands of spectators crowded around a tennis court at the West Side Tennis Club in Forest Hills, New York. Those who could not squeeze into the limited seating available tried to watch from under the fence or gratefully accepted standing room. They grumbled about tournament officials' poor scheduling. "The tennis fathers, in their infinite wisdom, must surely have realized that her appearance in the tournament was a matter of considerable interest to many," complained one reporter, "yet they staged her first-round match on the remotest possible court, where not more than three hundred spectators could watch, although about three thousand deserted the stadium and tried to." Who had generated such interest? It was a woman, Althea Gibson, the first "Negro" player to compete in the United States Lawn Tennis Association (USLTA) national outdoor championship. Fans were curious as to how a black player would do in the elite, white, and tradition-bound USLTA tournament.[1]

With bad luck in the draw, in her second match, Gibson had to face the reigning Wimbledon champ, Louise Brough, and in the first set Gibson's nerves showed. She settled down, though, and won the second set. Gibson fell behind in the third but rallied again, and according to a seasoned tennis observer, "her powerful service and mannish net attack . . . threaten[ed] the former national champion with defeat."[2] As the match tightened, the sky darkened, and peals of thunder punctuated their shots. Rain was moments away, but hardly anyone left. "Everyone in the stands sensed that a fabulous upset was in the making."[3] Finally, with Gibson leading 7–6 in the third set, the clouds released a deluge and the match was halted. Disappointed fans raced for cover and journalists to their typewriters. That a black woman was playing on the grass courts at Forest Hills was a story in itself, but now she had the white champ on the ropes. As if to confirm the drama, lightning struck one of the stone eagles on top of the stadium, and it toppled to the ground.

Excerpted from "Members Only: Class, Race, and Amateur Tennis for Women in the 1950s," *Playing Nice: Politics and Apologies in Women's Sports,* by Mary Jo Festle. Copyright © 1996 Columbia University Press. Reprinted with permission of the publisher.

Gibson's appearance at Forest Hills indeed toppled a long-standing tradition in a game known for its traditions. But when play resumed the next day, the excitement soon dissipated. Brough made short work of Gibson, defeating her in three straight games to finish the match in just eleven minutes. In the same way, the previous day's impression of dramatic change in the tennis world also proved illusory: despite some challenges like Gibson's, most of tennis's traditions remained intact in the 1950s. The USLTA retained its tight grasp on the game. Forest Hills remained an amateur tournament, and the game still kept its white, clubby, elitist atmosphere. Tennis fathers still wielded enormous power in deciding things like who would be allowed to enter tournaments, how to define amateur, and who played on which courts. And as the Gibson-Brough match illustrated, rarely did women grace the center courts. Still, although tennis authorities often relegated women to the fringes, it is significant that certain women were included at Forest Hills and that fans crowded to see them. Tennis traditions meant female tennis stars enjoyed greater status than other female athletes, but as the description of Gibson's "mannish" game suggests, their acceptance was far from unqualified.

Historically, tennis was considered a genteel sport. Upper-class sportsmen developed the modern game of lawn tennis in England in the late nineteenth century. After seeing it in Bermuda, Mary Outerbridge reportedly introduced the game in the United States in 1874.[4] Tennis became fashionable in elite circles (especially at seaside resorts on the East Coast) and was an expensive luxury—equipment came only from England, and only country estates or clubs could provide the grass courts. "Lawn tennis remained the game of polite society[,] essentially one for ladies and gentlemen," wrote a sportsman in 1886.[5] Clubs formed in Boston, New York, and Philadelphia, and a group of male enthusiasts organized the USLTA in 1881. Power in the USLTA theoretically belonged to individual members and clubs, but as early as 1904 an observer claimed that "its actions are governed by a certain clique of men mostly in Boston and New York who re-elect themselves or choose their successors each year."[6]

Although tennis at the turn of the century was very exclusive in terms of class, it was less so by gender—women of the upper classes were included. As early as 1889, in fact, the USLTA extended "its protecting wing" to lady players.[7] [. . .]

The game's setting contributed to its acceptability for women. Country estates, clubs, and resorts were intended as refuge from the cold and crowded urban industrial world. As such, they excluded others on the basis of class, race, and ethnicity, but included the whole upper-class family. [. . .]

Upper-middle-class associations of tennis persisted into the 1950s. Although athletic skill could not be determined by class, access to courts could be. With the exception of a few places like California, which had an extensive system of outdoor public courts, most tennis in the United States was taught and played in private clubs, and players from those clubs were most likely to advance up the amateur tennis ladder. At clubs players were introduced to strict tennis etiquette, which included wearing the right clothes (pure white ones) and behaving correctly (e.g., remaining silent during opponents' serves, respecting umpires' decisions, and so on). [. . .]

The tradition of amateurism also kept tennis exclusive. In theory, professionals played for money and amateurs played for the love of sport. To protect the amateur nature of the game, the USLTA's earliest rules prohibited players from benefiting financially from their talent. They could not earn money from winning tournaments, teaching, advertising, or even writing about tennis. As a result, few of those who competed regionally were poor—a player had to be able to afford to travel to tournaments and to secure room and board. But as the game became more popular, both players and tournament directors (who wanted top players to perform at their events) became disgruntled. Therefore two separate changes occurred. First, the USLTA loosened some of its rules defining amateurism. (For example, during the 1930s the USLTA began allowing players to receive expense money for a limited number of weeks a year, and slowly the practice expanded.)[8] The other adaptation was that many players and tournament directors simply quietly broke the rules. [. . .]

Just as the code of amateurism blended with gender to make tennis more exclusive, so did the code of race. Few blacks in the United States during the 1950s belonged to the most elite level of society; nor did African-Americans often grace—as spectators or players—the same country clubs as whites. It was a segregated game. Exceptions did exist; for example New York's cosmopolitan Tennis Club (defunct by 1957) was mixed, and the University of Chicago's varsity tennis team had a black captain in 1929. But no black played in a major USLTA tournament until Reginald Weir did so in 1948.[9] Before then, black Junior Champions had been rejected from the nationals because of their race, just as in the 1920s Helen Wills Moody flatly refused to play Ora Washington, a legendary tennis and basketball star.[10]

Exclusion, it seems, was based as much on tradition as explicit rules; unwritten policies and private decision-making worked effectively to institutionalize racism.[11] When white former champion Alice Marble made informal inquiries to USLTA officials in 1949 about Althea Gibson's chances of entering the U.S. outdoor national championship at Forest Hills, she discovered exactly how the system worked. Marble was not told outright that Gibson would be refused, but that she would have to make a strong showing at the major Eastern grass tournaments preceding the nationals. Unfortunately, though, those tournaments were by invitation only, and a USLTA official informed Marble that Gibson probably would not be invited. Appalled, Marble wrote a guest editorial in *Lawn Tennis* magazine that denounced the ruse. "If she is not invited to participate in them, as my committeeman freely predicts, then she obviously will be unable to prove anything at all, and it will be the reluctant duty of the committee to reject her entry at Forest Hills. . . . Miss Gibson," she concluded, "is over a very cunningly wrought barrel."[12]

Marble had been surprised to learn how the USLTA subtly discriminated, but blacks knew all too well and tried to adjust accordingly. African-Americans started playing tennis shortly after it was introduced in the United States. Often prohibited from playing on public courts, they developed their own clubs in cities like Washington, Baltimore, Philadelphia, New York, and Chicago. The American Tennis Association, a race-separate organization parallel to USLTA, held annual championships for Negro men and women annually beginning in 1917. By 1951, 150 Negro tennis clubs were allied with the ATA.[13] Like the USLTA, the ATA was run by a small group of well-off men, and as in the white community, tennis was an elitist game among blacks. A poor girl often in trouble on the streets of Harlem, Althea Gibson shot pool, gambled at cards, and had crude manners. At first she was uncomfortable with all the rules and proper etiquette that were part of tennis traditions, but she understood their roots.

The Cosmopolitan [Tennis Club] members were the highest class of Harlem people and they had rigid ideas about what was socially acceptable behavior. They were undoubtedly more strict than white people of similar position, for the obvious reason that they felt they had to be doubly careful in order to overcome the prejudiced attitude that all Negroes lived eight to a room in dirty houses and drank gin all day and settled all their arguments with knives.[14]

The manners and propriety of tennis appealed to some of the wealthy blacks who patronized the game. They wanted a share of tennis's refined reputation and some association with the powerful people who played. Many other blacks supported the upper-middle-class efforts to integrate the white tennis world. *Ebony* described the galleries at USLTA tournaments as being populated by "snobbish people who said 'Who, us? Why we've never discriminated,'" and the magazine's editors applauded when

Gibson gained access to this audience. "When she made good in this so-ciety, Althea reached over the masses to win the support of the few who frequently influence the masses."[15]

Because they believed that achievement in sports could make a differ-ence in the perception of blacks by the dominant white culture, male black leaders *sometimes encouraged* female athletes. [. . .]

Therefore, ATA leaders ignored Gibson's gender and overlooked her class background in order to groom her for the hoped-for opportunity in the white championships. Pygmalion-like, Dr. Walter Johnson of Lynch-burg, Virginia, and Dr. Hubert Eaton of Wilmington, North Carolina, took Gibson under their wings. They worked on both her technique and her social skills. Eaton "tried to show Althea how to be a lady on the court" and to accept defeat with grace, and his wife "bought her a few dresses and tried to make her more feminine by getting her straight hair curled and showing her how to use lipstick."[16] Gibson lived with the Ea-tons while school was in session, and during the summer traveled the ATA circuit as one of Johnson's protégées. She won almost everything on it in 1947, including the ATA women's crown. After a good showing there, they allowed her to enter the national championship at Forest Hills in 1950, where she created such a stir against Brough.

The better Gibson did (her USLTA ranking rose to ninth in 1952), the more blacks' hopes were raised. "Althea Gibson is to the tennis world what Jackie Robinson was to major league baseball," asserted the *Chi-cago Defender*.[17] Newspaper coverage of her success encouraged African-Americans all over the country to rally around her, making her aspira-tions collective. They realized that a black tennis player faced all sorts of extra obstacles to becoming a champion.[18] "Everybody is pulling for you," wired a black sportswriter. In addition to sending prayers, then, De-troit blacks raised $770 toward her Wimbledon costs, and boxer Joe Louis gave her a plane ticket and hotel suite. Even after she lost in 1950 in the finals of the national indoors, she returned to Florida A. & M. Uni-versity to find an overwhelming welcome, in which the president of the college and a marching band greeted her. "Obviously," noted Gibson, "they all felt that what I had done was important not just to me but to all Negroes."[19]

Her image became tarnished, however. On a number of occasions she refused to grant interviews, and after one incident a sportswriter for the *Chicago Defender* lambasted her as "ungracious as a stubborn jackass" and "the most arrogant athlete it has been my displeasure to meet."[20] As her success spread, so did her reputation for being difficult to deal with—sulky, tight-lipped, temperamental, and discourteous. Even her coach acknowledged her "personality problem." Especially worrisome—

so much so that controversy over it filled the black press—was the impact her behavior had on the reputation of all blacks. *Ebony* politely suggested she felt out of place in the dainty, feminine world of tennis and that she was not ready to assume the public relations demands of her role. A *Pittsburgh Courier* editorialist insisted that the usually gracious Gibson should not have to be perfect. "Should she grin and show her teeth every time a reporter says, 'Come here, Althea'?" he asked rhetorically. But the *Defender*'s Russ Cowans declared that Gibson was ungrateful for black support and was not fulfilling her responsibilities as a race hero. "Her face is a badge and whether you like it or not, she represents 16 million of her people in the field of tennis. Therefore, she is obligated to act as a goodwill ambassador."[21]

Clearly Gibson struggled with her role as race representative. "It was a strain," she wrote, "always trying to say and do the right thing, so that I wouldn't give people the wrong idea of what Negroes are like."[22] When she lost important matches (as she increasingly did in the mid-1950s), she had to live with not only her own frustration but that of millions. Critics began labeling her "the biggest disappointment in sports" and hinted she did not have what it took.[23] Even when she won, she suspected people wanted things from her. The pressure of "feel[ing] responsibilities to Negroes" was a "burden," and she thought it contributed to her failures in the mid-1950s. So she decided to start playing to please simply herself and not the black community. Unlike Jackie Robinson, then, she shied away from the role of race hero and refused to speak out about racial injustice. She wanted to be appreciated as an individual achiever, not to be a spokesperson or crusader. "I don't consciously beat the drums for any special cause, not even the cause of the Negro in the United States, because I feel that our best chance to advance is to prove ourselves as individuals."[24] Gibson thought the black press turned on her precisely because she did not welcome her role as champion of the race. "A lot of those who disagree with me are members of the Negro press, and they beat my brains out regularly. I have always enjoyed a good press among regular [white] American newspapers and magazines, but I am uncomfortably close to being Public Enemy No. 1 to some sections of the Negro press."[25]

Thus the sense of community ownership of black athletes could cut a number of ways. For some female athletes, like the track stars from Tennessee State and the *Philadelphia Tribune* basketball team, a sense of racial mission gained them support and acceptance despite their gender. However, as Gibson's experience indicates, the same sense of community ownership could become burdensome. For having different ideas about her role and responsibility, Gibson was viewed by some blacks as ungrateful. In turn, Gibson felt more alienated from the black community that had such aspirations for her. As she looked back years later, Gibson said she would probably do things differently. But "at that time I felt I was just representing myself," she remembered. "My people weren't in that sport anyway."[26] Gibson's use of the phrase "my people" surely implies her identification with African-Americans but might also suggest her sense of class separateness from those elite blacks in the tennis world. Regardless, even before extensive criticism from the press, Gibson's frustration mounted. Tired of disappointments and the pressures of the amateur tour, she decided in 1955 to retire from tennis. "I'm sick of having people support me, taking up collections for me, buying me clothes and airplane tickets and every damn thing I eat or wear. I want to take care of myself for a change."[27] She planned to join the Women's Army Corps.

Suddenly, though, Gibson's luck changed. In the mid-fifties the federal government was aggressively trying to improve its international reputation and win the ideological Cold War. In particular, U.S. leaders wanted to counteract Communist propaganda which painted American freedom and democracy as a sham because of the nation's treatment of African-Americans. As part of this campaign, the State Department invited Gibson to participate in a "goodwill tour" to developing countries in Asia. Instead of joining the WACs, then, in 1956 Gibson traveled with three other athletes throughout the world playing exhibition matches and entering tournaments along the way. Gibson aided the country by providing the image of a successful black American, and at the same time benefited from playing tennis often and inexpensively—the first time a Negro was able to play the international tennis circuit. In some ways, however, this year was difficult.

Having to contend with crowds hostile to me because of my color, with newspapers demanding twice as much of me as they did of anybody else simply because my color made me more newsworthy, and even with powerful governments seeking to use me as an instrument of national policy because of my color, seemed to me to be more than anybody should have to bear.[28]

Still, the "experience did wonders for me."[29] In particular, it helped her game. Gibson won her first "significant" singles title as well as sixteen of the eighteen tournaments she entered.[30]

More comfortable and confident, Gibson finally appeared to be reaching her potential. That year, she made it to the quarterfinals at Wimbledon, and the next two summers (1957 and 1958) she won the championship. After her first Wimbledon victory, she came home to 100,000 New Yorkers cheering her at a ticker tape parade.

Gibson finally managed to "arrive" at the top by the late 1950s, but her success must be put in perspective. Compared to other champions, she had struggled disproportionately to get there. If she had been white and welcomed by the tennis elite, she probably would have been a U.S. and international champion all through her twenties. Instead, her rise took much longer. She did not win Wimbledon and the U.S. national outdoor championships until age twenty-nine. In addition, Gibson endured "a wicked amount of punishment along the way."[31] She may have hobnobbed with royalty, but right after winning Wimbledon she was not allowed to stay in a hotel in a Chicago suburb.[32]

Gibson attributed her success both to her ability to survive abuse and to people who cared enough to help her. Clearly her courage, the efforts of the ATA leaders, assistance from blacks all over the country, and the timely support of some liberal white players made an enormous difference. But Gibson was also lucky. At least as significant as the fact that she "made it" is that despite her enormous talent and dedicated friends, she very nearly did not. She was fortunate to come along at a moment when the postwar political climate meant white tennis authorities would be embarrassed if they excluded her, and lucky that the State Department entered the picture just before she quit so as to furnish opportunities that a talented and well-off white girl would have had years earlier.

Nor did Gibson's arrival mean that the racial and class hegemony of the tennis establishment had been overturned. When she published her autobiography in 1958, Gibson thought USLTA was becoming more open to black competitors. "U.S.L.T.A. works closely with A.T.A. in examining the qualifications of Negro players," she said, "and, in effect, any player strongly recommended for a place in the national championship draw is accepted without question."[33] However, history proved her hope illusory. Unlike basketball and baseball, where blacks entered in large numbers once racial barriers were lowered, tennis remained predominantly white.[34] Tennis's white fathers enjoyed positive publicity from accepting Gibson into their major tournaments, but proved unwilling to address the circumstances that continued to limit access to tennis. Besides remaining silent about racial discrimination at most country clubs, they seemed unperturbed by class exclusion.

The combination of class and racial factors proved extremely difficult for an African-American athlete to overcome. Throughout the 1950s USLTA allowed blacks into a few national tournaments but did not let them compete the rest of the year on the same footing. Blacks were not welcomed in the same lead-up tournaments and were evaluated in a different manner from white players. Blacks had "advanced" to the position where they might petition USLTA and expect some response, but USLTA's hegemonic position remained firmly in place. Historian William Chafe describes the "civilities" of race relations in Greensboro, North Carolina, during the 1950s, in which wealthy white "patrons" doled out occasional favors to black leaders as long as blacks remained in their "proper place."[35] The description seems to apply to the USLTA-ATA patron-client relationship as well. "The A.T.A., of course, is careful not to recommend any but the finest players, which is as it should be," explained Gibson.[36] Gibson and ATA leaders displayed gratitude and respect toward their USLTA patrons, but they really had no choice. Clearly they remained entrenched in a supplicating, subordinate, and ultimately submissive role, forced to ask for token favors from the powerful white organization.

NOTES

Note numbers and callouts have been changed from the original article.

1. P. W. W., Jr. "On the Courts," *New Yorker,* September 16, 1950.

2. Allison Danzig, "Miss Gibson Game from Victory Over Louise Brough as Rain Stops Match," *NYT,* August 30, 1950, 33.

3. David Eisenberg, *New York Journal-American,* quoted in Althea Gibson, *I Always Wanted To Be Somebody* (New York: Harper, 1958); Danzig, "Miss Gibson Game from Victory."

4. Davenport, "History and Interpretation of Amateurism in the USLTA," Ph.D. Diss., Ohio State University, 1966, 65–69.

5. Ibid., 65.

6. Ibid., 49.

7. Quoted in Davenport, "History and Interpretation of Amateurism," 41.

8. Davenport, "History and Interpretation of Amateurism," 79–127.

9. Marianna W. Davis, ed. *Contributions of Black Women to America,"* vol. 1 (Columbia, S.C.: Kenday Press, 1982).

10. Edwin B. Henderson, *The Negro in Sports,* ch. 10 (Washington, D.C.: Assoc. Pub., 1934).

11. Wendell Smith referred to the "ladies and gentlemen's agreement" keeping blacks out of Forest Hills. "Wendell Smith's Sports Beat," *Pittsburgh Courier,* July 29, 1950.

12. Gibson, *I Always Wanted to Be Somebody,* 63–64; "Another Budge," *Time,* July 17, 1950.

13. Edwin B. Henderson, "The Negro in Tennis," *Negro History Bulletin* 15 (December 1951): 54.

14. Gibson, *I Always Wanted to Be Somebody,* 29; description of Gibson's habits and manners from "Gibson Girl," *Time,* August 26, 1957, 44.

15. "Althea Has Finally Arrived," *Ebony,* August 1956, 35–38. And certainly Gibson's working-class neighbors appreciated her achievements by flocking to her apartment to greet and congratulate her after her victories in traditionally white tournaments. George Barner, "Ticker Tape Parade for Althea," *New York Amsterdam News,* July 13, 1957, 1, 35.

16. "Gibson Girl," *Time,* August 26, 1957, 44–48.

17. Frank A. Young, "Fay Says," *Chicago Defender* (city ed.), July 14, 1956, 17. Another reporter wrote that she "captured the admiration and won the hearts of millions." Chastine Everett, "Althea Gibson Looks Forward to Bid to Compete in Nationals This Summer, *Chicago Defender* (city ed.), June 17, 1950, 16.

18. "Well Done, Althea," *New York Amsterdam News,* July 13, 1957, 8; Frank A. Young, "Fay Says"; Betty Granger, "The Truth About Althea Gibson," *New York Amsterdam News,* July 21, 1956, 14.

19. Gibson, *I Always Wanted to Be Somebody,* 55–61; "Famcee Campus Turns Out for Althea Gibson," *Chicago Defender* (city ed.), April 8, 1950.

20. "Tennis Queen from Harlem," *Ebony,* October 1957; Russ J. Cowans (Russ' Corner"), "Sports Writers Sour on Althea, But She's Still Champ," *Chicago Defender* (city ed.), July 27, 1957, 1; Russ J. Cowans ("Russ' Corner"), "She Should Be Told," *Chicago Defender* (city ed.), July 27, 1957, 17.

21. Robert M. Ratcliffe, "Althea and the Press," *Pittsburgh Courier,* August 31, 1957; "Tennis Queen From Harlem," *Ebony,* October 1957.

22. Gibson, *I Always Wanted to Be Somebody,* 105.

23. "Tennis Queen from Harlem," *Ebony,* October 1957; "Gibson Girl," *Time,* August 26, 1957, 44.

24. Gibson, *I Always Wanted to Be Somebody,* 61–62, 158. Gibson said, "I am just another tennis player, not a Negro tennis player. Of course I am a Negro—everybody knows that—but you don't say somebody is a white tennis player, do you?" Kennett Love, "Althea Is at Home Abroad on Tennis Courts," *NYT,* June 24, 1956, 35.

25. Gibson, *I Always Wanted to Be Somebody,* 61–62, 158.

26. Virginia Wade and Jean Rafferty, *Ladies of the Court: A Century of Women at Wimbledon,* 104.

27. King and Starr, *We Have Come a Long Way,* 95.

28. Gibson, *I Always Wanted to Be Somebody,* 118.

29. Ibid., 105–106.

30. "That Gibson Girl," *Newsweek,* May 28, 1956, 62.

31. Gibson, *I Always Wanted to Be Somebody,* 2.

32. Quentin Reynolds, "Long Road to the Center Court," *Saturday Review of Books,* November 29, 1958. Nor would the Ambassador East Hotel's Pump Room hold a luncheon in her honor. See Gibson Girl," *Nation,* July 20, 1957, 22.

33. Gibson, *I Always Wanted to Be Somebody,* 159.

34. Arthur Ashe became a champion in the mid-1970s, but no other black male has broken into the top ranks since then. And not until the late 1980s did a black woman again win Wimbledon.

35. William Chafe, *Civilities and Civil Rights: Greensboro, North Carolina, and the Black Struggle for Freedom,* 7–9, 32–33, 38–34.

36. Gibson, *I Always Wanted to Be Somebody,* 159.

◀▶

PIONEERS

J. E. Vader

How do things change? We think of video clips on the evening news, of banners held high amid chanting throngs, of charismatic leaders speaking out. We think of mass movements, forces of history, swelling orchestral music.

On a chilly April morning 25 years ago, Roberta Gibb crouched in the bushes in Hopkinton, Massachusetts, and waited for scores of runners to pass her before she stood and blended in with the pack. She wore a hooded sweatshirt to disguise her hair and face. This was the way she had to start the 1966 Boston Marathon, the first marathon run by a woman. Gibb knew something that few people thought possible—that women can indeed run long distances. It was a shocking idea, so scandalous that some of the people who *knew* that women could not run long distances would naturally prove their point by stopping her before she ran 10 feet.

But the fact that she could run more than 26 miles was about all Gibb knew about distance running. The four days before the Boston races she blithely spent traveling on a bus from San Diego, sleeping in her seat, eating at the bus stops. The night before the race she feasted on pot roast, and then had cheese for breakfast, foods she would carry in her stomach, undigested throughout the race. She thought it was a mistake to drink fluids while exercising, and she wore brand new running shoes (made for boys). "I did everything wrong," Gibb says.

Diane Crump was sure of one thing: She didn't have a chance. She had never seen the horse before, or the trainer. "They told me: He's not much horse," Crump says. "He probably doesn't belong in here, but do the best you can. Those were my orders: Do the best you can."

At Hialeah Park in February 1969, Crump became the first woman to ride in a pari-mutuel race. She was 19 years old, and passionately obsessed with horses. In the starting gate she hunched in the saddle on her bay horse, Bridle 'N Bit, and waited for the bell to ring and the doors to slam open. "I really wasn't that nervous," she says. Crump was a veteran exercise rider; she knew what she was doing. She was ready to go. The

From *A Kind of Grace: A Treasury of Sportswriting by Women*, Ron Rapoport, ed., Berkeley: Zenobia Press, 1994. First published in *The National*. "Pioneers" by J. E. Vader © *The National*.

jockey in the next stall, Craig Perret, looked over, looked her up and down. He reminded her to put her goggles on.

Maria Pepe didn't have the faintest idea she was doing something significant. She just wanted to play baseball. Over and over again, before, during and after the furor, she kept repeating it like a mantra. Baseball, baseball, baseball. What do 11-year-old kids know from history, from politics? Maria was a nice Catholic girl. She was just playing a game, like always, with the kids in her neighborhood in Hoboken, New Jersey. Only this time they were all wearing real uniforms, and there were real umpires, real coaches—all the trappings of Little League.

Of course, in 1972 girls were not supposed to play organized baseball, but nobody on her team was going to make a big deal out of it. They didn't know then, as others would declare, that their very manhood was at stake. Maria's brown, curly hair was cut short under her baseball cap. In the local paper, Maria is in the background of the traditional picture of the mayor of Hoboken at the Little League opening ceremonies. The mayor takes his traditional awkward swing, and the caption notes: ". . . While Naria Pepe waits his turn at bat."

"Naria?" the editor must have thought as the caption was typed. "What an odd name for a boy."

How quaint it all seems, how distant. Of course women can run farther than a mile and a half. Of course women can ride racehorses, and the world does not fall apart when little girls play baseball with little boys. How could anyone think anything else?

The amazing thing is that this was all so recent. It is startling to look at the faces of these women—these pioneers—and realize that they are not ancient curiosities. They are *young*. Each, in her way, helped change sports forever, and each of their lives was changed by sports. They became famous, publicly celebrated and reviled. And now they are mostly forgotten.

Maria Pepe, 30, still has short, dark curly hair. She still lives in Hoboken. But she isn't stuck in the past. She is a young executive, a controller for a large teaching hospital in Hackensack. She teaches night classes in accounting and is working toward an MBA in corporate finance at Fairleigh Dickinson. She plays third base for the medical center's co-ed softball team. She seems amused to be talking, again, about her Little League days. And she does mean days.

"The one thing I really wanted to do was play," she says. "And I really didn't get to play—just three games. I still feel bad about that."

Pepe grew up playing with the boys in her neighborhood. "There were no activities for girls at the time," she says. "It was unusual to even see women wearing sneakers."

When the other kids in the neighborhood went to sign up for Little League, Pepe held back. "I guess I knew there wasn't ever a girl who played," she said. James Farima, a member of the Young Democrats club, which sponsored the team, asked her why she didn't register. "I guess he thought I was a boy," she says, laughing. But Farima encouraged her, and after three games, and with interest in the "Little League Libber" mounting, Little League headquarters threatened to revoke insurance for the entire Hoboken league and suspend its charter—all for allowing a girl to play. Farima went to Maria's house and told her she had to give back the uniform, but she would be allowed to keep score.

Off the team, the now-famous kid would read her name in the papers looking for only one thing. "I would read until I came to a part that would say whether they were going to allow me to play or not," Pepe says. Then she would toss the paper aside in disgust.

"Look at this," she says, and reads from a yellowed clipping: 'A 12-year-old curly haired girl who broke the sex barrier on the Little League team has been dropped from the roster because she is physiologically and medically unfit.' Can you imagine? Here I am a 12-year-old. You could grow up with a serious complex reading this stuff!"

A letter to the editor of the *Jersey Journal*: "It would be unfair to the boys to inflict a lower class of play that would surely result from playing at the girl's level. The whole purpose of Little League, aside from recreation, is to take boys and give them purpose and direction, strengthen character and prepare them for manhood."

Maria's purpose and direction was that she loved baseball and wanted to play with her friends. In the meantime, her character was strengthened by having camera crews film her walking home from school. She became skilled at ducking reporters, just like a big-time athlete.

"As a kid I always went to church and talked to God and said, 'If I'm a girl and I'm not supposed to play, then why did you give me the ability?' I could never reconcile that in my own mind. I figured I should have been a boy or something."

It was two years before Maria felt at peace; that's how long it took for Little League to cave in and allow little girls to play—only after a string of protests and lawsuits, spearheaded by one filed on Maria's behalf by the National Organization of Women. By then, of course, time had run out for Maria; she was too old to play

"Of all the people that have contacted me," she says, "there is still one entity that has never called. I'll give you one guess."

But then, why would Little League Baseball Inc. get in touch, give her credit or even apologize? The organization thwarted a kid's wish to play baseball by threatening to take the game away from all children in her town. And since then it has also, literally, rewritten history.

The official 50th anniversary book for Little League Baseball, *Growing Up At Bat,* was published last year. The book quotes Little League official John Lindemuth: "It wasn't that anyone had anything against girls. It was just that throughout most of the years of the program the issue never came up. Discrimination of any kind has always been frowned on by Little League Baseball." There is no mention of the threats to revoke charters and withhold insurance. No mention of the official Little League rule specifically forbidding girls.

Can Pepe ever foresee the day when women will play in the major leagues? She frowns. "I don't know what the restrictions are," she says. For one who learned early that success is not based on merit alone, the first thought is not of physical limitations, but of man-made barriers.

She wanted to be an athlete, not a historical footnote. Asked if she would rather have been born ten years later, she answers: "Yes!" with surprising force. "I would have gotten to play four full seasons." She would eagerly trade in the scrapbook of clippings, the day in the Yankee dugout, the appearance on "To Tell the Truth" ("Only Kitty Carlisle guessed it was me"), the chapter about her in a children's book written by Geraldo Rivera, all this minor celebrity, this footnote in history stuff, for a few more anonymous swings at bat.

Diane Crump has to really stretch to brush the filly's back, but there is never any doubt she is going to get the brush there. Crump, not surprisingly, is short—but she is by no means slight. The former jockey moves with brisk determination, speaks loudly and clearly. Every movement has a purpose—roll bandages, paint a hoof, comb the tail. Horses are too much work to allow superfluous action.

Crump is in the first year of her trainer's license. She rents ten stalls in a barn in the rolling hills of Virginia's horse country, running her horses at Charlestown or other small tracks. The neat buildings, the manicured hills, the iron entrance gates all connote money—but Crump is just a commuter. "The farther west you go, the less expensive it is," she says. She lives an hour's drive west, in Browntown, in a house with her parents and her 11-year-old daughter. She is divorced after a 17-year marriage, and her family has suffered some financial setbacks. "I'm over 40 now," she says with a sigh, "and right back where I was when I was 17."

Times are not easy. Two years ago, Crump was exercising a big, skittish, stupid thoroughbred named Proof Positive, who reared and fell over backward. Crump's left leg was crushed; the doctors removed her fibula, and replaced it with a steel rod. Under the eight-inch-long scar on her calf are a half dozen screws, and her knee is a metal plate. The wound still weeps. But it doesn't stop Crump from getting back on horses; she says she wouldn't train them if she couldn't ride them.

Crump may be newly licensed to train, but she's been handling horses ever since she was a horse-crazy kid. Her family moved to Tampa when she was 12, and she kept her first horse, an ornery gelding called Buckshot, just two miles from Florida Downs. From the first time she rode Buckshot to the race, she was hooked. At age 13 she started working for a nearby thoroughbred farm, helping break yearlings, then dropped out of school to follow the racing string to the big Miami tracks.

"I never wanted to be a jockey because it was something you just didn't think about," she says. "There were no women riders. Of course, I wanted to gallop on the track, I wanted to do everything everyone else did even though there were only one or two other women galloping and one or two ponying."

She became the first woman jockey almost by default. Kathy Kusner, an Olympic equestrian, applied for and was granted a jockey's license. Other women followed suit and, on the last day of the Churchill Downs meet in 1968, Penny Ann Early was scheduled to ride in a race—which caused the male jockeys to boycott. A few weeks later, at Tropical Park in Florida, jockeys boycotted a race in which Barbara Jo Rubin was named to ride a horse.

By the time the circuit moved to Hialeah, officials there made it clear they would not tolerate a boycott. Catherine Calumet, wife of trainer Tom, felt sorry for women who were trying to ride and she had her husband name Crump to a horse. That was how she found herself on 48-1 Bridle 'N Bit. The race went off without incident, and she finished 10th in a 12-horse field. The following day a headline read: SHE BEAT ONLY 2 HORSES IN HER HISTORIC RIDE.

Crump's scrapbook bulges with clippings with the word "jockette" in the headlines—including this popper: TAMPAN CRACKS JOCKETTE BARRIER.

What the jockette looked like, of course, was vital. The Associated Press report leads with it: "Miami, Fla., Feb. 7 (AP)—Pretty Diane Crump became the first woman today to ride in an American parimutuel horse race. . . . " Crump's light brown hair apparently offered a challenge to reporters' skills—it was described as blond, brunette, red, rust-colored, golden—and several stories duly noted her "doll-like blue eyes." A picture of Crump wiping mud off her face was captioned "Much in need of a powder puff. . . . "

Although the press may have been amused, there was a hard core of resentment at the track.

"I thought change would come faster than it did," she says. "I thought people's attitudes would change. But they didn't. It took ten years to make any difference at all."

Those ten years, when Crump was at her physical peak, she was out on the backstretch, every day, trying to get work. Even when she proved she was good, she didn't get mounts.

"I never had the chance to ride that many horses," she says. "I rode on a regular basis for 17 years, and in the last five or six, I think I rode my best races. But it took so many years to get the experience. At that point, I was as good a rider as there was."

She remembers a night at Latonia (Kentucky) racetrack, when jockey Steve Cauthen came in to ride as part of a special promotion. "In the feature we came down the stretch, neck and neck," Crump says. "We were on horses of equal ability—and I outfinished him! Well, I shouldn't say I outfinished him, but let's put it this way—I won."

Crump refuses to admit that her best is behind her. She grooms her big filly—a $5,000 claimer called Heavenly Wish—and thinks about building a stable of contenders. Then, after her leg has fully healed, she can start race riding again. This time, if she gets a good one, there's no telling how far she can go. "I don't care how old I get," she says. "I don't want to give up my dream."

Roberta Gibb makes tea in her cluttered kitchen, a room of pleasant disarray, filled with her clay sculptures of runners and presidents and with fur from white angora cats. Her home is an 18th century house in Rockport, Massachusetts, just north of Boston.

Gibb started to run when she was a student at Tufts in suburban Boston, after she met her boyfriend, a cross-country runner. "I had never even heard of something like running five miles," she says, softly. "I thought, 'How can you keep going?'" She started to run "for the joy of it—I had a feeling of joy and the only way I could express it was running."

When she first heard of the Boston Marathon, "I didn't believe it," she says. "I thought, 'It's not humanly possible to run 26 miles.' I was running about five miles at that point. Then I went to see the 1964 Boston Marathon and that was it. It was a gut level decision." She knew at that moment that she would enter the race. She didn't notice that everyone she saw going by was male.

Gibb began to train with no notion of *how* to train. She simply ran as far and fast as she could. In the autumn of 1965 she went to Woodstock, Vermont, and ran beside horses and riders competing in an equine endurance contest. The first day she ran 40 miles over rugged terrain; the next day she ran 25 miles before her knees gave out. She felt she was ready for the marathon and, in February 1966, sent away for an application.

"I received a curt reply that women were not physiologically able to run such distances. I was stunned. I assumed the marathon was open to every person in the world." And that is how she found herself hiding in the bushes in Hopkinton.

She not only finished the race—with painful blisters on her feet from her new shoes—she ran it in 3:21, placing her 135th out of more than 600 runners. It was a stunning achievement. Although Japanese runners had swept the first four spots, the story of the first woman marathoner was the news—although, of course, the word "woman" rarely appeared in the copy.

The Boston papers:

BLONDE WIFE, 23, RUNS MARATHON
GIRL SHOWS MARATHON'S BEST FORM
LADY RUNNER NO CRUSADER
WOMEN RUN HOME, ISN'T THAT ENOUGH?

Gibb laughs at the clippings. The front page of the *Record American* shows her cooking fudge after the race—"I guess to show that I was normal," Gibb says. "Can you imagine a headline: BLONDE HUSBAND RUNS MARATHON?" But at the time the press didn't seem strange to Gibb at all. "That was just the '60s," she says, laughing again.

Gibb thought, when she started all this, that change would be easy. "I thought once I showed that women could run, everything would just automatically open up," she says. "That's how naive I was. I thought: Well, they didn't believe women could run, but now they'll see they made a mistake. I didn't realize it was a lot more subtle than that."

Gibb assumed women would be allowed to compete not only in future Boston Marathons, but also in the Olympics, and she dreamed of running in the Games herself. But, of course, women did not have an Olympic long-distance race for another 18 years—in 1984, in Los Angeles—and only after hardball politicking.

Gibb also found her history rewritten. The year after that first Boston Marathon another woman, Katherine Switzer, entered the race under the name K. V. She apparently had a friend take the physical exam, and she started the race with an official number. When marathon official Jock Semple saw her running with the number he became enraged and tried to rip it off her shirt in mid-stride. News photographers were right there and the series of pictures—a short burly man attacking a woman runner—were published everywhere. Switzer finished the race and faced a media bonanza. Gibb, running in her second straight race without incident, finished virtually unnoticed more than an hour ahead of Switzer.

Somehow, in the years that followed, the perception grew that Switzer was the first woman marathoner—a notion that Switzer, who now works as a television sports commentator, did little to dispel.

"I would watch interviews where she would be introduced as the first woman to run the Boston Marathon and she would say, "Yes, thank you," Gibb says. "She was making her living off this. I would write letters, and call her and say if you keep doing this I'll be forced to sue you."

Switzer has gotten better about it, Gibb says, explaining that her resentment is not based solely on being denied her due credit. "She had her boyfriend take the physical and then she lied about it," Gibb says. "It really put women's running in a bad light. Plus, she took more than four hours to finish the race." The Switzer-Semple incident put running right on a men vs. women course—exactly what Gibb wanted to avoid.

She sees running as simple, natural, healthful—and doesn't "compete" in the conventional sense, although she would like to know just how good she could have been. "If I regret anything it's that after the first race, I didn't find a coach. I did continue to run marathons, but I got stuck in other aspects of life—getting married and having children and getting through law school. And of course it wasn't possible then to make a living as a woman runner."

Her husband left her 15 years ago, five days after her son was born, and she had to go to work as a real estate lawyer. She still ran, and continues to run almost every day, but not at the top level of competition. Now 48, with her son away at school, she finds she is restless for change.

"Maybe I'm going through a mid-life crisis," she says. "If I was radicalized by running I was even more radicalized by having a baby. I never realized what women were going through. I didn't feel anything running the marathon compared to that."

Gibb smiles and sips her tea. She is stretching her mind to places far beyond sports. If only she could demonstrate her beliefs as easily as she ran a marathon 25 years ago.

"I don't know if I would have come to all this consciousness without the marathon," she says. "And it has made me much more aware of how social change comes about. One person sees one little thing and does something about it. They never do get the credit. That's what makes ordinary people special."

◄❖►

RIGGS BUTCHERED BY MS. KING AS PROMOTERS SCORE A MILLION

Charles Maher

HOUSTON—Billie Jean King butchered the nation's No. 1 male chauvinist pig Thursday night.

Ms. King, among the more outspoken liberators of the tender gender, astonished Jimmy the Greek and frustrated at least a few million males by defeating Bobby Riggs—in straight sets yet—before the largest crowd in television history.

Jimmy the Greek and 30,471 others came to the Astrodome to watch what Ms. King later described as a turning point in women's sports and her own career.

She had succeeded, where Margaret Court had failed, in showing that one of the world's great female tennis players can defeat a very good middle-aged man.

If that doesn't sound like much, consider the possibility that she may also have stemmed the Niagaran flow from her adversary's oral aperture. First indications, however, were not promising. His mouth was considerably more mobile after the match than his legs were during it.

The contest was about as close as the Spanish-American War. Ms. King, like the U.S. Navy, had some difficulty in the early stages of the conflict. But she rallied for a 6–4 victory in the opening set and thrashed Riggs, 6–3, 6–3, in the last two.

When she got to the interview room, Billie Jean took off her shoes and socks, wiggled her toes, and said:

"I feel this is the culmination of my 19 years in tennis. Since that first day when I was 11 and I wasn't let in a picture because I wasn't wearing a white skirt, I knew I wanted to change tennis."

Riggs arrived a few minutes later.

"What happened?"

"Billie Jean is too good," he said. "Too quick. I got the ball past her but she not only returned it but made a better shot than I did. Too good. Too quick. She deserved to win it."

This second Battle of the Sexes was surely the most ambitious, hyperbolic promotion conceived on this continent since Barnum bumped into Bailey.

From the *Los Angeles Times,* 21 September 1973: 2. All Rights Reserved. Reprinted with permission.

Seats sold for up to $100. The match was seen on national television and, the promoters said, in 36 foreign countries. It attracted about 300 newsmen—and newswomen—from points as distant as Germany, England and Australia.

It also attracted Salvador Dali and such Hollywood tennis freaks as Glen Campbell, Claudine Longet, Robert Stack, Stephanie Powers, Rod Steiger, Janet Leigh, Jim Brown. Moreover, said promoter Jerry Perenchio, "there's a sheik from a Mideast country who has his own 707 and 60 people in his party." The 60 were said to include a harem. ("Ah," Riggs would say. "Very chic, sheik.")

The national television rights went for about $700,000; overseas rights went for $267,000. Talk was the thing would gross $900,000 to $1.2 million, including money from the many endorsements his return to prominence has fetched him.

The match must have set a record for commercial coloration. About every company this side of the Ithaca Drop Forge Tool & Die Corp. seemed involved, one way or another. Ladies' cigarets [sic] men's toiletries, a mint (which is striking a silver commemorative coin bearing the image of Bobby Riggs, "the emperor of male chauvinists"), a housing development (which sponsored practices), a local sporting goods chain (which paid the Astrodome $50,000 to be official sponsor of the match). Oh, yes, and there was the coincidental announcement at a pre-match news conference that Emperor Riggs is starting a chain of tennis clubs, the first to be built in the Astrodome complex.

Surely, given all the Madison Avenue madness, no one would take the match seriously. No one, that is, besides Ms. King and Riggs. Billy [sic] Jean considered it important because a loss might wrinkle the image of women's professional tennis, of which she is a principal architect. Riggs saw it as a serious thing (the match, not the buildup) because a loss might knock the Hollywood props out from under the hustle he began by defeating Margaret Court last spring in the first Battle of the Sexes.

But at least nobody else would get serious about it, right? Not quite.

The thing seemed to arouse a lot of sexperts. A sexpert is a man who insists any male player could beat any female, or a women who would almost argue the converse.

For the better part of a year, Riggs has been going on about how a women's place is in the kitchen and the bedroom—not necessarily in that order. Many in the women's movement, and some of their male sympathizers, seemed to seize the bait.

Strange they did not see through all the blather, as Nora Ephron did not long ago in a perceptive piece for *New York* magazine:

"What do you really think of women?" I ask.

"I'll tell you," (Riggs) says. "I say all this stuff about women staying in the home barefoot and pregnant, but here's what I really think . . . I maybe had two or three dates in high school, and I wasn't really good with girls . . . I was too busy playing tennis. I got married the first time when I was 20 and we were married for 13 years . . . I loved my second wife and enjoyed her and probably always will, but I loved the game on the golf course, on the tennis course, in the locker room, the excitement of being around the guys, more so, perhaps, than I enjoyed being just with a woman. I've never really developed any relationships with women other than the two that I married. So to answer your question—what do I think of women?—I really never thought about them much. I don't really know much about them."

"And what do you really know about women's liberation?"

"You're not going to believe this," says Bobby Riggs. "Nothing."

Another lady journalist, Elizabeth Bennett of the *Houston Post,* rode with Riggs the other day to a news conference in Belmont, Tex. "Back in the car en route to Houston," she wrote, "he slumps back in his seat, exhausted . . . He's talking about his ex-wife, who divorced him a year and a half ago . . . and his five children. And women's lib, which he admits he doesn't understand. All he knows is that it's been a good thing for him and it's helped make his upcoming match with Billie Jean King possible."

Precisely. The blather was mostly lather for the match. A harmless match, really, if you don't buy the preposterous proposition that it made a serious statement about the worth of women or men, athletically or otherwise. If women could never beat middle-aged men at tennis, they could still play entertaining matches.

What it was was the theater of the bizarre. Fifty-five-year-old guy with (as he likes to say) "one foot in the grave" vs. a lady 26 years his junior. Name a nuttier confrontation than that.

The promoters didn't just publicize the match. They flew bombardment missions. The publicity was almost suffocating. But it was salable. Riggs made the cover of *Time.* The match got nearly as much exposure on the sports page as Watergate did on the front page.

Trouble was Riggs had nearly eaten up all the material in his chauvinist pigpen halfway through the buildup and we started getting reruns.

The buildup hardly plunged Houston into a state of unendurable suspense, but everybody seemed to know about the match. It got plenteous play in the papers.

The press began appearing in numbers about Tuesday. Both players had workouts that evening in the Bubble. Billie Jean arrived about 6, wearing a lavender perspiration suit (the female equivalent of a sweat suit). She practiced about 1½ hours with Betty Stove, a pro on the Virginia Slims circuit, and Peter Collins, a resident pro at Hilton Head, S.C. For most of the workout both hit against Billie Jean at the same time. They warmed her up with hard shots, then began feeding her Riggsian lobs and slices.

There were stories Ms. King had a touch of virus last week, but she looked in superb condition, strong and quick. She made some great shots, the gallery responding with ahs and applause.

Speaking of the gallery, the promoters overlooked no opportunity to bring in a buck. They charged $5 a head for practices, plus $1 for parking.

"Billie Jean has always had ability to hit the junk," Collins said after the workout. ["]Riggs is going to have to be in shape. When I played her in the humidity down on the island (at Hilton Head), I was always the first to quit."

Billie Jean left before Riggs arrived for his workout. He wore white shorts and a gray sweat shirt with a pink pig on the chest and "Chauvinist" over that. (One night he turned up in a shirt with round cutouts that exposed his breasts. And across his tummy: "Men's Liberation.")

Lornie Kuhle, a Las Vegas pro who trains Riggs, announced on the p.a. system that Riggs would play a $200 challenge set with Hans Wichary, tennis coach at the University of San Diego. Kuhle also announced: "If there's any King money in the house, please contact me. We're taking all bets." (Jimmy the Greek's line was 5–2 Riggs. But Riggs was offering only 8–5. He wouldn't say how much he'd bet.)

Riggs struggled through his set with Wichary, winning 6–4. Then he played a challenge set with Phil Causey, a local shoe company executive. Causey, it soon became evident, was out of his depth. Riggs, taking a number from his hustler's handbook, brought the "chair game" into play. He put two chairs just inside the sidelines on each side of his half of the court. If Causey hit a chair, he got a point. Bobby won the first game easily, increased the number of chairs to 6, then 8, then 12 and finally 28. At the end, chairs were covering half the back line of the service courts. But Riggs prevailed, 6–2, winning $100 and a year's supply of shoes.

Next came an unscheduled challenge set between Riggs and King. Right, Riggs and King.

Among the spectators at the Riggs workout was Larry King, Billie Jean's lawyer husband. "Love Billie, Zero Bobby," it said on the front of his T-shirt. Riggs offered to play him, giving him six chairs. King declined but after further negotiation agreed to play one set with two bets going at once. Under bet No. 1, Larry would get a three-games-to-none head start. Under bet 2, he'd get a four-game advantage. Each bet was for $150.

King is a nice-looking blond who could drive a tennis ball through a bank vault if he could hit it. Trouble is he might often find the bank itself too small a target. He faulted repeatedly on his first serve, got taken out 6–0.

"It's going to be close because of the competition," King said. "They're going to be nervous and play conservatively."

There was a news conference (actually, a no-news conference, it turned out) the next afternoon. Ms. King and Riggs sat at a table facing a slew of microphones. Nearby, on an easel, was a painting of Billie Jean and Bobby, as sweet a couple as you ever saw. "Commissioned by the Lone Star Brewing Co.," said an inscription underneath.

Heavyweight George Foreman, who was to present the winner's check the next night, sat in on the news conference. Foreman lives in Houston. He picked Billie Jean.

(The press got up a pool before the news conference. Entry fee: $5, up $4 from the Court-Riggs match. Thirty-two entered, 22 picking Riggs.)

Riggs, responding to a question, said he didn't mind being called an egomaniac but resented it when Billie Jean called him a creep.

Billie Jean said "Any person who puts women down must be insecure, must feel women are a threat to their masculinity."

And so on.

Perenchio said the winner would get $100,000 and each player about $75,000 from ancillary rights. It was on this occasion he said Riggs might wind up with $1 million or more overall[.] "I handle his endorsements," Perenchio said. "I don't handle hers, but Larry says there's been a tremendous increase."

A reporter dropped by Riggs' hotel suite later and asked about his condition. Bobby's answer was a little vague. His nutritional advisor, Rheo H. Blair, here from L.A. to supervise Riggs' diet, said Bobby was in better shape for the Court match. "He lived it up too much in Beverly Hills," Blair said, referring to an interlude during which Riggs was making commercials, TV appearances, and starlets.

"But he's still in good condition," Blair said. "We took him to Dr. Denton-Cooley's hospital—he's the top heart surgeon in the world—and they were envious of his condition."

"But the Beverly Hills caper hurt?"

"I had a ball," Bobby said.

Billie Jean, who let Bobby do most of the talking right along, granted no interviews here. But a cheering section was getting ready to make noise for her. At the Net Set Tennis Club Wednesday, 14 or 15 women players were practicing yells:

"One set, two sets, three sets to none.

"Hang up your racket, Riggs, you're all done.

"Hey! Hey! Hey! Oink! Oink! Oink!"

The other camp held a pep rally for Riggs at a late-afternoon party sponsored by Hai Karate toiletries.

Riggs also had lady backers. Somebody rounded up 10 or 12 young ladies and named them "Bobby Riggs' Bosom Buddies."

ABC televised the match—over CBS's dead body, or bodies. There were all kinds of bodies on CBS Thursday night, and they were there for a purpose.

The sports departments of the two networks have fallen madly out of love in recent months. First, CBS outbid ABC for NBS television rights, taking a package ABC held for years. That made ABC mad. Then ABC outbid CBS for the King-Riggs match. That made CBS mad. So it unloaded the bodies, running "Bonnie and Clyde" in some time zones, but not Los Angeles opposite Billie and Bobby. We'll have to wait for the ratings to get the score of that one. But at least the final is in on King and Riggs. Bad night for pigs.

◄❖►

"MIA" CULPA

The All–Too Quiet Retirement of Mia Hamm

David Zirin

Washington Post columnist Michael Wilbon called soccer star Mia Hamm, "Perhaps the most important athlete of the last 15 years." This may sell her a bit short. Ms. Hamm, with little fanfare, retired this past week at the age of 32. She and her bobbing signature ponytail walked away from the U.S. National team that signed her up at the age of 15. Ms. Hamm departs as the all time leading goal scorer, male or female, in the history of international soccer competition, with 158 scores. She also leaves the field of play with the one name stature accorded a select few: Magic, Peyton, Michael, Larry, Mia.

Mia Hamm's retirement should have been *Sports Illustrated* cover material. We should be able to wallpaper the halls of congress with tributes to her greatness. Instead, the broad media silence that greeted her departure— beyond the ghettoes of soccer sports writing—was deafening.

It tempts the spirit to say that Ms. Hamm, always quiet, always humble, never the one to rip off her shirt after a goal or criticize teammates

First published on Dave Zirin's Web site, www.edgeofsports.com. Reprinted in *Political Affairs*, December 2004. http://politicalaffairs.net/article/view/456/1/50.

who did, left with the same reserved dignity that defined her play. It would be tempting, but as Samuel L. Jackson said in *Pulp Fiction,* "That sh*t just aint the truth."

The yipping testosterone-addled heads of sports talk always moan and groan about the lack of role models, difference makers, and dignity in sports. Yet when faced with the opportunity to highlight a career defined by these ideals, they looked the other way. Instead, we had another week about what Barry Bonds was or was not ingesting, who Ron Artest did or did not punch, and what Ricky Williams is or is not smoking.

This stands as yet another example of women's place on the back of the athletic bus. Call it the "Kournikova effect" (named after Anna Kournikova who made it to the cover of *Sports Illustrated* without having won a single tournament). It's not enough for a woman to have blistering athletic talent. She also has to date cheesy celebrities, strip to her skivvies, and basically become Paris Hilton with muscle tone to generate any attention. If Mia Hamm was shtupping Justin Timberlake, or had appeared in *Playboy*'s "Women of the Olympics" issue, her retirement may have generated some more immediate coverage. Good thing she married fading shortstop Nomar Garciaparra, a fact that forced its way into every story written about her this week.

The shame of it is that—even absent paparazzi puke—Hamm's story justifies thorough examination. At 32, she is roughly the same age as Title IX, the law that guarantees equal funding for men and women's sports. A product of the women's movement of the 1960s, Title IX has radically changed the lives of millions throughout the U.S. According to the Women's Sports Foundation, one in twenty-seven high school girls played sports 25 years ago; one in three do today.

Before Title IX, fewer than 32,000 women participated in college sports; today that number exceeds 150,000. Young girls who play sports are less likely to suffer from eating disorders, be involved in abusive relationships, or drop out of high school. Despite this record of achievement it's subject to constant attack. Like all of the 1960s reforms that improved the lives of women, people of color, and the poor, Title IX has been subject to a well-organized and well-funded backlash. Mia Hamm, who can be painfully shy, has carried through her play the symbolic weight of everything about Title IX that is indomitable and will not be turned back.

She bears this burden because of all athletic programs affected by Title IX, the most profound impact has been on soccer. Women's soccer is now offered on nearly 88 percent of college campuses compared to only 2.8 percent in 1977. Through these openings denied women of previous generations, Ms. Hamm dazzled and became the first team superstar that U.S. women's sports ever produced. She was the focal point for the national team that beat China in the historic 1999 World Cup final that drew a crowd of 90,000 to the Rose Bowl and attracted a television audience of 40 million. She also starred for the U.S. team that won the 1991 World Cup championships and Olympic gold medals last summer and in 1996. Throughout her brilliant career, in the words of one writer, Hamm "undoubtedly inspired more girls to step onto a playing surface than all other female athletes combined."

In honoring the retiring Hamm, along with teammates Julie Foudy and Joy Fawcett, U.S. national team coach April Heinrichs said, "Think of it this way: Imagine that Magic, Larry Bird, Michael Jordan, Shaq, Kobe and LeBron were all on one team for 15 years. That's what we have had with our women's national team."

Their play was so inspired, and the attention they received so profound, they were harnessed with the ultimate "compliment" when Bill Clinton joined the players' husbands and partners in a special stadium box for that game against China. Women were perhaps for the first time deemed a worthy vehicle for the ugly side of international competition that breeds the kind of nationalism and saber rattling usually reserved for men's contests. The success against China spawned a Women's Professional Soccer League, sponsorship and fan frenzy when not playing the evil Chinese.

The failure of the WUSA undoubtedly dimmed the light on Mia Hamm in recent years, but her last game was a fitting athletic epitaph. Hamm racked up two stellar assists that defy description. On the first assist, Hamm took a pass in the right corner of the box, started dribbling to her left, then to her right, faked back to her left, then raced around an off-balance defender. With goalkeeper Pamela Tajonar sliding to her left to cut off the angle, Hamm rolled a well-paced pass across the center of the box, and a hard charging teammate crushed a shot into the net. Hamm recorded another assist on a corner kick, when her curling kick sailed just over the goalie's outstretched hands and into the center of the box, where a teammate headed the ball into the net. "Scoring is fun," she said. "But it's also fun to watch your teammates enjoying the game."

Hamm made a point of going to the stands to sign autographs, with some of the young fans lingering for more than an hour after the game. This is par for the course for an athlete who never shirked from the responsibility to tirelessly promote her sport, or personifying the athletic hopes and dreams of a generation of young girls. Mia Hamm earned this place by showing through her everyday plan that women could equal or exceed a man's blood, sweat, and tears. She exhibited in practice that men do not own exclusive rights to the wicked dynamism that is athletic greatness.

As Heinrichs said when the retirement celebration drew to a close, "They had an impact on America's consciousness, on women's sports, on women's voices." Having an "impact on women's voices" won't get you in *People Magazine,* but it means a legacy for Mia Hamm that is richer and more resonant than yesterday's tabloids. Her legacy is one that will echo in our demands for women's equality in the generations to come.

PART II

Negotiating Masculinity and Femininity: The Female Athlete as Oxymoron

Part II explores a central issue in the history of women in sport. If society defines sport as basically masculine, what message does that definition convey about sportswomen? Do women become less feminine, less womanly, when they take up sport? Or are women who gravitate toward sport, especially more successful athletes, less feminine to begin with? Any answer to these questions must first grapple with the issue of what, exactly, the terms *masculine* and *feminine* mean.

As editors, our perspective is that sport is neither inherently masculine nor feminine. Sports are games that require, nourish, and reward a variety of human qualities available to women and men. But the fact that popular perceptions of sport as masculine have made women's athletic involvement controversial suggests that there are larger issues at stake. After all, what does it matter if women take on culturally defined masculine qualities like strength, speed, power, or unconcealed ambition, qualities men are rewarded for on and off the playing fields? The persistent social, cultural, and political resistance to women's full and equitable participation in sports shows that it does matter.

At least two issues are at stake here. First, there is the threat to the traditional social and cultural practice of differentiating *woman* from *man* by assigning a cluster of descriptors to each sex, with the expectation that every woman will be feminine, every man, masculine. This expectation underlies arguments by leading physical educators Senda Berenson (writing in 1903) and Dudley Sargent (1912) in support of modified rules for women's sports. Miss Berenson, gymnasium director and instructor of Physical Culture at Smith College from 1892 until her marriage in 1911, introduced the first rules of women's basketball and organized the first women's collegiate basketball game. Dr. Sargent, director of Harvard's Hemenway Gymnasium from 1879 to 1919, founded the Sargent Normal School in Boston to train physical education teachers.

Three decades after the publication of Sargent's essay, the concern for sportswomen's loss of femininity fueled many of the AAGPBL's Rules of Conduct.

A careful look at the lists of required and prohibited behaviors provides useful insight into mid-century beliefs about gender and sport. If a woman can be too masculine, perhaps even more masculine than the man who disdains sports and prefers cooking over football for instance, then what do these categories really mean? If culturally assigned norms of *gender* have no necessary association with biological *sex,* then we must ask what gender really describes and what purpose it serves. If we argue that gender is an erroneous assignment of human attributes to two falsely dichotomized biological classes, the so-called opposite sexes, then why preserve the categories of masculinity and femininity at all?

Hostile reactions to "masculine" women athletes reveal a second issue at stake, the fact that gender is not only an arrangement of difference but also an arrangement of power. The qualities associated with sport and masculinity are the powers of dominance: physical superiority, violence, aggression, control, and victory. Sports sociologist Don Sabo identifies and attacks six "patriarchal myths" about women in sport, neatly illustrating that athletic skill is affected at least as much by access to knowledge and encouragement to practice as it is by biological difference. His essay maintains that if women and men cease to be defined by, respectively, femininity and masculinity, women may come to rival men not only on the athletic field but in all realms of society. James Fallows' essay, "Throwing Like a Girl," raises the idea that athletic skill is not inherently masculine, but rather is culturally imparted to boys "in training" for masculinity. The stereotypical girl does not throw badly because she is female, but because she has not been taught—as boys are—how to throw. Throwing is defined in our culture as a masculine activity, something girls need not learn how to do. In Fallows' analysis, we might see "throwing like a girl" as something other than an insult, indicating a gender-neutral lack of skill, and possibly encouragement to acquire that skill, rather than a gender-based attribute.

The threat, real or imagined, that sport presents to conventional femininity remains an issue for today's collegiate sportswomen, even as they revel in the physical power and personal confidence they have developed from pursuing their sports. That much is evident in some of the interview responses Vikki Krane et al. record in "Living the Paradox," which explores the ways in which female athletes reconcile conflicting social expectations surrounding femininity and athleticism. Part II thus raises the twin issues of gendered difference and power, themes that will reappear throughout the book because they are so fundamental to the experience of sport in America.

THE SIGNIFICANCE OF BASKET BALL FOR WOMEN

Senda Berenson

Within the last few years athletic games for women have made such wonderful strides in popularity that there are few directors of physical training who do not value them as an important part of their work. They have become popular, too, not as the outcome of a "fad," but because educators everywhere see the great value games may have in any scheme of education. Gymnastics and games for women are meeting less and less opposition, and gaining larger numbers of warm supporters because our younger generation of women are already showing the good results that may be obtained from them in better physiques and greater strength and endurance.

Now that the woman's sphere of usefulness is constantly widening, now that she is proving that her work in certain fields of labor is equal to man's work and hence should have equal reward, now that all fields of labor and all professions are opening their doors to her, she needs more than ever the physical strength to meet these ever increasing demands. And not only does she need a strong physique, but physical and moral courage as well.

Games are invaluable for women in that they bring out as nothing else just these elements that women find necessary today in their enlarged field of activities. Basket ball is the game above all others that has proved of the greatest value to them. Foot ball will never be played by women, and base ball is seldom entered into with spirit. Basket ball is played with deep earnestness and utter unconsciousness of self. Certain elements of false education for centuries have made woman self-conscious. She is becoming less so, but one finds women posing even in tennis and golf. It is impossible to pose in basket ball. The game is too quick, too vigorous, the action too continuous to allow any element to enter which is foreign to it. It develops quick perception and judgment—in one moment a person must judge space and time in order to run and catch the ball at the right place, must decide to whom it may best be thrown, and at the same time must remember not to "foul." It develops physical and moral courage, self-reliance and self-control, the ability to meet success and defeat with dignity.

Excerpted from Senda Berenson, *Basket Ball for Women*. Park Place, N.Y.: American Sports Publishing Company, 1903.

It is said that one of woman's weaknesses is her inability to leave the personal element out of thought or action. If this is so—and there is some ground for such a supposition—a competitive game like basket ball does much to do away with it. Success in this game can be brought about only by good team-play. A team with a number of brilliant individual players lacking team-work will be beaten always by a team of conscientious players who play for each other. This develops traits of character which organization brings: fair play, impersonal interest, earnestness of purpose, the ability to give one's best not for one's own glorification but for the good of the team—the cause.

But just as basket ball may be made an influence for good so may it be made a strong influence for evil. The gravest objection to the game is the rough element it contains. Since athletics for women are still in their infancy, it is well to bring up the large and significant question: shall women blindly imitate the athletics of men without reference to their different organizations and purpose in life; or shall their athletics be such as shall develop those physical and moral elements that are particularly necessary for them? We can profit by the experience of our brothers and therefore save ourselves from allowing those objectionable features to creep into our athletics that many men are seriously working to eliminate from theirs. Since all new movements swing from the extreme of degeneracy or inertness to the extreme of newly acquired powers, unless we are most careful we shall allow that enthusiasm and power to run away with our reason. It is a well known fact that women abandon themselves more readily to an impulse than men. Lombroso tells us that women are more open to suggestion, more open to run to extremes than men. This shows us that unless we guard our athletics carefully in the beginning many objectionable elements will quickly come in. It also shows us that unless a game as exciting as basket ball is carefully guided by such rules as will eliminate roughness, the great desire to win and the excitement of the game will make our women do sadly unwomanly things.

This has already been proved. A basket ball match game was played several years ago between the teams of two of our normal schools. One team had been trained to play with the Y.M.C.A. rules; the other with modified rules. Since neither team wished to change its method of play, the first half was played by each team according to its own rules. The game was so rough that the second half was played by both teams with the modified rules. Let me quote from a paper commenting on this game:

"Probably no finer exhibition of basket ball playing by women has ever been seen in this country than the game played by these two teams during the *last* half of their contest. As a possibility of what women can show in the way of skill, alertness, accuracy, coolness and presence of mind under trying circumstances, and still be ladies, the game was a revelation to many present.

"To my mind the important lesson of this game, and the one that should make it a memorable one, is that a courteous consideration of an opponent, even in an antagonistic game, does not necessarily diminish a team's chances for victory."

Another instance; a basket ball team composed of refined women, in one of our New York cities, was challenged to play a game by a team just out of their town. The occasion was not only to be an athletic but a great social event. The visiting team had played with modified rules; the other with rules for men. The playing was not only rough to a degree, but the spirit shown toward the guests who were beaten, by their opponents and their friends, was what one would think quite impossible in women who had any regard for the ordinary courtesies of life. Rough and vicious play seems worse in women than in men. A certain amount of roughness is deemed necessary to bring out manliness in our young men. Surely rough play can have no possible excuse in our young women.

Of course, these two cases and similar instances of which I have heard do not prove that many of our women who play basket ball do so in an undesirable way. They are sufficient, however, to make us pause and consider whether they are not enough to prove that we need to free the game from anything that might lead to objectionable play. And here a serious question may be raised as to whether it is for the best interests of women to go into inter-scholastic games.

However, just this fact that women are more open to suggestion is an encouraging one, for it shows us that they can the more easily be led to right thought and action. This can be seen by the splendid results of clean sport and good spirit gained wherever basket ball has been guarded by careful rules and strict discipline.

But just here I must say that not only is it necessary to modify the game somewhat, but the physical director and umpire cannot appreciate too fully the responsibility of their positions. The best of rules will be no protection to one who does not insist on fair play and does not umpire most conscientiously. It is also important that the captain of the team shall not only be a good basket ball player, but one who represents the best athletic spirit. I may say that the spirit of athletics in our colleges and schools for women is what the director of the gymnasium makes it. The right spirit is not gained by autocratic methods, but by almost imperceptible suggestion and strong example. If the physical director takes it for granted that athletics can be no other than fair and honorable, her spirit will be imbibed unconsciously by her pupils.

◀▮▶

ARE ATHLETICS MAKING GIRLS MASCULINE?

A Practical Answer to a Question Every Girl Asks

Dudley A. Sargent, M.D.

Many persons honestly believe that athletics are making girls bold, masculine and overassertive; that they are destroying the beautiful lines and curves of her figure, and are robbing her of that charm and elusiveness that has so long characterized the female sex. Others, including many physicians, incline to the belief that athletics are injurious to the health. This double charge, of course, gives a serious aspect to the whole question, and it should be met.

What Athletics Really Are

Now, what are athletics and how are women affected by them? An athlete is one who contends against another for a victory; athletics are the events in which one contends. A gymnasium is a place for the performance of athletic exercises; a gymnast is a person who trains athletes, and gymnastics are the exercises practiced in the gymnasium for the purpose of putting one's self in proper condition for competing in the athletic contests. In our times the terms athletics, gymnastics and physical training are often used synonymously, while actually they are not alike and may bring about very different results.

If a schoolgirl practices jumping a bar with other girls, as one of the physical exercises prescribed for general development, she is engaging in gymnastics. If, however, the bar is jumped with the purpose of finding out which girl can clear the bar at the greatest height the performance becomes an athletic one. In the first instance the exercise would be undertaken as a means of physical improvement for its own sake. In the second instance, if the spirit of emulation ran high the girls would be engaging in a course of special physical training, not primarily to benefit themselves physically but for the set purpose of improving their jumping powers so as to vanquish their nearest competitor.

Excerpted from Dudley Sargent, "Are Athletics Making Girls Masculine? A Practical Answer to a Question Every Girl Asks," *Ladies' Home Journal*, March 1912.

This distinction, that gymnastics are pursued as a means to an end, and athletics as an end in themselves, would apply equally well to such forms of exercise as walking, running, vaulting, swimming and skating, which may be measured in time or space and thus be made competitive. The element of competition and "sport" must, therefore, enter into what we now term athletics. [. . .]

These Make Women More Masculine

Physically all forms of athletic sports and most physical exercises tend to make women's figures more masculine, inasmuch as they tend to broaden the shoulders, deepen the chest, narrow the hips, and develop the muscles of the arms, back and legs, which are masculine characteristics. Some exercises, like bowling, tennis, fencing, hurdling and swimming, tend to broaden the hips, which is a feminine characteristic. But archery, skating and canoeing, which are thought to be especially adapted to women, tend to develop respectively broad shoulders, long feet and deep muscular chests, which are essentially masculine; while rowing, which is thought to be the most masculine of all exercises, tends to broaden the hips, narrow the waist, develop the large front and back thighs and give many of the lines of the feminine figure.

Just how all-round athletics tend to modify woman's form may be judged by comparing the conventional with the athletic type of woman. The conventional woman has a narrow waist, broad and massive hips and large thighs. In the athletic type of woman sex characteristics are less accentuated, and there is a suggestion of reserve power in both trunk and limbs. Even the mental and moral qualities that accompany the development of such a figure are largely masculine, but this is because women have not yet had as many opportunities to exercise them.

Sports Should Be Adapted to Women

Some of the specific mental and physical qualities which are developed by athletics are increased powers of attention, will, concentration, accuracy, alertness, quickness of perception, perseverance, reason, judgment, forbearance, patience, obedience, self-control, loyalty to leaders, self-denial, submergence of self, grace, poise, suppleness, courage, strength and endurance. These qualities are as valuable to women as to men. While there is some danger that women who try to excel in men's sports may take on more marked masculine characteristics [. . .] this danger is greatly lessened if the sports are modified so as to meet their peculiar qualifications as to strength, height, weight, etc. inasmuch as the average woman is inferior to the average man in nearly all physical qualifications, all the apparatus used and the weights lifted, as well as the height and distance to be attained in running, jumping, etc., should be modified to meet her limitations. Considering also the peculiar constitution of her nervous system and the great emotional disturbances to which she is subjected, changes should be made in many of the rules and regulations governing the sports and games for men, to adapt them to the requirements of women.

Modify Men's Athletics for Women

Any one who has had much experience in teaching or training women must have observed these facts in regard to them: Women as a class cannot stand a prolonged mental or physical strain as well as men. Exact it of them and they will try to do the work, but they will do it at a fearful cost to themselves and eventually to their children. Give women frequent intervals of rest and relaxation and they will often accomplish as much in twenty-four hours as men accomplish. So firmly have I become convinced of this fact that I have arranged the schedule of work at both the winter and summer Normal Schools at Cambridge so that periods of mental and physical activity follow each other alternately, and both are interspersed with frequent intervals of rest.

The modifications that I would suggest in men's athletics so as to adapt them to women are as follows: Reduce the time of playing in all games and lengthen the periods of rest between the halves. Reduce the heights of high and low hurdles and lessen the distance between them. Lessen the weight of the shot and hammer and all other heavy-weight appliances. In heavy gymnastics have bars, horses, swings, ladders, etc., adjustable so that they may be easily adapted to the requirements of women. In basket-ball, a favorite game with women and girls, divide the field of play into three equal parts by lines, and insist upon the players confining themselves to the space prescribed for them. This insures that every one shall be in the game, and prevents some players from exhausting themselves. If the field of play is large enough seven or nine players on a side are preferable to the five required by the men's rules. As the game is played today by men, with only five on a side and without lines, it brings a harder strain on the heart, lungs and nervous system than the game of football does.

I am often asked: "Are girls overdoing athletics at school and college?" I have no hesitation in saying that in many of the schools where basketball is being played according to rules for boys many girls are injuring themselves in playing this game. The numerous reports of these girls breaking down with heart trouble or a nervous collapse are mostly too well founded. Other instances are recorded where schoolgirls have broken down in training for tennis tournaments, or for running, jumping and swimming contests. These instances generally occur in schools or colleges where efforts are made to arouse interest in athletics by arranging matches between rival teams, clubs and institutions, and appealing to school pride, loyalty, etc., to furnish the driving power. Under the sway of these powerful impulses the individual is not only forced to do her best, but to do even better than her best, though she breaks down in her efforts to surpass her previous records.

There will be little honor or glory in winning a race, playing a game or doing a "stunt" which every other girl could do. It is in the attempt to win distinction by doing something that others cannot do that the girl who is over-zealous or too ambitious is likely to do herself an injury. For this reason girls who are ambitious to enter athletic contests should be carefully examined and selected by a physician or trained woman expert, and the usual method of trying out unprepared candidates by actual contests in order to determine "the survival of the fittest" should not be allowed.

◆❀▶

ALL-AMERICAN GIRLS PROFESSIONAL BASEBALL LEAGUE RULES OF CONDUCT, 1943–1954

The Rules of Conduct for Players as Set Up by The All-American Girls Professional Baseball League

The management sets a high standard for the girls selected for the different clubs and expects them to live up to the code of conduct which recognizes that standard. There are general regulations necessary as a means of maintaining order and organizing clubs into a working procedure.

1. ALWAYS appear in feminine attire when not actively engaged in practice or playing ball. This regulation continues through the playoffs for all, even though your team is not participating. AT NO TIME MAY A PLAYER APPEAR IN THE STANDS IN HER UNIFORM, OR WEAR SLACKS OR SHORTS IN PUBLIC.

From The Official Web Site of the AAGPBL Players Assoc., http://www.aagpbl.org/index.cfm.

2. Boyish bobs are not permissible and in general your hair should be well groomed at all times with longer hair preferable to short hair cuts. Lipstick should always be on.

3. Smoking or drinking is not permissible in public places. Liquor drinking will not be permissible under any circumstances. Other intoxicating drinks in limited portions with after-game meal only, will be allowed. Obscene language will not be allowed at any time.

4. All social engagements must be approved by chaperone. Legitimate requests for dates can be allowed by chaperones.

5. Jewelry must not be worn during game or practice, regardless of type.

6. All living quarters and eating places must be approved by the chaperones. No player shall change her residence without the permission of the chaperone.

7. For emergency purposes, it is necessary that you leave notice of your whereabouts and your home phone.

8. Each club will establish a satisfactory place to eat, and a time when all members must be in their individual rooms. In general, the lapse of time will be two hours after the finish of the last game, but in no case later than 12:30 a.m. Players must respect hotel regulations as to other guests after this hour, maintaining conduct in accordance with high standards set by the league.

9. Always carry your employee's pass as a means of identification for entering the various parks. This pass is NOT transferable.

10. Relatives, friends, and visitors are not allowed on the bench at any time.

11. Due to shortage of equipment, baseballs must not be given as souvenirs without permission from the Management.

12. Baseball uniform skirts shall not be shorter than six inches above the knee-cap.

13. In order to sustain the complete spirit of rivalry between clubs, the members of different clubs must not fraternize at any time during the season. After the opening day of the season, fraternizing will be subject to heavy penalties. This also means in particular: room parties, auto trips to out of the way eating places, etc. However, friendly discussions in lobbies with opposing players are permissible. Players should never approach the opposing manager or chaperone about being transferred.

14. When traveling, the members of the clubs must be at the station thirty minutes before departure time. Anyone missing her arranged transportation will have to pay her own fare.

15. Players will not be allowed to drive their cars past their city's limits without the special permission of their manager. Each team will travel as a unit via method of travel provided for the league.

Fines of five dollars for first offense, ten dollars for second, and suspension for third, will automatically be imposed for breaking any of the above rules.

◀▓▶

PSYCHOSOCIAL IMPACTS OF ATHLETIC PARTICIPATION ON AMERICAN WOMEN

Facts and Fables

Don Sabo

Patriarchal myths are encoded within American culture and transmitted through art and literature, religion and law, fables and folkways. These myths help to legitimate structured sex inequality in all sectors of society, including sport. Feminist theorists argue that patriarchal myths in American sport are more than mere cultural beliefs or "gender stereotypes." They are historically constructed ideologies that exaggerate and naturalize sex differences and, in effect, sustain men's power and privilege in [relation] to women (Messner and Sabo, in press; Birrell and Cole, 1986; Hargreaves, 1986). These same ideologies have also kept sport researchers from seeing women athletes as they really are as well as what they are capable of becoming.

This paper identifies six beliefs about American women athletes which are grounded more in myth than empirical reality. Each myth is examined in light of current sport research which includes findings from three recent nationwide surveys which the author helped to design and execute. The first of these latter studies, the *American High School Survey* (AHSS), is a longitudinal analysis of a national, two-state, stratified probability sample of 569 female students. This study is unique because it overcomes a critical defect present in most previous studies of the effects of athletic participation, namely, their reliance on cross-sectional rather than longitudinal analysis and the resulting inability to adequately discuss change (see Melnick, Sabo, & Vanfossen, 1988). The second study, the 1985 *Miller Lite Report on Women in Sports* (MLR),

From Don Sabo, *Journal of Sport and Social Issues* (12:2) pp. 83–93, copyright 1988. Reprinted in *Sport in Contemporary Society: An Anthology*, D. Stanley Eitzen, ed. New York: St. Martin's Press, 1992. Reprinted by permission of Sage Publications, Inc.

is the first nationwide survey of "active and committed" adult female athletes (Pollock, 1985). A random sample of 7,000 members of the Women's Sports Foundation were surveyed in fall of 1985 and questioned about participation in sports and fitness activities. Finally, *The Wilson Report: Moms, Dads, Daughters and Sports* (TWR) focused on how family factors influence girls' athletic participation (Garfield, 1988). Telephone interviews were conducted with a national random sample of 702 mothers, 302 fathers, and 513 of their daughters aged 7–18. Whereas the AHSS provides solid methodological grounds for making causal inferences, the data reported in the MLR and TWR are descriptive and interpretations are made with caution.

The goals of this paper are to (1) identify several "myth-conceptions" about women athletes, and (2) scrutinize their merit in light of sport research. The intent is to move sport research and theory away from androcentric assumptions and their resultant biases (Hall, 1987).

The Myth of Female Frailty

The "myth of female frailty" in sports holds that women lack the necessary physical strength and energy to fully participate in athletics. As Lenskyj amply documents, such beliefs helped justify women's exclusion from sports and fitness activities. The belief in the fragility of female physiology is evident in 19th century medical writings which depict upper-class women as being inherently weak, sickly, hypochondriacal, and intellectually incapable of understanding medical matters and their own bodies. Well-to-do women were considered especially vulnerable to a variety of ailments. Because of their "innate" frailness, many medical scientists reasoned that women's activities had to be limited to the more moderate demands of motherhood and homemaking (Ehrenreich and English, 1979). Likewise, American sociologist W. I. Thomas argued in 1907 that women's peculiar anatomical traits were "very striking evidence of the ineptitude of women for the expenditure of physiological energy through motor action" (1907).

The most recent evidence of the belief in female frailty issued in May of 1986 when the American College of Obstetricians and Gynecologists (ACOG) issued thirteen pages of "Safety Guidelines for Women." Women were advised to consider 30 minutes of moderate exercise followed by a "day of rest" as a safe limit to avoid injury. These prescriptions were challenged by women's sports advocates and researchers who point out that ACOG's recommendations were not based on rigorously scientific studies of women athletes. In contrast to ACOG's medical prescriptions, studies show that very few physical obstructions stand in the way of women's full participation in sport and fitness activities (Harris 1973, 1986; Wilmore, 1974, Ryan 1974: Adrian and Brame 1977; Hudson 1978).

ACOG's recommendations also do not reflect the life experiences of active American athletes who, according to MLS and TWR data, feel their health is bettered by participation. Seventy-four percent of the MLS respondents ranked "improved health" and "stress reduction" as main reasons for engaging in sports activity (Pollock, 1985:17). Fifty-five percent of the TWR parents interviewed cited fitness and health as chief benefits of their daughters' participation in sports (Garfield, 1988:15). Finally, data from both studies show that, while the exercise regimen of many of the female subjects exceeded ACOG's guidelines, there were no negative physiological effects other than a normal incidence of athletic injury.

Rather than "excessive" exercise, socialization for physical passivity and the more sedentary character of many women's roles may in fact be responsible for many of women's health problems. For example, about 43.4% of American women between the ages of 25–34 are obese (National Center for Health Statistics, 1983). American children are growing fatter. The National Children and Youth Fitness found significant increases in the percentage of body fat in young people since 1960 (U.S. Department of Health and Human Services, 1985). Obesity is a risk factor in the development of hyperlipidemia, hypercholesterolemia, hypertension, and diabetes, which are also cardiac risk factors (Schroeder, 1982). Obesity increases the risk of osteoarthritis, a crippling disease prevalent among elderly women (Braye, 1978; Mayer, 1968). Similarly, osteoporosis afflicts 25% of American women over age 60, a disease which is propitiated by sedentary lifestyles (Veninga, 1984). Moreover, emerging research shows that regular and strenuous exercise curtails or prevents the development of osteoarthritic symptoms (Larson & Shannon, 1984; Yeaker & Martin, 1984; Huddleston, et al. 1980; Nilsson and Westlin, 1971).

In summary, both the increased number and apparent vitality of female athletes debunk the sexist assumptions of many health professionals. Feminist scholars are challenging the purportedly "objective" and "neutral" pronouncements of medical science, especially as regards to women's bodies (Lenskyj, 1986; MacPherson, 1985; Hubbard, 1983). Women athletes themselves, the MLS shows, want unbiased information about the effects of participation; 70% selected "Physiology of Women as Athletes" as one of the "most important areas for future research on women in sport" (Pollock, 1985:31). What appears to be needed is a more accurate assessment of women's athletic capabilities and the formation of sound health policy which encourages rather than squelches their physical potentials.

The Myth of Psychic Damage

The "myth of psychic damage" contends that women do not have the necessary psychological assets for athletic competition and, in contrast to men, women do not reap psychological benefit from sport. These notions are partly rooted in psychological theory. Around 1900, the American school of functionalism developed the view that female psychology and behavior are molded by evolution and instincts. Within this biologistic framework, the observable differences between women's and men's physiology, intellectual interests, and cultural achievements were interpreted as evidence of women's inferiority. Women's subordination to men thus found scientific legitimacy (Williams, 1977). These views (and their implicit values) became fused within the development of psychoanalytic theory and psychiatric practice (Efron, 1985; Smith, 1975). Within the framework of psychoanalytic theory, for example, nonconformity to traditional roles and stereotypes was considered pathological. Hence, women's interest and involvement in business, engineering, athletics, or other "masculine" activities were clinically suspect.

What does empirical research say about the psychological impacts of athletic participation on women? Generally, sport researchers have found sport involvement betters rather than worsens psychological health. Prior research suggests that, compared to nonathletes, female athletes are more achievement-motivated, independent, poised, and inner-controlled (Burke et al., 1977; Kleiber et al., 1981). Some studies find that women athletes feel that their sport involvement contributes to their self-confidence, higher energy levels, better health and a general well-being (Snyder & Kivlin, 1977; Snyder and Spreitzer, 1983). Other research shows women are deriving elevated self-esteem, self-image, and self-actualization from athletic participation (Harris, 1975, 1973; Snyder and Kivlin, 1975; Snyder and Spreitzer, 1976). As regards to body image, a widely accepted index of overall, psychological health, the 1985 MLR found that 62% of respondents felt much more positively about their bodies now than five years ago, and another 23% felt the same. Also, 41% of the TWR parents believed their daughters derived character benefits from athletic participation.

The AHSS findings, however, indicate that understanding the psychological impacts of athletic participation on women (and men) may be more complex than previously assumed. Earlier studies of both female and male athletes have mainly used convenient samples and cross-sectional data, hence it has been impossible to untangle the effects of selectivity into and out of the sport stream from the socialization that occurs within sport itself. Almost all studies to date, moreover, fail to systematically account for the confounding impacts of race and/or social class on psychological well-being. In contract, the NHSS yielded no discernable psychological effects which were directly attributable to athletic participation itself (Melnick, Sabo, and Vanfossen, 1986). The researchers initially uncovered several correlations between athletic participation and self-esteem, self-mastery, and body-concept. When controls for socio-economic status and sophomore participation were introduced, however, these associations disappeared.

There are two interpretations of this outcome. First, since greater numbers of middle-class than working-class girls participate in high school athletic programs, the initial correlations may be picking up class differences rather than differential outcomes of athletic socialization. Secondly, the NHSS focused solely on athletic socialization between the sophomore and senior years. That no psychological affects accruing from athletic participation were found, therefore, might suggest that the impact of sport involvement upon overall personality development for many girls occurs before the sophomore year (Melnick, Sabo, & Vanfossen, 1986). In any event, contrary to patriarchal myth, no evidence of negative psychological outcomes emerged in any study!

The Myth of the "Macho" Female Athlete

The "myth of the 'macho' female athlete" holds that playing sports makes women think, act, and feel like men. It derives from the cultural assumption that sport is a "man's domain" and being an "athlete" means being "masculine." In this view, athletic participation is believed to exert a "masculinizing" effect on women's gender identities and, in turn, results in "abnormal" personality traits. This view was so well entrenched in American culture in the early 20th century that Dr. Dudley Sargent, a physician and physical educationist, created a stir in 1912 when he wrote in the *Ladies Home Journal* that women and men shared the same athletic potential. Sargent observed that "Many persons honestly believe that athletics are making girls bold, masculine and overassertive; that they are destroying the beautiful lines and curves of her figure, and are robbing her of that charm and elusiveness that has so long characterized the female sex" (quoted in Twin, 1979:53–54). Today, one often hears the assertion that sports turn women into lesbians which, according to some sexual stereotypes, means "masculine" women. Is there any empirical basis for these assumptions?

Research shows that athletic participation more probably "androgynizes" rather than "masculinizes" women's identities. Psychological androgyny means that a mixture or balance of feminine and masculine traits reside in the same personality (Bem, 1979). The outcomes of athletic socialization vis à vis androgyny are different for males and females (Sabo 1985). Traditional sport endorses stereotypical gender expectations and idealizes manliness. For boys, sport socialization represents a CONTINUATION of previous gender learning; traditionally masculine expectations often become exaggerated as boys spend more time in the athletic subculture. In contrast, when girls enter the "masculine" world of sport, their experiences are apt to have an androgynizing effect on gender identity development. Athletic involvement for girls is a source of social and psychological counterpoint but, for boys, just another variation on a theme. Theoretically, therefore, gender socialization in sport is often onesided and narrowing for boys and multifaceted and expansive for girls.

The expansion of women's gender identity in sport does not appear to produce psychological ill effects (Oglesby, 1983; Duquin, 1978). For example, Harris and Jennings (1977, 1978) studied college women athletes and found that those with androgynous identities also scored significantly higher on self-esteem than "masculine," "feminine," or "undifferentiated" individuals. These findings parallel studies of non-athletic subgroups which indicate that, regardless of their sex, androgynous individuals enjoy the highest level of self-esteem when compared with "masculine" (next highest), "feminine" (third highest) and "undifferentiated" (lowest) (Spence, Helmreich, and Stapp, 1974). Finally, data on female athletes and high achievers show they "are more likely than their male counterparts to possess masculine and feminine attributes without suffering any deficit to their femininity" (Harris, 1980:234). In other words, there does not appear to be any trade-off between women's sports involvement and "femininity" or self-esteem.

Sport researchers must recognize that the discussion of female athleticism within the conceptual framework of "androgyny" can be a form of psychological reductionism which actually reinforces patriarchal notions about gender differences. If athletic participation helps females to expand gender identity and behavior beyond narrow patriarchal standards (which include passivity, weakness, heterosexual appeal, etc.), then this means that the dominant cultural standard for femininity, or what Connell (1987) calls "emphasized femininity," is being challenged. Hence, the social construction of alternative definitions of femininity in sport depart from hegemonic views of gender which reflect and reinforce male dominance. So-called "psychological androgyny" in sport, therefore, is more accurately seen as a challenge to the social and political status quo. Indeed, data from the TWR show that most adults now accept sport as an appropriate cultural terrain for girls: 97% of parents were pleased with their daughters' involvement or want them to be more highly involved;

87% of parents believed that sports are just as important for daughters as sons; 85% of daughters felt it is no more important for boys to play sports than it is for girls.

The Myth of the "Female Apologetic"

A variety of sport researchers have suggested that female athletes tend to espouse a more traditional or conventional view of the women's role in society, in effect, to "apologize" for their participation in a non-traditional and "manly" activity. More recently the usefulness of the "apologetic" concept has fallen into disfavor among researchers and it is sometimes vehemently denied by feminists who claim women athletes have nothing for which to apologize. Where does the truth lie?

Research on college samples has not demonstrated the existence of the apologetic (Colker and Widom, 1980; Del Ray, 1977; Snyder & Kivlin, 1977; Uguccioni & Ballantine, 1980). The AHSS found no evidence that the "female apologetic" is a pervasive reality among American female high school athletes; female athletes were no more apt to endorse conservative gender expectations than nonathletes. In addition, the MLS found that 94% of the respondents disagreed with the statement "Participation in sports diminishes a woman's femininity." However, at the same time, 57% of the sample agreed with the statement that "In this society, a woman is forced to choose between being an athlete and being feminine." This latter finding may mean that, while women athletes are aware of other people's (especially men's) reservations or hang-ups about sports and femininity, they themselves are generally self-confident about their participation. Finally, the TWR findings revealed that, while some girls still feel that "boys will make fun of them" for playing sports (22% of the 7–10 year olds), this concern ebbs as they grow older (10% of 11–14 year olds and only 3% of 15–18 year olds).

On one hand, the data may indicate that generally favorable attitudes toward women's sports now exist among American girls and women. Negative attitudes toward female athletic participation were more pervasive and intense in earlier decades. In short, during the last two decades of women's increased participation in American sport, the "masculinizing" taint surrounding women's athletic involvements may have lost its former venom. On the other hand, the very existence of the apologetic in previous decades has never received unambiguous empirical documentation. Hence, the "apologetic" may have been more of a figment of the social scientific imagination rather than a fixture in the psyche of women athletes. In any event, there is no evidence for its existence in the 1980s.

The Myth of Coed Catastrophe

The "myth of coed catastrophe" assumes that athletic competition between or among BOTH sexes is harmful to women, men, and society. Negative assumptions are that physiological disparities between the sexes (size and strength differences) would make females injury prone, that men's masculine self-esteem and women's feminine self-image would be destroyed, that any further erosion of gender differences would lead to individual pathology and social anarchy. In contrast, proponents of cross-sex sport see a potential for positive outcomes: e.g., destructive gender stereotypes would be eroded; greater contact between the sexes would translate into enhanced respect and empathy; girls would learn competitive and team skills which would help them function more effectively in adult occupational settings; boys would learn how to work WITH rather than against women and apply these lessons to other sectors of their lives; many women athletes would gain access to the higher levels of competition they desire. Where does the truth lie?

Chief among myth-conceptions about cross-sex sport is that it is a "totally new" and scarce phenomenon. In fact, many types of cross-sex sport have emerged during the last few decades; e.g., coed volley ball leagues, baseball and softball leagues, racquetball, touch or flag football, floor and ice hockey, and team tennis. Whereas some forms of cross-sex sport pit individual females against males, team-sports most often mix males and females on the same team; competition between all-female and all-male teams is comparatively rare.

Reliable data on the actual extent of coed participation is scarce, but the MLR offers some intriguing descriptive statistics which may serve as a starting point for further theory and research. Table 1 shows the percentage of times the respondents participated in the 11 most popular athletic and fitness activities as either single-sex or coed participants. The overall data show that the subjects participate in coed sports about half the time.

A second myth is that women do not want to participate in cross-sex sport. Emerging evidence only partly disconfirms this notion. On one hand, the desire for coed athletic alternatives is growing in some sectors. The TWR found that most girls (58%) would prefer to play coed sports while only 33% would prefer to play with girls only; no significant differences issued across age subgroups. Among the MLR respondents, 79% indicated that, when playing sports, they "seek out people with the same skill level REGARDLESS OF SEX." On the other hand, however, women's desire for male competitors with similar athletic skills NEED NOT stem from personal preferences as much as from social necessity. The fact is that women's athletic skills have greatly expanded in recent decades. For

Table 1

Percentage of Single-Sex and Cross-Sex Participation in the 11 Most Popular Athletic and Fitness Activities among Active, Committed Women Athletes

	Single Sex %	Cross Sex %	Total Number
Calisthenics/Aerobics	66	34	987
Jogging/Running	66	34	1010
Softball/Baseball	56	44	874
Walking	55	45	1117
Bicycling	54	46	996
Weightlifting	53	47	821
Basketball	49	51	774
Tennis, Squash	41	59	1076
Swimming	40	60	1025
Volleyball	40	60	854
Dance	25	75	773

Adapted from the *1985 Miller Lite Report on Women in Sports,* in cooperation with the Women's Sports Foundation.

highly-skilled women athletes, it may be easier to find accessible and challenging competition among men than women simply for demographic reasons; i.e., there are more highly-skilled male athletes than women athletes within the general population.

Reservations about coed competition were also evident among the MLR respondents. For example, only about half (52%) of the sample were generally WILLING to play with members of the opposite sex, and 69% believed women's sports should be "kept separate from men's." Moreover, 78% felt that "women have something to teach men about humane competition" and 82% felt that "in coed sports men are often threatened by losing to a woman." Finally, though 82% disagreed that sports diminish a woman's PERSONAL SENSE of her femininity, 57% recognized that women are often forced by social pressures to choose between being athletes and being feminine. In summary, therefore, the issue of whether many women athletes actually prefer or simply settle for coed sport remains blurred. What does seem clear is that, for personal and socio-political reasons, they are wading rather than diving headlong into the waters of coed sport.

One final question clouded by patriarchal myth and sadly in need of empirical scrutiny is whether cross-sex participation eroticizes male-female relations. The argument is sometimes made that cross-sex sport would lead to sexual contact, especially where boys and girls are playing contact sports together such as wrestling or basketball. This position conjures up visions of sexually aroused adolescents spending their post-game hours in heated, coital clinches. There are reasons to suspect this kind of thinking. First of all, sex research consistently shows that physical familiarity usually de-eroticizes male-female relations; e.g., coital frequency decreases the longer a couple is married (Kinsey, 1948, 1953; Hunt, 1974). Secondly, the proposition that physical contact automatically leads to sexual arousal assumes that the human sexual response is physiologically or instinctually motivated. This is not so. For humans, sexual behavior is orchestrated by the mind's capacity to internalize cultural meanings rather than some primeval or genetically triggered instinctual program (Davis, 1971). It is culture that establishes what is sexual and what is not; e.g., hand-to-genital petting in a movie theater is sexual and a gynecological examination is not. Thirdly, there is no scientific evidence that SAME-SEX contact in sport results in excessive amounts of homosexual arousal or behavior. It is theoretically inconsistent, therefore, to assert that CROSS-SEX athletic activity would inflame heterosexual passion.

In summary, the "myth of coed catastrophe" reflects and shores up patriarchy's mandate for sex segregation. To propose that men and women enter direct competition with one another violates this structural imperative. Such a proposition also challenges patriarchal beliefs about men's athletic superiority and physical powers and women's athletic inferiority and physical vulnerability. Sport researchers can inject needed empirical clarity into current controversies surrounding cross-sex sport by separating fact from fancy, reason from sentiment, and theory from ideology.

The Myth of Immobility

Many sport researchers conclude that, for males, athletic participation leads to increased status among peers, greater educational attainment and aspiration, and upward mobility (Curry & Jibou, 1984; Sack & Theil, 1979; Loy, 1969). In comparison, researchers are less contentious about whether sport involvement favorably impacts on the status and mobility of females. Whereas many researchers lean toward inferring upward mobility for men, they hesitate to do so for women. Are these dispositions based on social fact or patriarchal bias?

To begin with, most of the research on this question has focused on MALES and not FEMALES. This very disparity may reflect underlying and unconscious patriarchal norms which emphasize upward mobility and achievement for men but not women. Secondly, statements about upward mobility and male athletes remain methodologically suspect because most are based on studies using cross-sectional data and convenient samples.

Finally, the few studies of women athletes to date have produced mixed findings. For example, Feltz (1978) discovered that sports involvement ranked low among a variety of status criteria among high school students. She suggests that this is due to the stigma associated with female athletes in the high school subculture. Wells and Picou (1980), in contrast, found that among Louisiana high school females, athletes were more apt to be members of the college-oriented crowd and to hold higher educational aspirations than nonathletes. Finally, the MLR indicates that female athletes themselves endorse the view that sport involvement is related to social mobility for women. Ninety-three percent of the respondents agreed with the statement "if young girls compete successfully on the athletic fields, they will be better able to compete successfully in later life."

The AHSS generated several significant findings which may help dispel some of the current ambiguity. First, athletic participation exerted a modest impact on female athletes' self-reported popularity in the high school. Though socioeconomic status explained most of the variance in popularity, athletic participation exerted an independent effect between the sophomore and senior years. Findings also showed that athletic participation produced a slight but statistically significant effect on educational aspiration; athletes aspired toward greater educational attainment. Finally, athletic participation significantly increased the extent of girls' extracurricular activities; athletes were more involved in school and community activities than non-athletes. Melnick, Sabo, and Vanfossen (1986) infer that athletic participation expands the spectrum of activities which girls consider appropriate for self-expression. They add that, "As the high school career unfolds, the personal lessons learned through athletic socialization may interact with the status gains gleaned from sports activity thereby facilitating social experimentation and involvement within and outside the school social network" (p. 15).

Conclusion

This paper has identified six patriarchal myths about women athletes and examined them in light of current research knowledge. Several conclusions can be made.

1. There is no evidence that women are too physiologically frail for athletic involvement. In fact, data indicate that strenuous exercise is a health asset while women's traditional socialization for physical passivity is a risk factor for several diseases.

2. Contrary to the "myth of psychic damage," the evidence does not suggest that women are psychologically harmed by athletic participation.

3. Rather than becoming "masculinized" by athletic participation, girls and women appear to be adopting a wider array of psychological traits and behaviors which goes beyond narrow, patriarchal definitions of femininity.
4. Findings indicate that American girls and women in the 1980s no longer feel defensive or "apologetic" about their athletic involvement.
5. Research on psychosocial impacts of coed sport on participants is so sparse at this time that inferences are not warranted. However, many young females prefer coed activities, and active and committed adult athletes frequently engage in coed sports and with no apparent negative social or psychological effects.
6. The data show that, though participation in sport slightly heightens high school girls' educational aspirations, it significantly expands the extent of their involvement in extracurricular activities. In addition, athletic participation modestly increases girls' perceived status within the high school.

Patriarchal myths may be fading within American culture but they continue to influence perceptions of women athletes. All cultures defend their fictions and, ordinarily, we see only what we assume we know. When new information challenges mythic assumptions, two alternatives emerge: to discard the myths that establish the realities, or to cling unquestionably to the beliefs which emanate from and invigorate the status quo. Both women athletes and sport researchers now find themselves between these two alternatives. Simone de Beauvoir stated, "It is always difficult to describe a myth; it cannot be grasped or encompassed; it haunts the human consciousness without ever appearing before it in fixed form. The myth is so various, so contradictory, that at first its unity is not discerned: (1953).

The patriarchal myths described in this paper are only part of a large, unified web of beliefs which not only contain and conceal the true abilities and potentials of women athletes, but women in ALL sectors of North American society. Empirical research will hopefully continue to play an important role in sifting fact from fable, and reality from sexist ideology.

REFERENCES

Adrian, M. & Brame, J. (eds.). 1977. National Association of Girls' and Women's Sports. Research Reports, 3. Washington, DC: American Alliance for Health, Physical Education, and Recreation.
Aloia, J. F., Chn, S. J. & Ostuni, J. A. 1978. Prevention of involutional bone loss by exercise. *Annals of Internal Medicine,* 89 (3): 356–358.
Bem, S. 1975. Sex-role adaptability: One consequence of psychological androgyny. *Journal of Personality and Social Psychology,* 31: 534–43.

Birrell, S. & Cole, C. 1986. Resisting the canon: Feminist cultural studies and sport. Paper presented at NASSS meeting, Las Vegas, Oct.

Bray, G. A. (ed.) 1978. Obesity in perspective: Proceedings of the conference. Washington, DC: U.S. Government Printing Office.

Burke, E. J., Straub, W. F. & Bonney, A. R. 1975. Psycho-social parameters in young female long distance runners. *Movement, actes du 7, Symposium en apopresntissage psycho-moteur et psychologie du sport,* 367–371.

Carpenter & Acosta. 1983. The status of women in intercollegiate athletics. Cited in P. Miller, The organization and regulation of sport proceedings of The New Agenda, Nov. 3–6, Washington, DC.

Colker, R. & Widom, C. S. 1980. Correlates of female athletic participation: Masculinity, femininity, self-esteem and attitudes toward women. *Sex Roles,* 6:47–58.

Connell, R. W. 1987. *Gender and power.* Stanford, CA: Stanford University Press.

Curry, T. J. & Jibou, R. M. 1984. *Sports: A social perspective.* Englewood Cliffs, NJ: Prentice Hall.

Davis, K. 1971. The prostitute: Developing a deviant identity. In J. M. Harris (ed.) *Studies in the sociology of sex.* New York: Appleton-Century-Crofts.

de Beauvoir, S. 1953. *The second sex.* New York: Knopf.

Duquin, M. 1978. Effects of culture on women's experience in sport. *Sport Sociology Bulletin,* 6:20–25.

Effron, A. 1985. The sexual body: An interdisciplinary perspective. *The Journal of Mind and Behavior,* 6: (1 & 2).

Ehrenreich, B. & English, D. 1979. *For her own good.* New York: Anchor Books.

Feltz, D. L. 1978. Athletics in the status system of female adolescents. *Review of Sport & Leisure,* 3:98–108.

Garfield, E. 1988. The Wilson report: Moms, dads, daughters and sport. Copies may be secured by writing Women's Sports Foundation, 342 Madison Avenue, Suite 728, New York, NY 10017.

Hall, M. A. 1987. The gendering of sport, leisure, and physical education. *Women's Studies International Forum,* 10 (4).

Hargreaves, J. A. 1986. Where's the virtue? where's the grace? A discussion of the social production of gender through sport. *Theory, Culture & Society,* 3: 109–121.

Harris, D. V. 1973. *Involvement in sport.* Philadelphia: Lea & Febiger.

Harris, D. V. 1975. Research studies on the female athletes: Psychosocial considerations. *Journal of Physical Education and Recreation,* 46: 32–6.

Harris, D. V. 1980. Femininity and athleticism: Conflict or consonance: pp. 222–239 in D. Sabo & R. Runfola (eds.) *Jock: Sports & Male Identity.* Englewood Cliffs, NJ: Prentice Hall.

Harris, D. & Jennings, S. E. 1977. Self-perception of female distance runners, in P. Milvy (ed.) *The marathon: physiological, medic, epidemiologist and psychological studies.* NY: New York Academy of Sciences.

Harris, D. & Jennings, S. E. 1978. Achievement motivation: There is no fear of success among female athletes. A paper presented at the Fall Conference of the Eastern Association of Physical Education of College Women. Hershey, PA. October.

Hubbard, R. 1983. Social effects of some contemporary myths about women. Pp. 1–8 in M. Lowe & R. Hubbard (eds.). *Women's nature: Rationalization of inequality.* New York: Pergamon Press.

Huddleston, A. L., Rockwell, D., Kulund, D. N. & Harrison, B. 1980. Bone mass in lifetime tennis athletes. In C. A. Oglesby (ed.), *Women and Sport: From Myth to Reality*. Philadelphia: Lea & Febiger.

Hudson, J. 1978. Physical parameters used for female exclusion from law enforcement and athletics. In C. A. Oglesby (ed.), *Women and Sport: From Myth to Reality*. Philadelphia: Lea & Febiger.

Hunt, M. H. 1974. *Sexual behavior in the 1970's*. New York: Dell Publishing Company.

Kinsey, A. 1948. *Sexual behavior in the human male*. Philadelphia, PA: Saunders Publishing Company.

———. 1948. *Sexual behavior in the human female*. Philadelphia, PA: Saunders Publishing Company.

Kleiber, D. A. & Hemmer, J. D. 1981. Sex differences in the relationship of locus of control and recreational sport participation. *Sex Roles*, 7: 801–810.

Larson, K. A. & Shannon, S. C. 1985. Decreasing the incidence of osteoporosis-related injuries through diet and exercise, Public Health Reports, 99 (6): 609–613.

Lenskyj, H. 1986. *Out of bounds: women, sport and sexuality*. Toronto: The Women's Press.

Loy, J. 1969. The Study of sport and social mobility. Pp. 112–117 in G. S. Kenyon, *Aspects of Contemporary Sport Psychology*. Chicago, IL: The Athletic Institute.

MacPherson, K. 1985. Osteoporosis and menopause: A feminist analysis of the social construction of a syndrome. *Advances in Nursing Science*, 7 (4): 11–22.

Mayer, J. 1968. *Overweight: causes, costs, controls*. Englewood Cliffs, NJ: Prentice Hall.

Melnick, M., Sabo, D., & Vanfossen, B. 1988. Developmental effects of athletic participation among high school girls. *Sociology of Sport Journal*, 5 (1): 22–36.

Messner, M., & Sabo, D. (In press.) *Sport, man, and the gender order: Critical feminist perspectives*. Champaign, IL: Human Kinetics Press.

Nilsson, D. E. Westlin, N. W. 1971. Bone density in athletics. *Clinical Orthopedics and Related Research*, 77: 179–182.

Oglesby, C. 1973. Athleticism and sex role. A paper presented at The New Agenda Conference, Washington, D.C., November 3–6.

Pollock, J. 1985. *The 1985 Miller Lite report on women in sports*. Copies can be obtained from New World Decisions, Ltd., 120 Wood Avenue South, Iselin, NJ 08830.

Ryan, J. 1975. Gynecological considerations. *Journal of Physical Education and Recreation*, 46:40.

Sabo, D. & Runfola, R. (eds.). 1980. *Jock: Sports and male identity*. Englewood Cliffs, NJ: Prentice Hall.

Sabo, D. 1985. Sports, patriarchy & male identity. *Arena Review*, 9 (2): 1–30.

Sack, A. L. & Theil, R. 1979. College football and social mobility: A case study of Notre Dame football players. *Sociology of Education*, 52:63.

Schroeder, M. A. (ed.). (1982). Symposia on obesity. *The Nursing Clinics of North America*, 17 (2): 189–251.

Smith, Dorothy. 1975. Women and psychiatry. Pp. 1–19 in D. Smith and S. David (eds.), *Women look at psychiatry*. Vancouver: Press Gange Publishers.

Snyder, E. E. & Kivlin, J. E. 1975. Women athletes and aspects of psychological well-being and body image. *Research Quarterly*, 46: 191–199.

Snyder, E. E. & Kivlin, J. E. 1977. Perceptions of the sex role among female athletes and nonathletes. *Adolescence*. 12; 25–29.

Snyder, E. C. & Spreitzer, E. A. 1976. Correlates of sport participation among adolescent girls. *Research Quarterly*, 47: 804–09.

Snyder, E. D. & Spreitzer, E. A. 1983. *Social aspects of sport*. Englewood Cliffs, NJ: Prentice Hall.

Spence, J. T. & Helmreich, R. L. 1978. *Masculinity and femininity: Their psychological dimensions, correlates, and antecedents*. Austin: University of Texas Press.

Thomas, W. I. 1907. *Sex and society*. Chicago: University of Chicago Press.

Twin, S. 1979. *Out of the bleachers: Writings on women and sport*. New York: McGraw-Hill.

Uguccioni, S. M. & Ballantine, R. H. 1980. Comparison of attitudes and sex roles for female athletic participants and nonparticipants. *International Journal of Sport Psychology*, 11: 42–48.

U.S. Department of Health and Human Services. 1985. The national children and youth fitness study. Office of Disease Prevention and Health Promotion, Washington, D. C. 20201. This study is also published in the *Journal of Physical Education, Recreation & Dance*, 56 (1): NCYFS 1-NCYFS 48.

Velinga, K. S. 1984. Osteoporosis: Implications for community health nursing. *Journal of Community Health Nursing*, 1 (4): 227–233.

Wells, R. H. & Picou, J. S. 1980. Interscholastic athletes and socialization for educational achievement. *Journal of Sport Behavior*, 3: 119–128.

Williams, Juanita H. 1977. *Psychology of women: Behavior in a biosocial context*. New York: W. W. Norton.

Willhelm, S. 1983. *Black in a White America*. Cambridge, MA: Schenkman Publishing Company.

Wilmore, J. (ed.), 1974. Research methodology in the sociology of sport. *Exercise and Sport Sciences Review*, 2, New York: Academic Press.

Yeaker, R. A. & Martin, R. B. 1984. Senile osteoporosis: The effects of calcium. *Postgraduate Medicine*, 75 (2): 147–159.

THROWING LIKE A GIRL

James Fallows

Most people remember the 1994 baseball season for the way it ended—with a strike rather than a World Series. I keep thinking about the way it began. On opening day, April 4, Bill Clinton went to Cleveland and, like many Presidents before him, threw out a ceremonial first pitch. That same day Hillary Rodham Clinton went to Chicago and, like no First Lady before her, also threw out a first ball, at a Cubs game in Wrigley Field.

From *The Atlantic Monthly* 278:2 (August, 1996): 84–87.

The next day photos of the Clintons in action appeared in newspapers around the country. Many papers, including *The New York Times* and *The Washington Post,* chose the same two photos to run. The one of Bill Clinton showed him wearing an Indians cap and warm-up jacket. The President, throwing lefty, had turned his shoulders sideways to the plate in preparation for delivery. He was bringing the ball forward from behind his head in a clean-looking throwing action as the photo was snapped. Hillary Clinton was pictured wearing a dark jacket, a scarf, and an oversized Cubs hat. In preparation for her throw she was standing directly facing the plate. A right-hander, she had the elbow of her throwing arm pointed out in front of her. Her forearm was tilted back, toward her shoulder. The ball rested on her upturned palm. As the picture was taken, she was in the middle of an action that can only be described as throwing like a girl.

The phrase "throwing like a girl" has become an embattled and offensive one. Feminists smart at its implication that to do something "like a girl" is to do it the wrong way. Recently, on the heels of the O. J. Simpson case, a book appeared in which the phrase was used to help explain why male athletes, especially football players, were involved in so many assaults against women. Having been trained (like most American boys) to dread the accusation of doing anything "like a girl," athletes were said to grow into the assumption that women were valueless, and natural prey.

I grant the justice of such complaints. I am attuned to the hurt caused by similar broad-brush stereotypes when they apply to groups I belong to—"dancing like a white man," for instance, or "speaking foreign languages like an American," or "thinking like a Washingtonian."

Still, whatever we want to call it, the difference between the two Clintons in what they were doing that day is real, and it is instantly recognizable. And since seeing those photos I have been wondering, Why, exactly, do so many women throw "like a girl"? If the motion were easy to change, presumably a woman as motivated and self-possessed as Hillary Clinton would have changed it. (According to her press secretary, Lisa Caputo, Mrs. Clinton spent the weekend before opening day tossing a ball in the Rose Garden with her husband, for practice.) Presumably, too, the answer to the question cannot be anything quite as simple as, Because they *are* girls.

A surprising number of people think that there is a structural difference between male and female arms or shoulders—in the famous "rotator cuff," perhaps—that dictates different throwing motions. "It's in the shoulder joint," a well-educated woman told me recently. "They're hinged differently." Someday researchers may find evidence to support a biological theory of throwing actions. For now, what you'll hear if you ask an orthopedist, an anatomist, or (especially) the coach of a women's softball team is that there is no structural reason why men and women should throw in different ways. This point will be obvious to any male who grew up around girls who liked to play baseball and became good at it. It should be obvious on a larger scale this summer, in broadcasts of the Olympic Games. This year, for the first time, women's fast-pitch softball teams will compete in the Olympics. Although the pitchers in these games will deliver the ball underhand, viewers will see female shortstops, center fielders, catchers, and so on pegging the ball to one another at speeds few male viewers could match.

Even women's tennis is a constant if indirect reminder that men's and women's shoulders are "hinged" the same way. The serving motion in tennis is like a throw—but more difficult, because it must be coordinated with the toss of the tennis ball. The men in professional tennis serve harder than the women, because they are bigger and stronger. But women pros serve harder than most male amateurs have ever done, and the service motion for good players is the same for men and women alike. There is no expectation in college or pro tennis that because of their anatomy female players must "serve like a girl." "I know many women who can throw a lot harder and better than the normal male," says Linda Wells, the coach of the highly successful women's softball team at Arizona State University. "It's not gender that makes the difference in how they throw."

So what is it, then? Since Hillary Clinton's ceremonial visit to Wrigley Field, I have asked men and women how they learned to throw, or didn't. Why did I care? My impetus was the knowledge that eventually my sons would be grown and gone. If my wife, in all other ways a talented athlete, could learn how to throw, I would still have someone to play catch with. My research left some women, including my wife, thinking that I am some kind of obsessed lout, but it has led me to the solution to the mystery. First let's be clear about what there is to be explained.

At a superficial level it's easy to tick off the traits of an awkward-looking throw. The fundamental mistake is the one Mrs. Clinton appeared to be making in the photo: trying to throw the ball with your body facing the target, rather than rotating your shoulders and hips ninety degrees away from the target and then swinging them around in order to accelerate the ball. A throw looks bad if your elbow is lower than your shoulder as your arm comes forward (unless you're throwing sidearm). A throw looks really bad if, as the ball leaves your hand, your wrist is "inside your elbow"—that is, your elbow joint is bent in such a way that your forearm angles back toward your body and your wrist is closer to your head than your elbow is. Slow-motion film of big-league pitchers shows that when they release the ball, the throwing arm is fully extended and straight from shoulder to wrist. The combination of these three elements—head-on stance, dropped elbow, and wrist inside the elbow—mechanically dictates a pushing rather than a hurling motion, creating the familiar pattern of "throwing like a girl."

It is surprisingly hard to find in the literature of baseball a deeper explanation of the mechanics of good and bad throws. Tom Seaver's pitching for the Mets and the White Sox got him into the Hall of Fame, but his book *The Art of Pitching* is full of bromides that hardly clarify the process of throwing, even if they might mean something to accomplished pitchers. His chapter "The Absolutes of Pitching Mechanics," for instance, lays out these four unhelpful principles: "Keep the Front Leg Flexible!" "Rub Up the Baseball," "Hide the Baseball!" "Get it Out, Get it Up!" (The fourth refers to the need to get the ball out of the glove and into the throwing hand in a quick motion.)

A variety of other instructional documents, from *Little League's Official How-to-Play Baseball Book* to *Softball for Girls & Women*, mainly reveal the difficulty of finding words to describe a simple motor activity that everyone can recognize. The challenge, I suppose, is like that of writing a manual on how to ride a bike, or how to kiss. Indeed, the most useful description I've found of the mechanics of throwing comes from a man whose specialty is another sport: Vic Braden made his name as a tennis coach, but he has attempted to analyze the physics of a wide variety of sports so that they all will be easier to teach.

Braden says that an effective throw involves connecting a series of links in a "kinetic chain." The kinetic chain, which is Braden's tool for analyzing most sporting activity, operates on a principle like that of crack-the-whip. Momentum builds up in one part of the body. When that part is suddenly stopped, as the end of the "whip" is stopped in crack-the-whip, the momentum is transferred to and concentrated in the next link in the chain. A good throw uses six links of chain, Braden says. The first two links involve the lower body, from feet to waist. The first motion of a throw (after the body has been rotated away from the target) is to rotate the legs and hips back in the direction of the throw, building up momentum as large muscles move body mass. Then those links stop—a pitcher stops turning his hips once they face the plate—and the momentum is transferred to the next link. This is the torso, from waist to shoulders, and since its mass is less than that of the legs, momentum makes it rotate faster than the hips and legs did. The torso stops when it is facing the plate, and the momentum is transferred to the next link—the upper arm. As the upper arm comes past the head, it stops moving forward, and the momentum goes into the final links—the forearm and wrist, which snap forward at tremendous speed.

This may sound arcane and jerkily mechanical, but it makes perfect sense when one sees Braden's slow-mo movies of pitchers in action. And it explains why people do, or don't, learn how to throw. The implication of

Braden's analysis is that throwing is a perfectly natural action (millions and millions of people can do it), but not at all innate. A successful throw involves an intricate series of actions coordinated among muscle groups, as each link of the chain is timed to interact with the next. Like bike riding or skating, it can be learned by anyone—male or female. No one starts out knowing how to ride a bike or throw a ball. Everyone has to learn.

Readers who are happy with their throwing skills can prove this to themselves in about two seconds. If you are right-handed, pick up a ball with your left hand and throw it. Unless you are ambidextrous or have some other odd advantage, you will throw it "like a girl." The problem is not that your left shoulder is hinged strangely or that you don't know what a good throw looks like. It is that you have not spent time training your leg, hip, shoulder, and arm muscles on that side to work together as required for a throw. The actor John Goodman, who played football seriously and baseball casually when he was in high school, is right-handed. When cast in the 1992 movie *The Babe*, he had to learn how to bat and throw left-handed, for realism in the role of Babe Ruth. For weeks before the filming began he would arrive an hour early at the set of his TV show, *Roseanne*, so that he could practice throwing a tennis ball against a wall left-handed. "I made damn sure no one could see me," Goodman told me recently. "I'm hard enough on myself without the derisive laughter of my so-called friends." When *The Babe* was released, Goodman told a newspaper interviewer, "I'll never say something like 'He throws like a girl' again. It's not easy to learn how to throw."

What Goodman discovered is what most men have forgotten: that if they know how to throw now, it is because they spent time learning at some point long ago. (Goodman says that he can remember learning to ride a bicycle but not learning to throw with his right hand.) This brings us back to the roots of the "throwing like a girl" phenomenon. The crucial factor is not that males and females are put together differently but that they typically spend their early years in different ways. Little boys often learn to throw without noticing that they are throwing. Little girls are more rarely in environments that encourage them in the same way. A boy who wonders why a girl throws the way she does is like a Frenchman who wonders why so many Americans speak French "with an accent."

"For young boys it is culturally acceptable and politically correct to develop these skills," says Linda Wells, of the Arizona State softball team. "They are mentored and networked. Usually girls are not coached at all, or are coached by Mom—or if it's by Dad, he may not be much of an athlete. Girls are often stuck with the bottom of the male talent pool as examples. I would argue that rather than learning to 'throw like a girl,' they learn to throw like poor male athletes. I say that a bad throw is 'throwing like an old man.' This is not gender, it's acculturation."

Almost any motor skill, from doing handstands to dribbling a basketball, is easier to learn if you start young, which is why John Goodman did not realize that learning to throw is difficult until he attempted it as an adult. Many girls reach adulthood having missed the chance to learn to throw when that would have been easiest to do. And as adults they have neither John Goodman's incentive to teach their muscles a new set of skills nor his confidence that the feat is possible. Five years ago Joseph Russo, long a baseball coach at St. John's University, gave athletic-talent tests to actresses who were trying out for roles in *A League of Their Own,* a movie about women's baseball. Most of them were "well coordinated in general, like for dancing," he says. But those who had not happened to play baseball or softball when they were young had a problem: "It sounds silly to say it, but they kept throwing like girls." (The best ballfield talents, by the way, were Madonna, Demi Moore, and the rock singer Joan Jett, who according to Russo "can really hit it hard." Careful viewers of *A League of Their Own* will note that only in a fleeting instant in one scene is the star, Geena Davis, shown actually throwing a ball.)

I'm not sure that I buy Linda Wells's theory that most boys are "mentored" or "networked" into developing ball skills. Those who make the baseball team, maybe. But for a far larger number the decisive ingredient seems to be the hundreds of idle hours spent throwing balls, sticks, rocks, and so on in the playground or the back yard. Children on the playground, I think, demonstrate the moment when the kinetic chain begins to work. It is when a little boys tries to throw a rock farther than his friend can, or to throw a stick over a telephone wire thirty feet up. A toddler's first, instinctive throw is a push from the shoulder, showing the essential traits of "throwing like a girl." But when a child is really trying to put some oomph into the throw, his natural instinct is to wind up his body and let fly with the links of the chain. Little girls who do the same thing—compete with each other in distance throwing—learn the same way; but whereas many boys do this, few girls do. Tammy Richards, a woman who was raised on a farm in central California, says that she learned to throw by trying to heave dried cow chips farther than her brother could. It may have helped that her father, Bob Richards, was a former Olympic competitor in the decathlon (and two-time Olympic champion in the pole vault), and that he taught all his sons and daughters to throw not only the ball but also the discus, the shotput, and the javelin.

Is there a way to make up for lost time if you failed to invest those long hours on the playground years ago? Of course. Adults may not be able to learn to speak unaccented French, but they can learn to ride a bike, or skate, or throw. All that is required for developing any of these motor skills is time for practice—and spending that time requires overcoming the sense of embarrassment and futility that adults often have when attempting something new. Here are two tips that may help.

One is a surprisingly valuable drill suggested by the Little League's *How-to-Play* handbook. Play catch with a partner who is ten or fifteen feet away—but do so while squatting with the knee of your throwing side touching the ground. When you start out this low, you have to keep the throw high to get the ball to your partner without bouncing it. This encourages a throw with the elbow held well above the shoulder, where it belongs.

The other is to play catch with a person who can throw like an athlete but is using his or her off hand. The typical adult woman hates to play catch with the typical adult man. She is well aware that she's not looking graceful, and reacts murderously to the condescending tone in his voice ("That's more like it, honey!") Forcing a right-handed man to throw left-handed is the great equalizer. He suddenly concentrates his attention on what it takes to get hips, shoulder, and elbow working together. He is suddenly aware of the strength of character needed to ignore the snickers of onlookers while learning new motor skills. He can no longer be condescending. He may even be nervous, wondering what he'll do if his partner makes the breakthrough first and he's the one still throwing like a girl.

◀▮▶

LIVING THE PARADOX

Female Athletes Negotiate Femininity and Muscularity

Vikki Krane, Y. L. Choi, Shannon M. Baird, Christine M. Aimar, and Kerrie J. Kauer

Physically active women and girls face an intriguing paradox: Western culture emphasizes a feminine ideal body and demeanor that contrasts with an athletic body and demeanor. Sportswomen, therefore, live in two cultures, the sport culture and their larger social culture, wherein social and sport

Excerpt from Krane, et al., "Living the Paradox: Female Athletes Negotiate Femininity and Muscularity," *Sex Roles: A Journal of Research* 50: 5–6 (March 2004): 315–329. Reprinted with kind permission of Springer Science and Business Media.

ideals clash. This lived paradox may have a multitude of effects on female athletes, and the research provides varied accounts of their body image, eating behaviors, self-presentation, and self-esteem. Some researchers have found that female athletes have a more positive body image, healthier eating patterns, and are less likely to become pregnant accidentally than their nonathletic peers (Marten-DiBartolo and Shaffer, 2002; Miller, Sabo, Farrell, Barnes, and Melnick, 1999). Yet, other researchers have found that the sport environment creates pressures that lead to unhealthy practices such as disordered eating, excessive exercising, and training through injuries (e.g., Duquin, 1994; Johns, 1996; Krane, Greenleaf, and Snow, 1997).

To comprehend the sporting experiences of female athletes it is important to consider the cultural influences that can potentially alter their experiences, behaviors, and psychological states. [. . .]

An important cultural ideal that affects all women, and especially athletic women, is femininity. Femininity is a socially constructed standard for women's appearance, demeanor, and values (Bordo, 1993). There are multiple permutations of femininity; femininity is bound to historical context (i.e., it changes over time), and "acceptable" femininity may be perceived differently on the basis of, for example, race and sexual orientation (Chow, 1999). Although there are multiple femininities in the Western world, there also is a privileged, or hegemonic, form of femininity (Choi, 2000; Krane, 2001a; Lenskyj, 1994). This hegemonic femininity is constructed within a White, heterosexual, and class-based structure, and it has strong associations with heterosexual sex and romance (Ussher, 1997). Hegemonic femininity, therefore, has a strong emphasis on appearance with the dominant notion of an ideal feminine body as thin and toned. [. . .]

Within the context of the masculine domain of sport, sportswomen are expected to perform hegemonic femininity while distancing themselves from behavior perceived as masculine (Choi, 2000; Krane, 2001a). However, negotiating the performance of hegemonic femininity while avoiding masculine behaviors becomes problematic for these physically active women. They face the contradiction that to be successful in athletics they must develop characteristics associated with masculinity (e.g., strength, assertiveness, independence, competitiveness), which contradict hegemonic femininity (Krane, 2001a). Female athletes learn what behaviors and appearances are privileged, and femininity is "performed" to gain social acceptance and status. For example, professional female boxers (Halbert, 1995) and elite ice hockey players (Etu and Williams, 1996) often present a feminine image even during competition (e.g., wearing pink).

It is evident that the privilege, and concomitant power, afforded sportswomen who adhere to the social expectations for women (i.e., perform hegemonic femininity) eludes masculine-perceived female athletes.

As female athletes who perform femininity correctly accrue power and privilege, female athletes perceived as masculine are labeled as social deviants (Blinde and Taub, 1992), and they experience discrimination (Crawley, 1998; Krane, 1997). Feminine women in sport reap benefits such as positive media attention, fan adoration, and sponsorship (Kolnes, 1995; Krane, 2001a; Pirinen, 1997). As these feminine athletes gain acclaim, they become spokespeople for their sport (e.g., Mia Hamm for professional soccer, Lisa Leslie for the Women's Professional Basketball League). They also garner respect for their ability to be successful athletes while remaining true to their gender. As these feminine female athletes are highlighted by the media and receive financial and political clout, they reinforce the socially constructed expectations for feminine behavior and appearance of sportswomen.

A problematic expression of hegemonic femininity for female athletes is the presentation of a feminine body. Ideally, sportswomen have toned bodies, yet they also must avoid excessive, masculine-perceived, muscular bodies. Successful athletes must be powerful and strong, yet obvious signs of this power are construed negatively, as contradicting hegemonic femininity. Consequently, female athletes struggle with the contradiction of the desire to be strong and successful, but not to develop "oversized" musculature (Wright and Clarke, 1999; Young, 1997). Muscle development for athletes, therefore, creates a paradox in which a tight, toned body is perceived as ideal, yet large muscles symbolize strength and masculinity (Bordo, 1993).

Two recent studies clearly showed the contradiction between the performance of hegemonic femininity and sport performance in female athletes. Krane, Waldron, et al. (2001) interviewed American college athletes, who revealed that they had conflicting body images. As athletes, the women had developed strong, muscular bodies to meet their aspirations in sport; however, their muscular physiques were a source of personal concern in social settings. This manifestation of concern was tied to their knowledge that their bodies did not fit the cultural ideal of a toned but not-too-muscular female body. Similarly, Russell (2002), in a study of British female rugby, cricket, and netball players, identified tensions between the "sporting body" and "the social body." The women in Russell's study were satisfied with their sporting bodies as strong, useful, and admired while participating in their sport, yet they expressed dissatisfaction with their bodies when they considered social contexts. In addition, Krane, Waldron, et al. found that athletes who wore revealing athletic uniforms (e.g., swimmers, gymnasts), expressed concern about how they looked in their uniforms. Their worries that they would be perceived as fat or too big, in some cases, led to unhealthy behaviors (e.g., dieting, excessive exercise, disordered eating).

The findings of those two studies (Krane, Waldron, et al., 2001; Russell, 2002) piqued our interest to understand further how female athletes negotiate social expectations of femininity and their athleticism. Specifically, we investigated relationships among body image and perceptions of muscularity and femininity in female collegiate athletes. Our research question was: How do female athletes negotiate and reconcile the social expectations of femininity with their muscularity and athleticism?

Method

Participants

Female athletes who were competing for a midwestern, NCAA Division I university participated in this study (n = 21). The college varsity athletes included three cross-country distance runners, two track athletes, one soccer player, two volleyball players, two gymnasts, one swimmer, one basketball player, three softball players, and three tennis players. Club sport athletes included one rugby player and two ice hockey players. One of the volleyball players also competed in club hockey. The athletes averaged 20.48 (SD = 1.83) years of age, had an average of 9.36 years of experience (SD = 4.31) in their current sport, and had been on their current team for an average of 2.76 years (SD = 1.26). Body size varied among these women, but, overall, they were quite fit with low body fat. Their average self-reported height was 66.88 in. (SD = 2.94) and weight was 141.7 lbs (SD = 21.03). Body mass index (BMI) averaged 22.22 (SD = 2.20, range 18.6–26.6); all but three athletes had a BMI of less than 24. All of the athletes were White. We did not ask them about their sexual orientation, but all of the athletes presented a heterosexual stance (i.e., no one identified as lesbian, bisexual, or transgendered). [. . .]

Results

Influence of Hegemonic Femininity

The theme "the influence of hegemonic femininity" addressed the ramifications of constant comparison to the cultural ideal of femininity. As the athletes contrasted their bodies with feminine bodies, the following data categories emerged: "the ideal body," "femininity defined," "muscular but not too muscular," and "uniform concerns."

The Ideal Body

It is important to understand how these athletes constructed the ideal body, their own bodies, and femininity. Their discussion of these topics reflected the influence of hegemonic femininity. These women expressed a narrow rendering of femininity—that from a White, heterosexual perspective. Perhaps this is partly an effect of their social environment at a university with a predominantly White student body and because none of the athletes acknowledged an identity as other than heterosexual in the interviews.

The cultural ideal body that the athletes described was "perfect" and "real good looking and they don't have much muscle," but they have "definition." The ideal body is exemplified by "people in magazines," actresses, and models. A volleyball player said:

You're surrounded by it. Like in the media, you're shown this perfect image, . . . you know the Barbie doll, and models and everything. And then you see the female athletes, all the popular athletes, and they've got like the athletic physique and now that's becoming more popular.

A hockey player responded to this comment as follows:

How many people would rather look like Rachel Hunter [a model] rather than Mia Hamm [a soccer player]? Because Rachel Hunter is this little skinny thing, waif-like person and then Mia Hamm's thicker, and that's not as cool. I still think that's not gonna change.

The athletes also acknowledged that the cultural ideal body was unrealistic: "all the perfect people and like no one looks like that, they're all air brushed and stuff."

In the focus groups, the athletes discussed their personal ideal bodies. Each woman identified something that could be different such as "longer legs," "smaller stomach," "smaller rear end," and "smaller thighs." Overall, they lamented their size and muscularity. Distance Runner 1 stated: "I wish I was littler. . . . Sometimes I just wish I had like a regular size body." Volleyball 1 concurred: "we have our muscle and I don't like it, I'd rather not have that." Still, most of the athletes wanted more muscular definition, but without muscular bulk. As they said: "I would be more defined," and "I always wanted to have a six pack [well defined abdominals]."

Femininity Defined
Discussion regarding femininity was intriguing; their definitions of femininity typically were based on contrasting it with athleticism. "You lose all femininity when you put on a hockey uniform." In general, their definitions of femininity concerned being "petite and dainty" and engaging in specific behaviors. For example, femininity was defined as "having a gentle spirit," "more laid back," "having proper etiquette," "being clean," and "being girly." Generally, it was easier for the athletes to state what femininity was not: "not sweaty," "opposite of being a tomboy," "not

wearing baggy jeans," and "like hitting the weight room is not feminine." The following exchange further expressed these beliefs:

GYMNAST 2: When you think of being feminine, you don't think of the person being like really outgoing, it's really reserved.
VOLLEYBALL PLAYER 1: Yeah and like grunting. You know how like people grunt in the weight room.
ALL: laughter
VOLLEYBALL PLAYER 1: Farting and belching are definitely not feminine. . . . Making noises is not.
DISTANCE RUNNER 1: [I am not feminine] because I grunt, I fart, I burp. (laughter) I'm loud, I'm obnoxious, I swear worse than any guy you'll probably ever meet. I don't have the body structure, I don't act like it, I'm . . . I dunno, aggressive.

The athletes reconciled their perceived lack of femininity by saying that it was not essential to being athletic. As two athletes said:

HOCKEY PLAYER 1: It doesn't count [on the ice], nobody is going to give me points for having my hair done or whatever. No way, I'm looking to be the toughest person out there, the meanest person out there, the dirtiest person, whatever I can get away with, all I get away with, whatever. That's not feminine, that's not feminine at all, and I spit and hack and cuss and everything that you're not supposed to do when you're a girl.
VB/HOCKEY PLAYER: When you're sitting in pre-game, we're having our locker room talk or whatever, you're not thinking about 'ok we need to go out there and cross our legs when we sit on the bench because that's the feminine thing to do, we need to sit up straight.' We're not trying to look like women out there because that's not the whole point of why we're playing the sport. We're out there 'cause we enjoy it, we want competition and we're out there to beat the crap out of somebody. I mean it's just not a focus at all.

Most of the athletes believed that being soft, girly, dainty, and clean implied femininity, whereas being aggressive, outgoing, and sweaty implied being an athlete. Further, being athletic was equated with being masculine. Feminine was socially acceptable, and athletic was not. The athletes consistently expressed this conflict throughout the focus groups.

Muscular but Not Too Muscular
The athletes struggled with their perceptions of their own bodies. They recognized the cultural ideal body as one shape, and they viewed their own bodies as contrary to that ideal. These athletes clearly were in great physical condition with low body fat, yet their muscularity was a source of consternation. Having or building muscles was associated with being unfeminine or "like men." Gymnast 1 said: "You don't feel feminine when you're big and buff." By building "excess" muscle the athletes were being "like guys." Soccer 1, when talking about working out in the weight room, said: "I feel like when I am in there like we are getting . . . we're being like men or something like that."

The participants described a seemingly arbitrary line that demarcated too much muscle from attractive muscle tone in women. Once women surpassed this subjective limit of musculature, they were no longer perceived as feminine. As Distance Runner 2 said: "Muscle tone, yeah that's sexy. But, I guess I don't want to get too big or anything." Similarly, Softball Player 2 stated: "I like muscle a lot, [but] I mean, there is a point . . ." Concern about becoming too big often was expressed. The Basketball player noted, "I wouldn't want to be like real big and buff." Softball 3 elaborated on that point:

I like the way I feel when I get the muscle . . . but yet, in the back of my mind I get scared that I'm gonna get big and people are gonna look at me like 'oh my god.'. . . I get scared of looking too much like a guy, like having too much muscle.

In addition to being conscious of how much muscle mass they were building, the women were concerned with their body weight. Not only did they perceive themselves as too muscular, they interpreted their body weight negatively regardless of their low body fat. When describing her first reaction to her weight gain from muscle development Tennis Player 3 said:

When I came in my freshman year and started lifting, it was weird because then you develop and you're like 'whoa!' You're very self-conscious about getting bigger and 'oh, I'm getting fat or I'm getting too big there.'

The following interaction shows how the athletes sometimes misinterpreted body weight:

VB/HOCKEY PLAYER: Me being 5'11", I weigh 187 and so I look at the number of the scale and I'm like 'holy crap I'm fat,' but then [laughter] we get our fat tested and we find out you're like 15, 16, 17 percent body fat and you're like 'oh, okay maybe I'm not that fat.' Sometimes you just need that reinforcement, you know that reinforcement behind it just to be like 'okay, I'm not fat' right, cause you look at the numbers and you're like 'Oh God.'
SWIMMER: I agree with her [Laughing].
RUGBY PLAYER: You pretty much summed it up [laughing].

The athletes in this study initially felt that their increased body weight was traumatic. They didn't like getting bigger because it detracted from femininity and contradicted the cultural ideal body.

Uniform Concerns
Uniform concerns emerged as a unique category for those athletes who wore "revealing" uniforms (e.g., track, gymnastics, swimming, and volleyball). Uniforms were considered revealing when they were tight and exposed the shape of the women's bodies. These athletes were concerned with how they looked in revealing uniforms, and two different

perspectives emerged: (a) they looked too big and (b) they were sexualized in their uniforms.

Athletes described their revealing uniforms in a variety of ways. The runners described their uniform as "butt-huggers, like basically underwear. And then like, a real tight tank top." Gymnast 2 explained that their uniforms were like bathing suits. The tennis players described one of their uniforms as:

TENNIS PLAYER 3: Like a miniskirt.
TENNIS PLAYER 2: 8 inches above your knees, like barely covering your butt.

The volley team wore spandex shorts and "short sleeve jerseys which they're starting to get tighter as the years go on."

In these tight and revealing uniforms, the athletes felt "exposed." Distance Runner 2 said: "I was so scared when I saw them. Ours is like a one-piece swimsuit. I was so scared the first time I wore this, I'm like, 'my butt's gonna be jiggling all over the place.'" Similarly, VB/Hockey Player said:

First day of practice, my coach hands me this pair of spandex about this big [indicating very small] and she's like, 'here fit your butt into those.' And I'm like, 'I can't even fit my hand into those let alone my entire butt.' [laughing] Okay, and I almost cried and I put those things on, I walked out, and I'm like, 'I don't feel comfortable at all.'

Track Athlete 3 best articulated the general feelings of discomfort associated with these uniforms when she said: "you feel completely naked . . . your butt's right there."

Ironically, although the athletes thought that their "excessive" size and musculature was exposed in their uniforms, they also acknowledged that they were perceived as sexy in their revealing uniforms. Generally they stated that men attended their sporting events just to see them in their revealing uniforms: "Guys, like you know, 'Oh yeah, come to gymnastics, girls in leotards," and "Yeah, we've had comments like, 'oh you wear those spandex, I'll come to your games'" (Volleyball). Distance Runner 1 explained:

Guys will come to our races because we wear those things. They're like, 'You guys wear those? Oh my gosh, we're coming!'. . . Of course nobody would come see a cross-country race unless they knew we wore those things.

The women complained that they were sexualized rather than appreciated for their athletic achievement. To minimize feeling exposed and reduce being sexualized, the athletes tended to wear additional clothes over their uniforms when not competing. Gymnast 2 explained:

After you compete, you put something on, like even if it's just a T-shirt or if it's something else. The only time you're really standing around with your leotard on is if you're about to go out there or if you're competing. Usually we don't really just sit around. . . . I personally just don't like to stand around in it [laughter] because people are constantly looking at you. I just feel uncomfortable if that happens.

Distance Runner 1 stated: "we definitely don't wear our [uniforms] until we're racing. . . . We don't run around in those things. No way." A tennis player agreed: "I usually just put my sweatpants on [when not playing]."

The athletes knew that their bodies differed from the feminine ideal body. This incompatibility negatively affected their body image (i.e., a desire to be less muscular) and resulted in concerns about how others perceived them, even during competitions. Their uniforms were a unique source of stress because of the exposure of their bodies in front of an audience. Yet immediately prior to competing, the athletes were able to shift their focus from body image concerns to performance. Distance Runner 1 said: "When I'm racing I'm not caring what I'm looking like at all, if it's like sexual or not. I'm just out there to feel comfortable in my uniform and race." The athletes articulated that they became used to wearing their revealing uniforms.

GYMNAST 2: How do I feel about them? I've been in them all my life. Umm, I don't know.
VOLLEYBALL PLAYER 1: Well I'm comfortable in them now because we've worn them for a long time and you just get used to them.
VB/HOCKEY PLAYER: You grow into it 'cause you have to wear them everyday.

The athletes also seemed to have incorporated wearing their uniforms into their competitive mental preparation routines. They described wearing their uniforms as putting on "your game face" and feeling ready to compete. This sentiment was expressed in the following interaction among the track athletes:

TRACK ATHLETE 3: I feel faster when I put on my little bathing suit. . . . I feel like I'm ready to race, I'm in like a certain mode.
TRACK ATHLETE 2: Yeah, plus you're in the right like mind set, like. . .
TRACK ATHLETE 3: Yeah.
TRACK ATHLETE 2: . . . when you're wearing your uniform it feels like a lot different, like mentally almost than when you're just running in like a t-shirt and shorts.
TRACK ATHLETE 3: To me it does.

Although the athletes noted that their uniforms were a source of trepidation, they also had learned to cope with them and to refocus their attention during competition.

Athlete as "Other"

The higher order theme of "athlete as 'other'" emerged from the women's descriptions of female athletes as marginalized and perceived as different from "normal girls." Within the context of the interviews, "normal" was used to refer to nonathletic girls and women. The participants were aware that as athletes they differed from women who were not athletes in (un)feminine appearance and behavior. The most common description of this perception was they were "like guys," or "like men" and particularly as "not girls." They often made comments such as "I wish I was a girl," "I want to look like a girl," and "sometimes I'm just not like a girl." All of the participants agreed with the basketball player's statement, "I just feel so different than everybody else." Additional indications of "other" status were supported by the data categories of discrepancy, clothes (not) doing femininity, social attention, and dating.

Discrepancy

This data category highlights the conflict the athletes had between being athletic and being feminine. The athletes clearly distinguished between their identities as a woman and as an athlete [. . .].

Their strength and muscularity are acceptable in a sport environment, but a more feminine demeanor and image is desired in a social setting. The athletes recognized these different identities and distinguished between fitting into the different environments. As Rugby Player 2 stated: "if you're an athlete, then you have to like transform into entirely someone else when you come off the field or the ice or whatever." A softball player said:

In sports I don't really think about my body that much. Or when like I'm in my uniform and everything, it's pretty much, it's irrelevant, you know? I think that people look at us and how good do we play our sports, but when we're out [socially], you know, like just using like chest size for example. I like feel really self-conscious about it, like if you see the girls that have big chests and little stomachs, and do that sort of stuff. And when you're out at that scene, out of the athletic scene, you know you're just a person that doesn't really have that good of a body. . . . Well I don't really care that I don't have big boobs, I can still throw a ball way harder than you can (laughs) you know what I mean, but I definitely, I mean I can see a difference between the two settings. I think about that a lot actually. (Softball Player 2)

Thus, the athletes constantly juxtaposed their athletic behaviors with "being a girl" (i.e., being feminine). Gender and femininity, therefore, have to be put aside in order to focus on the task at hand (i.e., sport). This may not seem surprising or important until one takes into account why gender is being put aside—because sport is not consistent with hegemonic femininity.

Clothes

Attempts to find clothes that fit their muscular bodies were a constant reminder that the athletes were different from nonathletic women. The following interaction expresses this concern:

VOLLEYBALL PLAYER 1: I hate shopping for pants and also when I shop for jeans, because my thighs are bigger (laughter) and it's from squatting, like if I didn't squat [an exercise with weights for strengthening leg muscles] I could probably fit into like three sizes smaller. But it's frustrating because like here I am fitting into the size like 12, 14, whatever when I never used to be that before I came to college.

GYMNAST 2: It's so frustrating to go shopping for any type of clothing because, like I'd have to have it too big or like, my size, just can't get into shirts and stuff like that, especially jeans. It's just so tight like, around your thighs.

DISTANCE RUNNER 2: And your quads . . .

GYMNAST 2: And then the rest is just loose. Like you can be sitting down and be bulging out you know. You have no control over it. So . . .

VOLLEYBALL PLAYER 1: My roommates are athletes too. One plays softball, and the two other ones play volleyball, and last year they were talking about opening a "Big Buns and Big Guns" clothing store for athletes (laughter) because, like we have bigger, like arms and then bigger butts. (laughter) We don't fit in normal clothes.

Not only was finding clothes problematic, but the women were not happy with the way they looked in skirts and dresses because of their muscular bodies. Their descriptions of themselves reiterate their other status (i.e., not a normal woman). For example, "I've got huge arms, and like you like wear a dress or you dress up or something and you feel like a monkey" (Gymnast 1) and "[in a dress] you don't look like a girl" (Distance Runner 2). Distance Runner 1 remarked: "It's kinda like an oxymoron, you're like you have these little skirts on and then you have this body. And it looks kind of funny." She later added:

I look so stupid in a dress. It's like my dress, and then I have these legs. (laughter) They just don't match. Like it looks so weird. Like I have fancy shoes on, and I have these legs that are just like muscles, and they look really weird.

The clothes problem was merely pragmatic, yet a deeper issue remains. Athletes do not fit into regular clothes and, consequently, they were reminded about how they differ from "normal" women.

Social Attention

Another reminder that female athletes were perceived as different came through the social attention that the athletes received. As the athletes said:

I don't feel like less of a girl [because of my muscles] but I feel like other people think I'm less of one. (Track Athlete 1)

Some people that don't [know that I'm an athlete], they'll come up to me like, 'what the heck is she?' (Distance Runner 1)

Social attention from men particularly reinforced that athletes differed from other women. [. . .] "When I dress up or anything it's like 'wow, you are a girl.'. . . even my boyfriend comes up and is like 'oh my gosh, you're all done up" (Gymnast 2). All of the athletes described situations when friends and other people acted surprised when they wore feminine attire.

Dating

The distinction between being a "normal girl" and an athlete also was acknowledged during discussions about attractiveness and dating. All references to dating were in a heterosexual context and were consistent with the script of hegemonic femininity as heterosexual. The athletes explained that to be attractive to men, it was important to act in an "appropriate" manner. As Hockey Player 2 stated: "If you want to attract a guy, then you have to be [feminine] sometimes." VB/Hockey Player explained:

If you're trying to attract a guy, you're not gonna be like (laughs) punching them in the shoulder, be like 'did you catch the game Friday?' You're gonna be, you know, tiny, cute, demure, and whatever. Not that I can pull off the demure thing, but I mean you're gonna want to act more like a female than a male or, you know, than more so a female than an athlete.

Similarly, Tennis Player 1 stated: "[it's important to be feminine] when you go out and you want to, you know, look nice and impress the boys (laughs)."

The athletes also complained that men were not attracted to women with large, athletic bodies. A hockey player said: "it's really hard to date around here, if you're not like this big [gestures making hands in small box]. . . . The ones that get chased after all the time it always seems to be like the little itty bitty girls." VB/Hockey Player agreed, "I'm so tall and big and it's hard to get a date."

(Not) Doing Femininity

With the constant reminders that athletes were something other than normal women, these women engaged in behaviors to reinforce the notion that "we can be athletes and feminine too." VB/Hockey Player stated:

We don't look very feminine when we're out there playing, and you know just to grasp on to that one last thing that makes us a girl, we'll put a ribbon in our hair. We do it to remind all you people in the stands, we are still girls. We're athletes first, but just remind everybody that we're girls too.

The athletes engaged in many typical behaviors to enhance their femininity: "doing my hair, putting makeup on," "putting on nice clothes," "wearing the latest trends," and "wearing French braids." Ironically, al-though well-fitting clothes were a source of contention, "wearing normal clothes" and "dressing up" were essential for appearing feminine. The athletes stressed that they could be feminine: "I can be more girly." [. . .]

Throughout the discussions, appearing feminine was equated with being a "normal girl." As Softball 3 stated: "I like doing my hair, putting makeup on so people know that I'm not just an athlete, like I am a girl too." The traditional script of femininity is incongruous with sport, so these athletes also constructed a feminine appearance to be perceived as normal women.

It is interesting that the athletes also equated eating with unfeminine behavior. Because of their physical activity, these women ate more than their nonathletic peers, which further reinforced their other status. Ap-parently, feminine women do not eat large amounts of food, as indicated in the following conversation:

HOCKEY PLAYER 1: In season at our house, you can't keep enough food in there. Oh my god, last year, three of us were playing hockey and [VB/Hockey Player] was playing volleyball and hockey, and we'd eat like you would not believe in that house. Everything in the place was a mess. The fridge was constantly stocked full of stuff. That makes me feel very unfeminine, but you're hungry you just keep eat-ing. (Everyone nods in agreement)
VB/HOCKEY PLAYER: You're wolfing down food and you eat like seven times a day.
HOCKEY PLAYER 1: Every three hours.
VB/HOCKEY PLAYER: Yeah, like every three hours you're stuffing your face with something.
RUGBY PLAYER: Your friends go all day with just one meal and you're just like . . .
VB/HOCKEY PLAYER: I'm hungry again.

Other athletes also noted that their eating differentiated them from their nonathletic peers. Their nonathlete female friends often commented about how much they ate compared to normal women. For example, Dis-tance Runner 2 described that friends stated: "I'll go out to dinner with [nonathlete friends] and I'll have like three big plates and they'll have like one little one, and I'll be done with everything and they're still eating."

Through many different avenues, the athletes were reminded that they were different. They were larger, more assertive, more muscular, and they ate more than normal women. The athletes also were not considered fem-inine because of their body shape and their casual attire. To be considered socially acceptable, they sometimes created an alternate identity from athlete—that of a feminine woman.

Physicality
An intriguing higher order theme emerged related to the Physicality of Sport. Although the athletes struggled with the conflict between being

perceived in a socially desirable manner and excelling in their sport, they also discussed the benefits of their sport participation. The data categories of function, pride, and empowerment described some of these benefits.

Function
One mechanism of reconciling the contradiction between having a culturally ideal body and being athletic women was their focus on the function of their size and strength. To be competitive, it was essential that they were strong and muscular. Throughout the interviews, they stated that they gained much muscle size because of their weight lifting. Yet, they also described the benefits of weightlifting as "it does make me stronger," "it makes me hit harder and maybe even quicker" (tennis player), and "help[s] you take off more on the ice if you want to pick your legs up faster" (hockey player). [. . .]

Pride
The athletes discussed the pride they felt in their athletic achievements. These sportswomen worked hard to be competitive at the college level. Their commitment and effort resulted in pride in being an athlete. Distance Runner 2 stated: "I think girl athletes are sexy. . . . I think it's cool that we go out there and do that." Although these athletes acknowledged that models portray the culturally ideal body, the following interaction shows how they reconciled the difference between being valued for one's looks versus being valued for one's skill:

TRACK ATHLETE 3: I would rather be an athlete; I'd rather not be a model out there getting pictures taken just for her body, I'd rather have muscles, you know, and do the sport, and be recognized for it and know that I'm doing something good for myself.
SOCCER PLAYER: I think that people look up to athletes more than they look up to models. . . . They give them more respect.
TRACK ATHLETE 1: I'd rather be respected for running rather than my looks.
SOCCER PLAYER: 'Cause it's something you can control.

Part of becoming a successful athlete is developing a strong muscular body. They recognized that the cultural ideal exemplified a smaller physique, yet these athletes were proud of their strong, developed bodies. As a rugby player stated:

It doesn't bug me to see people a lot smaller than me or whatever because I know I'm healthy and I know most of it's muscle. Like when I work out and stuff, like I can just see the muscles when I move, like them flexing. And I think if someone says 'you're thick' and 'you're like a healthy muscular,' and it's more muscle than fat, then it's cool.

[. . .]

The essence of this data category was exemplified by VB/Hockey Player, who explained:

I used to be like more self-conscious about my size, but I mean I look around and I see so many more athletes around on campus that are big, you know, but they're built like Mack trucks. I don't think it's anything to be ashamed about. I'm very proud that I'm a big girl.

These athletes appeared to redefine what it meant to be a muscular woman. They focused on how they are strong and healthy even if they are different than other women. They were proud of their status as athletes and the bodies they developed through training and competition.

Empowerment
Not only were these women proud of being athletic, they also felt empowered because of their strength and skill. As they discussed, being an athlete "helps your self-esteem," "it gives us more of a sense of time management and confidence," "you feel stronger and you feel independent," and it leads to "self-respect." These feelings of empowerment generalized beyond the sport context and helped the women to feel self-sufficient:

I know people won't mess with me. 'You mess with me and look you gotta deal with this.' Like in the real world I think it will help me out in the long run because I don't think people will mess with me, you know. . . . Whether it be on a job or like walking down New York City in the middle of the night and I think my chances of getting mugged will be lower than some waif-like person walking around. (VB/Hockey Player)

A hockey player expressed the same sentiment:

I feel more, this is gonna sound cheesey, but I feel more independent. I feel like I can take care of myself rather than if I was just some weakling. I feel like I could run away from someone if I had to, or whatever, you know what I mean. I don't need somebody to take care of me.

Although there were constant reminders that female athletes were not considered normal women, these athletes savored the benefits of their athletic participation. They were accomplished, confident, independent women in both athletic and social situations.

Discussion

The findings of this study illustrate how, because of the influence of hegemonic femininity, sportswomen live a paradox of dual and dueling identities. The athletes in our study recognized the status and privilege of "normal girls" that contrasted with their "other" or marginalized position. This circumstance reinforced the importance of portraying a heterosexually feminine appearance in social settings and sometimes in sport settings. Consistent with previous research (Krane, Waldron, et al., 2001), the athletes described the ideal feminine body as small, thin, and model-like. As expected, their description of the ideal female body was consistent with media portrayals of feminine women (Bordo, 1993; Duncan, 1994).

The athletes considered their muscular bodies as the primary hindrance to being perceived as heterosexually feminine in social settings. When they considered their athletic bodies in comparison to "normal girls" or the culturally ideal body, the athletes felt "different." They were larger and more muscular, and they did not fit into trendy clothing. Even though they embraced the function of their bodies, being too muscular was disconcerting. It was an unwanted source of social attention, a constant reminder that they were different from other women. [. . .]

As we pursued the examination of perceptions of muscular bodies, we found as much pride as consternation in athletic bodies. The athletes acknowledged the positive distinctiveness of the athletic female body, yet each athlete also expressed some desire to look different—that is, normal. Further, several athletes noted that when they came to college and began intensive weight lifting, they were not sure how to interpret the changes in their bodies. Weight gain initially was perceived negatively and was assumed to be due to increased body fat. However, the athletes appeared to have learned to focus on the function of their musculature and size, which resulted in satisfaction and pride. They worked hard to be strong and successful and were proud of their efforts. This was consistent with previous studies that revealed that female athletes expressed empowerment, satisfaction, and enjoyment through physically assertive sport (Baird, 2001; Hargreaves, 1993; Rail, 1992; Russell, 2002; Theberge, 1997). Although these women were reminded in many ways that they did not conform to the culturally accepted, hegemonic script of femininity, they were able to highlight the benefits associated with sport performance. They enjoyed their sport participation and gained strength and confidence that positively affected them outside of sport as well as in the athletic environment.

It appears that, in negotiating and reconciling the social expectations of femininity with athleticism, sportswomen develop two identities—athlete and woman. Sometimes these two contrasting identities are kept separate but at other times they merge. This can be seen in their different performances of femininity and gender. Drawing on Ussher's (1997) scripts of doing girl, being girl, resisting girl, and subverting girl, Choi (2000) suggested that "being girl" is unlikely to be common among sportswomen, whereas "resisting girl" is likely to be prevalent. The athletes in this study understood that being feminine was important for feeling like normal women, but they were unanimous in the view that, as athletes, they did not have the time required to work on their appearance on a daily basis. Being feminine in our society is an effortful exercise, but so too is being an athlete. These women's priorities as athletes did not include taking time to use makeup, style their hair, and dress nicely. Femininity, therefore, had to be "put aside" and resisted when they were being athletes as opposed to "girls." The athletes in our study simply displaced femininity with their "game face" or competitive zeal and left "doing girl" for social situations. This type of performance also was found in female rugby players who constantly negotiated being highly competitive (i.e., masculine) on the rugby pitch with being "real women" (i.e., feminine) in social contexts (Baird, 2001).

For some athletes, "doing girl" was seen as important in sport, such as when the volleyball players wore bows in their hair to remind people that although they were athletes, they were still women. [. . .] These findings illustrated that the position of "doing girl" can be taken up at the same time as "resisting girl." The two identities of athlete and woman are not, or perhaps cannot, always be kept separate because of the requirements of hegemonic femininity. This conflict also emerged from the athletes' concerns about how other people perceived their bodies. The athletes who wore revealing uniforms thought that their bodies were sexualized while in their uniforms, which was a source of discomfort. [. . .] The imposition of this perception upon the female athlete prevents the two identities of athlete and woman from being kept completely separate, as the unwanted attention from men is a reminder that she is a woman and subject to the male gaze.

Although the athletes' descriptions of the ideal feminine body were consistent with the dominant ideal as portrayed in the media, it is important to situate this within a White, heterosexual prototype, or what Dewar (1993) referred to as the "generic sporting woman." All of the athletes in this study were White and presented as heterosexual. It is very likely that athletes of color and lesbian or bisexual athletes may not aspire to this same ideal. Yet, as Dewar noted, these other women are rendered invisible in sport and hegemonic femininity is privileged. For this reason, it also is important to note that although the athletes presented as heterosexual, it is possible that some of them identify as lesbian or bisexual. However, as Braun (2000) pointed out, focus groups offer many benefits, but they also may perpetuate heterosexism. The dominant heterosexual focus within the groups with discussions of dating and being attractive to men may have created an environment where women were not comfortable revealing another identity. How to challenge and not collude in heterosexism is an important issue for researchers to consider (Braun, 2000).

It also is important to point out that although there were commonalities among these athletes' construction of femininity and its consequences, they were not a wholly homogeneous group. In general, the tennis players were more concerned with portraying a traditionally feminine appearance and the rugby and hockey players most pushed the boundaries of femininity. Ice hockey and rugby were club sports, organized or managed by the women on the team. They were not governed within the traditional male-dominated sport setting, and the women were not compelled to adhere to hegemonic standards. Also of interest is that these athletes revealed positions contrary to popular beliefs. For example, although gymnasts and distance runners are stereotyped to be excessively thin, the women in this study were just as concerned about being too muscular as the athletes more commonly expected to be large and muscular (e.g., basketball, softball, and soccer players).

In conclusion, this study has extended our understanding of female athletes' perceptions of their bodies and their selves in sport and society. Rather than simply being passive victims of hegemonic femininity however, women can actively choose how the paradox of dueling identities is lived through different gender and femininity performances. Our study has illustrated the complexity of this process as women move among scripts as well as perform different scripts simultaneously. Moreover, "choices" are not always freely chosen. The complexity of living this paradox might lead to negative behaviors such as poor body image, disordered eating, and low self-esteem, although this did not seem to be the case for the women in our study. Indeed, through their negotiations of femininity they redefined the acceptable female body and behavior, reveling in their self-descriptions of their "nonfeminine" behaviors such as being noisy, assertive, competitive, and tough, as well as swearing, sweating, and eating. Although the athletes noted that other people may not consider this acceptable feminine behavior, for them it was normal, and being an athlete was reconciled by the many physical and psychological benefits that empowered them both inside and outside of the sport context.

REFERENCES

Baird, S. (2001). Femininity on the pitch: An ethnography of women's rugby. Unpublished master's thesis, Bowling Green State University, Ohio.
Blinde, E. M., and Taub, D. E. (1992). Women athletes as falsely accused deviants: Managing the lesbian stigma. Sociological Quarterly, 33, 521–533.
Bordo, S. (1993). Unbearable weight: Feminism, Western culture, and the body. Berkeley: University of California Press.
Braun, V. (2000). Heterosexism in focus group research: Collusion and challenge. Feminism and Psychology, 10, 133–140.

Choi, P. Y. L. (2000). Femininity and the physically active woman. London: Routledge.

Chow, R. (1999). When Whiteness feminizes . . . : Some consequences of a supplementary logic. Differences, 11(3), 137–168.

Crawley, S. L. (1998). Gender, class and the construction masculinity in professional sailing. International Review for the Sociology of Sport, 33, 35–41.

Dewar, A. (1993). Would all the generic women in sport please stand up? Challenges facing feminist sport sociology. Quest, 45, 211–229.

Duncan, M. C. (1994). The politics of women's body images and practices: Foucault, the panopticon, and Shape magazine. Journal of Sport and Social Issues, 18, 48–65.

Duquin, M. E. (1994). The body snatchers and Dr. Frankenstein revisited: Social construction and deconstruction of bodies and sport. Journal of Sport and Social Issues, 18, 268–281.

Etu, E., and Williams, M. K. (1996). On the edge: Women making hockey history. Toronto: Second Story Press.

Halbert, C. (1995). Tough enough and woman enough: Stereotypes discrimination and impression management among women professional boxes. Journal of Sport and Social Issues, 21, 7–36.

Hargreaves, J. A. (1993). Sporting females: Critical issues in the history and sociology of women's sports. New York: Routledge.

Johns, D. (1996). Fasting and feasting: Paradoxes of the sport ethic. Sociology of Sport Journal, 15, 41–63.

Kolnes, L. J. (1995). Heterosexuality as an organizing principle in women's sport. International Review for Sociology of Sport, 30, 61–79.

Krane, V. (1997). Homonegativism experienced by lesbian collegiate athletes. Women in Sport and Physical Activity Journal, 6(1), 141–163.

Krane, V. (2001a). "We can be athletic and feminine," but do we want to? Challenges to femininity and heterosexuality in women's sport. Quest, 53, 115–133.

Krane, V., Greenleaf, C., and Snow, J. (1997). Reaching for gold and the price of glory: A motivational case study of a former elite gymnast. The Sport Psychologist, 11, 53–71.

Krane, V., Waldron, J., Michalenok, J., and Stiles-Shipley, J. (2001). Body image, and eating and exercise behaviors: A feminist cultural studies perspective. Women in Sport and Physical Activity Journal, 10(1), 17–54.

Lenskyj, H. J. (1994). Sexuality and femininity in sport context: Issues and alternatives. Journal of Sport and Social Issues, 18, 356–376.

Marten-DiBartolo, P., and Shaffer, C. (2002). A comparison of female college athletes and nonathletes: Eating disorder symptomatology and psychological well-being. Journal of Sport and Exercise Psychology, 24, 33–41.

Miller, K. E., Sabo, D. F., Farrell, M. P., Barnes, G. M., and Melnick, M. J. (1999). Sports, sexual behavior, contraceptive use, and pregnancy among female and male high school students: Testing cultural resource theory. Sociology of Sport Journal, 16, 366–387.

Pirinen, R. M. (1997). The construction of women's positions in sport: A textual analysis of articles on female athletes in Finnish women's magazines. Sociology of Sport Journal, 14, 290–301.

Rail, G. (1992). Physical contact in women's basketball: A phenomenological construction and contextualization. International Review for the Sociology of Sport, 27, 1–27.

Russell, K. (2002). Women's participation motivation in rugby, cricket, and net-ball: Body satisfaction and self identity. Unpublished doctoral dissertation, Coventry University, Coventry, UK.

Theberge, N. (1997). "It's part of the game": Physicality and the production of gender in women's hockey. Gender and Society, 11, 69–87.

Ussher, J. M. (1997). Fantasies of femininity: Reframing the boundaries of sex. New Brunswick, NJ: Rutgers University Press.

Wright, J., and Clarke, G. (1999). Sport, the media and the construction of com-pulsory heterosexuality. International Review for the Sociology of Sport, 34, 227–243.

Young, K. (1997). Women, sport, and physicality. International Review for the Sociology of Sport, 32, 297–305.

PART III

Competing Bodies: Physiological, Biological and Psychological Issues

Part III looks deep into the body to ask the most basic of questions: what is the difference between a female body and a male body? A question that at first glance appears obvious turns out to be surprisingly complicated, as shown by Alison Carlson's history of sex tests required of female Olympic competitors and Ann Crittenden's exploration of the narrowing gap between male and female athletic performance. By testing for chromosome patterns, a test designed to verify a woman's genetic status as a female, the assumed dichotomy between XX females and XY males is refuted by findings that there are multiple chromosomal (and hormonal) patterns. Many scientists claim that there is no such thing as a clear-cut definition that separates biological females from males, arguing that sex is socially determined, much as gender is (a topic explored in Part II). The Olympic sex tests, administered ostensibly to weed out any potential male "cheaters" passing as women—and thus not given to competitors in men's events—in the end destabilizes the very notion of two separate and irrefutable biological sexes. The implicit question, then, is what difference does sex make in sports? Again, we find evidence of a range of answers: few Olympic spectators find it strange that men and women compete against each other in equestrian events, but the IOC is unlikely to introduce mixed-sex boxing anytime soon.

For the vast majority of people with a female sex assignment who are raised as girls and who identify and compete as women, however, there are legitimate scientific questions to be asked about female bodies in competition. The relationship between sport and menstruation, for example, has long been a subject of scientific study, pseudo-scientific myth, and social controversy. Irene McCormick's essay, "Understanding the Female Athlete Triad," explains the important role menstruation plays in the health of adult women and how the intensive pursuit of high levels of fitness in a woman's early years can affect her health in later life. Studies of the kinds and rates of athletic injuries found in women's sport, and how they compare with those in men's sports, have been an important addition to the fields of physiology and kinesiology, as evidenced by Maureen Madden's article on ACL injuries (which hobble female athletes far more often than male athletes). The short statistical article that classifies catastrophic injuries in female athletes by sport provides sobering evidence of what can happen when athletes—male or female—are not properly trained in safety techniques as their sport becomes more demanding. Cheerleading, long denied the honor of the title *sport*, has over the past twenty-five years evolved into an activity far beyond the waving of pom-poms, as we can see both here and in Emily Badger's related article in Part VII.

The question of who deserves the title *athlete* arises as well when women with disabilities engage in sports and fitness training. Disabled women's insistence that they are talented athletes equally entitled to compete suggests that commonplace notions of what makes an athletic body, or more generally an able or a disabled body, need reconsideration. In their article, "Women, Disability, and Sport and Physical Fitness Activity," Elaine M. Blinde and Sarah G. McCallister show that their subjects make self-conscious decisions to engage in athletic activity for its psychological and physical benefits.

No exploration of biological imperatives and athletic performance would be complete without a look at the ways in which the female body can be nudged toward physiological indicators of maleness and improved performance levels through the use of anabolic steroids. Although the most notorious case of steroid use in women's athletic competition occurred at the 1976 Olympics, where the East German women's swim team with the help of Oral-Turinabol claimed eleven gold medals and set astounding new records, any female athlete at any level of competition who wants to improve her performance dramatically is open to the steroid temptation. Weightlifter Tam Thompson's account of her brush with anabolic steroid use, as chronicled by Terry Todd, neatly explains both the great rewards and the high price of steroid use.

The latter portion of Part III focuses on positive and negative psychological dimensions of sport, ways that athletic competition can increase self-confidence and self-esteem or, quite the opposite, cause confusion, doubt, and psychological pain. Questions of success and failure, which may seem self-evident because athletic contests always produce winners and losers, are complicated by other forms of loss and gain. For instance, researchers have documented a significant correlation between female athletes and eating disorders. Ana Cintado's essay, "Eating Disorders and Gymnastics," is a good example of that type of scholarship. Why would athletic activity, touted as a means of strengthening the body and empowering women's sense of self, sometimes have the unintended effect of encouraging women to dislike and harm their bodies? Other authors from this section ask equally difficult questions. Why, asks Frank Murphy, would talented, record-setting runner Kathy Ormsby abandon the 10,000 meter race at the NCAA Outdoor Track and Field Championships, in which she was performing well with more than eight laps to go, and throw herself off a bridge? Why, questions former track and field coach Joli Sandoz, would her female athletes in the 1970s balk at the weightlifting, long practices, and teamwork that was so evidently improving their performances? These questions lead directly into the realm of psychology and the mind/body connection that forms such a powerful dimension of athletic experience.

Lest we lose sight of the great advantages sport brings to women, we end Part III with Mariah Burton Nelson's essay, "Stronger Women." Perhaps better than any other writer, Nelson, a former professional basketball player and competitive swimmer, expresses the joy and freedom so many women experience when they take up a sport and learn to do it well. Nelson also raises the intriguing idea that a woman's participation in sports is an intrinsically feminist activity.

◀▦▶

CHROMOSOME COUNT

Alison Carlson

I am an athlete, and I am a woman. At least I think I'm a woman. But if I were among that dazzlingly gifted number of female athletes preparing to compete in Seoul, my gender, like theirs, would be considered suspect. So much so, that before any athlete is allowed to compete in women's events at the Games or in most other major international competitions, she must first submit to a "gender verification" test of her chromosomes. As a tennis pro who has competed on the regional level, I have never had to subject myself to this "Orwellian" inspection, nor contemplate the traumatic possibility of being told I am not female. But this is precisely what has happened to other women athletes, despite the fact that gender is far too complex to be evaluated by a laboratory test.

Since 1968, the International Olympic Committee (IOC) has been screening the chromosomes of all women competitors, to "insure femininity in the competitors" and "establish equality among athletes." Passing the test, which is called the buccal smear, has nothing to do with the way a woman looks, her birth records, or her sense of self. Getting "certified feminine" depends on the results of a microscopic analysis of cells, scraped from inside the athlete's cheek to determine the pattern of her sex chromosomes. Normally, the female pattern is XX, and the male is XY. But that is not always the case. And when an abnormality appears, the athlete is subjected to a battery of gynecological and clinical exams to determine whether she is "feminine" enough to compete. So far, it is

From *Ms.* 17:4 (October 1988): 40–44. Reprinted by permission of Ms. Magazine, © 1988.

estimated that a dozen women have been disqualified from Olympic competition.

Those numbers don't begin to tell the chilling story of what's happening to young girls who are being pretested today at lower levels of competition, or of the inaccuracies in the test itself and the flawed assumptions about the very nature of sexuality, or the narrow definitions of femininity that its use is based upon. Neither do they reflect the havoc it wreaks in the lives of those who do not pass, or the stress the test imposes on female athletes on the eve of their competition. As Olympic high jump champion Debbie Brill, who was first "certified feminine" in 1972, says, "It is scary having to report to a 'sex-control' station. You go through all these 'what ifs.' You know you are a girl, but what if the test doesn't show that?"

Which is what happened to Eva Klobukowska. The Polish sprinter was the first woman to be disqualified by the test when it was used on a trial basis at the European Track and Field Championships in 1967. Klobukowska may have had some internal male organs due to a birth defect, which is not unusual. Estimates of the incidence of sex chromosomal defects range from one in 1,000 to one in 4,000 births. At one end of the spectrum are people who look female; while at the other extreme are those who can have some ambiguity in their sex organs and secondary sex characteristics and are almost always treated medically and surgically to produce as concordant a sexual identity as possible.

What the officials told the 21-year-old Klobukowska was that her test revealed an irregularity. Upon further examination, they said she showed "male-like characteristics." Despite the fact that she was neither hypermuscular nor particularly more successful than her peers, their conclusion was that she had been competing "unwittingly as a man." Klobukowska was quoted as saying, "I know what I am and how I feel. . . . It's a dirty and a stupid thing to do to me." After her disqualification, she went through severe and long-lasting depressions; it was rumoured that she even submitted to surgery to try to correct her internal abnormalities and retain her eligibility. Although Klobukowska was an Olympic gold medalist and world record holder in the 100-meter dash, her name was removed from the books, and all public recognition of her awards taken away. Today, she works for a Polish computer firm in Czechoslovakia and has broken off all contact with the sports world.

"What is so ridiculously sad about the whole affair is that she was probably just as much a woman as anyone else, especially if she had male internal organs that were removed and she was given the female hormone estrogen, which is a standard procedure," says John Money, a psychologist at Johns Hopkins who is one of the world's authorities on disorders of sexual differentiation.

So why are female athletes being subjected to this? Because of rumors of men masquerading as women, and of women "who were not really women" competing at the Games. Although these allegations were not unfounded, they were greatly exaggerated and reflected a fundamental ignorance of the biological conditions of women like Klobukowska, who were singled out.

There is only one documented case of a man masquerading as a woman at the Olympics. In 1957, Hermann a.k.a. "Dora" Ratjen from Bremen, Germany, went public with the news that in the 1930s he had been forced to pose as a woman for three years by officials of the Nazi Youth Movement. Entered in the women's high jump in the Berlin Games in 1936, he qualified for the finals and came in fourth. And then in 1938 Ratjen went on to set a world record in the event at a lesser meet.

Other cases cited as justification for the IOC's sex-testing policy involve individuals who lived and competed as females, but later through surgery became males. Between the late thirties and the mid-sixties, there were reports that three track and field athletes and one top skier had sex-change operations after winning medals in women's competitions. It was generally assumed that these athletes, described as "imposters" by the IOC, had had an unfair physical advantage.

As a result of those cases and the persistent rumors, the sex of some of the very dominant eastern bloc athletes came into question. Because of their strength and masculine appearance, suspicion focused on Tamara and Irina Press, two famous Soviet athletes who from 1959 to 1965 won five gold medals and set 26 world records between them. At the same time, men from one eastern European nation were rumoured to be binding their genitals and taking estrogen in order to develop breasts and pass for females in competition.

And so for the first time, at the 1966 European Track and Field Championships in Budapest, women were required to undress for what the press called a "nude parade" in front of a panel of gynecologists. All 235 competitors were inspected and all of them, including Klobukowska, passed. But several of those dominating eastern bloc athletes, among them the Press sisters, failed to appear. Their absence was construed as confirmation that they were afraid of failing the sex test.

By 1968, the visual check was not enough. A year after Klobukowska's very public disqualification, the IOC decided to adopt the newly discovered buccal smear test, which it considered a simpler, more objective, and more dignified method of distinguishing the sexes. The IOC Medical Commission further justified its use by stating, "It would be unfair in a women's competition to allow chromosomally abnormal athletes with male-like characteristics."

From the first, concerned medical specialists have protested using the buccal smear in this context. The American College of Physicians and the American College of Obstetricians and Gynecologists recently passed resolutions calling for the test to be banned. Not surprisingly, critics are labeling the entire theory and practice of sex testing discriminatory—not just because men are not tested—but because athletes are disqualified on the basis of a postulated advantage that may not be an advantage at all. But at the very heart of the debate is a far more disturbing and complex question of whether testing should be done in the first place.

For twenty years the Finnish geneticist Albert de la Chapelle has spearheaded a movement to get the IOC to reconsider its policy. He reasons that if the intent of the test is to exclude men and women whose body structure or muscle strength confers a "male-like" advantage, then "the buccal smear is the wrong test." He contends it catches some women with genetic abnormalities that bear no relation to any conceivable advantage in strength, while it fails to detect up to 90 percent of the women who might have such an "advantage," the majority of whom have normal chromosome patterns but increase their muscle bulk and strength by taking steroids or who have other disorders that give them a similar advantage.

Although all normal women and men produce both male and female hormones—it is their relative proportion that is important in sexual development—there are also genetically normal women with medical conditions causing an overabundance of the male hormone testosterone. One of these, congenital adrenal hyperplasia, accounts for many, if not most, innately hypermuscular women. Then there are women who have testosterone-producing tumours on their ovaries, which can induce "male-like" characteristics. Even some hermaphrodites, who are born with both male and female internal organs, have the female XX pattern. And there are men who have the XX chromosome pattern, although this is extremely rare. All of these people would pass through the chromosome screen undetected, would never be subjected to further examination, and would not be banned. Considering the IOC's standards, de la Chapelle points this out as "inconsistent" and "unfair" to those with similar characteristics who do get disqualified.

And what of those women with abnormal chromosomes who fail the test but have no hormonal or physical advantage? The most common example is a child born with the male chromosome pattern and testes but an impaired ability to either produce or respond to testosterone. Most are raised female and, if necessary, treated surgically and hormonally to correct their abnormalities.

As psychologist John Money explains in his book *Sexual Signatures: On Being a Man or a Woman*, "The easy assumption has been that there are two quite separate roads [to gender identity], one leading from XY chromosomes at conception to manhood, the other from XX chromosomes at conception to womanhood. But . . . scientists are uncovering a different picture. The fact is that there are not two roads, but one road with a number of forks where each of us turns in either the male or the female direction. You became male or female by stages. Most of us turn smoothly in the same direction at each fork."

If there is complete nonresponsivity to testosterone at each of the forks after the embryonic development of testes, the child develops as a female, except that she has no uterus or Fallopian tubes and is sterile. She has a vagina, and what is commonly perceived as female body proportions and muscle strength. Most of these people don't even know they have discordant chromosomes, and wouldn't find out unless they investigated their infertility or got tested by a sporting federation or at international competitions.

When a person is born with a high degree of apparent sexual ambiguity, it can be the result of having both ovaries and testes. According to prevailing medical opinion, it is more than likely that all the historical cases of sex change cited as justification for gender testing were in fact not imposters, but hermaphrodites who were assigned to the female gender at birth.

An IOC magazine editorial asserted when the buccal smear was adopted that "the chromosome formula indicates quite definitely the sex of a person." But the critics disagree, countering that a person's "genetic sex" is the least relevant parameter of gender. Once the chromosomes have given their message to the embryo to develop testes or ovaries at the first fork in the road, they never again play a role in the process of sexual differentiation. Hormone levels, internal and external organs, and overall body build all have a greater influence on gender. Money, who considers psychosocial influences a major factor, says, "The label 'boy' or 'girl' has tremendous force as a self-fulfilling prophesy."

Asking, "How often do competitors wittingly seek to deceive the IOC?" an editorial in the *Journal of the American Medical Association* took the position that genetic males raised as females universally believe they are women. "We physicians tell them so! To accuse such individuals of willful deception would be churlish."

"It is imperative that this minority of individuals not get discriminated against," added Dr. Jean Wilson, an endocrinologist who wrote a letter to the IOC in 1968 elaborating on the dangers of the buccal smear. "It would be better for individual athletes to receive a competitive advantage than for underlying diagnoses to be exposed in this cruel and heartless manner."

For a young girl, the news could be utterly devastating. In cases where a patient has to be informed of her condition, most doctors wait until she reaches her mid-twenties and is mature enough to handle it. Yet most of the athletes getting tested these days are in their teens. What Dr. de la Chapelle views as the worst consequence of the IOC's position is this testing of younger and younger girls, often in situations where there isn't even the guarantee of quality control. And technical inaccuracies in the test itself are not unusual. De la Chapelle estimates that between 6 and 15 percent of the time, individuals tested for the presence of a Y will score falsely positive, as was the case with U.S. swimmer Kirsten Wengler.

Myron Genel, a pediatric endocrinologist who is an associate dean at the Yale University School of Medicine, is concerned about the philosophical implications of the test as well. Asking, "What makes a woman a woman?" Genel says, "What it comes down to is the definition of femininity. Should it be left to a handful of people at the IOC, most of whom are men, to decide who is 'feminine enough' to compete?"

The IOC Medical commission says its intention is not to issue "ex cathedra" decisions about who is a man or a woman. Eduardo Hay, a 73-year-old gynecologist from Mexico City, is ultimately responsible for making all disqualification decisions at the Olympics. He emphasizes that the buccal smear was never meant to be more than an initial screen, and that it is always followed by more detailed chromosomal analysis, as well as gynecological and clinical exams. If the woman refuses these, she can quietly withdraw from competition. If she is disqualified, the IOC will help her invent an "injury" or some other excuse for withdrawal.

According to Hay, the IOC's aim is simply to prevent unfair competition. "At the moment when you have genetic abnormalities such as hermaphroditism, you also see anatomical differences. If there is a classically male-shaped pelvis and body configuration, then you can assume there is an advantage. You can see very well that men's records are better than women's, generally by a margin of 8 to 17 percent, depending on the sport. That difference overall is only on account of anatomical differences."

But to assert that a woman's "male-like" characteristics automatically account for her success dismisses the many interactive factors that contribute to athletic victory, such as training, intelligence, coordination, and discipline. According to Dr. Genel, not only is the assumption of advantage based on such anatomical measures scientifically unsound, but the issue of whether the presence of typically male traits creates an advantage is far from being settled.

John Money emphasizes: "The difference between male and female is not black and white; it is a biologic continuum. I don't know of any statistical studies anywhere that could tell you what isn't overlap between men and women on anatomical scales. . . . really, the range of difference within the same sex can be as great as that between men and women. Any dividing line is a matter of context."

Inevitably, drawing that line is a subjective decision. Just how much "male-likeness" is too much? When does it start to mean an unfair advantage?

Dr. Genel deems it absurd that the IOC is trying to guarantee such things as "physical equality," "unfair advantage," and "fair competition:—concepts that he says can't even be defined consistently in the first place. "If some women get disqualified for being extra strong, then why not also disqualify those with unusual height or more oxygen capacity?"

Or for that matter why disqualify only some women who have so-called genetic advantages? Genel cites the case of Flo Hyman, who suffered from Marfan's syndrome, a genetic disorder that causes extra height. At six feet five, she was one of the best volleyball players in the world. If anything, height is the anatomical parameter that correlates best with athletic success. Following the IOC's standards, should she have been disqualified?

If authorities begin selecting out designated bits of anatomy, John Money wonders, "What of the Masai with their huge long legs, or the Mexican-Indian tribals with their extraordinary oxygenation capacity? Who gets excluded?" He contends that "sports are not democratic; they are elitist. The tallest play basketball, the shortest are jockeys. The ultimate would be to break the Olympics into biological classes and run them like the Westminster Dog Show."

Dr. Genel says, "If the test were applied across the board to men as well, people would quickly see how useless it is because it sure wouldn't tell which men had an unfair advantage." Although not convinced that someone who is an intersex is more successful athletically because of that condition he concedes that if the results achieved by intersex individuals could be proven to be unattainable by "genetically normal women, then the IOC might have a leg to stand on." But the records of those athletes have consistently been superseded by women of normal genetic makeup, generally within an Olympics or two.

Not surprisingly, women athletes are divided on the subject. Long jumper Willye White had the world record she set at a U.S.–USSR meet in 1964 broken soon afterwards at the same event by a Russian whose femininity was in question. Today, White unconditionally supports sex testing: "If she hadn't been a man I would have been the world record holder."

Kate Schmidt, a world-class javelin thrower who competed in the 1972 and 1976 Olympics, considers sex-testing "just another us-against-them thing that is being done in the name of protecting women. It is Cold War mentality, because most of the athletes involved were eastern bloc." Schmidt would never protest the presence of people with birth defects, or make them feel bad for being good: "That is a sour grapes, ungracious, win-at-any-cost attitude. People like that are bad sports."

Heptathlete Jane Frederick says she doesn't believe the official explanation of the test. "I think they are just saying, 'You are so good, we can't believe you're a woman. So prove it.'"

The IOC's response to the debate? "If there is a better way, we would welcome suggestions," said IOC Medical Commission Chairman Prince Alexandre de Merode. After 20 years, the IOC has finally agreed to set up a "working group" to address the problem. Chairman de Merode promises that by Seoul the medical commission will have decided "how and when the IOC will look into the issue."

Dr. de la Chapelle, although a member of that group, is somewhat skeptical, saying: "For so long I have asked the IOC to reassess their policy, and every four years they tell me, 'Let us just get through these next games, and then we will look into it.' I know the IOC means no harm, but the policy is misguided."

One of the suggestions sure to be made will be to replace the chromosome test with a simple physical exam by female doctors. Another might be the introduction of a hormone test for allowable testosterone limits, but that is fraught with the same technical and ethical inconsistencies engendered by chromosome testing. A postcompetition "appeal system" for cases where there is controversy has been proposed. But the resulting publicity could potentially damage an unwitting athlete's psyche and reputation. Some just want to see testing dropped altogether.

Whatever is decided, the people the IOC claims it is trying to protect should be included in the discussion. To date, there has been no indication that women athletes have ever been asked.

◂▦▸

CLOSING THE MUSCLE GAP

Ann Crittenden

The author of nature gave man strength of body and intrepidity of mind to enable him to face great hardships, and to woman was given a weak and delicate constitution, accompanied by a natural softness and modest timidity, which fit her for sedentary life.
— Aristotle, "Physiognomics" (4th century B.C.)

Woman is "defective and accidental . . . a male gone awry . . . the result of some weakness in the [father's] generative power. . . .   — St. Thomas Aquinas (13th century)

From *Ms.,* vol. 3 (September 1974): 49. Ms. Crittenden's Web site is www.anncrittenden .com.

I will make you acquainted with the proportions of a man; I omit those of a woman, because there is not one of them perfectly proportioned.
—Author (unknown) of a Renaissance treatise on painting (16th century)

One way of dealing with these disparities between the athletic promise and achievement of men and women is to view women as truncated males. As such they should be permitted to engage in such sports as men do . . . but in foreshortened versions.
—Paul Weiss, Professor of Philosophy at Yale,
Sport: A Philosophical Inquiry (1969: Southern Illinois University Press)

Of all the repressions visited on woman by the heavy-handed centuries of paternalism, perhaps the most insidious has been the denial of her physical powers. Despite the fact that the average man is larger, heavier, and stronger than the average woman, it is now clear that those differences are far less than it formerly appeared. Evidence shows that the difference in strength between trained male and female athletes is far less than that between average or untrained men and women. And it is equally clear that the differences of strength within either sex are far greater than the differences between them.

The male's "overwhelming" superiority of strength and endurance may be, as Dr. Jack Wilmore of the University of California at Davis has written, more an "artifact of social or cultural restriction imposed on the female . . . than a result of true biological difference in performance potential between the sexes." The physically inferior, it turns out, are not women, but any human beings who do not develop the body's potential—exactly what women have been taught not to do for centuries. Just how much that indoctrination has cost them is only now being revealed, as more and more girls challenge the age-old prejudices defining their physical capacities.

Nowhere is the narrowing gap between young men and women so well demonstrated as in the record books of international competitions. Twenty-five years ago the women's outdoor world record for the 100-meter dash was 11.5 seconds, compared with a men's record of 10.2. Today men can cover the 100 meters in 9.9 seconds, an improvement of .3 seconds, while women have shaved a full .7 seconds off their time—now 10.8, or only .9 seconds off the time of the men.

Even more dramatic gains have been made in swimming, where women have been competing on an international level for a longer period, and therefore come closer to fulfilling their potential. In the 1924 Olympic games, for example, the men's winning time in the 400-meter freestyle was 16 percent faster than the women's. This lead was reduced to 11.66 percent by 1948, and cut to only 7.3 percent in Munich in 1972. Today's stars, like Debbie Meyer and Shane Gould, could have driven Tarzan back into the trees; Gould's current women's world record for the

400-meter freestyle is 4:21.2, a pool-length ahead of Johnny Weissmuller's men's record of 4:52.0 in 1927.

Track experts expect that the present 15.9 percent faster performance of men in the mile run will soon be reduced just as impressively. A few physiologists, such as Dr. Jerry Mogel at Queens College in New York, even refuse to rule out the possibility that a woman might eventually turn out to be the fastest runner in the world, at least in the distance runs, where brute muscle strength counts for less. At the very least, as more women compete and stay in competition until full maturity, the gap between the sexes in most physical tests could well be narrowed to 10 percent or less.

For the moment, however, such speculations about women's athletic potential remain just that, for the truth of female power still lies buried under centuries of sexist dogma. Even today the secrecy and ignorance surrounding the subject of female physiology are staggering if not surprising. Only a fraction of physical education research deals with women's performance or compares men and women under conditions of maximum effort. "It's almost as if there were a cultural or professional taboo against designing a research study involving women," comments Dr. Clayton L. Thomas, vice-president of medical affairs for Tampax and one of the few experts on female physiology in the male-dominated medical field. (Only 7 percent of American doctors are women, and of some 250 exercise physiologists in the country, fewer than 10 are female.)

There are almost no studies of the long-range effects of strenuous conditioning programs on women. There is virtually no information on the physical capabilities of older women, and little is known about the physical advantage that girls aged 12 to 14 have over boys of the same age. The influence of sexual activity on women's performance has never been studied. (Masters and Johnson found it had no effect on the muscular performance of men.) Nor has anyone studied the influence of menstrual cramps (dysmenorrhea), although as Thomas points out, "If men had cramps, we'd have had a National Institute of Dysmenorrhea for years." Worst of all, the effects of birth-control pills on a woman's strength, coordination, timing, endurance, and emotional stability are still a mystery, although one 1969 experiment indicated that the additional estrogen in most pills might cause women to be less physically active.

"All in all, what we know, compared to what we don't know, is a drop in the bucket," according to Dr. Dorothy Harris, whose new Center for Women in Sport at Penn State University in College Park, Pennsylvania, is attempting to dispel some of the uncertainties.

What we *do* know is that throughout childhood, boys and girls are roughly similar in size, strength, and reaction times. Girls aged 9 to 12 are, if anything, larger and stronger than their male peers because their bone structure and musculature begin developing earlier and mature by age 12 or 13. Boys do not generally achieve the same stage of development until age 14, 15, or 16.

At adolescence, however, a sharp divergence between untrained male and female performance begins and continues until well after middle age. When physical maturity is reached, young men are on the average about 10 percent larger than young women, and their muscle mass is about twice that of girls. They perform two to four times as well in tests of strength, according to Dr. Thomas Shaffer, pediatrics professor at Ohio State University. In sum, the skimpy evidence that exists indicates that adult men are at least 30 percent stronger than women until both subside into a more or less equally feeble old age.

The question is, why?

Much of the answer lies in the male hormone, androgen, which produces denser bones and stimulates the growth of muscle tissue. As a result, men are not only larger and heavier than women in general, but a normal man of any given size will have more muscle, or lean body mass, than a woman of similar build (or than a man with a lower androgen level). Athletes know all this very well, and those dependent on brute strength, such as football players and weight lifters, frequently (and illicitly) beef themselves up with male hormones in the form of anabolic steroids. Even a few female athletes have been known to indulge in order to perk up a performance. But no one takes female hormones for the same purpose—they simply wouldn't do the job.

From infancy, males also display a smaller amount of fat tissue than females, a distinction which increases after adolescence. Apparently no amount of conditioning can make women as lean, proportionately, as men. College-age men in the United States, for example, average 15 percent body fat, women some 25 percent. In trained athletes, however, the difference is far less, although males are still lower on the average than females. (One national study of 27 female track stars showed that seven had less than 10 percent body fat. Two had fat values of less than 7.5 percent, which was the average for 114 male competitors at the 1968 U.S. Olympic Marathon Trial.) Despite the exceptions, even most women athletes are like racehorses with a heavier handicap: that extra load of fat they have to carry around has a direct and negative effect on their work capacity and stamina.

(It is important to note, however, that fatty tissue gives women extra buoyancy and an added insulation against cold. It is no accident that women hold the records for swimming the English Channel, and that the daring food divers off the coast of Korea and Japan are predominantly women.)

Women's stamina—their ability to perform at maximum capacity and over an extended period of time—may be genetically less than men's for two other reasons. Endurance depends on the ability to take oxygen from the air and then send it to the muscles. Men have proportionately larger hearts and lungs, enabling them to pump more blood to the tissues, and they have higher concentrations of hemoglobin, the oxygen carrier in the blood. It is still unclear to what extent these factors limit female endurance, or if they actually do at all, but it is at least true that in all comparisons so far between men and women with equal degrees of conditioning, the men's maximum oxygen intake is higher.

But far more significant than the "anything you can do I can do better" comparison game is the fact that when encouraged, women can shatter all the stereotypes about the gentle, weaker sex. Young 14- to 17-year-old female athletes are handling weights of up to 40 pounds without reaching maximum capacity, and female swimmers are covering 8,000 to 12,000 yards in two two-hour sessions a day. Women distance runners, limited in the Olympics to nothing longer than the 1500-meter race (approximately one mile), chalk up to 100 miles a week in training sessions. And after a few weeks in a conditioning course at Queens College in New York, sedentary coeds can do 200 sit-ups and run a half hour without stopping. "Women have been babied in the past," says Dr. Frank Katch, their instructor. "They've never been pushed hard enough or given strenuous training. I predict there'll be a revolution in the next five years in what women can do."

There may well be, for women are discovering that the secret of their physical intimidation by men is as simple as a saying of Mao and as close as the nearest gym: conditioning. By developing her powers to the fullest, any woman, from Olympic star to the weekend tennis player, can be a match for any man she chooses to take on. More importantly, she will inherit the essential source of human self-confidence—pride in and control over a finely tuned body. That alone would be a revolution.

◆◈◆

UNDERSTANDING THE FEMALE ATHLETE TRIAD

Irene McCormick

With Olympic gold in her sights, gymnast Christy Henrich trained over several years with a goal of achieving contender status on the U.S. Olympic Women's Gymnastics Team. But then a judge at a national competition

From *IDEA Personal Trainer* 15:5 (May 2004): 28–33. Reproduced with permission of IDEA Health and Fitness Association, www.IDEAfit.com.

told the 95-pound Henrich that if she expected to win Olympic gold, she would have to lose weight—"advice" that eventually proved fatal for the 15-year-old girl.

Although Henrich believed that her intense training and disciplined diet would contribute significantly to her success, she developed the severe eating disorders known as bulimia and anorexia nervosa. She struggled with these eating disorders for 6 years before dying in 1994, weighing only 47 pounds. Henrich has been called a "poster child" for the syndrome that has become known as the female athlete triad (Porter 2000).

Discovery of the Female Athlete Triad

Gymnasts, figure skaters, runners and female athletes in other sports wherein body composition is perceived to play an integral role in performance, are under ever-increasing pressure to maintain specific weight and body fat percentage. Many female athletes are encouraged by coaches to be unrealistically thin. "In the early 1980s, I began to see women athletes at UCLA who came in and told me that they were vomiting, and they stated they had a lot of body dissatisfaction," recalls Los Angeles–based sports medicine physician Carol Otis, a former UCLA team physician, chairperson on the women's health initiative and the lead author of the 1992 American College of Sports Medicine (ACSM) "Position Stand on Female Athlete Triad."

"We didn't even know about bulimia then, but these women were talking about their experiences and conveying symptoms associated with bulimia, depression, eating disorders and other weight-related problems. We thought we'd better get a group together and talk about how we would deal with this issue moving forward," she explained recently.

In the early 1990s, researchers at the National Institutes of Health (NIH) and ACSM had a consensus conference simply to talk about the problem. Following the conference, research efforts were directed at uncovering the relationship between the prevalence of disordered eating and menstrual irregularities that occur in female athletes. It was revealed that when they occur in tandem, irregular menstrual cycles and eating disorders are associated with premature bone loss and osteoporosis. Together, disordered eating, menstrual dysfunction and decreased bone mineral density became known as the female athlete triad.

Raising Awareness

According to the 1992 ACSM position statement, it is important for coaches and parents to tell female athletes about the female athlete triad syndrome. "There are three interrelated components to the triad," Otis explains. "Disordered eating—poor nutritional habits that are less severe than anorexia or bulimia—which leads to amenorrhea, or the loss of regular menstrual cycles, and, finally, the early onset of bone mineral density or osteoporosis, a condition that is irreversible for women between the ages of 18 and 30."

This is a potentially serious condition occurring in many physically active girls, and women. The position statement concludes that the syndrome is triggered by eating disorders coupled with overtraining that is characteristic in many sports, but especially in the "appearance" sports, or those sports that encourage the athlete to look and be thin. Gymnastics, figure skating, dancing and distance running have a higher percentage of athletes with eating disorders, according to ACSM's position.

Triad Factor #1: Disordered Eating

What can begin with a harmless diet may develop into a clinically defined disordered eating pattern. Disordered eating can range from moderate restriction of food intake to binge eating and purging to severe food restrictions. However, it is important to understand the difference between clinically defined eating disorders, such as anorexia nervosa or bulimia nervosa, and "disordered" eating patterns, defined as unsafe and flawed practices used to lose weight fast.

The use of diuretics, self-induced vomiting, fad diets, fasting and attempts to sweat off weight are examples of techniques used for weight loss that are part of disordered eating patterns. One of the first signs of the triad is the use of these practices to lose weight. Female athletes may experiment with these techniques occasionally , or as frequently as several times a day. When female athletes want to lose weight and it does not come off quickly enough, they may embrace these techniques. These practices can be classified as harmful eating behaviors that do not result in true weight loss (Corsini and Reitz 2003).

The American Psychiatric Association's Diagnostic and Statistical Manual of Mental Disorders describes self-induced vomiting, the use of laxatives and short-term, self-induced starvation as part of a large and assorted category of disordered eating patterns termed eating disorder, not otherwise specified (EDNOS) (1994). EDNOS is a category reserved for individuals with clinically significant disordered eating patterns who fail to meet all of the diagnostic criteria for anorexia nervosa or bulimia nervosa.

However, EDNOS as a term may understate the significance of these practices, and they may mistakenly be perceived as less important. Despite the differences in classification, females in either category share at least one common feature of the disordered eating behaviors, which is the measure of body weight as a self-assessment.

Triad Factor #2: Amenorrhea

When an athlete is developing symptoms of the triad, she is typically exercising intensely while simultaneously reducing her weight. Some athletes do not see missing their periods as an issue, but neither do they relate missed periods to future damage to their bodies.

Primary amenorrhea (pronounced ay-meh-nuh-ree-uh) is defined as a female reaching the age of 16 without starting a regular menstrual cycle. If menstrual cycles cease without reasonable cause (such as pregnancy) for at least three consecutive periods, and the athlete is increasing her training and changing eating habits, this is secondary amenorrhea (Otis and Goldingay 2000; Boeckner 1998).

Estrogen levels are typically low during amenorrhea and decreased estrogen levels lead to decreased bone mass and increased cardiac risk (Otis and Goldingay 2000). The prevalence of amenorrhea among the general population is between two and five percent. But among female athletes it has been reported in ranges of three percent to 66 percent (Otis and Goldingay 2000).

Triad Factor #3: Osteopenia to Osteoporosis

Estrogen is necessary for proper bone density development and skeletal construction. Low estrogen levels and poor nutritional intake can lead to osteopenia, a milder form of osteoporosis, which is one of the most common and serious bone diseases (Thibodeau and Patton 1997).

"If estrogen levels are low and calcium intake is reduced because of food restrictions, there is a strong possibility that bones will be weakened. One needs a certain amount of calcium in order to grow requisite bone mass, especially athletes who participate in sports," said Malhar Gore, team physician at Iowa State University, in a 1996 interview. "Female athletes are at an increased risk for injuries such as stress fractures because their bone mineral density is diminished. Weakened bones that are exercised repeatedly and excessively will eventually fail.

"Athletic women who combine low body fat levels with overexercise and an inadequate diet stop experiencing regular menstrual cycles. At this point their estrogen levels tend to drop below normal levels to maintain healthy bone, which may lead to a catastrophic event. A minimum of

1,500 mg of calcium per day is needed to build and maintain bone, and most female athletes don't get that much," Gore said.

Evidence to date suggests that between the ages of 15 and 30 women form 30 percent of their bone density. "Without the appropriate requisite bone matrix formed during this particular period, bones do not progress to their fullest density, and this becomes an irreversible problem," Otis adds.

Body Image and the Media

In the new millennium, sports participation by girls and women is growing quickly. New opportunities in both amateur and professional sports once closed to women are now open. Research has proven that physical activity, including participation in physically demanding sports and activities, is not only healthy, but the exercise and increased strength associated with training for such activity is linked to decreased mortality and an improved psychological outlook (Smith 1996).

Despite the interest in healthy exercise, mixed messages abound. "The media can have such a negative influence. Women with the skinny appearance of an ectomorph are almost always shown on magazine covers, and this has become the ideal body image," Otis observes. "It is important for consumers to understand that genetics plays such an important role in physical development and how one will appear as an adult."

"Those at greatest risk for these negative body influences are children," said former Iowa State University associate professor Deborah Rhea, in a 1996 interview. Rhea has concentrated her research efforts on eating disorders among high school and college athletes.

A study performed by the American Association of University Women found the self-esteem of pre-adolescent (middle school) and adolescent girls plummets as much as 30 percent from the self-esteem of girls in elementary school. "Since the majority of recreational, competitive and elite athletes are in middle and high school, this poses a very real threat to the health of our nation's young athletic women," Rhea said.

With the constant attention given to achieving and maintaining a prescribed weight goal, the female athlete is at a very real risk to experience lifelong health problems. "Today's healthy look is thin, according to society's current definition," Rhea observed. Unfortunately very unhealthy behaviors are associated with this slender appearance. "Eating disorders are generally considered to be psychological disorders and are extremely difficult to treat. The most desired body image for a young, female athlete is slim, with very small, almost androgynous hips combined with voluptuous breasts—unattainable by most. Eating disorders among female athletes are among the most serious problems facing this population and parallels the seriousness of anabolic steroid use in male athletes," Rhea said.

USA Gymnastics Takes Action

Although the number of gymnasts affected by the triad is unclear at present, USA Gymnastics has created a task force to examine its response to the female athlete triad. With more than 50,000 mostly adolescent female athletes registered with USA Gymnastics, the organization is "attempting to actively pursue policies that will provide a healthy environment in which gymnasts can pursue their goals as athletes, yet maintain a healthy body image." The organization created a task force, which developed a position stand, to cope with the effects of the triad on its athletes (USA Gymnastics 1995).

The Role of Health Professionals

According to a paper published through the University of Nebraska Extension Office, it may be easy for girls with symptoms of the triad to keep such information a secret because information about their menstrual periods and any damage done to bones usually isn't visible to friends, teammates, coaches and family members. For these reasons alone, females found to have one component of the triad should be screened for the other two.

As an example, if a female is found to have irregular menstrual cycles, or regular cycles have ceased, the athlete should be questioned by team physicians, coaches and/or parents about her eating patterns, weight loss history and whether she is prone to stress fractures. Alternatively, if she had repeated stress fractures, she should be screened to see if she experiences irregularities in her eating patterns or if she is having regular menstrual cycles. The repeated presence of stress fractures is a more visible triad symptom (Bockner 1998).

The Triad on a Continuum

Otis reminds us that the components of the triad affect not only female athletes but also fitness enthusiasts of a variety of ages. "Although 20 years ago we were initially talking about the triad being described in female adolescents and young women, we are now beginning to see that this problem is occurring in Baby Boomers," she says. "Fitness industry professionals such as personal trainers do not think the triad applies to them or their clients."

She adds that in these populations, "The triad can tend to run on a continuum." The three components have a wide range of how they appear and affect people in a variety of ways."

Although Otis admits there are no long-term studies on the triad, she says that development of the triad will result in compromised bone mineral development. "A personal trainer can use several techniques to screen for components of the triad such as asking specific questions that include 'I' statements. Repeated or frequent stress fractures are also a tip-off."

Not Everybody Agrees

Contrary to the stand and the consensus of the NIH, Judy Mahle-Lutter, co-author of *The Bodywise Woman* and co-founder and president of the Melpomene Institute in St. Paul, Minnesota, disagrees with the level of severity with which the female athlete triad has become associated. "It's easy for coaches and the press to latch onto a name like the female athlete triad, making it look more deadly than it is—to play on people's fears," she says. "It's good to have a name so coaches and parents can be aware of the potential damage of this situation—the fact that it could be an issue for elite-level athletes. But the naming of this condition is often overstated. The data does not support the prevalence of the triad among the general exercising population, and I don't think it would be accurate to state that it is something of this level of severity."

The Melpomene Institute performs research devoted to health issues affecting physically active women and attempts to educate women in a variety of ways including providing educational resources. "We did not see a high number of female athletes with this condition. It is more of an elite athlete that we are dealing with," Mahle-Lutter observes. Further, to synthesize the words of Carol Oglesby, a member of the Melpomene's advisory board, "the [number of] women suffering from the female athlete triad is miniscule compared to the number of women who are not participating in exercise."

Mahle-Lutter concluded by stating that the research is still not conclusive. The big picture is that coaches do not know enough about it, but at least they bring it up, and they may be able to refer the female athletes who exhibit these symptoms to appropriate treatment without the panic that all exercising females will experience this problem.

What Can Fitness Professionals Do?

The ACSM position stand warns that female athlete triad occurs not only in elite athletes, but also in physically active girls and women participating in a wide range of physical activities. Otis reminds us that fitness professionals are in a great position to make a positive impact on this condition. "Fitness industry people do not think that it applies to them, but it definitely does. This is for your clients, not just for thin celebrities and elite athletes who work with personal trainers and coaches."

How can you deal with such situations? Be honest about what you observe. If you notice that statements made by the client are negative and degrading, ask her about them. Bring to her attention that she is using negative self-talk. Ask if her feelings about her body dissatisfaction are affecting other parts of her life. If she agrees that they are, refer her to her primary physician or other health professional.

Although individuals with components of the triad (disordered eating or amenorrhea) may deny any nutritional or health problems, it is important that medical attention is sought. If the client is reminded that proper nutrition and appropriate medical care may enhance performance, she may be more likely to get the help she needs. Also, if the risk factors are described to the athlete in a non-judgmental way, she may in turn be more likely to get the medical help she needs.

Treatment of the triad often requires intervention through a team approach. A medical professional aligned with a psychologist, a nutritionist, parents and coaches can create a healthy and full-range approach.

More research continues in many areas related to the triad. Monitoring young women to avert and treat the female athlete triad is the best way to prevent the disastrous outcomes.

Signs and Symptoms of the Female Athlete Triad

- undue fatigue
- erosion of dental enamel from frequent vomiting
- anemia
- abdominal pain and bloating
- depression
- constipation
- dry skin
- sore throat
- decreased ability to concentrate
- lightheadedness

- cold intolerance
- chest pain
- cold and discolored hands and feet
- irregular or loss of menstrual cycles
- lanugo (fine, downy hair covering the body)
- stress fractures (micro fractures of bones that may progress to complete bone breakage)

Some Warning Signs of Disordered Eating Patterns

- preoccupation with food and weight
- excessive leanness or rapid weight loss
- expressed concern with being too fat
- frequent eating alone
- use of laxatives
- trips to the bathroom during or immediately following a meal
- increased criticism of self
- continual drinking of no-calorie beverages
- many dental cavities, foul breath (from self-induced vomiting)
- depression, low self-esteem
- daily vigorous exercise in addition to regular training
- chipmunk-like cheeks from swollen parotid glands (self-induced vomiting)

More on Female Athlete Triad from ACSM

The following are excerpts from the ACSM "Position Stand on Female Athlete Triad" as presented by the American Family Physician in a clinical brief.

- The female athlete triad occurs not only in elite athletes, but also in physically active girls and women participating in a wide variety of sports and other physical activities. The triad can result in waning overall physical performance, as well as physical and psychological illness, and even death.
- The triad is often denied by athletes, not recognized by parents, coaches or health care professionals and, as a result, is underreported. Health care professionals need to be aware of the interrelated components of the triad and be able to recognize, diagnose and treat or refer women when at least one component of the triad is identified.

- Women with at least one component of the triad identified should be screened for the other two components of the triad. Frequently occurring stress fractures, recent or sporadic weight loss and missed periods should be discussed openly without judgment. This can be done at the pre-participation physical exam and during routine clinical evaluations.
- All sports medicine professionals should learn the symptoms and risks of the triad. They should have basic nutrition information and should have access to referral sources for nutritional counseling and medical and mental health evaluation.
- Education for physically active girls and women, coaches, fitness professionals working with women, and parents is key to prevention of the triad. These individuals should be aware of basic proper nutrition, safe training practices and the warning signs of the risk of the triad.

EAT-26

It is believed that early identification of an eating disorder can lead to earlier treatment thereby reducing serious physical and psychological complications or even death (Boeckner 1998). The Eating Attitudes Test (EAT-26) is a screening test primarily used for early identification of an eating disorder and is designed to assess concerns and attitudes common in those with eating disorders. Only a qualified professional in a formal psychological evaluation can diagnose an eating disorder, but EAT-26 is probably the most widely used standardized measure of symptoms and concerns characteristic of eating disorders.

RESOURCES

The Athletic Woman's Survival Guide, by Carol Otis and Roger Goldingay. 2000. Champaign, IL: Human Kinetics Publishers.
"The Female Athlete Triad" (video). 2002. Produced in cooperation with the American College of Sports Medicine and Megafitness Fitness Videos, www.megafitness.com.
"Female Athlete Triad: Disordered Eating, Amenorrhea, and Osteoporosis," 2001. Published consumer handout, www.acsm.org.
The Bodywise Woman, 2d ed., by Judy Mahle-Lutter and Lynn Jaffee of the Melpomene Institute. 1990. Champaign, IL: Human Kinetics Publishers.

WEBSITES

American Academy of Family Physicians, www.aafp.org
The American College of Sports Medicine, www.adsm.org

Human Kinetics Online Education Center, www.hkeducationcenter.com. Select "Course Catalog," then select "Fitness for Women," and select either the course with or without materials.

KidsHealth, a website created by the Nemours Foundation's Center for Children's Health Media, www.kidshealth.org.

USA Gymnastics, www.usa-gymnastics.org

REFERENCES

American Family Physician. (1997). Clinical brief: Position stand on female athlete triad, 56(6), 1676–77.

Boeckner, L. 1998. The female athlete triad. University of Nebraska, Lincoln Facts Nebraska Cooperative Extension, Institute of Agricultural and Natural Resources, NF98–361. University of Nebraska, Lincoln. Retrieved December 23, 2003 from www.ianr.unl.edu/pubs/foods/nf361.htm.

Corsini, M., and Reitz, J. (2003). The prevalence of risk factors for the female athlete triad in college level female athletes at the University of South Dakota. Retrieved December 23, 2003 from www.med.usa.edu/communityprojects/cp2003sf/2003_corsini_reitz.htm.

Diagnostic and Statistical Manual of Mental Disorders (4th ed.). Washington, D.C.: American Psychiatric Association.

Garner, D. M., et al. (1982). The eating attitudes test: Psychometric features and clinical correlates. *Psychological Medicine*, 12 871–8.

Garner, D. M. (1997). Psychoeducational principles in treatment. In D. M. Garner and P. E. Garfinkel (Eds.), *Handbook of Treatment for Eating Disorders*. New York: Guilford Press.

Hobart, J. A., and Smicker, D. R. (2000). The female athlete triad. *American Family Physician*, 61(11), 3357–70.

Otis, C. L., and Goldingay, R. (2000). *The Athletic Woman's Survival Guide*. Champaign, IL: Human Kinetics Publishers.

Porter, Y. (2000). Tumbling down: Eating disorders and the female athlete triad. *The Village Voice*, April, 19–24.

Smith, A. D. (1996). The female athlete triad: Causes, diagnosis, and treatment. *The Physician and Sports Medicine*, 24(7), 67–72.

Thibodeau, G. A., and Patton, K. T. (1997). *The Human Body in Health and Disease*, 3d ed. St. Louis: Mosby.

USA Gymnastics Online. (1995). Technique: Task force on USA gymnastics response to the female athlete triad preliminary report. Retrieved December 23, 2003 from www.usa-gymnastics.org/publications/technique/1995/9/triad.html.

◆❖◆

WOMEN AND ACL INJURIES

Taking the Bad News with the Good

Maureen Madden, PT, CSCS

The Bad News

The statistics are impressive. Women are two to eight times more likely to sustain an ACL tear in sports that are at the highest risk such as basketball and soccer. The incidence of significant knee injury among females is roughly five times higher per player per hour than for males. The volume of injury is significant. It is estimated that 350,000 ACL injuries occur annually in the U.S. alone. More of those injured will still be men by virtue of a greater number of male participation in sports. The data suggests that women who choose to participate in sports are taking a greater risk than men. With the help of Title IX in 1972 and the trend of adolescents to participate in a single sport year round, the number of women and the level of competition in many sports continues to rise. There is no sign of a slowdown in female athletic endeavors, nor should there be. The increasing interest and study in the causes of this disparity among men and women is helping lead to discoveries that can benefit both male and female athletes.

Early research was primarily focused on the anatomical and hormonal differences among men and women. Unfortunately, the studies have not led to obvious answers or methods of injury prevention. Although differences exist, ultimately there would be no reasonable course of action available to change one's anatomy or biochemistry for the sake of basketball. For example, there have been studies on the relationship between femoral notch width to ACL injuries with conclusions that smaller notch width (which on average is smaller in women) shows a higher incidence of unilateral and bilateral ACL tears. There have been studies about the relationship of ACL injuries in women and the menstrual cycle. Wojts et al. found that women are three times more likely to injure their ACL during ovulation (when levels of estrogen peak) than during other times of their cycle. Others along similar lines include studies showing greater joint and ligament laxity in women. However, none of these studies could conclusively find a direct relationship to increased ACL tears.

From the Web site of The Stone Clinic, 21 March 2003, http://www.stoneclinic.com /acl_womenbadgood.htm.

Additional anatomic differences can be more easily observed. On average, women have greater pelvis widths, a larger "Q angle," greater hip varus, hip ante version, knee valgus and foot pronation. All combined, these biomechanics may put the ligament at a disadvantage even before any jump or landing is ever made. The exact effect that these characteristics have individually or in combination on ACL vulnerability continues to be explored, but may help identify risk factors. Again, other than possible orthotic intervention in some cases, or the unlikely result of "quitting soccer because of my Q angle," little else can reasonably be done to influence these anatomical traits in women.

The Good News

The most encouraging aspect of the bad news about ACL tears is that 70% are noncontact injuries. This can be viewed with optimism because it says there may be something we can do about one aspect of the problem at a neuromuscular level, rather than hope to accomplish an impossible task by trying to control outside forces such as a tackle from another player. Since there has been no solid evidence to support the benefit of prophylactic bracing for knee injuries, neuromuscular training had to be looked at.

In the neuromuscular arena, women appear, yet again, to have a general disadvantage. There have been reports of women having electromechanical delay in muscle recruitment, poor hamstring recruitment patterns, and less functional joint stiffness (the stability of the joint brought about by muscular constraints). Others have noted less hamstring and gluteus medius activation in females than males. Still others have noted the functional outcome of all these factors seems to be that women tend to use less hip and ankle musculature during sport, therefore, exposing the knee and ACL to greater amounts of uncontrolled movement.

ACL injuries appear to occur most frequently during deceleration activity such as a sudden stop, change in direction, or landing from a jump. Therefore, eccentric strength and proprioception play a critical role. Both are factors that can be influenced substantially through training. The answer is not simply sport specific training, but functional training, which takes into account quality of movement and the inherent efficiency of muscle integration.

Making the Best of It

There has been documented success with a jumping program that takes into account form, flexibility, and plyometric strength. This program is essentially a progressive jump-training program that emphasizes form and technique of jumping and landing. It progressively builds on plyometric training over a six-week period. Noted benefits are increased overall strength of the hamstrings and an increase in vertical jump. Jump training led to a significant decrease in the incidence of ACL injury among women trained in this manner versus untrained women. The power building ability of plyometrics has long been recognized so it is no surprise that a program like this, when implemented carefully, can help athletes with joint protection as well as performance.

Deceleration training, in which the athlete practices landing from a jump, accelerating, changing direction, and then decelerating, has also been proposed. These programs pick up where pure jump training leaves off and put another functional dimension into the obvious strength and power gains made with a pure jumping program. Although the program emphasizes teaching the athlete to use short quick steps to decelerate and to keep her center of gravity over the knee, this may not always be possible to control during the intensity of competition.

Functional training programs blend the benefits of jumping and deceleration training with exercises that help the athlete prepare for stresses placed in multiple planes concurrently, which is most likely when injury takes place. The addition of various proprioceptive challenges combined with strength building fill in the missing piece to ACL prevention training programs. In addition to jump training, it seems necessary for the athlete to practice recovering from a precarious position that may occur during competition. For example in basketball, a player may have the hip, knee, and arm extended, with the trunk and head rotated while reaching back for a bad pass in basketball. In a game situation, this type of complex movement pattern cannot always simply be avoided. The body may be better prepared for this potentially dangerous situation through exercises that are gradually increased in complexity, and in proprioceptive challenge. The goal being to build a neuromuscular system in the athlete that can efficiently deal with the many proprioceptive challenges inherent to sport. The therapist or trainer must drive the training by imposing various demands at the appropriate level to obtain efficient and safe mechanics. The clinician must be able to recognize poor functional form and correct it through "tweaking" the exercise. Functional training is "quality of movement" training that requires careful progression and the understanding of biomechanical and neurological principles.

What to Do with the News

Unfortunately for women, there seems to be a confluence of factors that put them at risk for ACL and other knee injury. It is imperative that coaches, athletes, and parents be educated in the risks, not to discourage participation, but to encourage pre-season programs. Girls should also be encouraged to participate in numerous sports and cross training activities while growing and developing in order to be exposed to various proprioceptive challenges. It seems counterproductive to funnel children into programs that concentrate on one sport year round. Although the child may become quite skilled, poor habits can develop but not be recognized until injury occurs. Cross training works for all athletes.

The physical therapist has a responsibility to evaluate the athlete thoroughly (whether pre or post injury) in order to combine various parts of the above programs to focus on the individual's weaknesses. It appears that eccentric control of the muscles throughout the lower extremity, good quadriceps to hamstring ratios, and good proprioceptive skills are the cornerstones for training women and men to reduce injury risk. The athlete must be aware of the benefits of pre-season and in-season functional training. These programs must become readily available and clearly taught to coaches and trainers. It should be emphasized that more is not necessarily better, but the right training done with quality and variety may be the key.

REFERENCES

Arendtt, E., Dick R. Knee injury patterns among men and women in collegiate basketball and soccer; NCAA data and review of literature. *American Journal of Sports Medicine*, 1995; 23:694–701.

Frank, C. B., Jackson, D. W. The science of reconstruction of the anterior cruciate ligament. *Journal of Bone Surg Am*, 1997; 79:1556–1576.

Griffin, L. Y. et al., Noncontact anterior cruciate ligament injuries: Risk factors and prevention strategies. *J Am Acad Orthop Surg*, 2000, vol. 8, pp. 141–150.

Wojts, E. M., Huston, L. J., Lindenfeld, T. N., Hewett, T. E., Geenfield, M. L. V. H. Association between the menstrual cycle and interior cruciate ligament injuries in female athletes. *American Journal of Sports Medicine*, 1998; 26:614–619.

Vescovi, J. D., Brown, T. Decelerating injuries. *Training and Conditioning*, March 2002; 12.2.

Gambetta, V., Leap of strength. *Coaching Management*, April 2000, 8.3.

◀▓▶

CATASTROPHIC INJURIES IN FEMALE ATHLETES

Cheerleading Leads the List

Robert C. Cantu, M.D., and Frederick O. Mueller, Ph.D.

From 1982 through 1997, 60 direct fatalities and catastrophic injuries and 25 indirect fatalities occurred among high school and college female athletes, including cheerleaders (table A). Cheerleading, in fact, accounted for 34 (57 percent) of the direct fatalities and catastrophic injuries. A major factor in these injuries was the change in cheerleading activity, which now involves gymnastic-type stunts such as front and back flips, dives from mini-trampolines, and pyramid building.

Many state high school associations have responded to these changes and the increase in injuries by banning stunts such as pyramid building and the tossing of cheerleaders. Others have designated cheerleading as a sport. The American Association of Cheerleading Coaches and Advisors implemented a Safety Certification Program, which has certified over 500 coaches and been adopted by some states and some college conferences.

Safety initiatives have resulted in a number of recommendations, including the following:

- Coaches should supervise all practices and be safety certified
- Cheerleaders should have a preparticipation exam, be trained in gymnastics, spotting, and conditioning, and participate only in stunts that they have mastered
- Stunts should be limited; e.g., pyramids should be limited to two levels and performed on mats
- Emergency procedures should be written and available
- Cheerleaders who have signs of head trauma should receive immediate medical attention and return to cheerleading only with permission from a physician

Excerpted from Robert C. Cantu, M.D., and Frederick O. Mueller, Ph.D., "Fatalities and Catastrophic Injuries in High School and College Sports, 1982–1997: Lessons for Improving Safety," *The Physician and Sportsmedicine* 27:8 (August 1999).

Table 1

Fatalities and Catastrophic and Serious Injuries in US Female Student Athletes, 1982–1997

Direct Fatalities[a] and Catastrophic Injuries[b]		Indirect Fatalities[c]	
High School			
Cheerleading	18	Basketball	8
Gymnastics	9	Swimming	5
Track	3	Track	4
Swimming	2	Cheerleading	3
Basketball	2	Soccer	1
Softball	2	Cross Country	1
Field Hockey	2	Volleyball	1
Volleyball	1		
Total	39		23
College			
Cheerleading	16	Tennis	1
Gymnastics	2	Basketball	1
Field Hockey	1		
Downhill Skiing	1		
Lacrosse	1		
Total	21		2

[a] Caused by performing the activities of a sport.

[b] Resulting in transient or permanent severe functional spinal cord disability.

[c] Caused by systemic failure as a result of exertion while participating in a sport.

◀▦▶

WOMEN, DISABILITY, AND SPORT AND PHYSICAL FITNESS ACTIVITY

The Intersection of Gender and Disability Dynamics

Elaine M. Blinde and Sarah G. McCallister

[. . .] Existing work exploring the experiences of women with disabilities in sport and physical fitness activity has often focused on participants in organized sport or elite-level athletes (Brasile, 1988; Brasile, Kleiber, and Harnisch, 1991; Hopper, 1986; Horvat, French, and Henschen, 1986; Sherrill, 1993b). Although research has highlighted the experiences of a small number of women with disabilities, findings cannot be assumed to generalize to the vast majority of women with disabilities who participate in less structured sport and physical fitness activities.

Henderson and Bedini (1995) conducted one of the few studies exploring the physical activity experiences of adult women with physical disabilities who were not athletes or elite-level sport participants. In their interviews of 16 women with mobility impairments, Henderson and Bedini examined how this group experienced physical activity, recreation, and leisure. In general, these women reported various perspectives from which to view the value of these activities, including leisure, therapeutic gains, and maintaining mental and physical health. On the other hand, some respondents indicated that these activities had limited value in their lives. In a related study, Henderson, Bedini, and Hecht (1944) interviewed 30 adult women with various sensory and physical disabilities about their physical activity participation. Increasingly, most of these women did not experience their bodies in active or physical ways when engaging in these activities. Rather than seeing physical activity as leisure, it was more commonly viewed as a form of therapy.

The purpose of the present paper was to enhance our limited knowledge of the experiences of women with physical disabilities in sport and physical fitness activity. [. . .]

The various questions asked during the interview assisted the investigators in learning more about the nature of outcomes experienced from

Reprinted with permission from *Research Quarterly for Exercise and Sport*, Vol. 70, No. 3, 303+, Copyright 1999 by the American Alliance for Health, Physical Education, Recreation and Dance, 1900 Association Drive, Reston, VA 20191.

the participants' sport and physical fitness activity participation. Questions focused on areas such as positive and negative aspects of participation, meanings and feelings associated with participation, and things learned about oneself and one's physical capabilities from participation.

The one unifying theme among their responses was the intrinsic nature of what they gained from participation. Rather than focusing on extrinsic factors such as winning, status, awards, recognition, or visibility, the women almost exclusively discussed outcomes reflecting intrinsic gains of participation. Although their initial motives for participation often focused on maintaining a functional level of the body, they saw sport and physical fitness activity participation as an enlightening experience impacting several aspects of their lives. Common areas discussed during the interviews included an enhanced view of one's capabilities, seeing the body as a source of strength, viewing sport and physical fitness activity as a motivational outlet, and experiencing a greater sense of control in their lives. Despite efforts to identify both positive and negative outcomes derived from the participation experience, most responses were positive. Where appropriate, however, examples of negative experiences are noted.

Enhanced Views of Capabilities

When discussing participation outcomes from sport and physical fitness activities, one of the most commonly mentioned gains was an enhanced view of one's capabilities. Despite the physical limitations or constraints a disability can impose on an individual's lifestyle, approximately half of the women discussed how participating in sport and physical fitness activities often provided them with an expanded sense of their physical capabilities. For example, comments such as, "I can do a lot more than, you know, before [participation]," and, "I think it makes me feel more confident about what I can do," were not unusual. Similarly, the statement, "I think it helps me at times not feel like I'm quite as disabled," typified these feelings. Sandy, a 34-year-old with cerebral palsy who had received a college degree in special education, provided some interesting insight into how she felt about herself when she participated in sport and physical fitness activities:

I tend to feel a whole lot more capable when I'm in the midst of doing something in terms of fitness and sports or, um, even if I'm not particularly successful at it, just the fact that I'm actively doing something. . . . It seems to be a real, like, freeing experience type thing for me.

Or, as Jackie, a 20-year-old college junior with paraplegia commented, "I can do more than, you know, than just pushing around [my wheelchair]."

However, perceptions of enhanced capability were not limited to sport or physical fitness activity. Again, approximately half the respondents discussed the impact of participation on their capabilities in general life situations. Examples of areas impacted included social life, community integration, work place, interpersonal relationships, and student role. These women felt that sport and physical fitness activity provided them with a renewed (or, in some cases, first-time) sense of confidence in a variety of situations. For example, when asked what she had learned about herself from participating in sport and physical fitness activity, Kathy, a 25-year-old graduate student with paraplegia for the past 10 years, stated:

I'm probably a stronger person physically and mentally than I thought I was, that I'm more persistent than, maybe, I thought I could be.

When asked if this information will help her in other areas of life, Kathy continued:

Oh, yeah. I think, um, in terms of, you know, just school, I think it improves my drive and my desire to succeed there. . . . I think it'll help me in the work place, um, in dealing with other people, um, and being assertive, and also, um, in terms of commitment to work.

Body as Source of Strength

A second theme was seeing the body as a source of strength. Approximately half the women mentioned outcomes that challenged the stereotypical portrayal of disability as weakness. Their comments frequently highlighted how sport and physical fitness activity enhanced views of the body and its potential. For example, they sometimes mentioned participation outcomes such as "building up your strength" and "keeping your body fit." Jennifer, a 21-year-old high school graduate with cerebral palsy, talked about how walking, swimming, and lifting weights made her feel:

Good. I think it makes my body feel better, it makes . . . you know, I think from the outside and the inside, I mean, mentally and physically, I think it's better.

Sandy, who previously discussed how sport and physical fitness activity enhanced perceptions of her capabilities, also commented on how she felt about her body when participating in these activities:

It tends to be a[n] invigorating experience, and I tend to be, um, feel more positive about my body and, um, less self-conscious about how I look, because I'm usually focused on specific goals.

Although many of the women talked about seeing the body as a source of strength, this perception did not characterize all the respondents' views. To the contrary, some still struggled with the assumed contradictions between disability and sport and physical fitness activity. Julie mentioned feeling "frustrated once in a while when I try and do something" and "not being able to do what I used to do." When asked how she viewed her body in this context, Wanda, a 47-year-old woman with incomplete hemiplegia for the past 26 years, responded:

Like I view [a] calculator that's misfunctioning, well, something without all the gears, something, you know, it's not doing what it's supposed to. . . . I catch myself saying to myself, "Can we stop now?" and it's funny, because I'm the one who started it and yet I'm the one that wants to stop.

Participation as a Motivational Outlet

As respondents discussed their varied experiences in sport and physical fitness activity, several women mentioned how this context provided them with an important motivational outlet. They sometimes saw participation in sport and physical fitness activity as providing a reason "to get out of the apartment" and be "with other people."

In a similar light, Cheryl, a 36-year-old with hemiplegia for 19 years, credited participation with giving her "something to look forward to when I wake up in the morning." Connie, a 49-year-old woman with cerebral palsy, provided several related comments about the importance of participation:

It gives me something to look forward to. . . . I just like to do it, and I think it's good for me. And I just enjoy it. . . . [It] give[s] me more to think about, and you talk about with other people.

Other women mentioned the newness or unique aspect of this form of activity. Sport and physical fitness represented variety in many of their lives. For example, Sandy talked about how participation made her feel:

It's that feeling of, like, new challenges and new horizons and . . . just, you know, newness, whereas like physical therapy and that kind of thing. I mean, I'm 34, and I've been doing physical therapy since I was, like, 5 years old. And physical therapy, they tend not to vary the routine a whole lot, you know, whereas, I mean, recreation, I mean, it has a little different twist because you're working and you're doing physical activity.

Or, as Julie stated about the positive aspects of participation, "getting to do activities which, you know you wouldn't be doing otherwise."

Greater Sense of Control in Lives

Many women viewed participation in sport and physical fitness activity as enhancing the perceived degree of control in their lives. Their responses highlighted several different aspects of control, including attaining a sense of freedom, accomplishing what they set out to do, doing something for themselves, feeling empowered, believing that no obstacles can stop them, and experiencing a sense of mastery.

Kelly, a 19-year-old with cerebral palsy, felt strongly about what she had learned about herself through participating in sport and physical fitness activity. She stated, "I can do anything I want to. Nothing can stop me." Similarly, when asked about her overall experiences in sport and physical fitness activity, Judy, a 32-year-old college student with partial paralysis, commented:

I feel fit. . . . I feel like I have control over it, over myself, you know, I feel it's important. . . . It gives you a better mental health . . . feeling happier about myself.

Julie added that having "control over things" was important to her and that sport and physical fitness activity provided a "sense of empowerment." Wanda, a 47-year-old with incomplete hemiplegia, mentioned a "feeling of mastery" when asked what participation meant to her. Finally, Alice, a 54-year-old with muscular dystrophy who had taught school for about 14 years, commented that participation "give[s] me a certain, um, freedom." [. . .]

[The women in this study] participated in sport and physical fitness activity primarily to preserve or maintain a body already at risk. Rather than participating in sport and physical fitness activity to build a body with new capabilities and potential, many of the women acknowledged that their involvement was motivated by a desire to prevent further loss of bodily function. This finding parallels that of Henderson et al. (1994) in their interviews of adult women with disabilities. Also, comments focusing on the desire to construct a more attractive or aesthetically pleasing body were not common.

While maintenance and functionality were major motives for participation, the sense of empowerment experienced through sport and physical fitness activity was noteworthy for these women. Sport and physical fitness activity often represented a means through which women with disabilities reevaluated their capabilities and potential. Although sport and physical fitness activity participation stood in sharp contrast to societal constructions of a disability, several women talked about how participation was a "freeing experience" for them. Moreover, participation often challenged feelings of being disabled and resulted in altered perceptions of the body as a source of strength. Participation also enhanced perceptions of having "control" over certain aspects of their lives.

Sport and physical fitness activity also provided women with disabilities an intrinsically rewarding experience. Despite the range of participation outcomes these women discussed, most of the gains were foundational in nature. Being able to engage in some form of sport or physical fitness activity was often sufficient to enhance their sense of physical capabilities. The women interviewed generally did not hold high or unrealistic expectations in terms of what they desired to obtain from sport or physical fitness activity participation. In many cases, success in the activity was secondary to the fact that they were actually able to do something physical. Or, in other cases, merely getting "out of the apartment," "being with people," or having "something to look forward to" made sport and physical fitness activity extremely rewarding. [. . .]

REFERENCES

Balsamo, A. 1994. Feminist bodybuilding. In S. Birrell and C. L. Cole (Eds.), *Women, sport, and culture* (pp. 341–352). Champaign, IL: Human Kinetics.

Benefield, L., and Head, D. W. 1984. Discrimination and disabled women. *Journal of Humanistic Education and Development*, 23(2), 60–68.

Birrell, S., and Cole, C. L. (Eds.) 1994. *Women, sport, and culture*. Champaign, IL: Human Kinetics.

Blinde, E. M., and McClung, L. R. 1997. Enhancing the physical and social self through recreational activity: Accounts of individuals with physical disabilities. Adapted *Physical Activity Quarterly*, 14, 327–344.

Blinde, E. M., and Taub, D. E. 1999. Personal empowerment through sport and physical fitness activity: Perspectives from male college students with physical and sensory disabilities. *Journal of Sport Behavior*, 22, 181–202.

Blinde, E. M., Taub, D. E., and Han, L. 1993. Sport participation and women's personal empowerment: Experiences of the college athlete. *Journal of Sport and Social Issues*, 17, 47–60.

Brasile, F. M. 1988. Psychological factors that influence participation in wheelchair basketball. *Palaestra*, 4(3), 16–19, 25–27.

Brasile, F. M., Kleiber, D. A., and Harnish, D. 1991. Analysis of participation incentives among athletes with and without disabilities. *Therapeutic Recreation Journal*, 25, 18–33.

Bryson, L. 1987. Sport and the maintenance of masculine hegemony. *Women's Studies International Forum*, 10, 349–360.

Cole, C. L. 1994. Resisting the canon: Feminist cultural studies, sport, and technologies of the body. In S. Birrell and C. L. Cole (Eds.), *Women, sport, and culture* (pp. 5–29). Champaign, IL: Human Kinetics.

Deegan, M. J. 1985. Multiple minority groups: A case study of physically disabled women. In M. J. Deegan and N. A. Brooks (Eds.), *Women and disability: The double handicap* (pp. 37–55). New Brunswick, NJ: Transaction Books.

Deegan, M. J., and Brooks, N. A. (Eds.), *Women and disability: The double handicap.* New Brunswick, NJ: Transaction Books.

DePauw, K. P. 1994. A feminist perspective on sports and sports organizations for persons with disabilities. In R. D. Steadward, E. R. Nelson, and G. D. Wheeler (Eds.), VISTA '93—The Outlook (pp. 457–477). Edmonton, Alberta: Rick Hansen Centre.

DePauw, K. P. 1994. Sport and physical fitness activity in the life-cycle of girls and women with disabilities. *Women in Sport and Physical Activity Journal,* 6(2), 225–237.

DePauw, K. P. 1997b. The (in)visibility of disability: Cultural contexts and "sporting bodies." *Quest,* 49, 416–430.

Fine, M., and Asch, A. 1985. Disabled women: Sexism without the pedestal. In M. J. Deegan and N. A. Brooks (Eds.), *Women and disability: The double handicap* (pp. 6–22). New Brunswick, NJ: Transaction books.

Fine, M., and Asch, A. (Eds.) 1988. *Women with disabilities: Essays in psychology, culture, and politics.* Philadelphia: Temple University Press.

Guthrie, S. R. 1997. Defending the self: Martial arts and women's self-esteem. *Women in Sport and Physical Activity Journal,* 6(1), 1–28.

Hall, M. A. 1996. *Feminism and sporting bodies: Essays on theory and practice.* Champaign, IL: Human Kinetics.

Hanna, W. J., and Rogovsky, B. 1993. Women with disabilities: Two handicaps plus. In M. Nagler (Ed.), *Perspectives on disability* (2nd ed., pp. 109–120). Palo Alto, CA: Health Markets Research.

Henderson, K. A., and Bedini, L A . 1995. "I have a soul that dances like Tina Turner, but my body can't": Physical activity and women with mobility impairments. *Research Quarterly for Exercise and Sport,* 66, 151–161.

Henderson, K. A., Bedini, L. A., and Hecht, L. 1994. "Not just a wheelchair, not just a woman": Self-identity and leisure. *Therapeutic Recreation Journal,* 28(2), 73–86.

Highlen, P. S., and Finley, H. C. 1996. Doing qualitative analysis. In F. T. L. Leong and J. T. Austin (Eds.), *The psychology research handbook* (pp. 177–192). Thousand Oaks, CA: Sage.

Hopper, C. A. 1986. Socialization of wheelchair athletes. In C. Sherill (Ed.), *Sport and disabled athletes* (pp. 197–202). Champaign, IL: Human Kinetics.

Horvat, M., French, R., and Henschen, K. 1986. A comparison of the psychological characteristics of male and female able-bodied and wheelchair athletes. *Paraplegia,* 24, 115–122.

Locke, L. F. 1989. Qualitative research as a form of scientific inquiry in sport and physical education. *Research Quarterly for Exercise and Sport,* 60, 1–20.

Lonsdale, S. 1990. *Women and disability: The experience of physical disability among women.* New York: St. Martin's Press.

Markula, P. 1993. Looking good, feeling good: Strengthening mind and body in aerobics. In L. Laine (Ed.), *On the fringes of sport* (pp. 93–99). St. Augustin, Germany: Academia.

Messner, M. S. 1988. Sports and male domination: The female athlete as contested ideological terrain. *Sociology of Sport Journal,* 5, 197–211.

Morris, J. 1993. Gender and disability. In J. Swain, V. Finkelstein, S. French, and M. Oliver (Eds.), *Disabling barriers—Enabling environments* (pp. 85–92). London: Sage.

Nilges, L. M. 1997. Five years of *Women in Sport and Physical Activity Journal*: A content review. *Women in Sport and Physical Activity Journal,* 6(1), 109–129.

Patrick, D. R., and Bignall, J. E. 1984. Creating the component self: The case of the wheelchair runner. In J. A. Kotarba and A. Fontana (Eds.), *The existential self in society* (pp. 207–221). Chicago: University of Chicago Press.

Sherrill, C. 1993a. Women with disabilities. In G. L. Cohen (Ed.), *Women in sport: Issues and controversies* (pp. 238–248). Newbury Park, CA: Sage.

Sherrill, C. 1993b. Women with disability, paralympics, and reasoned action contact theory. *Women in Sport and Physical Activity Journal,* 2(2), 51–60.

Strauss, A., and Corbin, J. 1990. *Basics of qualitative research: Grounded theory procedures and techniques.* Newbury Park, CA: Sage.

Taub, D. W., Blinde, E. M., and Greer, K. R. (in press). Stigma management through participation in sport and physical activity: Experiences of male college students with physical disabilities. Human Relations.

Theberge, N. 1985. Toward a feminist alternative to sport as a male preserve. *Quest,* 37, 193–202.

Wendell, S. 1989. Toward a feminist theory of disability. *Hypathia,* 4, 104–124.

Whitson, D. 1990. Sport in the social construction of masculinity. In M. A. Messner and D. F. Sabo (Eds.), *Sport, men, and the gender order: Critical feminist perspectives* (pp. 12–29. Champaign, IL: Human Kinetics.

Willis, P. 1994. Women in sport in ideology. In S. Birrell and C. L. Cole (Eds.), *Women, sport, and culture* (pp. 31–45). Champaign, IL: Human Kinetics.

◆◈▶

ANABOLIC STEROIDS

The Gremlins of Sport

Terry Todd

Tam Thompson, a 27-year-old graduate student in physical education, has competed in the sport of powerlifting since 1982 and admits having used anabolic steroids to improve her performance. Like many other athletes in an increasingly wide variety of sports, Tam felt that using anabolic steroids (synthetic derivatives of the male hormone, testosterone, which helps in the building of muscle size and strength) would give her a competitive edge. Before using steroids, Tam had never won a national title nor set any official records and she hoped steroids would allow her to catch the top women. In this quest she was ultimately successful. Two years ago, Tam decided to stop using the drugs and the result was a significant drop in her level of strength.

Excerpted from Terry Todd, "Anabolic Steroids: The Gremlins of Sport," *Journal of Sport History* 14:1 (1987): 87–88.

The following interview represents one of the few times a woman athlete has discussed her drug usage for the record.[1] Much of what Tam has to say may seem extraordinary to those who are removed from the world of competitive sports, but neither the amounts of drugs she took, her attitude toward those drugs, nor the side effects she experienced are atypical of what many observers now see regularly among men and women who use these substances. Tam's interest in, involvement with, and ultimate opposition to anabolic steroids began shortly after her first competition in powerlifting.

I remember after my first powerlifting meet thinking, "I can't believe I finished sixth out of the nine women in my weight class. I know I'm stronger than they are." And so, instead of training harder or going to better techniques, I figured they were taking drugs and I would too. I'd catch up. "And besides," I told myself, "if I decide this is a bad thing, I can simply stop."

The dealer was steering me. He told me, "Stay away from Dianabol and testosterone, they're not good for women." And of course, that was tantalizing to me. I thought, "What is this? This is chauvinistic. Why can the men take these stronger drugs and not me?"

I started on Anavar and decided it didn't work, so I switched to injections of Equipoise—you know, the new veterinary steroid everyone's using—and decadurabolin. Then I added some Dianabol on top—generally five to six a day, and then, when I was about five weeks out from the U.S. Women's Nationals I started a cycle of testosterone, too. I started off with one half cc a week, then one cc the next week, then to one and one-half, then two cc's, and finally, the week before the meet, I took three cc's. I was pretty well tanked.

And then three days before the meet I started taking shots of aqueous testosterone—the real nasty stuff that hurts when it goes in. I mean you put that thing in your hip and it feels like it's dripping all down the back of your hamstring. It makes the hamstrings cramp really bad. I took one cc in the morning and one cc at night for the first two days, then the day before the meet one cc in the morning and two cc's at night and the morning of the meet I took two more cc's, and then three more right before the meet started. And during the meet I took some of those sublingual testosterones—I don't remember how many—and right before the deadlifts I took an injection of adrenalin backstage—about one-half cc, I guess.

How did I feel? Like I was on top of he world. Not high, just a very super feeling. I thought I could do anything.

Unwanted side effects? I didn't really notice anything the first cycle. So I figured, "OK, we're safe, this isn't going to do anything to me." And it didn't, not the first time. But the second cycle, my voice started getting lower, and I noticed those strange hairs showing up. I thought, "Well, that's no big deal. A hair here, a hair there. Big deal. I can live with it." Some of it was on my face, some on my chest. And the next cycle it got worse. But by then, I figured the damage had already been done, and I went ahead with the full cycle of steroids because I had a meet coming up. It's hard to explain to people that once you're on the drugs you lose sight of everything but winning. That's one thing they don't understand. I mean, I could look at myself, back then, and I could sort of see what was happening, but I didn't care. I don't feel that way now. I've been off the drugs for almost two years now, but I still have to shave every day.[2]

Tam admits that she was obsessive, even fanatical, in her approach to sport. But so, apparently, are thousands of other athletes in a variety of sports. Consider the comments of Harold Connally, gold medal winner in the hammer throw in the 1956 Olympic Games. "I think that any athlete should take any steps necessary, short of killing himself, to maximize his performance." Or consider a study done by Dr. Gabe Mirkin. He once asked more than 100 competitive runners if they would take a "magic pill" that guaranteed them an Olympic gold medal but would also kill them within the year and found, "to my amazement, more than one-half of the athletes responding stated they would take my magic pill." A comparable study involving lifters found similar results. And sports scientist Gideon Ariel admitted that if he had had to choose during his days as an Olympic discus thrower between an extra five inches in distance or an extra five years of life he'd have chosen the distance.[3]

The use of ergogenic—performance enhancing—drugs by athletes is certainly not a new phenomenon. What *is* new, and distressing to many who observe sport, is that these more recent additions to the athletes' bag of tricks—anabolic steroids—have the power to do more than simply enhance an athlete for a single, isolated athletic event. They can physically alter the athlete, sometimes permanently. Tam's use of steroids, for instance, left her with noticeable hair on her chest, enough facial hair to produce a beard and mustache, the beginnings of male pattern baldness, clitoral enlargement and a significantly lowered voice. Whether she also suffered internal side-effects is unclear. She did not get her drugs from a doctor and she had no tests made. But she knows, just as the many thousands of other athletes who regularly take steroids know, that liver dysfunction and an increased susceptibility to cancer, cardiovascular disease, prostate enlargement, and infertility are also associated with the use of steroids.

Steroids also affect athletes psychologically. Some experts think, in fact, that the greatest benefit to athletes from steroids is not the fact that they allow the body to build more muscle, but that, as central nervous system stimulants, they make the athlete more aggressive about training and competition.[4] Many athletes would even argue, as Tam does, that the use of these drugs fundamentally changes who they are.

There's no doubt in my mind that when I took the drugs I was no longer the same person I was before I took them. And I'm not simply talking about the facial hair and the lower voice. My personality completely changed. I trained harder. I wanted to win more. And I got much more aggressive. There was one woman at the nationals last year who looked at me the wrong way, so I invited her out in the hall.[5]

By anyone's lexicography, powerlifting is a minor sport. Though national and world championships are held, these contests are not part of the Olympic Games and they have recently attracted very little media attention, in part because of the ubiquitous drug use in the sport.[6] Nor is prize money offered in powerlifting; it is strictly an amateur affair and the greatest reward one can achieve is the holding of a world record or being named to a national team. Seen in this light, the risks Tam Thompson took seem astonishing. Yet she is certainly not unique. Nor is she without historical precedent.

NOTES

Note numbers and callouts have been changed from the original article.

1. Another woman who openly admits to steroid use is the bodybuilder "Pillow," who began an anti-steroid campaign in 1984. See Jan Todd, "Pillow Talks," *Strength Training for Beauty*, 2 (September, 1985), 65–68.

2. Taped interview with powerlifter Tammy (Tam) Thompson, 15 April 1986. Tape on file at Todd-McLean Sport History Collection. The University of Texas, Austin, Texas.

3. Conally quoted in Jan Todd, "Former Powerlifter Calls for Steroid Curbs," *Austin American Statesman*, 13 September 1983, p. 6. Mirkin in "High Risk Gamble to Obtain Winning Edge," *San Diego Union*, 13 July 1982, sec. C, p. 1; weightlifting study is from Goldman, *Death in the Locker Room*, p. 32; Ariel in Jan Todd, "Former Powerlifter Calls for Steroid Curbs," p. 6.

4. Terry Todd, "The Steroid Predicament," *Sports Illustrated* 59 (August 1, 1983), 70–73.

5. Tam Thompson interview.

6. Both women's and men's powerlifting attracted a good deal of media attention in the latter part of the 1970s and early part of the 1980s. Both the national and world championships were regularly covered by CBS's *Sports Spectacular* and NBC's *Sports World*, and several positive articles in *Sports Illustrated* and other mainstream publications appeared. However, as powerlifting became more closely identified as a sport which abused anabolic steroids—and, in particular, as many of the women who dominated the sport looked more androgynous and in some cases were growling and sprouting facial hair—the sport became harder to sell to the national networks. NBC announcer, Mike Adamlie, put this concern in words at the 1981 Women's World Championships, when he told Jan Todd, head of the IPF Women's Committee, that powerlifting simply had to do something to clean up its image. According to Adamlie, his viewers might be interested in watching these women once—as he put it, just as people will pay to see the freaks in the sideshow—but he did not see them becoming interested in the sport or the women on a long-term basis.

◄❖►

EATING DISORDERS AND GYMNASTICS

Ana Cintado

Why Are Eating Disorders More Prevalent Among Athletes in General?

Eating disorders are especially common among athletes because the pressure of the sport environment frequently precipitates the onset of these problems. In this population, certain compulsive behaviors such as excessive exercise and restricted eating patterns are seen as acceptable, and pathogenic methods of weight control are often introduced. In addition, concern about body size and shape is increased because of the "social influence for thinness [from coaches and peers], anxiety about athletic performance, and negative self-appraisal of athletic achievement" (Williamson et al. 1995). Finally, the competitive nature of sports reinforces characteristics such as "perfectionism, high achievement motivation, obsessive behavior, control of physique, and attention to detail" (Ludwig 1996). Most successful athletes are more determined and more disciplined than the average individual. They often set very high goals for themselves and work extra hours each day to reach them. These same attributes, however, can lead to eating disorders and are often found in anorexic and bulimic patients.

Are Certain Types of Sports More Prone to Develop Eating Disorders Than Others?

Eating disorders are obviously found in all sports, but athletes participating in activities that emphasize leanness for performance and appearance are at a significantly greater risk. Thus, gymnasts, long-distance runners, divers, and figure skaters are more prone to developing eating disorders and related problems than those who compete in nonweight-restricting sports such as volleyball or football. Furthermore, disordered eating patterns are found more in female athletes than in males. In a NCAA survey of collegiate athletics conducted in 1992, "93% of the

From the Vanderbilt University Psychology Department Home Page, http://healthpysch .psy.vanderbilt.edu/HealthPsych/gymnasts.htm.

programs reporting eating disorders were in women's sports" ("Dying to win" 1994). Some male athletes do use extreme methods for losing weight, but an important difference exists between these and the self-starvation strategies of anorexics. For instance, a wrestler's perception of his body is not distorted and when he is not competing, he can regain the weight with ease.

Do Female Gymnasts Suffer an Even Greater Risk?

As demonstrated by such famous gymnasts as Kathy Johnson and Nadia Comaneci who have struggled with eating disorders themselves, women's gymnastics seems "designed for the disease" ("Dying for a medal" 1994). In the 1992 NCAA survey, 51% of the gymnastics programs that responded reported this illness among its team members, "a far greater percentage than in any other sport" ("Dying to win" 1994). Unfortunately, the real number is probably even higher.

Why Might Gymnasts Be More Vulnerable to Eating Disorders?

Anorexia often strikes young women who try to evade the natural process of becoming adults and who use excessive measures to maintain a thin and girlish figure—the exact description of what today's female gymnast must accomplish to stay competitive at its highest levels. For these athletes, the onset of womanhood is their biggest fear because it means developing hips or breasts that might hinder their performance. Thus, starving themselves offers the most convenient solution to their problem. In addition, many of these girls begin training specifically for this sport since the time they are toddlers. Engaging in such targeted training before the body matures could prevent them from choosing a sport that best suits their adult body type. As a result, "this could provoke a conflict in which the athlete struggles to prevent or counter the natural physical changes precipitated by growth and maturity" (Sundgot-Borgen 1994).

The second reason for gymnasts' greater drive for thinness and body dissatisfaction is the subjectivity of their judging system. A runner's achievement, for example, relies completely on speed and endurance. Even though a lean physique is important for performance in this sport, it does not determine which person is awarded first or second place. Instead, the winner is chosen according to the exact time they reach the finish line. Judging a gymnastics routine, however, is not as objective. Each judge assigns a score according to his or her own beliefs. Thus, the appearance of the performer may actually influence their perceptions and affect their ultimate decision. A tragic example of the judges' power over these athletes is an incident with gymnast Christy Henrich—a top competitor of the late 1980's who died of multiple organ failure due to her battle with bulimia and anorexia nervosa. At a meet in Budapest, a U.S. judge commented that Henrich would have to lose weight if she wanted to make the Olympic team. Upon returning to the states, her mother recalls the first words out of her daughter's mouth: she was fat and she would have to lose weight—that was the only way she would reach her dreams.

A third reason for the greater prevalence of eating disorders among these gymnasts is their authoritarian coaches. A large percentage of coaches are constantly instructing the girls on "how to count calories, how to act, what to wear, [and] what to say in public" ("Dying to win" 1994). As a result, the only aspect of their lives they can truly control is the food they put into their bodies. Furthermore, as role models to these girls, any comment made by their coaches is taken very seriously. The reason so many of them even begin dieting is because their coach recommends that they lose weight. These athletes are so young and impressionable that such a recommendation may be seen as a requirement for improved performance. One gymnast recalls how her club coach would punish team members if they exceeded their assigned weight by "abusing them verbally, withholding meals, and confining them to a 'fat room'" ("Dying to win" 1994). This gymnast remembers vomiting 12 times a day before she finally quit the team.

Weight Concerns Among Gymnasts

Although discrepancies exist in the percentages of eating-related disturbances in gymnasts, a majority of the available evidence does suggest that these athletes are more preoccupied with their body weight than are both nonathletes and most other athlete groups.

Is It Pathological?
It is unclear whether the increased weight preoccupation observed in gymnasts is the result of a mental illness or if it "represents a healthy commitment to the achievement of athletic excellence." It has been argued that a pathological disease of any kind is "inconsistent with optimal athletic performance, and there is substantial evidence that athletes tend to have healthy psychological profiles" (O'Connor et al. 1996). Another study challenged this proposition, however, by finding a relationship between eating-disorder problems in gymnasts and personality/attitudinal pathologies. In this study, the bulimic subjects displayed significantly higher levels

of pathology than the "normals" and "exercisers" across the four measures of body satisfaction, beliefs about attractiveness, self-esteem, and weight difference. For example, they wanted to lose more weight and reported less satisfaction with their bodies than both of the other groups. The exercising gymnasts were also shown to be different psychologically from the "dieters/restricters" by exhibiting higher levels of self-esteem and body satisfaction (Petrie 1993).

How Are These Concerns Reflected?
Over the past thirty years, the trend shows that elite gymnasts have become significantly smaller in terms of body size and weight. At the 1964 Olympics, the all-around title was given to 26-year-old Vera Caslavska who at 5'3", 121 pounds would be considered a "geriatric giant by today's standards" ("Dying to win" 1994). In 1968, however, she was soon upstaged by 13-year-old Olga Korbut who at 4'11", 85 pounds changed the history of gymnastics forever.

During the last two decades, the image of the world-class gymnast as a very thin prepubescent girl has become even more exaggerated. For example, the average size of the U.S. team alone has declined from 5'3", 105 pounds in 1976 to 4'9", 88 pounds in 1992. Even more alarming is the all-around gold medalist of the 1993 world championships: 16-year-old Shannon Miller who at the time was only 4'10", 79 pounds.

What Effects Do These Concerns Have on Gymnasts?
Although their weight, body mass index, and percentage of body fat are extremely low, a large percentage of these athletes consider themselves too fat and feel that others perceive them in a similar fashion. Eager to lose the "extra pounds," most of them weigh themselves frequently and spend a significant portion of their day thinking about and talking about their weight. Furthermore, most of them believe that even a small weight gain of three pounds would be detrimental to their performance. Thus, they experience unpleasant feelings when they weigh more than they desire (which is most of the time).

How Does Weight Actually Affect Performance?
In general, it is argued that a negative relationship exists between body weight or composition and athletic performance. Thus, the higher the body weight, the poorer the athletic performance will be in most cases. Although weight can limit an athlete significantly, it is the actual percentage of body fat that tends to be the determining factor (meaning that a leaner athlete will typically perform better in competition). One particular study examined the physiological performance variables needed for skills in the routines of elite gymnasts, such as running speed, jumping

height, and hand strength. This investigation found that there was no correlation between body weight and the performance of these behaviors. In a different study, however, the actual gymnastics performance was looked at in terms of its relationship to body fat composition. The study determined that college gymnasts who placed first, second, or third in a competition at the national level had significantly lower body fat than the other team members who did not place at all. However, these two groups of gymnasts did not differ in any way in terms of height and weight.

Another study that looked at the body mass index and performance among elite gymnasts found that "although there was a trend toward thinner athletes performing better, the athletes who performed best were neither the thinnest nor the heaviest: (Sherman 1996). These findings suggested that a lower body mass index is related to better performance, but that the performance can actually be affected negatively if the BMI becomes too low. In other words, weight loss only enhances performance up to a certain point. Losing weight beyond this point only leads to a deterioration of athletic performance because the gymnast starts to lose lean tissue and body fluid instead of fat. She becomes too unhealthy and weak to perform with the same strength and endurance that she did in the past. Thus, increasing muscle content would improve performance more than decreasing body fat.

What Happens to Concerns about Body Weight After Retirement?
An investigation recently conducted found that not many symptoms of eating disorders are present 15 years after retirement from the sport. In addition, it discovered that former gymnasts claim to be more satisfied with the shape of their bodies and less weight-preoccupied than when they were competitive athletes. Despite having less body fat than most of the women their age, these women had reported low levels of satisfaction with their bodies during their college years. This suggests that they gave more importance to how they differed from their ideal weight than to their actual percentage of body fat. After retirement, however, the gymnasts "subscribed to a different ideal body weight that was less discrepant from their actual body weight, resulting in less body dissatisfaction" (O'Connor et al. 1996).

What Are the Consequences of Weight Loss Associated with Eating Disorders?

The use of rapid weight loss techniques leads to severe consequences that affect both the performance and the overall health of gymnasts. These consequences include fatigue, nutrient inadequacies, and impaired growth.

Another major consequence includes amenorrhea, the suspension of the menstrual cycle. This severe estrogen deficiency eventually leads to bone loss, a side effect that contributes to osteoporosis later in life.

Finally, in the most extreme cases, eating disorders can also end in tragic death.

What Measures Are Being Taken to Improve Conditions?

As a means of remedying the current situation, the U.S. Gymnastics Federation is beginning a nationwide club for gymnasts. This club will include a hot line the young athletes can call if they are receiving too much pressure from their coaches, parents, or peers to lose more weight than necessary. It will also train coaches in their program on how to detect and prevent eating disorders in their team members. In addition, the Federation Internationale de Gymnastique, a group that governs international gymnastics competitions, raised the age eligibility by one year. This age change may have psychological benefits regarding body image issues because it may create a more realistic body figure as the ideal for gymnasts. Finally, the USA Gymnastic Athlete Wellness Program has been assigned to "promote wellness education and develop a national referral network of specialists in athletic training, nutrition psychology, and medicine who will be available as resources for gymnastics clubs and coaches" (Anderson 1997). Hopefully, these measures will prevent the development of more severe eating disorders and reduce the frequency with which the athletes engage in these unhealthy behaviors. Maybe one day the sport will lose its fame as "the fertile ground for anorexia" ("Dying for a medal" 1994).

REFERENCES

Anderson, Van (1997). "Female gymnasts: older and healthier?" *The Physician and Sportsmedicine*, 25, 25–27.
"Athletes and eating disorders" (1995). *Better Homes and Gardens*, 73, 68–69.
"Dying for a medal" (1994). *People Weekly*, 42, 36–38.
"Dying to win" 1994). *Sports Illustrated*, 81, 52–59.
Harris, B., and Greco, D. (1990). "Weight control and weight concern in competitive female gymnasts." *Journal of Sport and Exercise Psychology*, 12, 427–433.
Ludwig, M. (1996). "A sport psychology perspective." *Journal of Physical Education Recreation and Dance*, 67, 31–35.
O'Connor, P., Lewis, R., and Kirchner, E. (1995). "Eating disorder symptoms in female college gymnasts." *Medicine and Science in Sports and Exercise*, 550–554.

O' Connor, P., et al. (1996). "Eating disorder symptoms in former female college gymnasts: Relations with body composition." *The American Journal of Clinical Nutrition, 64,* 840–846.

Petrie, T. (1993). "Disordered eating in female collegiate gymnasts: Prevalence and personality/attitudinal correlates." *Journal of Sport and Exercise Psychology, 15,* 424–436.

Sherman, R., Thompson, R., and Rose, J. (1996). "Body mass index and athletic performance in elite female gymnasts." *Journal of Sport Behavior, 19,* 338–344.

Steen, Suzanne (1996). "Timely statement of the American Dietetic Association: Nutrition guidance for adolescent athletes in organized sports." *Journal of the American Dietetic Association, 96,* 611–615.

Stoutjesdyk, D., and Jevne, R. (1993). "Eating disorders among high performance athletes." *Journal of Youth and Adolescence, 22,* 271–281.

Sundgot-Borgen, J. (1994). "Risk and trigger factors for the development of eating disorders in female elite athletes." *Medicine and Science in Sports and Exercise,* 414–418.

"Ultra slim and fast" (1996). *Psychology Today, 29,* 17–18.

Vuori, Ilkka (1996). "Peak bone mass and physical activity: A short review." *Nutrition Reviews, 54,* S11–17.

Warren, B., Stanton, A., and Blessing, D. (1990). "Disordered eating patterns in competitive female athletes." *International Journal of Eating Disorders, 9,* 565–569.

Williamson, D., et al. (1995). "Structural equation modeling of risk factors for the development of eating disorder symptoms in female athletes." *International Journal of Eating Disorders, 17,* 387–393.

◈▶

THE SILENCE OF GREAT DISTANCE

Women Running Long

Frank Murphy

The difference between a jump and a fall is intention. The difference between falling and being pushed is a matter of proximity. Kathy Ormsby may have jumped, she may have fallen, and she may have been pushed. She may have been faint from the heat of the evening, the great tension of the race, from the stress of her own heavy expectations and from the misapprehension of other people's best wishes and her reconstruction of them as demands. She may have been physically unprepared for the challenges by

Excerpted from Frank Murphy, *The Silence of Great Distance*, Kansas City, Mo.: Windsprint Press, 2000.

virtue of her light weight, her eating habits, a faltering heart that fluttered once or twice at the wrong instant and left her; and she may in fact have felt the terrible brunt of depression, anger, and despair. And yet, from all the possibilities, she picked only one when she said to her coach at the base of the bridge, I jumped. It was a mechanical explanation which was misleading by its simplicity. It had only the virtue of bringing to Kathy Ormsby accountability for her own action, and incidentally of freeing any other person of blame. It also relieved the sport itself, and the conditions it engendered, from scrutiny. In that regard, Kathy's statement was a selfless, brave act. Of course, no one believed her. Certainly, the other women did not. They would have believed the simple fact of the statement, that she jumped, but no one believed that the jump, if any, was the conduct of a person acting in response to singly felt impulses. Empathy, understanding, and shared experience, as well as the instinctive sense among many runners of the day that they, too, could have traveled Kathy's road, foreclosed that conclusion. Kathy Ormsby got in trouble because the demands of her sport, inseparable from the demands of her nature and of the larger social environment, brought her to the bridge and impelled her. That ultimately was the determination made by Kathy's parents. It is the view that Kathy has approached in the many years since the accident. Without delay, however, it was the shocked and chastened sentiment of many of the women in Indianapolis with Kathy. They never understood the event any other way. Speaking with reporters, the women had the choice to stand with Kathy or apart from her. They stood with her, even as they regretted the consequence of the accident. In fact, they drew Kathy across the terrible divide of her unique experience and into a world they identified as their own. As a result, the building story of June 4 was written from an epicenter and then in expanding concentric rings. The epicenter was Kathy Ormsby, whose sparely rendered life provided the opportunity for endless speculation. The next ring was composed entirely of Stephanie Herbst, the winner upon whom survivor's guilt might be visited. The remaining rings gathered up the other women in the race, then women distance runners as a group, and finally women athletes generally. No woman in any sport was outside the last circle. To visualize the media reaction, throw a pebble in a still pond. With more time, visit Vienna, Austria. Start at the Cathedral of St. Stephen and walk away.

In the first ring, Kathy was an historical collection of words and phrases selected to build a picture of anxiety, nervousness, and tension—definably, a person who tried so hard to be good that she was bound to break under the strain. She was, the reports indicated, unforgiving of herself, a pusher, a serious Christian woman who pulled pressure on herself and then struggled to find an air pocket. "Running and school are her life," one college teammate was quoted as saying. "She'd even bring her notes to our workouts so she could study." One of the coaches from North Carolina State referred to the record and its effect: "She's a perfectionist and being the record holder for the 10,000 meters put too much pressure on her. It gave her a tremendous amount of pressure she couldn't handle." Her father, Dale, agreed that it was "a question of pressure," which originated with Kathy's desire to succeed. As to the accident itself, he felt "it was physical, and maybe it was mental, and it blotted out the ability to think rationally. I know she wanted to do well, and it was important to her. Her coach always told her to run within herself. But that was hard for her." Administrators, teachers, friends, and coaches from her hometown were also called into the account. This was, after all, a young woman honored at her high school with "Kathy Ormsby Day" shortly before her graduation, and an athlete whose number had been retired by the school, the only time that had happened. A friend from high school described Kathy as quiet, intense, deeply religious, unassuming, and as his "hero." One of her former coaches said that Kathy just would not complain, not even if she was injured, because she thought she would let her teammates and coaches down. "She pushed herself so hard," the coach said, "that we tried to get her to let up." An assistant principal added her impression, "Kathy was a strong, driven lady. She drove and drove herself." Capturing nearly identical images, another teacher and coach said that Kathy had always "driven herself very, very hard," and that "she's not the type of person who can accept second best for herself. If there's any pressure, Kathy was putting it on herself. She's always been very much a perfectionist. She was always very, very serious about everything she did." The high school's athletic director summed up Kathy's athletic persona when he said that "as far as who worked hard to be better than anybody else, I've never seen anybody like her." Finally, a high school math teacher described Kathy as a special person. "She was perfect; she was really perfect," the teacher said. "She was the most conscientious student I ever had. I don't think she competed with other people. I think she competed with herself. She wanted to excel. She just pushed herself too hard and was expecting too much from herself. And I think she kept a lot of things inside. She was quiet, a quiet girl." All the people back home were surprised and shocked about the events in Indianapolis—shocked that at the 6,500-meter mark of the 10,000-meter final the quiet girl just disappeared, figuratively carried away when the rain of many days became the flood of one day.

Any reference to Kathy's personal history tended to explain the event in terms of that personal history. Which is, Kathy had the accident because she asked too much of herself, felt too keenly the disappointment of a bad race, and over-reacted. The contrary view, or at least the view that provided balance, was that Kathy competed in a sporting environment which, in and of itself, uniformly asked a great deal from the participants and subjected all of them to risk, although the nature and extent of the risk varied from person to person. This case became stronger as fellow athletes, coaches, and teachers at North Carolina State softened the image of Kathy Ormsby by making it clear that, although she worked hard and aimed to do her best, she was also dearly loved by her teammates, as Rollie Geiger said; that she was sweet, courteous, diligent, sensible, and not afraid to reach out for help if she needed it, as her physics professor said; that she was caring enough even as she lay in her hospital bed—embarrassed, stunned, worried, in considerable pain, and struggling to adjust to a new physical reality—to write a note of encouragement to Janet Smith who was entered in the 5,000 meters on Saturday night; and that she was capable of earning the compliment of Ellen Reynolds, who stated directly that Kathy Ormsby was and remained one of the nicest people she knew. Kathy's image was also enhanced by the report that she was an all-American and the most valuable performer for each of her first two years on the NC State track teams, accomplishments that were possible precisely because she faced many nerve-racking athletic tests without flinching; and by reports that she accepted the news of her paralysis courageously, puzzled and anguished by what had happened, but not broken. These bits and pieces of information about Kathy made it difficult to dismiss her as a stern perfectionist unsuited for the unpredictable, uncontrolled world of competitive athletics. To the contrary, the more complete information identified Kathy Ormsby as the sort who would flourish if given a fair opportunity; a person who would not, in fact, panic in the face of adversity or flee from the fight, but would turn intentionally to face it. That was her record. The conclusion that she was a fighter overborne by events outside her control would have been even more clear if her prior experience with falls and blackouts had been immediately available, which it was not.

The testimony from her coach, from her teammates, and from other athletes, as well as from her prior performances, confused the question of causation. It was obviously not going to be sufficient to look only to Kathy Ormsby and leave the matter there. Connie Jo Robinson of North Carolina State, who finished sixth in the 10,000 meters, took the next step necessary to focus the evaluation correctly. When asked about the reaction by other runners, she presented Kathy as merely one among many. "No one has come up to me and asked why," said Connie Jo in the days after the accident. "They've just come up and said we're sorry and we're praying for her. Athletes don't need to know why. They know why. We're all in the same boat. We all have the same pressures." After Connie Jo visited Kathy at the hospital, she was asked whether Kathy explained what happened. Kathy had not, nor was there any need to do so. "She knows we understand," Connie Jo said. The runners understood because they stood where Kathy did, felt what she felt, and did not fall—they had to wonder—only by God's mercy. This point was ironically emphasized by a small, unverified report that appeared in the local newspaper two days after the 10,000 meters:

NCAA RECORDS: Wisconsin's Stephanie Herbst had a meet record (32:32.75) to win the women's 10,000-meter run on the opening day of the NCAA Outdoor Track and Field Championship in Indianapolis. Boston College senior Michele Hallett became disoriented during the race, ran out of the stadium and was found at the White River Bridge of New York Avenue about 1,000 feet from the Stadium. Indianapolis Fire Department Capt. Robert Eads said Hallett was taken to Wishard Memorial Hospital where she was treated for heat prostration. He said she was expected to be released today. During the race, temperatures were in the mid-70s and humidity was high.

Accepting the report as written, there were two women at the bridge that fateful night. One was stopped before she suffered serious harm; the other was alone when she needed help.

COMING HOME

Joli Sandoz

Homecoming weekend 1987. On the long drive south, I search for calm. I own a successful business now; it's ridiculous to relive battles a decade old. Still, my palms slip slightly on the wheel. If coaching is a home, it's one to which I dread returning.

First, the requisite football game. Just like old times. I park and walk across campus in the general direction of the Redwood Bowl. Yellow and orange flowers in neat beds nod among the spiky green leaves which decorate California. The university apparently still holds its ground. Making my way between aging buildings, I wonder—cynically—if the new paint is standard alumni whitewash. But there's also that faint, undeniable stirring. . . . The grandstand roof rises ahead, and I think with some surprise, *We were heroes here.* [. . .]

Excerpted from Joli Sandoz, "Coming Home," *Whatever it Takes: Women on Women's Sport.* Joli Sanoz, ed. New York: Farrar, Straus and Giroux, 1999.

. . .

I coached at Humboldt State University for two years in the late 1970s, at age twenty-four the youngest faculty member in my department but already a veteran of three seasons of intercollegiate coaching. My own average performance on teams in college convinced me that coaching would take me further than playing; I didn't think much about what coaching might do *to* (as apart from *for*) me. Besides teaching courses in recreation administration, I came to this far northern outpost of the California state university system to rebuild a sagging women's track and field program.

Down on the field in front of us the football moves back and forth. This is sport as drama of beef and bluff; my attention soon wanders. At halftime I slip out the stadium gates, around the back of the practice field, and down a shaded forest trail. On the dark earth of this very path, I conducted my first workouts as head coach. My shrill new whistle echoed from these massive redwood trunks. For two years here, teaching young women to pursue their own excellence—fiercely—formed the axis of my life.

In my journal I wrote:

1978 and 1979
Coaching. I feel myself coming alive on the deepest levels. Coaching challenges me to the core, forcing me to use all of my capacities and abilities, demanding everything I can give. I love the exhilarating feel of being used fully, of concentrating everything I have been and am in the hope that what is possible will be. The spiral of hope lifts—striving, discipline, patience, beauty—and I am everywhere forced to evaluate, to stretch out, in, up. [I feel] the immense satisfaction of stretching others, of knowing how to teach and inspire people to do difficult things well, of molding community from the crossings of diverse lives. The price is the weight of example and authenticity. No one can share the risk and fine-drawn pride and pain with the coach, not even most of her athletes. If the whole thing wasn't so much your own creation, your baby, it wouldn't bring such incredible tension: the chance of high-flying consummation, the looming possibility of defeat. Sometimes it's like riding a bike at breakneck speed down an immense hill—without the possibility (likelihood) of a crash, there couldn't be so much beauty.

Coaching seemed to me then a commitment to care—about life and its living. I privileged the team experience. The quality of our togetherness would take us through a very long season. At the same time, I believed strongly in individual effort and responsibility. Each athlete had to do her job in the throwing circles, and on the track and jumping aprons, and live with whatever the consequences turned out to be. If this team was my baby, then I saw my job as helping it to grow up.

In company with many parents, though, my joy and caring at times slid into protective anger. College coaches by tradition enjoy almost complete autonomy in their work with their team members; outsiders' interference with discipline or training schedules is serious trespass, analogous to walking into someone's living room and telling her children what to do. Nevertheless, at HSU the athletes and I soon began to receive unsolicited advice. One community member, a man, told a frosh that the weight workouts I'd written for her training were wrong, and pressured her—an inexperienced young athlete—to follow a strength program used by pro football players. Another man, this one a visiting high school coach, walked up to a group of us at practice and simply interrupted me to criticize an athlete's running form. Unasked-for guidance from male students, faculty, and staff became a constant sore point. As the months passed, I grew adept at warning them off. And more and more angry.

May 1977
If as a female you lose, men laugh at you contemptuously and treat you patronizingly, even if they themselves are losers. ("After all, I can beat her.") If you win, you are considered subnormal, a dyke, "too muscular," and probably a bad lay in the bargain. Bets are laid on you, males crowd around offering advice—something they wouldn't think of doing to a male winner—and everyone tries to get a piece of the action, to build his ego on and from you. ("Yep, I can *still* beat her.") . . . The insidious effect of all this is that women listen to this pompous patronizing and let it ruin the joy they gain from improvement. . . . How many times has a fledgling female athlete, spreading her new wings, had them clipped by the coarse and unfeeling remarks of a self-styled Mr. Superstar, himself by all outward indications a "failure" in athletics? It's time for women to say "to hell with you" and turn their attention from the color and cut of their uniforms to the incomparable grace and beauty of the female body in disciplined motion.

These particular men—not every man, I hasten to add, and not often those associated with the HSU men's track team—insulted the athletes and me by assuming that their expertise was more valid than our own and that we would be grateful for their help. Even harder for me to accept were the female athletes who asked if they could travel and compete as team members but train with their boyfriends or a male coach. (One simply said she just couldn't get used to obeying a woman.) Curiously enough, the man in question was never our own assistant coach, a highly competent grad student and former wrestler named Lloyd Wilson, who combined an intuitive understanding of people with a well-known penchant for hard work.

Where I once loved sport for the fun, the laughter, the physical highs, I became fierce in pursuing the wins which would show the men and women who rejected my coaching that I could be competent on their terms.

Each season at HSU began with a scramble for athletes. Phone calls, letters, recruiting talks in PE classes, bulletin boards extolling the pleasures and challenges of taking up track and field—Lloyd and I did everything we could to make five months of hard work sound special. We didn't have scholarships or a strong tradition, so we sold the sport on its merits, often to women who had not competed in athletics before. Our you-can-do attitude perforce extended year-round; the bulletin board in the locker room became a long collage of photos, pictures cut from magazines, our own and rivals' results. I typed every quote I could find which modeled the approach I wanted "my" athletes, as I called them, to take.

Some of those slogans came from mimeographed cards my own college coach handed out after practice: "Luck is what happens when *preparation* meets *opportunity*." "Enthusiasm *creates* momentum." "Act as if it were *impossible to fail*." Athletics still seemed to me a moral world, one which rewarded effort. Except for my increasing brusqueness toward male would-be "colleagues," I taught what had been taught to me.

And—following yet another sporting custom—I placed myself in charge. I knew just two models for women wielding authority. The first I thought of as the "do as I say" method, the one my own teachers and coaches used with me. It wasn't ideal; I knew being told what to do kept me for years from taking responsibility for my own training. But it worked in the short term. While I hated the idea of ordering other women around, and wondered sometimes about my fitness to lead, I needed something effective. The second way I'd seen women use power involved the self-sacrificing, nurturing-as-service paradigm of the proverbial mother, which seemed soft in comparison. Soft was something a too-young head coach with eyes upon her could not afford to be. Authoritarian got things done, reached the measurable goal; it seemed safer, especially in the face of aggressive masculinity. Everything in the athletic world, right down to the HSU locker-room bulletin board, supported my choice.

My notebook for the 1977–78 track and field year still contains every training plan and result. An athlete readying herself for practice on Monday read one of these mimeographed schedules, pinned of course on the bulletin board. There she found her personal plan for the next seven days, detailing what to run, how fast, and where, accompanied by goals, perhaps "constant effort" or "concentration." A typical March workout for half-milers and milers might consist of a mile or more of easy warm-up running; stretching; five repeats of 1,000 yards (just over half a mile) run faster than a specified time and separated by a timed rest period; then 1.5-plus miles of easy warm-down followed by more stretching. Sprinters added hopping and bounding drills designed to build speed. Throwers drilled for speed and strength, the components of physical power. Most athletes lifted weights two or three times a week.

Much of this activity took place under a coach's eye. My tension about the workout to come began to build in mid-morning, as I lectured or read student papers. By two or two-thirty, I stood on the track with watch and clipboard in hand. For the next four hours I encouraged, teased, cajoled, brow-beat and criticized people into choosing to perform. In any fifteen minutes I might jog from the track to the practice field behind the stands, there to instruct a discus thrower in "blocking," the strong bracing and extension of her left leg which would enhance the whiplike sling of her right arm, resulting in a longer throw. Then back to the track to time a mile repeat, watching closely for the slight wobble and too-hard breathing which signaled overexhaustion while shouting encouragement and at the same time looking out of the corner of my eye for male kibitzers and checking to see that athletes finishing their workout stretched their muscles before escaping inside. Up, again, to the practice field, to work with javelin throwers on the crossover steps taken to bend the body back— draw the bow—just before the spear sails into the sky. At the same time, Lloyd performed his own circuit, moving between jumpers, hurdlers, and sprinters. Evenings and weekends we met, or I pored over pieces of paper, making lists comparing our distances and times to those of athletes from other schools. Computer-generated tables awarded points for each result in competition, which allowed comparison rankings across events; lines on a big chart I posted for all to see showed an athlete's relative position on the team, and across the weeks her rise . . . or fall.

On paper, all the effort paid off. By my second season we had a team of twenty-two young women, including nine who had never competed in track and field before and eight frosh; among them were three national-class athletes, a shot-putter and two distance runners. Although we would again finish last in the conference, we won two meets—the first in five years—and broke school records forty-one times, setting fourteen conference marks. Five of us traveled to Tennessee for the national championship.

Told simply, my coaching at HSU sounds like success. It was and it wasn't. A month or two into my second season, an athlete thrust at me a hand-lettered Notice of Declaration. It served notice from "the plebeians of the Humboldt State Redwood Runners" to the "czar" that the latter's "autocratic tendencies" in requiring weight lifting endangered "the femininity of the female populace." This, coupled with the amount of time practices took, "might increase the spinsterhood rate," and so, I was to understand, the "peasants" hereby took the "evanescence of decision-making" into their own hands. Laughter graces my memories of almost all HSU team interactions. But I'm quite sure the Declaration's authors had a point or two to make with me, their czar. Points I chose, finally, not to heed.

The athletes who gave me the Declaration took sport very seriously; at the same time, their understanding of femininity formed a barrier beyond which they could not easily step. This bothered me, to say the least. What we should be about, I felt, was not a mere expansion of gender roles (by being that unusual thing, female athletes) but a radical recasting of them. A new definition of what women could do. For me back then, in sport, that meant everything honorable society labeled "masculine." All the leadership advice I'd received or read—coaching how-to books, articles in *Sports Illustrated,* and male-authored sport and war fiction—told me never to let my subordinates see me sweat. So I laughed as I read the Notice of Declaration, its authors' eyes on my face, and treated it thereafter as a joke. I did, I thought, something new, even radical, for a woman. I played it tough and aggressive. Just like a man.

The ultimate challenge to my authority, when it came, didn't play out prettily. I posted on the board our list of entries for the conference championship. One team member, a senior I'll call Connie, told me she would not run in the races in which I'd entered her. My decisions had been based on probable team points and were subject to adjustment on meet day, but in her final season, Connie wanted to run well in the races she enjoyed. I saw that as selfish and, despite her exemplary year of team leadership and very hard work, refused to let her compete. The situation passed beyond fixing.

I understood quite soon that the lines I'd spoken as the authoritarian female coach came from a much larger script. Sporting conventions of obedience to leadership can teach—had, in fact, taught me—a certain relationship to power, one benefiting those who already have it. As power's representative in this situation, I showed those watching what can happen, and too often does, to a lone individual with courage enough to voice a challenge. I wonder now, too, about the dynamics of power among us women. We'd all internalized certain expectations about the way coaches and athletes interact. At the same time, most of us carried scars from power expressed and experienced as domination. Would Connie have argued with a male coach? When he argued back, would she have listened?

We lost the meet anyway, and would have even had Connie run the races I wanted. Some part of me knew that even before it played out. Our argument had been partly about the team's best interest, but also about our individual, unmatching expectations and my ability to win by acting tough. I still feel badly about it.

Yet of course power was part, a large part, of what I loved about coaching. The athletes were "my" athletes; the team "my" team. I saw sport then as a wager, a gamble; mainlined adrenaline. Coaching appealed to me because it upped the stakes. Suddenly, I had many more cards to play than just running my own races. And much more to lose. But aren't the stakes part of what makes the game? As long as I filled that central role in our small corner of sport—where I *mattered* (rare for a woman)—I could win. For even while I hated the sexism and misogyny in sport, and despite all my talk of blazing new trails for women, I remained a bona fide member of the sporting world. And very, very angry. I was in charge, responsible. Winning, I see now, was damn near everything.

At least in public. Privately I wrote about power's cost, envisioning coaching at times as a predator sucking away my energy and creativity. I worried that, like those men I could not abide, I simply wanted an ego massage. And without much support for the difficult task of teaching women to value their own strength when too many others did not, I wondered why I bothered.

March 1978
There is a raw power in coaching that both excites and frightens me in the sense that the team is an extension of me, dressing, behaving, competing according to my rules and wishes. Who am I? Others' rules and ways are just as good. . . . Track is incredibly fulfilling to me in a way classroom teaching is not, yet what is it? Teaching women to run with grace and strength—in meaningless circles on an artificial surface. . . . Training someone to jump backward over a bar into a foam-rubber pit. For what?

This need to question would, years later, bring me to answers. But first it fed my shame. As we mingle before the Homecoming Hall of Fame banquet, people ask, "And are you still coaching?" I mumble, eyes downcast, some unmemorable answer. I tell no one the truth: four years after leaving HSU, I simply realized one day that many of my actions as coach, despite the best of intentions, furthered inequities I'd come to abhor. The whole thing was much, much bigger than I felt able to change. I quit coaching the year the team co-captains skipped our own regional championship to cheer at a race their boyfriends ran. Twenty years after my own introduction to organized sport, not much had changed, except that it was now by choice—not solely for lack of options—that young women sat on sidelines watching boys and men play.

I had so wanted to make things different for women. The sport creed's slogans and myths taught me that we control our own fates. I was the leader; if I found myself unable to teach women a sense of free agency, to pursue athletic excellence regardless of parents' or boyfriends' agendas and actions, then the fault must lie in me. What I took away from coaching, besides this haunting sense of my own failure to effect what truly mattered, was only more questions. How, specifically, does muscularity threaten a female's "femininity"? Why would women's pursuit of sporting excellence jeopardize relationships with men? And what, in any case, are issues of women's relationship to men and men's judgment of women's physical appearance doing in *women's* sport?

◀◈▶

STRONGER WOMEN

Mariah Burton Nelson

Boy, don't you men wish you could hit a ball like that!   —Babe Didrikson Zaharias

Laughing, Patrick would scoop his wife, Gail, off the floor and carry her around the house like a squirming child. This was early in the marriage, and Patrick, an ecologist from Maryland, thought it was funny, a joke. Gail, a history professor, didn't like it. Feeling helpless and angry, she would ask to be put down. He would refuse.

Later, Gail became a dedicated runner. Patrick argued that she was running too much, or in the wrong way, or at the wrong times. They would quarrel, and he would yell. Patrick didn't literally lift her off the ground then, but to Gail the sensation was similar: Patrick's criticisms felt like physical restraints, as if he were trying to prevent her from going where she wanted to go.

Patrick says Gail used running as a "weapon" against him, a way "to escape out of our relationship—to literally put physical distance between us."

Gail says running became "the focus of a power struggle over who would control me."

.   .   .

The way Gail gained strength, and keeps gaining strength, is through sports. Women can become strong in other ways, without being athletes, but athletic strength holds particular meaning in this culture. It's tangible, visible, measurable. It has a history of symbolic importance. Joe Louis, Jackie Robinson, Jesse Owens, Billie Jean King: their athletic feats have represented to many Americans key victories over racism and sexism, key "wins" in a game that has historically been dominated by white men.

Sports have particular salience for men, who share childhood memories of having their masculinity confirmed or questioned because of their athletic ability or inability. Along with money and sex, sports in this culture define men to men. Sports embody a language men understand.

Women also understand sports—their power, their allure—but historically, most women were limited to a spectator's perspective. When a woman steps out of the bleachers or slips off her cheerleader's costume

Excerpted from Mariah Burton Nelson, "Strong Women," *The Stronger Women Get, the More Men Love Football*. Dare Press, 2005. http://www.mariahburtonnelson.com.

and becomes an athlete herself, she implicitly challenges the association between masculinity and sports. She refutes the traditional feminine role (primarily for white women) of passivity, frailty, subservience. If a woman can play a sport—especially if she can play it better than many men—then that sport can no longer be used as a yardstick of masculinity. The more women play a variety of sports, the more the entire notion of masculine and feminine roles—or any roles at all assigned by gender—becomes as ludicrous as the notion of roles assigned by race.

Female athletes provide obvious, confrontational evidence—"in your face" evidence, some might say—of women's physical prowess, tangible examples of just what women can achieve.

. . .

An avid equestrian as a child, Gail thought of herself as "just one of those girls who loved horses." No one suggested that a girl who trains and competes in equestrian events is every bit as athletic as the boys her age who earn letters in baseball or track. Lately, thinking about her lifelong love affair with sports, she realized that she "was really being an athlete the whole time."

She rode during her first marriage, which lasted 13 years. She taught riding and spent an inordinate amount of time at the barn, as equestrians do. Her husband did not object, but nor did he ask questions about her teaching, or speak proudly of her to his friends, or take an interest in her career. "What I did was okay because it was not considered important," says Gail. "He never took it seriously."

During her second marriage, Gail's horse grew lame and had to be put out to pasture. She discovered she "couldn't just sit around" so she began running. For three months she was "in agony," then she fell in love with the hypnotic process of landing, step by step, on the earth, as well as the fleeting moments of flight in between. She was 42.

At first, Patrick did not object. When her training was occasional, her schedule flexible, he didn't mind. "I was supportive when she started out because she had gotten a little overweight," Patrick recalls. "I was surprised she stuck with it as long as she did."

Gail increased her mileage. She joined a running club, where she learned about interval training, track workouts, and the value of taking one's pulse. She memorized *Runner's World* magazine. She went running for two, three hours at a time. Patrick started to get upset.

He didn't say he was upset, exactly. He said he was concerned. "A woman of your age shouldn't be doing this to her body," he would say.

Rapists also concerned him. "He would try to frighten me into not going out," Gail says. "I couldn't go out late in the afternoon because it would get dark. I couldn't go out at sunrise; he didn't like that either. It made it more difficult for me to exercise my judgment. It seemed like his conclusion was I should never go out."

Patrick's assessment: "It was a conflict between moral imperative and reality. Gail would say, 'A woman should be able to run freely.' I'd say, 'Of course, but in the real world, you can't.'"

He criticized her tactics, too, charging her with working too hard, risking damage to her joints. "I had been a runner myself," he explains. "I thought she should spend as much time stretching and doing yoga as running. I thought she should take some time off. She didn't."

"When you train hard, you run some risk of injury," Gail concedes. "But it was a double bind. No matter what I did, it wasn't right."

The more she ran the better she felt about herself, and the more she ran the more she believed that she had a right to this time, this pursuit of excellence. "I've always wanted to do everything as best I could, but women of my generation weren't supposed to try hard. That would mean you would sweat, you might make noises, you might fail." Running offered Gail an opportunity to test herself, to find out how good she might be.

The more she ran, the more running became "a lightning rod for the larger issues of who was in charge" in her marriage, Gail says. "Talking about it makes it sound like we sat down and had rational discussions about it. We didn't. Mainly I'd stomp out of the house and run, and he'd give me lectures about how I was hurting my knees and ankles."

As she was lacing her shoes, he would ask, "Where are you going?"

"Out," she would say.

"When will you be back?" he'd ask.

"Later," she'd answer.

"I was very determined to go out on my own and not tell him where I was going," she admits. "That did exacerbate the conflict between us."

Eventually, after an eleven-year relationship, they divorced.

Gail's still running—farther, up to 45 miles per week, at about an eight-minute-per-mile pace. She competes in 10K's. She lifts weights and swims. She has tried orienteering, and is intrigued by the idea of competing in triathlons and marathons. "I seem to enjoy everything I try," she marvels. "I tend to acquire strength fairly easily."

. . .

For a woman, especially for a married woman with a controlling husband, running is a feminist act. The athlete's feminism begins with the fact that her sports participation is, in Gail's words, "a declaration of independence." The runner runs on her own two feet, on her own time, in her own way, without male assistance. If a man wants to join her club, and trot along next to her, and watch her race, and leave a light on for her when she arrives home late, fine. If not, if she encounters male interference, she may not tolerate it. She may prioritize, instead, her own athletic joy. Running raises the possibility that the woman with the aggrieved husband will become the woman with no husband—that, in the process of running, women will run away from men.

Running also raises the possibility that mothers will leave fathers at home to wash dishes and put kids to bed. If a woman runs in the morning while her husband dresses the children, feeds them, and gets them off to school, she tips the balance of power not only within the marriage but within the family. The runner who has no children, no husband, and no boyfriend—who instead carves out a life for herself with other athletes, and other women—is likewise committing feminist acts. Her running represents a world in which women are neither running toward nor alongside nor away from men; where men and their ideas about what's too strenuous for women, what's acceptable for women, and what's attractive in women become irrelevant.

Female athletes don't necessarily see it this way. They don't necessarily call themselves feminists. They cycle or swim or surf because it's fun and challenging, because it feels good, because they like the way it makes them look, because it allows them to eat without gaining weight, because it gives them energy and confidence and time spent with friends, female or male. Many are ignorant about the women's rights movement. I've heard college students confuse feminism with feminine hygiene.

In fact, female athletes have a long tradition of dissociating themselves from feminism. Their desire to be accepted or to acquire or keep a boyfriend or a job has often equaled their passion for sports. Thus athletes have taken great pains—and it can hurt—to send reassuring signals to those who would oppose their play: "Don't worry, we're not feminists. We're not dykes, we're not aggressive, we're not muscular, we're not a threat to you. We just want to play ball." It has been a survival strategy.

It's time to tell the truth. Our behavior is feminist.[1] Some of us—including some pioneers who lobbied for Title IX, some coaches who volunteered to teach girls, and some athletes who competed in the first pro baseball and basketball leagues—are lesbians. Some of us are aggressive. Some of us are muscular. All of us, collectively, are a threat—not to men exactly, but to male privilege and to masculinity as defined through manly sports.

By reserving time each day for basketball dribbling, or for runs or rides or rows, women are changing themselves and society. Feminism is rarely an individual's motivating force but always the result: a woman's athletic training, regardless of the factors that lead to her involvement, implicitly challenges patriarchal constraints on her behavior. Sport for women changes the woman's experience of herself and others' experience of her. It is feminist: It alters the balance of power between the sexes. It is daring. It is life-changing. It is happening every day.

Feminism is about freedom: the individual and collective liberty to make our own decisions. For women, sports embody freedom: unrestricted physical expression, travel across great distances, liberated movement. Sports give meaning to the phrase "free time." We find it, use it, and insist on retaining it. Our time for sports becomes a time when we free ourselves of all the other people and projects we usually tend to. We become the person, the project, who needs care. We take care of ourselves. For a group of people who have historically been defined by our ability to nurture others, the commitment to nurture ourselves is radical.

Sports give a woman the confidence to try new things, including things previously defined as dangerous or unfeminine. "Boys grow up trying lots of new physical activities," notes University of Virginia sports psychologist Linda Bunker. "They develop an overall sense of their ability to handle unknown situations. Ask a male tennis player if he wants to play racquetball; he'll say 'sure,' even if he's never seen a racquetball court. But ask a nonathletic woman to play racquetball, and she'll say, 'Gee, I don't know if I can do it.'

Several writers have used sports as metaphor, depicting women emancipated by the process of building muscle and endurance. In Fannie Flagg's film *Fried Green Tomatoes*, a meek and depressed Evelyn Couch (played by Kathy Bates) takes aerobics classes, meets with a women's support group, and develops a deep friendship with an old woman. Soon she has acquired a new persona, Tawanda, who skips up steps, knocks down walls, and asserts herself with her husband. "I'm trying to save our marriage," she tells him. "What's the point of my trying if you're gonna sit on your butt drinking beer and watching baseball, basketball, football, hockey, bowling, golf, and challenge of the gladiators?" [. . .]

Feminism is about bodies: birth control, sexual harassment, child sexual abuse, pornography, rape, date rape, battering, breast cancer, breast enlargement, dieting, Liposuction, abortion, anorexia, bulimia, sexuality.

Sports.

"The repossession by women of our bodies," wrote the poet and author Adrienne Rich in *Of Woman Born*, "will bring far more essential change to human society than the seizing of the means of production by workers."

As athletes, we repossess our bodies. Told that we're weak, we develop our strengths. Told that certain sports are wrong for women, we decide what feels right. Told that our bodies are too dark, big, old, flabby, or wrinkly to be attractive to men, we look at naked women in locker rooms and discover for ourselves the beauty of actual women's bodies in all their colors, shapes, and sizes. Told that certain sports make women look "like men," we notice the truth: working out doesn't make us look like men, it makes us look happy. It makes us smile. More important, it makes us healthy and powerful. It makes us feel good. [. . .]

In a country where male politicians and judges make key decisions about our bodies and all of us are vulnerable to random attacks of male violence, the simple act of taking control of our own bodies—including their health, their pleasure and their power—is radical. In a society in which real female bodies (as opposed to media images of female bodies) are unappreciated at best, the act of enjoying one's own female body is radical. It contradicts all feminine training to move, to extend our arms, to claim public space as our own, to use our bodies aggressively, instrumentally, to make rough contact with other bodies.

Temple University doctoral student Frances Johnston interviewed dozens of female ice hockey and rugby players and found that "physicality" was one of the most appealing aspects of the games. "They enjoyed the tackling, the checking, the falling down and getting up, the discovery that they had 'survived' another hard hit or rough game." Besides body contact, they enjoyed "kicking the ball, getting rid of the ball right before a tackle, the power of a well hit slapshot."[2]

Lunging for a soccer ball, we do not worry if our hair looks attractive. Leaping over a high bar, we do not wish we had bigger breasts. Strapped snugly into a race car, roaring around a track at 220 miles per hour, we do not smile or wave. While playing sports our bodies are ours to do with as we please. If in that process our bodies look unfeminine—if they become bruised or bloody or simply unattractive—that seems irrelevant. Our bodies are ours. We own them. While running to catch a ball, we remember that.

NOTES

Note numbers and callouts have been changed from the original article.

1. Susan Greendorfer, professor of kinesiology at the University of Illinois, Urbana-Champaign, was the first or one of the first to assert that women's sports are inherently a political act. Susan Greendorfer, "Making Connections: Women's Sport Participation as a Political Act." Paper presented at the National Girls and Women in Sports Symposium, Slippery Rock State University, Slippery Rock, Pennsylvania (February 13, 1993).

2. Frances Johnson, "Life on the Fringe: The Experience of Rugby and Ice Hockey Playing Women." Paper presented at the annual meeting of the North American Society for the Sociology of Sport (Toledo, Ohio: November 5, 1992).

PART IV

Building Inequality into Sport: Institutionalized Bias

Part IV explores the many ways in which both athletic organizations and the games they promote are often structured to discourage the participation of specific social groups. We begin this section with the essay "Structural Constraints Facing Women in Sport," in which scholars Nancy Theberge and Susan Birrell outline the ways in which gender bias in sport presents itself, and how the resulting inequalities continue to function despite the influence of Title IX. They then deepen their investigation to address two particular aspects of bias in women's sport, the lack of respect generally accorded disabled athletes and the widespread effects of homophobia in women's sports, an issue hinted at in Part II and explored in greater depth in Part V.

The two articles that follow, Heather Ross Miller's "Half-Court Basketball: Power and Sex" and Mark Starr's "'I Can See the Finish Line'," provide illustrative accounts of the obstacles female athletes encounter in the pursuit of their sports. Miller's memoir about playing by the rules of girls' basketball from an earlier period gives the modern reader some insight into the effects of the dominant modes of thought represented by Berenson's and Sargent's essays in Part II. Mark Starr's article offers a personal view of the experience of disabled athletes through the story of visually impaired middle-distance runner Marla Runyan. Runyan's bid to compete as an athlete in the 2000 Olympic Games (rather than in the Paralympic Games) was eventually successful: she placed eighth in the 1500-meter women's race in Sydney and in doing so became the first Paralympian to compete in the Olympic Games.

The story of institutionalized inequality extends from the most remote high school gymnasium to the grand stage of international tennis and ice skating, and includes discrimination on the basis of race and class as well as gender, ability, and sexual orientation. It is not coincidental that the "glamour" sports of tennis and figure skating, which have the reputation of being more feminine than sports like boxing or softball, have historically been off limits to women of color and to working-class women who lack the financial resources needed to succeed at elite levels. The phenomenal success of Venus and Serena Williams in tennis, as explored by Raquel Cepeda in "Courting Destiny," reveals the complex dynamic of disparagement and celebrity at work as the two African-American sisters pushed through the unwritten rules of racial and class privilege that have long sustained tennis as a country club sport. In both tennis and ice skating we see how the image of the ideal female champion and the rules and requirements of the sport have operated as a form of (un)natural selection, limiting the participation of girls and women who do not resemble the ideal. In Joan Ryan's essay on Tonya Harding and Bill Wong's on Michelle Kwan, skaters from a white working-class and a Chinese-American background respectively, we see how the promises of victory and fame affect both athletes and their fans. These and other essays in Part IV raise questions about the motivations of athletes, their different strategies for success, and the interaction between athlete and spectators through the power of image and association.

The last two items in this section look at how family and cultural expectations affect individual women's abilities to pursue sports. In "Breaking Cultural Traditions," MaryJo Sylwester studies the ways in which cultural traditions and family pressures discourage Latina girls from playing sports and affect their ability to become fully participating members of their school communities. In "On the Rez," Ian Frazier explores the importance of basketball to some Native American cultures and how one creative high school player confronted the racism of white spectators by using her knowledge of Lakota culture to stop cold their derisive taunts. In both items, it becomes clear that for some women the decision to play sports is also a decision to resist the dominant culture and perhaps to become the object of derision. The pioneering spirit explored in Part I lives on in women like Marla Runyan, Venus and Serena Williams, and SuAnne Marie Big Crow.

STRUCTURAL CONSTRAINTS FACING WOMEN IN SPORT

Nancy Theberge and Susan Birrell

You don't know anything about a woman until you meet her in court.
—Norman Mailer, quoted in *Words on Women*

Recent years have seen tremendous changes in women's social position and in gender relations in the wider society. Significant change also has occurred in women's sport and women's experiences of sport. These changes are intimately and dialectically connected: Developments in sport are inseparable from conditions in the wider society, so that changes in women's relationship to sport may signal or even influence transformations in women's position in society at large. In this chapter we review the status of women's participation in recreation and leisure settings, as well as collegiate and professional sport.

In this chapter we will examine sport as a *contested arena*. Sport historically has been a setting marked by struggles structured along lines of class, race, and gender. In recent years, barriers to women's participation have weakened, and cultural views of women athletes have been revised. Women's sport continues to be marked, however, by struggle for control of both the institutions that regulate women's participation and the meanings of our sporting experiences. Struggle for institutional control is evident in efforts to increase the opportunities for participation and the representation of women in administrative and coaching positions. Ideological struggle is evident in campaigns to increase and improve the coverage of women's sport in the media and to transform cultural images and ideas about women and physical activity.

Most information available on women and sport has focused on the needs and experiences of relatively young, middle- and upper-class, heterosexual, white women. Wherever possible, we attempt to broaden this homogenous and undifferentiated concept of women to suggest the limits of the current status of our knowledge.

From N. Theberge and S. Birrell, 1994, chapter 20: Structural Constraints Facing Women in Sport. In *Women and Sport: Interdisciplinary Perspectives,* edited by D.M. Costa and S.R. Guthrie, pages 331–340. © 1994 by D. Margaret Costa and Sharon R. Guthrie. Reprinted with permission from Human Kinetics (Champaign, IL).

Background to the Developments in Women's Sport

The changes that have occurred in women's sport in the United States in recent years can be understood against a background of broader social developments. In this section we consider the effects of legislative and political initiatives, the feminist movement, and the health and fitness movement. In quite different ways, each has had a significant impact on women and sport.

Legal and Political Initiatives

Some of the most important influences on women's sport have come from government efforts in the area of gender equity. The United States government has played a particularly active role in the transformation of school and university sport programs. Probably the single most important event affecting women's sport in the United States in the last 30 years was the passage of Title IX of the Educational Amendments Act of 1972. Title IX prohibits sex discrimination in educational institutions that receive federal funding, which includes virtually all institutions in the United States. Although Title IX did not single out sport as a target area, its obvious significance for sport was immediately apparent, because virtually all educational institutions had vastly unequal sport programs for females and males. [. . .]

The Feminist Movement

Until the late 1970s it appeared that the women's movement had few connections to sport, and it was not unusual to hear the lament that there were no feminists in sport. It would have been more accurate to say that those working on behalf of women in sport and, in particular, women athletic administrators had little or no visibility outside sport and few formal connections to the wider feminist movement. Since then there has been a growing feminist consciousness and movement in sport. A number of conferences have been held, and The Women's Sports Foundation in the United States has grown in size and influence. These activities have been complemented by a flourishing feminist scholarship and research. All of these developments have been part of the increasing impact of feminism on women's sport.

The Health and Fitness Movement

The "fitness boom" of the past two decades has had an undeniable impact on the expansion of women's physical activity and sport in North America. Not all of this influence, however, has been positive. Rader (1991) argues that North American preoccupation with "strenuous living" entails the "presentation of a particular self": The "new strenuosity" emphasizes style and appearance and often is explicitly sexualized. The most glaring instances of the sexualization of women's physical activity are exercise classes and videos that concentrate on body image and heterosexual attraction. Moreover, the fitness boom appeals particularly to members of the middle and upper classes, who have the means to purchase fitness club memberships, expensive equipment, and the fashionable leisure clothing that is now a signature of the "good life." The commodification and sexualization of women's physical activity seen in the health and fitness movement are alarming aspects of the expansion of this activity in recent years.

Women's Participation in Sport Today

The recent increases in girls' and women's physical activity have occurred at most levels and in most types of participation. The main exception is professional sport, where there continue to be few opportunities and there has been little change. Although opportunities and involvement by women have increased greatly, as we will see there remain significant differences in the participation of women and men. Moreover, these differences are exacerbated by racial and class barriers, and they become more pronounced at higher levels of involvement.

Recreational Sport and Physical Activity

One of the settings that has witnessed impressive changes in girls' and women's physical activity is recreational sport. Much of this activity is not well documented, and we have little reliable information on involvement in community and recreational sport leagues and programs. Data on patterns of unorganized physical activity, however, provide a picture of gender differences in activity, as well as details of women's involvement.

The annual surveys of the National Sporting Goods Association (NSGA, 1990, 1990a, 1990b) of 10,000 U.S. households show that females 7 years of age and older are more active in fitness activities than males: 62% of girls and women compared to 52% of boys and men regularly participated in fitness activities in 1989. These differences remain, but are less pronounced, when *frequency* of involvement is taken into consideration. According to the NSGA definition of a "frequent participant" as one who has participated in an activity at least twice a week, 22.5% of all women and 18.1% of all men fit that profile (NSGA, 1990a). These data also show, however, that men and boys are more likely than women and girls to participate in competitive sports, a pattern that no doubt reflects a history of greater opportunities for men in sport.

Information from the NSGA (1990a) does not provide analyses that take into account race, class, or age distinctions among women. The NSGA does report that for men and women together, household income is positively related and age is negatively related to involvement in fitness activities (NSGA, 1990a).

Women's Leisure Activities

Just how powerful women's domestic responsibilities are as barriers to leisure activity, including sport activity, is vividly described in research by the British sociologist Rosemary Deem (1987) in her study in Milton Keynes, a town in England. Two of the women Deem interviewed commented on the place of leisure in their lives.

"Leisure—that's a good one, alright—wouldn't know what it looked like—*if* and that is *if*, I ever get any time at the end of the day I generally fall asleep. . . . "Sport—no, definitely not—wouldn't catch me running nowhere or wearing one of them leotards—sport's what me husband does on Saturdays . . . a lot of silly men chasing a ball around—mind, I get asked to wash the kit." (p. 423)

As Deem indicates, for many women the difficulty in separating out periods in the day when uninterrupted leisure is possible is a major barrier to their participation in sport and physical activity.

The accounts provided by the women Deem interviewed capture graphically some of the conditions that continue to restrict women's experiences of sport and physical activity. Another important consideration is the types of activities in which women are participating. Although data on rising rates of involvement among women are encouraging, optimism should be tempered by a consideration of the feminization of physical activity present in some types of fitness activities. Exercise and training programs that emphasize weight control, appearance, and sex appeal are contemporary incarnations of the myth of female frailty in women's athletics. By emphasizing the connections between physical activity and sexuality, they maintain the image of feminine athleticism that was the foundation of an ideology that restricted women's sport involvement earlier in the century.

Governance of U.S. Collegiate Sport

The passage of Title IX was perhaps the most important event affecting women's sport participation in the United States. Because of Title IX and subsequent occurrences, most women's athletic programs are now governed by the NCAA, where control is largely in the hands of men. In 1991–92, women were 9% of the President's Commission, 32% of Council members (including the president of the Council), and 33% of the Executive Committee (National Collegiate Athletic Association, 1993).

Loss of control also took place in individual institutions. As women's sport grew and drew a larger share of resources, many institutions merged men's and women's programs under one administrator, who almost always was a man. The visibility and importance attributed to men's sport virtually ensured that the person judged to be the most "qualified" to head a newly combined program would be the head of the men's program. The wealth of experience that heads of women's programs possessed went largely unrecognized and unrewarded. As a result, since the passage of Title IX the proportion of women athletic administrators and coaches declined in both high schools and universities. In 1972, 90% of head athletic directors of women's collegiate programs were women; in 1990, 15.9% of women's programs were directed by women (Acosta and Carpenter, 1990).

Professional Sport
Professional sport remains largely a male preserve. Career opportunities for women athletes remain concentrated in a few sports, notably golf and tennis, which are nurtured in the private country clubs of the white upper classes. Although there has been some expansion of the professional tours in these sports, there has been little change overall in the gender imbalance at this level. Most opportunities in professional sport are still in men's sports.

Disparities are evident in comparisons of the earnings of individual men and women athletes. Of the 20 highest paid athletes in 1992, only three were women. One is Monica Seles, whose earnings from her winnings and bonuses totaled $3 million; however, Seles's endorsement income is estimated to be $6 million, putting her well below male athletes such as Evander Holyfield and Michael Jordan, whose incomes for 1992 are estimated to be more than $35 million each. Steffi Graf's income of $3.3 million from winnings and bonuses and $5.5 million from endorsements placed her number 15 on the list (Kiersh and Buchholz, 1993).

Further indications of the second-class status of women in professional sport are the problems encountered in efforts to establish women's sports leagues in North America. Both the Women's Professional Softball League (WPSL) and the Women's Professional Basketball League (WBL), which were organized in the 1970s, were plagued by inadequate financing and poor attendance. In the WBL, games were played in high-rent arenas and expensive promotions were directed toward the general sports audience rather than a narrower segment of sports fans who are followers of women's sport, particularly basketball. Coakley (1990) suggests the problems with the approach taken by the league:

They did not tap into the potential interest among people with personal connections to girls' basketball all over the United States. If two or three regional leagues had been organized, if teams had had lower budgets for coaches and less demand for returns on investment, if games had been played in smaller gyms, if marketing had been localized and directed at girls and their families connected with community and interscholastic leagues, the fate of women's professional basketball might have been different. (p. 241)

The failure of these leagues also may be attributed to lingering cultural biases that associate team sports and their potential for contact and physical aggression with racial, class, and heterosexist stereotypes. Perhaps for that reason, promotions for the Women's Professional Basketball League emphasized the coaches more than the athletes. All but one of these coaches were men, and many of these were former professional players or coaches. As well, the familiar pattern of trivialization of women's sport was evident in some of the team names, such as the California Dreams, Minnesota Fillies, Philadelphia Fox, and Milwaukee Does ("Scouting Reports: WBL," 1979).

Diversity in Women's Sport

Perhaps the most important issue facing feminist analysis and the women's movement today is the need to give voice to and better represent the interests of women who historically have been marginalized or excluded from dominant cultural forms. Cultural constraints on women's involvement in sport have been particularly pronounced for women of color, poor and working-class women, lesbians, older women, and physically challenged women. In this section we will consider two particular overlooked issues of diversity in women's sport: sport for the physically challenged and homophobia.

Sport and Physically Challenged Women
One of the most important changes in thinking about the place of sport and physical activity in women's lives in recent years is increased recognition of the needs and rights of physically challenged women. For too long, physical activity was viewed as an interest of only the able bodied and often was thought to be exclusively the prerogative of the skilled and talented. Not only were those with disabilities excluded from sport, but their exclusion contributed to an ideology of able bodiedness that further disadvantaged them in their struggle for dignity.

The physically challenged constitute a significant segment of our population. A 1986 survey by Harris and Associates estimated that 14% of all Americans 16 years of age or older are disabled, and of these 56% are women (cited in Grimes and French, 1987). The definition of *disabled* used in the survey is "an individual who has an impairment that significantly impairs them [*sic*] in one or more daily life activities, or are considered to have or have had such a condition" (Funk, 1986, cited in Grimes and French, 1987, p. 24).

Heterosexism, Homophobia, and Women Athletes

Women's full participation in sport also is restricted by homophobia, that is, "the irrational fear or intolerance of homosexuality, gay men or lesbians, and even behavior that is perceived to be outside the boundaries of traditional gender role expectations" (Griffin and Genasci, 1990, p. 211). Homophobia is at the heart of the long-standing concern with the supposed masculinizing effects of sport that underlies research on sex role conflict among women athletes. As Lenskyj (1991b) indicates, "Since the stereotype of 'female-athlete' and 'lesbian' share so-called masculine traits such as aggression and independence, the association between sport and lesbianism has frequently been made" (p. 49). Elsewhere Lenskyj (1986)notes that the popular association between sport and lesbianism is fundamentally an issue of male power:

[R]egardless of sexual preference, women who reject the traditional feminine role in their careers as athletes, coaches, or sport administrators, as in any other nontraditional pursuit, pose a threat to existing power relations between the sexes. For this reason, these women are the frequent targets of labels intended to devalue or dismiss their successes by calling their sexuality into question. (p. 383)

Homophobia directed against women in sport has produced numerous damaging consequences. In its most overt form, homophobia is the basis for discrimination in decisions about hiring and firing women in coaching and administrative positions. One study of college coaches found that the majority of both male and female coaches believe that "fear of a lesbian influence is a real consideration of administrators during the hiring process in women's programs" (Sweet and Malec, reported in Knoppers, 1988, p. 76). Lenskyj (1991a) cites additional evidence that sexual orientation is a key factor in administrators' decisions concerning women's employment in sport.

Homophobia operates in other ways to prevent women's full participation in sport. One of these is the denial of athletic opportunities to known or suspected lesbians. Another is through campaigns to discredit all women in sport through accusations about their sexual orientation, which is a form of sexual harassment. Yet another is the lack of support for team sports thought to be closely associated with masculine or lesbian images (e.g., rugby, football, softball).

Because of homophobia, all women face pressures to conform to a dominant image of feminine athleticism. Of course, not all women experience and deal with the pressure in the same ways; that is, some actively resist it, whereas others internalize the homophobia and conform quite closely by practicing "apologetic" behavior, such as devoting excessive attention to feminizing their appearance. Regardless of one's sexual preference or one's responses to homophobia, the power of these dominant images and expectations constitutes a form of oppression that all women face.

Perhaps the most insidious way that homophobia has harmed the cause of women in sport is by challenging the solidarity among them. As Boutilier and SanGiovanni (1983) note, "Lesbians are present in every type, level and degree of sport participation. While this point may be laughingly obvious to some, it is apparently vigorously denied by others" (p. 120). The denial of a lesbian presence in sport has resulted in barriers of ignorance and isolation that hurt heterosexual women as well as lesbians. In the decade since Boutilier and SanGiovanni's observations have been published, some discussion has begun (see in particular Kidd, 1983; Griffin, 1989; Griffin and Genasci, 1990; Lenskyj, 1991a); however, homophobia directed against women in sport continues to be inadequately addressed by athletes, coaches, administrators, and scholars. The result of this silence is a separation between lesbian and heterosexual women, which is often experienced as antagonism and divisiveness and which retards the progress of all women in sport.

It is critical to see heterosexism and homophobia as dynamics that are defined by wider patriarchal interests and that work to consolidate heterosexist male privilege. Homophobia acts as a means of social control, which not only keeps women out of the male preserve of sport but also invokes a fear of association that separates women from one another, effectively undercutting the potential for female solidarity and empowerment. To the extent that it manages to divide women, it further oppresses all of us.

Summary and Conclusions

The preceding discussion indicates that developments in women's sport in recent years are marked by a number of tendencies. On the one hand, the increasing involvement of girls and women in an expanding range of activities is cause for optimism. Other aspects of women's involvement, however, are less encouraging. Women continue to be excluded from most positions of power and influence in both the educational and amateur sport systems. In addition, the opportunities for skilled women athletes to pursue careers in professional sport remain severely restricted.

Inadequate opportunities for physically challenged women and the exclusion and oppression of lesbians are additional barriers to women's full participation in sport and physical activity.

An additional set of issues raised in this chapter concerns the persistence of ideological struggle over the values and meanings of women's sport. We examined the feminization of sport in the context of the "fitness boom" and the growing interest in "feminine" sports like gymnastics and synchronized swimming. The presence of these sports on the Olympic program, alongside sports like judo, marathoning, and other strength and distance events, indicates the varied images and ideals about women's athleticism in contemporary cultures.

REFERENCES

Acosta, R. V., and Carpenter, L. J. (1985). Women in sport. In D. Chu, J. O. Segrave, and B. Becker (Eds.). *Sport and Higher Education* (pp. 313–325). Champaign, IL: Human Kinetics.

Acosta, R. V., and Carpenter, L. J. (1990). Women in intercollegiate sport—a thirteen year update. Unpublished manuscript, Brooklyn College, Brooklyn, NY.

Boutilier, M., and SanGiovanni, L. (1983). *The sporting woman.* Champaign, IL: Human Kinetics.

Carpenter, L. J. (1985). The impact of Title IX on women's intercollegiate sports. In A. T. Johnson and J. H. Frey (Eds.), *Government and sport: The public policy issues* (pp. 62–78). Totowa, NJ: Rowman and Allenheld.

Coakley, J. (1990). *Sport in society: Issues and controversies* (4th ed.). St. Louis: C. V. Mosby.

Deem, R. (1987). Unleisured lives: Sport in the context of women's leisure. *Women's Studies International Forum,* 10(4), 423–432.

Farrell, C. S. (1986, August). Many women link anti-sex-bias law to outstanding Olympic performances. *Chronicle of Higher Education,* August 19, pp. 31–32.

Fitness Canada. (n.d.). Physical activity and women with disabilities. Ottawa: Fitness and Amateur Sport.

Geadelmann, P. L. (1977). *How can I determine if equality exists?* Reston, VA: AAHPERD.

Grant, C. (1984). The gender gap in sport: From intercollegiate to Olympic level. *Arena Review,* 8(2), 40–43

Greenberg, R. J. (1984). AIAW vs. NCAA: The takeover and implications. *Journal of the National Association of Women Deans, Administrators and Counsellors,* 47(2), 29.

Griffin, P. (1989). Homophobia in physical education. *Canadian Association for Physical Education and Recreation,* 11(2), 333–346.

Griffin, P., and Genasci, J. (1990). Addressing homophobia in physical education: Responsibilities for teachers and researchers. In M. A. Messner and D. F. Sabo (Eds.), *Sport, men, and the gender order* (pp. 211–221). Champaign, IL: Human Kinetics.

Grimes, P. S., and French, L. (1987). Barriers to disabled women's participation in sports. *Journal of Physical Education, Recreation and Dance,* 58(3), 24–27.

Kidd, D. (1983). Getting physical: Compulsory heterosexuality in sport. *Canadian Woman Studies, 4*, 62–65.

Kiersh, E., and Buchholz, B. (1993, April). Annual salary survey. *Inside Sports,* pp. 58–70.

Knoppers, A. (1988). Men working: Coaching as a male dominated and sex segregated occupation. *Arena Review,* 12(2) 69–80.

Lenskyj, H. (1986). Female sexuality and women's sport. *Women's Studies International Forum,* 10(4), 61–69.

Lenskyj, H. (1991a). Combating homophobia in sport and physical education. *Sociology of Sport Journal,* 8(1), 61–69.

Lenskyj, H. (1991b). Women's sport and physical activity: Research and bibliography (2nd ed.). Ottawa, ON. Ministry of Supply and Services.

National Sporting Goods Association. (1990, July). Women lead participation in ten sports activities. *National Sporting Goods Association News,* Mount Prospect, IL (press release).

National Sporting Goods Association (1990, August). Adult fitness participation. *National Sporting Goods Association News,* Mount Prospect, IL (press release).

National Sporting Goods Association (1990b, August). Women lead men in battle for fitness. *National Sporting Goods Association News,* Mount Prospect, IL (press release).

NCAA publicly censures Alcorn State: First action against women's program. (1984, May). *Chronicle of Higher Education,* p. 27.

National Collegiate Athletic Association. (1993). *Annual report of the NCAA: 1991-92* (pp. 5–10). Overland Park, KS: Author.

Rader, B. (1991). The quest for self-sufficiency and the new strenuosity: Reflections on the strenuous life of the 1970s and 1980s. *Journal of Sport History,* 18, 255–266.

Scouting reports: WBL. (1979, October 15). *Sports Illustrated,* pp. 64, 121–126.

Slatton, B. (1982). The greening of American athletics. In J. H. Frey (Ed.), *The governance of intercollegiate athletics* (pp. 144–154). West Point, NY: Leisure Press.

Sweet, K., and Malec, M. (1988). *Attitudes of male coaches of female basketball players.* Paper presented at the World Congress of the International Association of Physical Education, Madrid.

Theberge, N. (1989). Women's athletics and the myth of female frailty. In J. Freeman (Ed.), *Women: A feminist perspective* (4th ed.) (pp. 507–522). Mountain View, CA: Mayfield.

Throw a tantrum, sign a contract. (1990). *Forbes,* 146, 68–73.

◀◆▶

HALF-COURT BASKETBALL

Power and Sex

Heather Ross Miller

It took romance.

That old half-court ball we played in the '50s.

A blinding goofy romance flared every Tuesday and Friday night in the freckled gleam of long legs and white sneakers squeaking off the bright waxed floor of the Badin High School gymnasium. Our teenage breasts brushed against the ball before we slung it hard down the court to the tall forward who drove to sink the basket and run up the score for the 1957 Badin High Watts, the Aluminum City Kids, our magic kilowatts sparking every move. Such magnificent girls thundering to the center line.

You slung that ball hard and grinned and didn't care who got in the way.

Two! Four! Six! Eight!

The cheerleaders like dervishes in saddle oxfords and red skirts sweated through their heavy black turtleneck sweaters stitched with a big red B.

Who do we appreciate?

They didn't appreciate you. You were nothing but a guard. It was the tall forward they cheered. She got it all, you understood, that was the game. And but for the one hateful rule restricting girls to half-court play in 1957, keeping forwards and guards on the same team, six girls segregated into opposite ends of the hardwood, but for that one rule, you could have covered every polished inch of the floor, grabbing and passing and storming the opposition. Shooting baskets every bit as good as the forward. Mitzi Jane Blalock was her name.

What stopped you going the full length of the court?

Why didn't you?

Why didn't she?

We didn't know it was a sexual metaphor in 1957. We played that old half-court ball with vengeance and passion, like Amazons, like Valkyries, thundering to the center line. Then a dead hard stop at the center line, our ankles stinging from the concussion, and we slung the ball hard to one of the three forwards hovering there like bees at the comb. Mitzi Jane

From *Witness* 6:2 (1992): 42–49.

Blalock, the tall one, took it on to score, allowed only one bounce of the clumsy ball, no dribbling.

That's the way girls had to play until 1971 when five-on-five was allowed the full length of the court. But in our old game, three guards and three forwards circled in strict zones, a condition of cunningly segregated orbits. No dribbling. One bounce then pass. A dead stop at the center line. We thought it was the way you play girls' basketball. And playing was the thing.

And after the game, showered, pleasantly tired from winning this game of restrictions, we stretched on our beds and conjured up prizes for ourselves. Rich, good-looking men. Blue swimming pools. Strapless black evening dresses with thousands of sequins on the front.

Evening dresses! This old-fashioned garment is gone now. Now our daughters wear slinky gowns made of clinging stuff with spaghetti straps and plunging necklines down the *back,* their fashion sense sharp and demanding as Barbie's. In 1957, you were Scarlett, not Barbie. You played half-court basketball and wore evening dresses to dances, not proms. Always full-skirted, net and taffeta gathered to a tight strapless bodice, sometimes touching the floor, sometimes your ankles.

In the ninth grade, these garments were yellow stuff, ankle-length, strapless, with a little scrap of yellow stuff to throw around your shoulders, a stole you called it. Gold evening sandals with a slight French heel, the toes open, your toenails painted shocking pink. Carnations pinned to the bodice. Gold mesh evening bag with tiny hand-chain. And underneath these concoctions, a merry widow, a strapless item boned to the waist, pushed up your breasts, you hoped, toward a luscious cleavage.

Another blinding and goofy romance.

And gone for good like the half-court ball. The Howdy Doody days, the days of Fonz and The Three Bells singing "Jimmy Brown." A cozy American insularity. When basketball, not football, was the special pride of high school communities. And high schools were small two-story brick buildings still in communities, not big county conglomerates.

I'm stuck in my stereotypes here, lost in my nostalgia. How easy it is to make comparisons, to lament about the old days. Those good old days which probably are another kind of metaphor, another kind of hemmed-in half-court ball, sounding smug and coy, drowning in segregations.

I recently mentioned the old half-court ball to a good friend, an educated and sophisticated gentleman, and he said "But it was so nice, the way you girls played back then. So graceful and feminine. Why do you want to go make something out of it?"

The way he said that brought back my old anger at the goofy blinding and romantic way we obeyed such expectations in those days. Half-court basketball for women in the '50s was the same as racial segregation: separate but equal. Except in the case of basketball, we were not equal. Keeping women on the half court was a definite form of discrimination. They said we could play ball but not the way *they* played it. We had a silly little game that really didn't count. Half court. Halfway.

In 1954, in *Brown v. Board of Education of Topeka,* the Supreme Court held segregation unconstitutional and called for change "with all deliberate speed." This had nothing to do with segregation by gender, including rules for basketball. So equality did not reach to the half court in Badin High School or anywhere else for another seventeen years.

And keeping women on the half court was the same as keeping blacks in the back of the bus, keeping separate but equal water fountains, keeping lunch counters pure white.

High school basketball was a peculiar situation, trivial perhaps, but nevertheless peculiar. World War II brought promises and opportunities to women, that splendid carrot of equality: the workplace. Rosie the Riveter in her khaki jumpsuit, permed curls teasing over her kerchief knot, may not have been dainty and charming, but she was indeed equal.

And surely she would be allowed to continue into the fantastic '50s, enjoying all the benefits of that wartime equality. This was not to be the case. The '50s disenfranchised women again. The war should have changed things for good, but didn't. For isn't it obvious?—if you can rivet together a war plane, you can run up and down a basketball court.

Instead, a few miles up Highway 51 from Badin High School, Catawba College let one outstanding woman physical education major play with the Bobcats for a while because the war had depleted the bench. She ran the full length of the court, drove hard for the shot, and held her own with the sweating guys out there. She also got her picture in the local papers as the *Bobkitten!*

The feeling was one of generous amusement, you went to see the *Bobkitten* play because she was a girl playing with all those guys. Not because she was good with a basketball. The Bobcats were amused, absolutely carried away by their own generosity every time she entered the game. The fans roared and applauded and pointed their fingers, "Looka-there, the *Bobkitten!*"

Such subtle segregation in sports continued. After a world war, after a Supreme Court decision. And the game became one of power, not sport. Because when you set women against each other on a half court, you don't have one team set against another. You have teams within teams, factions, hatreds, territories. Forwards and guards despised each other, a feeling that rose beyond the emblems and colors of the uniforms and settled somewhere in the realm of survival of the fittest.

So you had four teams out there on that polished hardwood, two on either side of that holy center line over which *they shalt not cross*. Every girl struggling to be another Bobkitten, wanting to show herself as the best, the feistiest, the one who could drive just like a boy if she had to, the one who, if a war came, could play ball with the best.

And why did they do that to us?

And why did we let them?

I'm amazed at how little I actually know anymore about basketball. I don't know who it was, man or woman, who forced the issue of the half-court restrictions in women's basketball. Or who got the rules changed so we could run the full length of the court, five-on-five, the way men do. Was it Title III? Was it *Brown v. Topeka?*

The official pamphlet of the Basketball Hall of Fame in Springfield, Massachusetts features the original Springfield College teams, those handsome lads with their quaint handlebar moustaches. No information is shared concerning the rules for women's basketball. Little mention of women at all, except to chuckle on page seven that when Smith College played, the gym was closed to male spectators because the girls wore bloomers. The chuckle continues, "Regardless of what the encounter revealed or didn't reveal, this indicates the sweet young things were as quick to appreciate the merits of the game as were the more stalwart members of the opposite sex."

Ever since I left those red-brick gymnasiums of the '50s, I've never had a single concern about the old half-court handicaps they forced us to play. The old segregation and the way we obeyed it.

Except to make jokes.

Because what did they think would happen to the *sweet young things* if we ran the full length of the court? That we'd get our periods? Or give birth to little babies right out there on the court, in front of our mamas and daddies and boyfriends?

Of course, women were thought to be weaker. And although the pain of childbirth is said to be one of the highest levels of pain ever recorded, we still couldn't cross the center line on the basketball court.

Or was it a last hedge against what was coming—the feminism of the '80s and '90s—which, of course, nobody could predict in 1957, least of all we girls playing out there under the cage lights in our lightning-bolt suits?

Politics, power, maybe even money lay behind the sexual segregation we accepted. I remember the dizzying classifications our schools had, Double A, Triple A, Class A, too dizzying for clear explanations. These classifications had something to do with size and location, rural or city.

Whatever the motive behind the system, all rural or small schools had girls' basketball. Quite often city or bigger schools did not. But every school had men's basketball. And here's where it gets very peculiar. The bigger the school, the higher the classification, the more likely the school was not to have girls' basketball. This was never satisfactorily explained. More money and size ought to accommodate more teams.

And somewhere lurked a dark theory that when it came statewide tournament time, it wasn't seemly for the higher classification schools to compete with lower schools, especially when it came to putting girls out there on the court. It was okay for lower classification schools to put their girls on the court, but certainly not in competition with girls from bigger or so-called better schools.

So the game became not only sexist, but also elitist.

All the money, no doubt, went into men's basketball and their big statewide tournaments. Girls might compete at county levels, maybe even at small regional tournaments. But beyond that, not at all. The center-line rule was in effect in more places than the gym.

They never made any excuses to us about any of this or allowed any discussion. If you played girls' basketball, you stopped at the center line, got one bounce, and no dribbling. That was the way. You competed at certain lower classification levels. Your trophies came from the same hardware store as the men's trophies, but didn't really count. So it went. The happy blind obedient '50s.

And following the games, when we conjured up those fantasies I mentioned, the rich, good-looking men, the swimming pools, and the black evening dresses, we never conjured up lawsuits or test cases. We stayed on the half court and never crossed over. But I couldn't help thinking, what if, just once.

I used to fantasize driving around in a Thunderbird all over the small town of Badin, North Carolina, a white Thunderbird with portholes, like something the Bobkitten (wearing satin) might drive. I would pick up the two best-looking boys in Badin High school, Billy Trace who had exotic crossed eyes and Billy Rufty who had a five-inch scar down one cheek. They would peep in the portholes at me, then open the doors and say, Yes, sweet, anything you want, precious. And then they'd light my cigarette and hold their hands for the ashes and I'd say, Kiss my foot and they'd say, We'll kiss any part of you, precious.

This was in Badin, an obscure and pleasant North Carolina town where nothing exotic ever took place beyond the smelting of aluminum, the aluminum that appeared in piles of bright ingots inside the smelter yard and then disappeared into the boxcars of Maryland-Pacific,

Chesapeake-Ohio, Great Northern, Winston-Salem Southbound, gone in one night.

I was proud of my fantasies. I knew I wanted to get beyond the ingot yard, beyond the half-court segregation of the game I played so furiously. I didn't care much about Billy Trace or Billy Rufty with their crossed eyes and five-inch scars, except if I had to use them to crash the limits of my existence, I would.

I wish now I'd been clever enough to use the half-court basketball to take me places. Me and Mitzi Jane Blalock and all our other teammates in that peculiarly old-fashioned yet flashy Badin High Watts uniform: satiny black bloomer-shorts and a red knit tank top worn over a plain white T-shirt, the lightning-bolt emblem jagged between our breasts. The tank top fastened to little buttons concealed in the elastic waistband of the black bloomer-shorts. The other girls of the county teams wore more predictable uniforms resembling those of the men players: plain shirts tucked inside plain shorts. Or plain tank tops worn loose over plain shorts.

But the Badin High Watts were different. As the cheerleaders and the crowds assured us, not just our flashy uniforms, but our team effort, our origin, we were the Aluminum City Kids, you bet. Any girl who crossed this center line was doubtless doomed.

And all the time we went to school, all the afternoons we practiced in the big red-brick gymnasium, we heard, strong and rude as thunder, the booming of the Carolina Aluminum smelter at the edge of the town, Badin's never-sleeping industry, Badin's angry, overworked giant heaving away in the dark and the cold. Sparks showered from the crucibles and little flames clawed along the ingots as men sweated and aged. Everybody's father worked in the smelter in some capacity, carbon kiln, potroom, main office, rotary station, keeping the smelter going, turning out aluminum famous for its purity. Any man who crossed this center line was likewise doomed.

I meant to get free of such a place, such a game. My fantasies put me to sleep after each game won for the Badin High Watts. The smelter sprawled along Highway 740 and cooked furiously all night, devouring minerals, boiling up metal, and driving off the dross to produce silvery-white ingots we called pigs.

And all night I dreamed furiously about grabbing basketballs and slinging them down the court, hard, over the center line straight to Mitzi Jane Blalock. And then at some perfect moment in my dream, Mitzi Jane Blalock and I decided to run over the center line together, knock down the referees in their striped shirts, their whistles stuck in their mouths, and keep on running out of the gymnasium, downtown, past the aluminum smelter, and on up Highway 740, to the world, *the Bobkittens escape!*

We could have made it a circus ring, with snarling beasts and black whips and spotlights hot as sunshine beating down on Myrtle Beach. Men, emptying from the smelter potrooms, heading straight for the washhouse and the showers, would applaud our audacity. I'd tell them, Look at this, we are Venus di Milo twins in basketball uniforms, little stars twinkling in our teeth, stuck on our eyelashes, a hot burning light spilling out of both corners of our mouths. You never poured out any aluminum to match us.

But such daring, such a display, never happened. We played the game, anxious and swift, stopping like magic at the center line while the cheerleaders yay-yayed and rah-rahed us. We obeyed the zone. Stayed put. We couldn't tell what other maneuvers, other victories might wait on the other side of the center line—if we just broke through, just once. What futuristic ball courts dazzling with rich men and swimming pools, what black evening dresses with sequins might be our reward.

And maybe it's not even important in the history of American sports who first crossed over that center line in women's basketball, who broke the segregation of the old half-court ball. And maybe there's nothing to be made of the fact that Oklahoma and Iowa, those wholesome American heartland states, were the last to switch. There are no big deals in women's team sports. And except for the colorful stars in tennis or golf, the Olympic skaters and gymnasts, occasionally a swimmer or a runner—nobody really pays attention. Martina Navratilova and Chrissie Evert, Dorothy Hamill and Mary Lou Retton can get on a Wheaties box. And Florence Griffith Joyner can run in lace tights at the 1988 Olympics, an outfit almost as zany as our black satin and red lightning bolts of 1957. These women could wear merry widows and yellow net if they wanted. The old segregation is gone, that old half court, thank God, is dead.

In any case, to whomever she was who crossed first, I'd like to say I'm late with this—but I wanted to do it, too. My wind is gone now, my ankles and knees shot to hell, and my lower back crumbling into arthritis. But what I'd give to break across the center line, just once.

Running all the way in black satin, in lace, in sequins and lightning bolts.

◄❉►

"I CAN SEE THE FINISH LINE"

Mark Starr

If Marla Runyan had her wish, this story would be a straightforward account of her track-and-field odyssey. How she struggled with the heptathlon, the women's seven-event version of the decathlon, before switching to distance running. How she almost disappeared from competition for two years. And how, after injuries and coaching changes, Runyan, now 31, has emerged with a shot to make America's Olympic team in the 1,500 or 5,000 meters (she'll decide which race to run this week). But with success comes the media. Runyan is resigned to her journalistic fate. "It's always the human-interest story," she says with a sigh. "'There's this blind girl running! Isn't that great?'"

Sorry, Marla, but it *is* great. At the Olympic Track and Field Trials, which start this Friday in Sacramento, Calif., Runyan, who is legally blind, hopes to make one of the most remarkable leaps in sports: from 1996 gold-medal ParaOlympian (in the Games for the disabled) to Olympian-without-prefix in Sydney's 2000 Games. "I'll have done everything I can to make it—no holding back," says Runyan, who finished 10th at 1,500 meters in last year's world championships. "But I love this sport enough that if I don't, it's not the end of the world."

As if she hasn't already surmounted enough obstacles, Runyan now faces one more: a recent, nagging leg injury that has curtailed her training and could even force her withdrawal from the Trials. But Runyan can be oblivious to obstacles. She has never understood the fuss about her eyesight. At the age of 9, she began suffering from Stargardt's disease, a deteriorating retinal condition that left her with a vast blur at the center of her vision—20/300 in one eye, 20/400 in the other, even with the contact lenses that she wears to compete. But with sufficient peripheral vision to get a sense of the field around her, she doesn't believe she faces a competitive disadvantage. Her mantra: "I can see the finish line. It's at the end of the straightaway."

The literal truth is, she can't see the finish line—at least not the tape that marks it. And distance running at the Olympic level can be as treacherous as Roller Derby, with plenty of both accidental and intentional contact. Runyan can see the feet around her. Still, she appears

From *Newsweek*, July 17, 2000. © 2000 Newsweek Inc. All rights reserved. Reprinted by permission.

more comfortable running the early laps in the lead, which is mentally and physically draining, or on the outside of the pack, which adds yardage. And sometimes other racers can pull away from Marla without her noticing. In March she finished fourth in the prestigious 5K road race in Carlsbad, Calif. "The only way I could tell for sure I wasn't in first was by the cheers of the crowd," she says.

Runyan jokes that her visual "fog" can, at times, be a competitive advantage. Since the opposition runners are often indistinguishable, she's immune to the intimidation factor of racing alongside big stars. Her coach, Mike Manley, says her visual limitations may also eliminate distractions on the track and strengthen her mental focus.

As a student at San Diego State (she earned a master's degree in education), Runyan recognized her need for special treatment. She welcomed visual aids, including glasses fitted with a magnifying lens, audio books and assistants assigned to read to her. Still, she says she didn't comprehend that her experience on the track was different from anybody else's until the day a teammate suggested that she focus on the third hurdle down the track—and Runyan couldn't see it. "That was the first time it occurred to me," she says, "that I was the only one who couldn't see past the first hurdle."

Runyan is active in the disabled community and is a part-time teacher, working with vision- and hearing-impaired children. But she is reluctant to make her achievement part of any crusade, and uncomfortable with overstating the implications of her success. "What ParaOlympians do is incredible, and I don't want my message to be that every ParaOlympian can make it to the Olympic Games," she says. "I can't really even be an example for every blind person, 'cause I'm not totally blind. All I can do is represent a lot of misconceptions and stereotypes of the blind and vision-impaired being inept." That's another blind spot for a woman who has trouble recognizing that she's an inspiration to all who see her run.

❖

COURTING DESTINY

Raquel Cepeda

Venus Williams is stunning in the flesh. The 21-year-old tennis star glides into the quaint, dimly lit lobby of the West Palm Beach, Florida, Marriott more like a runway model than a pro athlete. She strolls in casually—all six feet two inches of mostly legs—clad in tiny jean shorts, a white Gucci fisherman's hat covering her braids, and a sleeveless spandex top that says, in royal blue script, "Real." I offer her my hand. She takes it firmly. I smile at her. She doesn't smile back.

I'll be straight with you: Before my interview with Venus and Serena, I know all the dish about how the sisters have been dubbed brash and un-friendly. But I also know what every person of color in America does—that merely stepping into a room and breathing is enough to make some folks label you "brash and unfriendly." So I've set aside the rumors and come to let Venus and Serena show me who they are—and to explain why, in a sport that they clearly redefined, they still get almost zero love on the tennis circuit.

Not until 19-year-old Serena steps into the room does Venus' face light up. At five feet ten inches, Serena is shorter than her sister and equally striking. She sports a look that screams "I'm here!"—gold braids, a black micromini, a white cotton midriff top and a diamond-studded belly-button ring. It's not hard to understand why just seeing the two sisters in the same room elicits comparisons, however unfair: Both are tennis Tro-jans who sport phat outfits as daring as those worn by the late sprinter Florence Griffith-Joyner. But don't get it twisted: Though Venus and Se-rena each have a killer game, they couldn't be more different.

In case you aren't one of the many proud Black folks who—though they don't give a rip about tennis—have held their collective breath for these sisters' victories, here's the 11-second version of what you've missed. In 1999 Serena, then 17, became the first Black since tennis great Althea Gibson in 1958 to win the U.S. Open. Then last year, Venus beat Lindsay Davenport and walked away with a Wimbledon victory—an-other feat that hadn't been accomplished by a Black person since Gibson did it 43 years ago. And at the 2000 Olympics in Sydney, Venus also be-came the first woman to win gold medals in both singles and in doubles, with Serena, since 1924.

From *Essence Magazine*, June 2001.

Yet the Williams sisters haven't been without their detractors. Since they entered the sport as children, critics and commentators have often dismissed their mental fierceness by overplaying their physical prowess. And that's just a piece of the drama of what it means to be them: They travel constantly. Sometimes for six days a week, they push themselves through marathon-long sessions of practice. At only 19 and 21, they struggle to carve out a personal life. And then, of course, each sister sometimes has to compete with her best friend—the other one.

But none of this means the girls are whiners: they aren't really even talkers. I spent more than an hour with the two but they must've been interview-weary, because I didn't exactly have to fight to squeeze a word in. Yet as a tennis player myself who grew up among the same well-heeled girls and opulent country clubs that have become their world, I can intuit a lot, and their mother and older sister fill in the details with comments they have never before shared in public. And in the end, I discover that what Venus and Serena don't say is often just as revealing as what they do.

Compton to Wimbledon

I'll do my part in debunking at least one urban legend. It's true that the Williams sisters didn't grow up on a prairie of white picket fences and privilege, but as tennis tots in Compton, California, Venus and Serena say they weren't dodging bullets and warding off junkies either. As the story of their rise onto the plush green grass of Wimbledon goes, Richard Williams, their father, once saw a tennis player receive a check for $30,000 after winning a tournament. It was at that moment that he decided to turn his two youngest children into tennis titans. There was just one tiny detail Richard had to work out: They hadn't yet been conceived.

As fortune would have it, his two youngest children turned out to be Venus and Serena. Richard, who back then oversaw a security agency, didn't know squat about how to play tennis—so he taught himself using an instructional video. As soon as his daughters were old enough to grip a racket, he began taking them every day to practice on a set of broken-down tennis courts near their home. By age 10, after Venus had gone unbeaten in 63 games, she won southern California's girls' title in the under-12 division. Serena, who entered her first tournament when she was only 4, soon succeeded her sister in that same division.

If their father was the gale wind of discipline at the girls' backs, their mother, Oracene, was the strong post that kept the gusts of strenuous work and stardom from toppling over their personal lives. "When Venus and Serena were very young, I would let them know that they had to be balanced, that they shouldn't think more of themselves than they actually were," says Oracene, who reared her children in the Jehovah's Witness faith. In all, Oracene and Richard have five daughters: Venus and Serena; 28-year-old Yetunde, a nurse; 26-year-old Isha, a law-school student; and 23-year-old Lyndrea, a television executive.

Even before her youngest daughters were born, Oracene, a tennis enthusiast herself, was already familiarizing them with their court of destiny. While pregnant with Venus and again with Serena, she played a match every morning at five-thirty—before going to her full-time gig as a nurse. Later, when the Williamses' preteen daughters practiced for six hours a day, six days a week, Oracene homeschooled them. And despite their father's zealous guidance of their tennis careers, he always demanded that hitting the books take precedence over slamming the balls. In 1996, after Richard removed Venus from the junior tennis circuit so she could focus on her studies, he told the *New York Times*, "People say, 'Richard, have her play tournaments.' But I'd rather see my daughter with an education— not a common education like I have, but one that's in demand."

That's a stance Richard's daughters certainly respect him for now. "Kudos to them," says Venus of her parents, "because they really brought us up well. They made sure we got our education so that we could become more than just athletes." Though their father has had his share of bad press, some self-inflicted, his hand in the sisters' ascent to dominance is certain. "It takes love to have that kind of dedication—and to do it at no cost," says the second-oldest daughter, Isha, of their father's unpaid tenure as Venus and Serena's coach. Even now, they try to keep things in the family: Isha, upon graduating from law school, will handle the Williamses' legal affairs.

Whatever anyone may think of Richard's sometimes offbeat statements and actions—for instance, it was reported that he climbed atop an NBC booth after Venus' victory at Wimbledon last year and held up a sign that read "It's Venus' party, and no one was invited"—he made one prediction that's proving to be on point. When Venus and Serena were only 13 and 12, Richard declared that they would one day become the top two tennis players in the world.

Girlfriend Has an Attitude?

It would be surprising if the Williams girls didn't come off as chilly at times. Being a powerful Black woman in a sport overrun with wealthy White girls who huddle for sherry hours and bond over Perrier is enough to send any 'round-the-way girl AWOL. And let's be real: What a White person calls a snub—like when one sports commentator remarked that it wouldn't kill Venus and Serena to say hello to the other players in their locker room—is what a Black woman simply calls a strategy for blocking out negativity.

I know. In the late eighties, as a formerly ranked junior tennis player myself, I received a scholarship to attend a prestigious tennis academy in New York, and it was my introduction to a sport fraught with racial tension and outright bigotry. "There's just a nasty disrespect you see on some people's faces," says Isha of her sisters' experience among the tennis elite. "It's like, 'They're not supposed to be here.'" In fact, from the time Venus and Serena began competing in junior tournaments, Isha recalls that some people would tell their kids things like, "Don't let that little Black girl beat you."

"We still get hate mail," Isha says. "That kind of thing gets put in your subconscious—in the far depths of your mind—and you just don't think about it." But that doesn't mean the hurt doesn't manifest itself in other ways. Some have accused Venus and Serena of being rude. But if that's true, sniping at those who attack them may be their way of handling the pain of a constant barrage of unfair criticism. And as two of only a handful of Blacks ever to dominate their sport, the sisters have to contend with one other ugly little reality: The same folks who dismiss them often fear them.

That's because Venus and Serena are to tennis what Tiger Woods is to golf—an unsettling symbol of change in America. "I don't think that White America will ever be ready to accept Black athletes who can think," says Peter Noel, an investigative reporter for New York's *The Village Voice* who witnessed firsthand the mixed reception Serena and Venus received at the 2000 U.S. Open. In one article he wrote, "Fear of the Williams Sisters," Noel dismisses the myth of the "superbred Black athlete" by pointing out Venus' and Serena's mental tenacity and strategic dominance. And still, Noel says, some White Americans view them as girls who came up from the ghetto who can't really help put it down on a blackboard or in a game plan.

Last September, even tennis pundit John McEnroe pummeled the girls in an article he wrote for London's *Telegraph*, charging the two with numerous counts of unfriendliness and bad character. This is the same John McEnroe who was thrown out of Long Island, New York's famed Port Washington Tennis Academy as a youngster for his, well, bratty behavior. The John McEnroe whose temper tantrums are more legendary than his mastery of the sport.

"When the sisters met in the semifinals at Wimbledon 2000, sports announcers suggested that their father had fixed the match," says New York writer Ayesha Grice, who has closely followed Venus' and Serena's careers. "Instead of pointing out that two sisters hadn't met in a match for decades—and had never met in the semifinals—the rumors kept seeping through in the media that something wasn't right." And still, after a six-month hiatus from the game and amid rumors of her early retirement, Venus went on to trounce her archrivals, Martina Hingis and Lindsay Davenport, to win both Wimbledon and, later, the U.S. Open.

But the criticism hasn't waned. World-ranked player Pete Sampras once dismissed Venus' 127-mph serve as sheer luck. Then former world-ranked player Martina Navratilova—once criticized for being too masculine and aggressive for women's tennis—was reported to have denounced the Williams sisters' interest in fashion as being arrogant and a sign of their lack of commitment to the game. "I prepared Venus and Serena for public scrutiny when they were very young, because I knew it would become part of their lives," says their mother, Oracene. "I wanted to make sure they were able to deal with the criticism and not take it personally—to keep it at a distance and to keep their lives private." That might be why when I mention Navratilova's comment to Serena, she says with indifference, "I didn't hear about that. People are entitled to their own opinions."

The Power Set

We've all heard the reports that Venus and Serena, although at times opponents on the court, couldn't be any tighter away from the game—in fact, they bought a Florida home together, which they've decorated in what they call a "contemporary classic" style. But all that love floating between them sort of makes you want to ask: Does their public camaraderie ever spiral into private competition?

Like all sisters you can be sure they've had their squabbles, though Isha says their kinship couldn't be more real. And no matter how many titles Serena wins, says Isha, Venus will always play the big-sister role. "Venus takes all blows," she says, "so Serena is able to be free-spirited. That's good, because that's who Serena really is."

Not that the youngest Williams daughter travels in her older sister's shadow. That became clear two years ago when Serena beat out Venus and all others vying for the coveted U.S. Open top spot—a moment of victory that was followed by that unforgettable image of an ecstatic Serena, gripping her trophy while tears of joy flooded her face. "For the first time, she was catapulted out of Venus' shadow and put in the spotlight," says Isha. "She accomplished that victory on her own, before anyone else in our family."

There were many reports of a somber Venus looking on as Serena won the family's first grand slam title. But according to Isha, that's quintessential Venus: serious and quiet. "She has carried much of the burden of their stardom," says Isha of Venus. "She's kind of world-weary. She has this attitude like, 'Been there, done that.' That's just the person she is."

It takes Serena to tell you about Venus Lite—the self-professed "introvert" who is also a *Golden Girls* junkie. In a *Tennis* magazine story in which the sisters interviewed each other, Serena wrote, "Most people consider Venus serious because they only see her on the court. . . . But beneath that introverted surface is 'Venus the Joker.' If you ever see us play a doubles match, you'll notice that the majority of the time, we're giggling—and it's usually at one of her jokes!" Serena continues, "Venus is more than a great tennis player—she is a great older sister, friend and person. Seeing that others are being helped, making sure her family is doing okay, and, above all, making sure that little sis is safe are what truly mean the most to her."

It was that kind of maturity and strength of character—along with Venus' graciousness while being constantly provoked—that led *Sports Illustrated for Women* to name her "Sportswoman of the Year 2000." After winning in a straight-set match over Lindsay Davenport at Wimbledon last year, Venus told the magazine, "I feel really calm. I love playing tennis, I love winning titles. And I realize I wouldn't be any happier in my life in general if I won or lost. Sure, in the tennis part of my life, I'd be much happier if I won. But winning, losing, money, riches or fame don't make you happy. For my tennis career, this is great. But as far as me being Venus, it doesn't really make a huge difference."

All About Business

Though Venus says she doesn't feel any extra pressure as one of the few African-American[s] on the pro circuit, her sister admits that racist undertones do permeate the sport. "And I'm sure there's a lot of hidden racism," says Serena. Yet because they keep winning tournaments and titles, they're in constant demand. "When you're a winner," Serena points out, "everyone—Black, White, Mexican or Hindu—wants to get on your team."

Indeed corporate sponsors are lining up to sign the sisters. Both Venus and Serena recently entered a three-year, $7 million contract to endorse Wrigley's Doublemint Gum. Venus also inked a $40 million contract with Reebok, while Serena sealed a $12 million deal with Puma. And the cosmetics company Avon recently signed the Williams sisters as spokeswomen in its first global campaign, "Let's Talk." "They are young, spirited, fun, beautiful women who just happen to be sisters with a very strong and loving relationship," says Janice Spector, vice-president of advertising for Avon. The television spots feature Venus and Serena in a personal dialogue, a snapshot of the beauty buzz that happens when women get together to talk about the products they love and use. "It's a great deal, and Avon is a great company," says Serena. "They're like a Mercedes, one of the best things you can get out there."

That leaves the girls with around three minutes a day for trivial endeavors like, say, sleep. But that doesn't stop Serena from keeping her personal life popping. "Besides being a tennis player," she says, "I'm a designer, a model, an actress and a rapper." While Serena did appear in rapper Memphis Bleek's *Do My* video featuring Jay-Z, the "I'm a rapper" line is a joke. Serena will, however, make a cameo appearance in *Black Knight,* a comedy starring Martin Lawrence, slated for release this fall. She also took a design job with Wilson's Leather to create her own line of clothing, which she'll unveil this August. With such a demanding schedule, no wonder Venus and Serena say they're "off the market"—not dating or even thinking about it.

Besides having a passion for collecting designer watches and bags—on the day of our interview, Venus shows up carrying an enviable chocolate-brown–and–tan checked Louis Vuitton purse—they are equally serious about clothes. "I've decided I want to design," says Venus, who along with her sister is a design student at the Art Institute of Fort Lauderdale in Florida. "It's fun, and it always keeps changing. It's kind of like tennis—you have to keep reinventing yourself and getting better in order to have something new to bring to the market."

Venus and Serena have made no apologies for being kick-butt tennis players. Or for being confident, independent thinkers. Or for making women's tennis exciting by fusing an aggressive game with fashionably bold statement. Maybe all the joking around with each other that they do on and off the court keeps Venus and Serena from internalizing the criticism lesser mortals might succumb to. Or maybe they just like to laugh.

◀◈▶

THE COLD WARS

Inside the Secret World of Figure Skating

Joan Ryan

[. . .] Only the top two finishers in Detroit would go on to the Olympics the following month in Lillehammer, Norway, and everyone in the competition knew they were fighting for second place. Nancy Kerrigan had a lock on

Excerpted from Joan Ryan, "The Cold Wars: Inside the Secret World of Figure Skating," *The Best American Sportswriting,* 1995. Dan Jenkins, ed., Glenn Stout series ed. Boston: Houghton Mifflin, 1995. First published in *The San Francisco Examiner Magazine.*

first. One skater, Nicole Bobek, went so far as to say before the competition, "I imagine if she doesn't do well, the judges will hold her up." Kerrigan was the one true star among the women in Detroit. She had risen like a real-life Cinderella from the working-class, hockey-playing, beer-and-pretzels Kerrigan clan to American Ice Princess, a stunning young woman with $13,000 designer costumes and a smile of newly capped teeth. She was the reigning national champion. She already had an Olympic medal, a bronze in 1992. She had national endorsement contracts for Campbell's, Reebok, Seiko, Evian.

The afternoon of January 6, a day before the start of the technical, or short, program, Kerrigan owned the ice. She glided around the rink in Cobo Hall in her white lace costume with six other women in her practice session, but she might as well have been alone. She drew the eyes of everyone in the arena. When the practice session ended, Kerrigan was first off the ice, pausing to slip skate guards on her blades, then striding through the blue curtains that separated the rink from the locker room hallway. Other skaters and coaches gathered their belongings to follow her. No one had noticed a man in black slip behind the curtains before Kerrigan. Unless you've been orbiting the earth or adrift at sea the past three months, you know the rest. The man whacked Kerrigan just above the right knee, knocking her from the competition.

With the field clear of Kerrigan—who had beaten 1991 national champion Tonya Harding in their last five meetings—Harding won her second national championship, securing a place on the Olympic team. Soon afterward, Jeff Gillooly, Harding's ex-husband, confessed to hiring the hit man. Thus began a media feeding frenzy that made last year's sordid accounts of Amy Fisher and Joey Buttafuoco look like *Masterpiece Theater*. Gillooly accused the skater of approving the plot and paying for it with training money she received from New York Yankees owner George Steinbrenner. Harding denied any wrongdoing and, because she had not been charged with any crime by the start of the Olympics, she was allowed to skate for the United States in Lillehammer.

One questioned dogged me as the bizarre story unfolded.

What would drive someone to risk everything in his or her life—freedom, career, reputation—for a skating title? [. . .]

The plot to attack Kerrigan apparently began late last year, when Harding finished fourth at the NHK Cup in Japan. The skating cards seemed stacked against her. Even though Kerrigan didn't compete at NHK, Harding, or at least Gillooly, decided that no matter how well Harding skated, Kerrigan would always stand between Harding and the shiniest medal. As long as Kerrigan was around, Kerrigan would get the commercial endorsements, the magazine covers, the starring roles in the ice shows. Harding would get nothing. Harding wasn't being paranoid. She was right. Kerrigan was the chosen. Skating is as much about politics and appearances as it is about athletics. Being the highest jumper and the fastest spinner guarantees a skater nothing. Athleticism counts—but so do beauty, grace, deportment, weight, hair, makeup, costume, music.

"Image is everything," said one skating coach. Judges regularly call the parents and coaches of a skater to suggest she wear more pink, or grow her hair back long, or see a dermatologist to clear up patches of teenage acne. One judge reportedly told one top skater to get a nose job because the girl's nose was "distracting." A skater who rebuffs a judge's suggestions risks repercussions come competition time. Skaters and coaches even invite local judges to come to the skater's rink and evaluate her program before she goes to a competition. Most skaters genuinely want the judge's input, others do it merely to stroke the ego of the judge, yes-yessing every suggestion the judge makes, then rolling their eyes when the judge leaves, changing nothing in their programs.

Some coaches, and even some parents, lobby the judges. Though Kerrigan's coach, Evy Scotvold, says he doesn't do it, he was spotted after practice one day in Lillehammer chatting and laughing with Margaret Weir, the only American on the women's judging panel. They likely were not talking about Kerrigan—she hardly needed a boost—but the appearance of a coach and a judge fraternizing just days before the most important competition of the skaters' lives couldn't have made Kerrigan's opponents sleep easier. Harding, or at least her coach, surely noticed. Parents frequently call local judges at home after a competition to ask them to explain their marks. Coaches ask other coaches, who might be particularly close to a judge, to put in a good word for their skater. Other coaches include judges on their Christmas card list. "One judge, if you told her she looked good in her jeans, she loved you," said Keith Lichtman, a pairs coach from Boston.

It's the game within the game, and Harding never learned to play. She refused to learn. Yes, she came from a family with little money or education, but she wasn't the only one from the working class. Kerrigan is as blue collar as a dime-store clerk. Nicole Bobek, too. Harding's unforgivable sin in the skating community was not that she had no class or taste but that she refused to allow anyone to give her some. She wore hideous, homemade costumes. She had a ratty ponytail, garish makeup, fake nails. She plowed through her routines like a bull, connecting one explosive jump after another with footwork about as complicated and graceful as a square dance. She had a pear-shaped body with heavy legs and beefy arms. "Hair and weight are everything in this sport," said ice dancer Susie Wynn, exaggerating only slightly.

It also didn't help that Harding was neither deferential nor sociable.

When she won the national championship in 1991 by landing the first triple axel by an American woman, she snubbed the formal champions dinner afterward. She put on jeans and a sweatshirt and shot eight ball with her friends in the hotel bar. During the week of the 1992 World Championships in Oakland, she refused to eat in the skater's dining room at the hotel, where the meals were free. Despite complaints of money problems, she ordered room service every night, which she had to pay for herself, rather than eat with the rest of the skaters, coaches and officials.

Harding refused to help her chances of winning by playing politics, yet she wanted to win more than she wanted anything in her life. She dropped out of school in tenth grade to concentrate full time on her skating, throwing all her eggs into this one precarious basket. Most elite skaters tend to live in a bubble, but Harding was particularly ignorant of the world beyond the rink and the pool tables. After the 1991 World Championships, where Harding finished second, the top skaters were invited on a European tour. Harding said she would go only if her husband could accompany her. As each skater was allowed to bring one guest, Gillooly went. Kristi Yamaguchi and Kerrigan, who finished first and third, respectively, went by themselves and roomed together. At the stop in Rome, the local skating club arranged for a special tour of the Vatican. When the team leader, an International Skating Union official from the United States, asked who wanted to go, everyone but Harding raised their hands. The team leader took Harding aside.

"You know, Tonya, this is a special tour of the Vatican; you might never get another chance to experience—"

"What," Harding asked, "is the Vatican? Some kind of religious place?"

The team leader, flabbergasted, tried to explain that it was also a place of great art, of Michelangelo's "Pietà" and the Sistine Chapel.

"Who's Michelangelo?" she asked.

As the rest of the group boarded the buses for the Vatican, Harding and Gillooly headed out to buy T-shirts.

Unlike Harding, Kerrigan allowed herself to be molded into a made-for-media princess by the expert hands of coaches Evy and Mary Scotvold. The Scotvolds performed magic with Kerrigan, considering that she has a less than scintillating personality. Her interviews came across as snippy and always, always dull. She mostly shrugs. But she looks the part. She's thin, beautiful, graceful, well groomed and polite to the judges. And, of course, on the ice, she's a dream.

"It's a packaging process, very much so," Evy Scotvold said. "You're trying to become a princess of the ice. . . . You try to make sure they know they have to behave, they have to have good manners and they have to be well dressed. They know they will be watched on and off the ice."

As for the skating itself, "The judges are all probably thirty-five to sixty-five, so you've got to give them something that they can understand," Scotvold said. "And if there's some new hip-hop kid thing from MTV, you're probably making a mistake [to use it as accompaniment to a skating program]. . . . You must not mistake who [judges] are and what their tastes are. You're trying to appeal to them, that's for sure. You're not trying to appeal to your own taste. If you don't have the right taste, learn it. But don't show them your bad taste."

It's a mistake Harding made over and over, even at the Olympics last month. The bordello-red sleeveless costume she wore for the short program was hideous, especially in contrast to Kerrigan's sophisticated black-and-white number. Harding's costume for her long program at Nationals was so awful—it gave the illusion that Harding was mostly bare-breasted—that the judges deducted points. So Harding wore a different costume in the Olympics. (Not that it made a difference. She finished eighth.)

Most concede judging is less political than a few years ago, now that school figures have been dropped from competition. Judges could rank a skater low enough in the figures portion of the competition—without fear of public reprisal since the press generally didn't cover the tedious event—that the skater would be out of medal contention before she even got to her technical program. But most everyone in figure skating agrees that allowances are—and should be—made for the top skaters.

"They're not going to keep Nancy Kerrigan off the Olympic team because she has an off night," Mary Lyn Gelderman, who coached former world champion Elaine Zayak, said before the U.S. championships. "That would be stupid. Everyone accepts that would be stupid. I would be shocked if they ever would do anything as dumb as that. That [kind of judging] will always exist. But it's not like it was before, when they could end your career if they wanted to."

Harding knew no such allowances would be made for her. She would have to make her own allowances. She had much at stake going into Nationals. She hadn't finished any competition in 1993 above third; now she had to finish in the top two in Detroit in order to qualify for the Olympic team. And she had to go to the Olympics. This was her last chance. Only an Olympic medal could reap a payback for everything she put into skating.

What a payback it could be. Agents said a gold was worth $10 million in endorsements, ice shows and appearances. Gold medalists spend the rest of their lives trading on their names. In fact, in a poll last year by the Dallas-based Sports Marketing Group, Dorothy Hamill—seventeen years after winning the gold—was named America's most beloved athlete along with gymnast Mary Lou Retton.

Figure skating is more popular now than ever before. Corporations that once sponsored tennis and golf are switching to figure skating. "Figure skating," John Bennett, a senior vice president at Visa, told *New York* magazine recently, "is the closest you can get to sex in the Olympics." Television ratings are phenomenal: an eight-month-old tape of the 1993 World Figure Skating Championships drew a larger audience last fall than a live broadcast of the Indiana-Kentucky college basketball game. The ratings for the women at the Olympics broke records. One billion people watched the women skate in Lillehammer, including more than 100 million in the States. The night of the women's technical program drew the highest ratings ever for an Olympics broadcast and the third-highest for a sporting event in the history of television. (Only the 1982 and 1983 Super Bowls did better.)

Those who shine on this stage can become icons. Figure skating champions represent an old-fashioned and, to many, a comforting feminine ideal not found in other female athletes. They are demure, beautiful, lithe, vulnerable and a bit spoiled. They're starlets in blades, with agents and fans fluttering about them.

In climbing toward this life, and knowing that talent alone might not carry them, skaters have resorted to unseemly measures to gain advantage. [. . .]

The attack, with all its bumbling and muddled objectives, was the work of desperate people. As events turned out, even if Kerrigan had not competed in the Olympics, Harding still would not have won a medal.

So what's the motivation behind attacking Kerrigan? My guess is jealousy and pathological denial. Harding still wasn't going to admit her own failures, such as not training hard enough, smoking despite her asthma, refusing to accept advice. She saw her failures only in relation to Kerrigan's success. Get Kerrigan out of the way and all would be fine.

Kerrigan represented everything Harding could never be. Nancy had beaten her at everything for two years. Everyone loved Nancy; it didn't seem to matter that she could be a bitch, too. (Did you see Kerrigan waiting for the awards ceremony to begin at the Olympics? CBS cameras caught her rolling her eyes in disgust and saying, "Oh come on, give me a break. So she's going to get out here and cry again," referring to sixteen-year-old gold medalist Oksana Baiul. Someone had told Kerrigan the holdup was so Baiul could apply fresh makeup after sobbing over her victory, when in fact the delay was caused by someone misplacing a tape of the Ukrainian national anthem.)

Nancy got every benefit of the doubt. Tonya got squat.

But Harding wasn't going to leave skating without a fight. Perhaps in some recess of her mind she figured the skating world didn't fight fair, so why should she? Perhaps the botched attack was a last-gasp stab at defeating Kerrigan and winning the prize she had eyed all her life, an Olympic medal. But the attack only served to make Kerrigan a bigger and even saintlier star. It backfired, like so much in Harding's career. She was always working at cross-purposes. She wanted to win more than anything, yet refused to play the games necessary to do it. She hired lawyers, filed lawsuits, put up with the media invading her life so she could compete at Lillehammer—then arrived there completely unprepared, from not training enough to not bringing the right skate laces.

Some say figure skating will never be the same. Yes, it will. As breathtakingly beautiful as the sport can be, beneath its sequins and lip liner, beneath its kittenish exterior, beats the heart of a tiger looking for its next meal. It was like this before the Kerrigan attack, it will continue after. The attack was an aberration, certainly. But when one stirs together politics, pressure, jealousy, money and ambition, as elite women's figure skating does to a degree unmatched by any other sport, one is likely to see an explosion now and then.

ROOTING FOR MICHELLE

Finding Contradictions at the Winter Olympics

Bill Wong

I was rooting for Michelle Kwan to win the gold medal in women's figure skating at the Nagano Winter Olympics, but that probably jinxed her.

Athletes and teams I root for don't do so well. I was cheering for the Green Bay Packers—a team I have followed faithfully for 40 years—and you know what happened to them in the Super Bowl last month. They lost to the Denver Broncos.

I have been known to put my faith in the Oakland Raiders, Oakland Athletics, and the Golden State Warriors. And if you are a sports fan, you know how pathetic those teams are. Even TV shows I like get canceled all the time.

So Michelle Kwan probably wishes I hadn't been in her corner last Friday night when she lost the gold medal she was favored to win.

Part of why I wanted her to win was the fact that she is Chinese American—simple ethnic pride. She also happens to be a graceful, elegant

From *Asian Week* 19:27 (26 February–4 March 1998). Copyright 1998 *Asian Week*. Reprinted with permission.

skater, although I am very much an amateur when it comes to judging the strange sport of women's figure skating.

It's strange because those charged with making judgments on the skaters' performances are sometimes so blatantly subjective (and nationalistic) that they make the sport a joke, even though women's figure skating is one of the most popular televised sports. Could it be a lot of dirty old men salivating over the nubile young female bodies swathed in tight, colorful dresses with heavy makeup and long exposed legs?

Nah. Women's figure skating garners a hefty female audience, a sharp counterpoint to the macho male sports of professional football and basketball.

Despite my own blithe ignorance, I do watch the Olympics women's figure skating competition because, as I revealed last week, I am a sheep. I can't seem to overcome the hype. That Michelle Kwan was a major contender helped ease my insouciance, although I recall with lurid imagination the 1994 epic battle between Nancy Kerrigan and Tonya Harding, a match watched by many millions of people.

Kwan versus tiny Tara Lipinski didn't have the tabloid fascination of the Kerrigan-Harding rivalry, but the duel was nonetheless the Olympics' star event. Kwan, only 17 years old, was favored because she won the U.S. championship last month in Philadelphia, scoring 15 (out of a possible 18) perfect marks of 6.0.

Her artistry was thought to be superior to that of Lipinski, all of 15 herself. Skating experts said Lipinski's jumps were possibly more athletic than Kwan's, but Kwan's overall maturity and ethereal artistry would most likely propel her to the top of the Olympic podium for a gold medal. Besides, these experts said, judges prefer artistry to technical skills.

After the Wednesday short program, Kwan was in the lead and Lipinski was in second place. Unless Kwan fell once or twice, experts said, the gold medal was hers to lose. Kwan didn't fall, yet she lost to Lipinski, who skated with great energy and had a more technically difficult program (more triple combination jumps).

To my eyes and those much more knowledgeable in the sport, Kwan skated beautifully, but was tentative and cautious. She admitted so herself afterwards. She didn't flow with the freedom and joy she showed in Philadelphia last month.

In one of numerous articles about the rivalry before the competition, *New York Times* writer Jere Longman recalled Kwan's difficult year. "There . . . appeared to be a timidity to her skating. Kwan seemed to be defending rather than attacking," he wrote.

As a front-runner, you can sometimes look over your shoulder rather than look ahead. Underdogs have less to lose.

After losing the gold and winning the silver medal (a tremendous accomplishment in its own right), Kwan was gracious. But her look during the medals' ceremony revealed deep disappointment.

I spoke earlier of my ethnic pride in Kwan, and I am certain other Chinese Americans felt the same way. Part of our emotional support for Kwan has to do with the fact that there are so few Chinese American and Asian American stars in American society.

No question many of us are good citizens who labor long hours and perform our jobs well. Many of us are good family people who abide by the laws of the land, but almost none of us possesses star status. Kwan had a good chance of achieving that status.

One writer observed that if Kwan won the gold medal, she would not experience the early difficulties Kristi Yamaguchi had in getting product endorsement deals after she won the gold medal in women's figure skating at the 1992 Winter Olympics. Yamaguchi's victory came at a time when there was resentment in the United States over Japanese economic successes. Even though Yamaguchi isn't Japanese, but rather Japanese American, her ethnicity was apparently held against her.

While many of us are easily seduced by stardom—however it is defined—I am wary of the celebrity culture that engulfs American society, even though I wish Michelle Kwan had become the top star in her field.

I don't mean to sound like a bundle of contradictions, but I guess I am. Because her family's story is close to mine and other Chinese Americans and Asian Americans—immigrants struggling for success—I felt it would be terrific if someone like us were held in high esteem by many other Americans. Yamaguchi served that purpose six years ago. Now it was time for Kwan.

This may sound like a sad confession about wanting acceptance, but I believe a lot of us have this desire.

At the same time, I kick myself for having such banal wishes. Why should who we are need to be validated by network TV, advertisers, and the American middle-class masses?

The Michelle Kwan phenomenon won't be the last time Asian America is wracked by the contradictions of wishing for fame and fortune and dismissing those desires for an undiluted sense of cultural integrity.

◀❖▶

BREAKING CULTURAL TRADITIONS

Culture, Family Play Role in Sports for Latina Girls

MaryJo Sylwester

GREELEY, COLO.—Korina Hernandez is one of only two Hispanics on the varsity girls basketball team at Greeley Central High School, where half the students are Hispanic. That's not unusual for girls teams here. Just 20% of Greeley Central's Hispanic girls play a sport, compared with 60% of the non-Hispanic girls, according to the athletics director.

Nationwide, this disparity is only slightly smaller. It worries school officials and others because girls who don't play sports miss a wide range of benefits for their health and academic success. They are also in more danger of feeling left out of their school.

Experts say promoting sports to prevent these problems is crucial for Hispanic girls because they are at greater risk for problems such as teen pregnancy and obesity and are more likely to drop out of school than non-Hispanics.

The number of girls involved is substantial. Hispanics have surpassed African-Americans as the nation's largest minority group. In October 2002, the census reported there were 1.8 million Hispanic females ages 14 to 19, slightly less than African-American males in the same age group.

Hernandez, 16, is an example of a growing number of Hispanic girls who are closing the athletic gap by casting aside cultural tradition and convincing reluctant parents that sports can be an avenue for staying out of trouble and getting better grades—and perhaps a ticket to a college education.

Many are the first females in their families to play sports, unbound by a custom that dictates girls help with the family after school; boys often have more freedom. Some families maintain this practice simply because everyone needs to help to survive financially.

For the Hernandez family, it was a difficult decision to let Korina play: Her parents were both working, and her mother needed someone to help care for younger daughter Ashley. "But it was something I really wanted to do," Korina says. "I kind of convinced her to let me play." Her parents found an after-school program for Ashley instead.

From *USA Today*, 28 March 2003. From USA TODAY, a division of Gannett Co., Inc. Reprinted with permission.

202 WOMEN AND SPORTS IN THE UNITED STATES

This type of situation is key to why Hispanic girls have a lower sports participation rate than non-Hispanic peers, according to numerous athletes, parents, athletic directors, coaches and researchers. Practical problems, such as lack of money or transportation, also are factors but are common for other girls, too.

Rosa Perez knows about this firsthand. She defied her parents' wishes and played softball in high school and at Stanford, where she graduated in 1971. Now she frequently meets with Hispanic parents who are reluctant to let their daughters play sports at Cañada College, a Redwood City, Calif., community college.

"The issue of participation in athletics first and foremost has to do with the responsibilities (Hispanic) girls still have in traditional households," says Perez, 55, who is president of the college. "A lot of our Latino families are still either first- or second-generation immigrants. . . . But it is changing, and especially with those people who were raised in the United States."

It's Not Just About Money

Nationally, about 36% of Hispanic sophomore girls played interscholastic sports, compared with 52% of non-Hispanics for the 2001–02 school year, according to a *USA Today* analysis of the most recent U.S. Department of Education survey data.

The data show the low participation rate isn't just about money. Hispanic girls from high-income homes also lag behind non-Hispanic peers, while the gap between boys of different ethnicities is much less pronounced. The participation rate for Hispanic boys is 50%, compared with 57% for non-Hispanics.

High school sports participation data, collected by state high school associations, do not include race or ethnicity. As a result, the education survey is the only available snapshot to quantify such participation.

Coaches and athletics directors across the country say they have had difficulty encouraging Hispanic girls to play sports, often because of parental reluctance.

"Most of these girls are athletically inclined," says Raul Hodgers, athletics director at Tucson's Desert View High School, which is 80% Hispanic. "But it's difficult to acclimate parents to the idea of kids staying after school."

Schools in Mexico, where the majority of Hispanic-Americans come from, don't have after-school activities, Hodgers says. That time is reserved for family obligations. When Mexican families arrive in the USA, the idea of after-school activities is even more problematic because they often don't have the money or time to shuttle kids to practice or to attend games.

Struggling to Make It Possible

This has been a struggle for Korina Hernandez's parents, Anita, 38, and Guadalupe, 39 "At first it was hard because I was working, and there were times when I couldn't be there," says her mother, who recently was laid off from a Wal-Mart distribution center and is studying at a local college to be a radiology technician. "It wasn't that I didn't support her."

Supporting Korina's wishes is important to Anita Hernandez because she had been denied that as a child. The daughter of migrant workers who spent the school year in Texas, Anita joined the band to play saxophone but her parents never came to performances. When she asked to become a cheerleader, her parents refused. They didn't have time, she says, but also "they didn't think it was important for me."

"I didn't want to do the same thing to my girls," she says. Her oldest, Ruby, now 21, was a cheerleader. Korina wants to play basketball in college. And now, Ashley, 11, plays basketball, too.

Ultimately, the deciding factor for the Hernandez family was the benefits after-school activities could provide. They made a deal: their daughters could participate as long as they help when their parents work overtime and they keep their grades up.

"My husband and I . . . thought it was something good for (Korina), and we knew that she was there practicing and not in the streets or hanging around with bad influences," Anita Hernandez says.

Greeley Central officials have stepped up their efforts in recent years to encourage more Hispanics, especially girls, to participate in school activities. This includes parent meetings for incoming freshmen in their own neighborhoods, instead of at the high school, and efforts by coaches to reach out to potential players, athletics director John Bettolo says.

Girls basketball coach John Steckel says talented girls play pickup basketball regularly in many Hispanic neighborhoods but don't join the school team.

"If we don't overcome this, I don't know if we'll ever recover from not making them a part of their school," says Steckel, who just finished his first season as head coach. "If you don't feel a part of your school, you're not going to have a very enjoyable high school career and possibly even postsecondary school. If they don't buy into it, we may never get them back."

Schools Sell Parents on Benefits

School officials in Greeley and at other schools across the country are focusing their efforts on telling Hispanic parents about the academic and other long-term benefits that sports can provide.

Bert Otero, who has coached softball at Tucson's Desert View High for 20 years, says, "It used to be that after high school you went to work. A lot of that was the old-school way of thinking. Now it's really being made the forefront that education is a path to further your goals in life."

The well-respected 1989 Women's Sports Foundation report *Minorities in Sports* found Hispanic female athletes are at least twice as likely as non-athletes to attend and stay in college. This report remains the only research linking minority involvement in sports with academic success. More recent studies also have found sports can reduce numerous health problems—such as obesity and diabetes—and reduce the likelihood of teen pregnancy, alcohol and drug use or eating disorders for all girls.

"The racial/ethnic sub-group to benefit the most from sports participation is Latina girls," Women's Sports Foundation executive director Donna Lopiano says. "There's no question that if we can solve the problem of parental support . . . and create a more nurturing, motivating environment . . . that we can make some great contributions to Hispanic girls in terms of their future health and well-being."

Crystl Bustos, a two-time Olympic gold medalist with the U.S. softball team, says lack of money shouldn't be an obstacle. Bustos, 27, says her family didn't always have the money to buy good equipment. When she speaks to Hispanic kids across the nation, Bustos talks of how she and her siblings made bats from broomsticks and balls from duct tape and stuffing while growing up in Granada Hills, Calif.

"I want them to understand it's hard, but there are ways," Bustos says. "You don't have to have the best equipment or the newest equipment. If you want it, you can do it." That's the mantra her father drilled into her.

"I was fortunate," Bustos says. "My parents, all my uncles and cousins were behind me since I was little. It took a whole family effort to get where I'm at right now."

Perez, gender equity committee chair for the Commission on Athletics for California Community Colleges, says hurdles remain in involving more Hispanic girls. Perez informally asked athletics directors at some of the community colleges with large Hispanic enrollments what they have done to attract Latinas. Reponses ranged from "not aware of anything" to some who had worked with high school parents to raise awareness of scholarship opportunities, Perez says.

At Kennedy High in Granada Hills, which is about 80% Hispanic, athletics director Rae Brittain says it's still common for girls to drop out because they need to stay home to babysit. But a push to encourage athletics as a positive step toward college is bringing more Hispanic girls to sports. "The tides are definitely changing," Brittain says. "In the past you didn't see that many Hispanic women (athletes). You will in the coming years start to see multitudes of them."

ON THE REZ

Ian Frazier

SuAnne Marie Big Crow was born on March 15, 1974, at Pine Ridge Hospital—the brick building, now no longer a hospital, just uphill from the four-way intersection in town. Her mother, Leatrice Big Crow, known as Chick, was twenty-five years old. Chick had two other daughters: Cecelia, Called Cee Cee, who was three, and Frances, called Pigeon, who was five. Chick had been born a Big Crow, and grew up in her grandmother Big Crow's house in Wolf Creek, a little community about seven miles east of Pine Ridge. Chick had a round, pretty face, dark eyes, a determined chin, and wiry reddish-brown hair. Her figure was big-shouldered and trim; she had been a good athlete as a girl. Now she worked as an administrative assistant for the tribal planning office and she was raising her daughters alone with the help of her sisters and other kin. [. . .]

As strongly as Chick forbade certain activities, she encouraged the girls in sports. At one time or another, they did them all—cross-country running and track, volleyball, cheerleading, basketball, softball. Some of the teams were at school and others were sponsored by organizations in town. Chick's sister, Yvonne "Tiny" De Cory, had a cheerleading drill team called the Tiny Tots, a group of girls eight years old and under who performed at local sporting events and gatherings. SuAnne became a featured star for the Tiny Tots when she was three; many in Pine Ridge remember first seeing her or hearing about her then. She began to play on her big sisters' league softball team at about the same time, when the bat was still taller than she was. Coaches would send SuAnne in to pinch-hit, hoping for a walk, and telling her not to swing. Often she swung anyway; once, in a tie game, she swung at the third strike, the catcher dropped it, and several errors later she had rounded the bases for the winning run.

Excerpted from Ian Frazier, *On the Rez*. New York: Picador, 2001.

Pine Ridge had a winter basketball league for girls aged seven to eleven, and SuAnne later recalled that she played her first organized game in that league when she was in kindergarten. She had gone with her sisters to a tournament in Rushville when a sudden snowstorm kept some of the players away. The coach, finding himself short-handed, put SuAnne in the game. "It was funny," SuAnne told a basketball magazine, "because all I really knew how to do was play defense, so that's all I did. I not only took the ball away from our opponents, but also from my own teammates!" A coach who watched her play then said, "If you ever saw the movie *Star Wars*—well, you remember the Ewoks? Well, SuAnne was so much smaller than the other kids, she looked like one of those little Ewoks out there runnin' around."

In the West, girls' basketball is a bigger deal than it is elsewhere. High school girls' basketball games in states like South Dakota and Montana draw full-house crowds, and newspapers and college recruiters give nearly the same attention to star players who are girls as they do to stars who are boys. There were many good players on the girls' teams at Pine Ridge High School and at the Red Cloud School when SuAnne was little. SuAnne idolized a star for the Pine Ridge Lady Thorpes named Lolly Steele, who set many records at the school. On a national level, SuAnne's hero was Earvin "Magic" Johnson, of the Los Angeles Lakers pro team. Women's professional basketball did not exist in those years, but men's pro games were reaching a level of popularity to challenge baseball and football. SuAnne had big posters of Magic Johnson on her bedroom walls.

She spent endless hours practicing basketball. When she was in the fifth grade she heard somewhere that to improve your dribbling you should bounce a basketball a thousand times a day with each hand. She followed this daily exercise faithfully on the cement floor of the patio; her mother and sisters got tired of the sound. For variety, she would shoot layups against the gutter and the drainpipe, until they came loose from the house and had to be repaired. She knew that no girl in an official game had ever dunked a basketball—that is, had leaped as high as the rim and stuffed the ball through the hoop from above—and she wanted to be the first in history to do it. To get the feel, she persuaded a younger boy cousin to kneel on all fours under the basket. With a running start and a leap using the boy's back as a springboard, she could dunk the ball.

Charles Zimiga, who would coach SuAnne in basketball during her high school years, remembered the first time he saw her. He was on the cross-country track on the old golf course coaching the high school boys' cross-country team—a team that later won the state championship—when SuAnne came running by. She was in seventh grade at the time. She practiced cross-country every fall, and ran in amateur meets, and sometimes placed high enough to be invited to tournaments in Boston and California. "The fluidness of her running amazed me, and the strength she had," Zimiga said. "I stood watching her go by and she stopped right in front of me—I'm a high school coach remember, and she's just a young little girl—and she said, 'What're you lookin' at?' I said, 'A runner.' She would've been a top cross-country runner, but in high school it never did work out, because the season conflicted with basketball. I had heard about her before, but that day on the golf course was the first time I really noticed her."

SuAnne went to elementary school in Wolf Creek, because of her family's connection there. Zimiga and others wanted her to come to Pine Ridge High School so she could play on the basketball team, and finally they persuaded Chick to let her transfer when she was in junior high. By the time SuAnne was in eighth grade, she had grown to five feet, five inches tall ("but she played six foot," Zimiga said); she was long-limbed, well-muscled, and quick. She had high cheekbones, a prominent, arched upper lip that lined up with the basket when she aimed the ball, and short hair that she wore in no particular style. She could have played every game for the varsity when she was in eighth grade, but Coach Zimiga, who took over girls' varsity basketball that year, wanted to keep peace among older players who had waited for their chance to be on the team. He kept SuAnne on the junior varsity during the regular season. The varsity team had a good year, and when it advanced to the district playoffs, Zimiga brought SuAnne up from the JVs for the play-off games. Several times she got into foul trouble; the referees rule strictly in tournament games, and SuAnne was used to a more headlong style of play. She and her cousin Doni De Cory, a 5'10" junior, combined for many long-break baskets, with Doni throwing downcourt passes to SuAnne on the scoring end. In the district play-off against the team from Red Cloud, SuAnne scored thirty-one points. In the regional play-off game, Pine Ridge beat a good Todd County team, but in the state tournament they lost all three games and finished eighth.

Some people who live in the cities and towns near reservations treat their Indian neighbors decently; some don't. In cities like Denver and Minneapolis and Rapid City, police have been known to harass Indian teenagers and rough up Indian drunks and needlessly stop and search Indian cars. Local banks whose deposits include millions in tribal funds sometimes charge Indians higher loan interest rates than they charge whites. Gift shops near reservations sell junky caricature Indian pictures and dolls, and until not long ago, beer coolers had signs on them that said, INDIAN POWER. In a big discount store in a reservation border town, a white clerk observes a lot of Indians waiting at the checkout and remarks,

"Oh, they're Indians—they're used to standing in line." Some people in South Dakota hate Indians, unapologetically, and will tell you why; in their voices you can hear a particular American meanness that is centuries old.

When teams from Pine Ridge play non-Indian teams, the question of race is always there. When Pine Ridge is the visiting team, usually their hosts are courteous, and the players and fans have a good time. But Pine Ridge coaches know that occasionally at away games their kids will be insulted, their fans will not feel welcome, the host gym will be dense with hostility, and the referees will call fouls on Indian players every chance they get. Sometimes in a game between Indian and non-Indian teams, the difference in race becomes an important and distracting part of the event.

One place where Pine Ridge teams used to get harassed regularly was in the high school gymnasium in Lead, South Dakota. Lead is a town of about 3,200 northwest of the reservation, in the Black Hills. It is laid out among the mines that are its main industry, and low, wooded mountains hedge it round. The brick high school building is set into a hillside. The school's only gym in those days was small, with tiers of gray-painted concrete on which the spectator benches descended from just below the steel-beamed roof to the very edge of the basketball court—an arrangement that greatly magnified the interior noise.

In the fall of 1988, the Pine Ridge Lady Thorpes went to Lead to play a basketball game. SuAnne was a full member of the team by then. She was a freshman, fourteen years old. Getting ready in the locker room, the Pine Ridge girls could hear the din from the fans. They were yelling fake-Indian war cries, a "woo-woo-woo" sound. The usual play for a pre-game warm-up was for the visiting team to run onto the court in a line, take a lap or two around the floor, shoot some baskets, and then go to their bench at courtside. After that, the home team would come out and do the same, and then the game would begin. Usually the Thorpes lined up for their entry more or less according to height, which meant that senior Doni De Cory, one of the tallest, went first. As the team waited in the hallway leading from the locker room, the heckling got louder. A typical kind of hollered remark was "Squaw!" or "Where's the cheese?" (the joke being that if Indians were lining up, it must be to get commodity cheese); today no one remembers exactly what was said. Doni De Cory looked out the door and told her teammates, "I can't handle this." SuAnne quickly offered to go first in her place. She was so eager that Doni became suspicious. "Don't embarrass us," Doni told her. SuAnne said, "I won't. I won't embarrass you." Doni gave her the ball, and SuAnne stood first in line.

She came running onto the court dribbling the basketball, with her teammates running behind. On the court, the noise was deafeningly loud. SuAnne went right down the middle; but instead of running a full lap, she suddenly stopped when she got to center court. Her teammates were taken by surprise, and some bumped into one another. Coach Zimiga at the rear of the line did not know why they had stopped. SuAnne turned to Doni De Cory and tossed her the ball. Then she stepped into the jump-ball circle at center court, in front of the Lead fans. She unbuttoned her warm-up jacket, took it off, draped it over her shoulders, and began to do the Lakota shawl dance. SuAnne knew all the traditional dances—she had competed in many powwows as a little girl—and the dance she chose is a young woman's dance, graceful and modest and show-offy all at the same time. "I couldn't believe it—she was powwowin', like 'get down!'" Doni De Cory recalled. "And then she started to sing." SuAnne began to sing in Lakota, swaying back and forth in the jump-ball circle, doing the shawl dance, using her warm-up jacket for a shawl. The crowd went completely silent. "All that stuff the Lead fans were yelling—it was like she *reversed* it somehow," a teammate said. In the sudden quiet, all you could hear was her Lakota song. SuAnne stood up, dropped her jacket, took the ball from Doni De Cory, and ran a lap around the court dribbling expertly and fast. The fans began to cheer and applaud. She sprinted to the basket, went up in the air, and laid the ball through the hoop, with the fans cheering loudly now. Of course, Pine Ridge went on to win the game.

This story, which was published first in a newspaper article at the time of SuAnne's death, is not quite accurate. The game took place not in 1988 but in 1987, when SuAnne was in eighth grade, and Pine Ridge did not win it, but lost in the last three seconds 66–64. Today no one in Lead seems to remember SuAnne's center-court dance. But because the story sums up so well the way people in Pine Ridge felt about SuAnne, and because it recounts one of the coolest and bravest deeds I ever heard of, I would like to consider it from a larger perspective that includes the town of Lead, all the Black Hills, and 125 years of history.

Lead, the town, does not get its name from the metal. The lead the name refers to is a mining term for a gold-bearing deposit, or vein, running through surrounding rock. The word, pronounced with a long *e,* is related to the word "lode." During the Black Hills gold rush of the 1870s, prospectors found a rich lead in what would become the town of Lead. In April 1876, Fred and Moses Manuel staked a claim to a mine they called the Homestake. Their lead led eventually to gold and more gold—a small mountain of gold—whose value may be guessed by the size of the hole its extraction has left in the middle of present-day Lead.

In 1877, a mining engineer from San Francisco named George Hearst came to the Hills, investigated the Manuels' mine, and advised his big-city

partners to buy it. The price was $70,000. At the time of Hearst's nego-
tiations, the illegal act of Congress which would take this land from the
Sioux had only recently passed. The partners followed Hearst's advice
and the Homestake Mine paid off its purchase price four times over in
dividends alone within three years. When George Hearst's only son, William Randolph, was kicked out of Harvard for giving his instructors
chamber pots with their names inscribed on the inside, George Hearst
suggested that he come West and take over his (George's) share in the
Homestake Mine. William Randolph Hearst chose to run the San Francisco *Examiner* instead. His father gave him a blank check to keep it
going for two years; gold from Lead helped start the Hearst newspaper
empire. Since the Homestake Mine was discovered, it has produced at
least $10 billion in gold. It is one of the richest gold mines in the world.

Almost from the moment of the Custer expedition's entry into the
Black Hills in 1874, there was no way the Sioux were going to be allowed to keep this land. By 1875, the Dakota Territorial Legislature had
already divided the Black Hills land into counties; Custer County, in the
southern Hills, was named in that general's honor while he was still
alive, and while the land still clearly belonged to the Sioux. Many people
in government and elsewhere knew at the time that taking this land was
wrong. At first, the Army even made halfhearted attempts to keep the
prospectors out. A high-ranking treaty negotiator told President Grant
that the Custer expedition was "a violation of the national honor." One
of the commissioners who worked on the "agreement" that gave paper
legitimacy to the theft said that Custer should not have gone into the
Hills in the first place; he and the other commissioners reminded the
government that it was making the Sioux homeless and that it owed
them protection and care. The taking of the Black Hills proceeded inex-
orably all the same.

Sioux leaders of Crazy Horse's generation began working to receive
fair compensation for the Hills in the early 1900s. The Black Hills claim
which the Sioux filed with the U.S. Court of Claims in the 1920s got nowhere. In 1946, the government established the Indian Claims Commission specifically to provide payment for wrongly taken Indian lands, and
in 1950 the Sioux filed a claim for the Black Hills with the ICC. After almost twenty-five years of historical research and esoteric legal back-and-
forth, the ICC finally ruled that the Sioux were entitled to a payment of
$17.5 million plus interest for the taking of the Hills. Further legal ma-
neuvering ensued. In 1980 the Supreme Court affirmed the ruling and
awarded the Sioux a total of $106 million. Justice Harry Blackmun, for
the majority, wrote: "A more ripe and rank case of dishonorable dealings
will never, in all probability, be found in our history"—which was to say
officially, and finally, that the Black Hills had been stolen.

By the time of the Supreme Court ruling, however, the Sioux had come to see their identity as linked to the Hills themselves, and the eight tribes involved decided unanimously not to accept the money. They said, "The Black Hills are not for sale." The Sioux now wanted the land back—some or all of it—and trespass damages as well. They especially wanted the Black Hills lands still owned by the federal government. These amount to about 1.3 million acres, a small proportion of what was stolen. At the moment, the chances of the Sioux getting these or any lands in the Black Hills appear remote. The untouched compensation money remains in a federal escrow account, where it, plus other compensation moneys, plus accumulated interest, is now over half a billion dollars.

Inescapably, this history is present when an Oglala team goes to Lead to play a basketball game. It may even explain why the fans in Lead were so mean: being in the wrong to begin with can make you ornerier sometimes. In all the accounts of this land grab and its aftermath, and among the many greedy and driven men who had a part, I cannot find evidence of a single act as elegant, as generous, or as transcendent as SuAnne's dance in the gym at Lead.

For the Oglala, what SuAnne did that day almost immediately took on the stature of myth. People from Pine Ridge still describe it in terms of awe and disbelief. Amazement swept through the younger kids when they heard. "I was, like, '*What* did she just do?'" recalled her cousin Angie Big Crow, an eighth-grader at the time. All over the reservation, people told and retold the story of SuAnne at Lead. Any time the subject of SuAnne came up when I was talking to people on Pine Ridge, I would always ask if they had heard about what she did at Lead, and always the answer was a smile and a nod—"Yeah, I heard about that." To the unnumbered big and small slights of local racism which the Oglala have known all their lives, SuAnne's exploit made an emphatic reply.

Back in the days when Lakota war parties still fought battles against other tribes and the Army, no deed of war was more honored than the act of counting coup. To count coup means to touch an armed enemy in full possession of his powers with a special stick called a coup stick, or with the hand. The touch is not a blow, and only serves to indicate how close to the enemy you came. As an act of bravery, counting coup was regarded as greater than killing an enemy in single combat, greater than taking a scalp or horses or any prize. Counting coup was an act of almost abstract courage, of pure playfulness taken to the most daring extreme. Very likely, to do it and survive brought an exhilaration to which nothing could compare. In an ancient sense which her Oglala kin could recognize, SuAnne counted coup on the hecklers at Lead.

And yet this coup was an act not of war but of peace. SuAnne's coup strike was an offering, an invitation. It took the hecklers at the best interpretation, as if their silly mocking chants were meant only in good-will. It showed that their fake Indian songs were just that—fake—and that the real thing was better, as real things usually are. We Lakota have been dancing like this for centuries, the dance said; we've been doing the shawl dance since long before you came, before you had gotten on the boat in Glasgow or Bremerhaven, before you stole this land, and we're still doing it today; and isn't it pretty, when you see how it's supposed to be done? Because finally what SuAnne proposed was to invite us—us on-lookers in the stands, which is the non-Lakota rest of this country—to dance, too. She was in the Lead gym to play, and she invited us all to play. The symbol she used to include us was the warm-up jacket. Every-one in America has a warm-up jacket. I've got one, probably so do you, so did (no doubt) many of the fans at Lead. By using the warm-up jacket as a shawl in her impromptu shawl dance, she made Lakota relatives of us all.

"It was funny," Doni De Cory said, "but after that game the relation-ship between Lead and us was tremendous. When we played Lead again, the games were really good, and we got to know some of the girls on the team. Later, when we went to a tournament and Lead was there, we were hanging out with the Lead girls and eating pizza with them. We got to know some of their parents, too. What SuAnne did made a lasting im-pression and changed the whole situation with us and Lead. We found out there are some really good people in Lead."

America is a leap of the imagination. From its beginning, people had only a persistent idea of what a good country should be. The idea involved freedom, equality, justice, and the pursuit of happiness; nowadays most of us probably could not describe it a lot more clearly than that. The truth is, it always has been a bit of a guess. No one has ever known for sure whether a country based on such an idea is really possible, but again and again we have leaped toward the idea and hoped. What SuAnne Big Crow demonstrated in the Lead high school gym is that making the leap is the whole point. The idea does not truly live unless it is expressed by an act; the country does not live unless we make the leap from our tribe or focus group or gated community or demographic, and land on the shaky platform of that idea of a good country which all kinds of different peo-ple share.

This leap is made in public, and it's made for free. It's not a product or a service that anyone will pay you for. You do it for reasons unexplain-able by economics—for ambition, out of conviction, for the heck of it, in playfulness, for love. It's done in public spaces, face-to-face, where any-one is free to go. It's not done on television, or the Internet, or over the telephone; our electronic systems can only tell us if the leap made elsewhere has succeeded or failed. The places you'll see it are high school gyms, city sidewalks, the subway, bus stations, public parks, parking lots, and wherever people gather during natural disasters. In those places and others like them, the leaps that continue to invent and knit the country continue to be made. When the leap fails, it looks like the L.A. riots, or Sherman's March through Georgia. When it succeeds, it looks like the New York City Bicentennial Celebration in July 1976, or the Civil Rights March on Washington in 1963. On that scale, whether it succeeds or fails, it's always something to see. The leap requires physical presence and physical risk. But the payoff—in terms of dreams realized, of understanding, of people getting along—can be so glorious as to make the risk seem minuscule.

I find all this hopefulness, and more, in SuAnne's dance in the gym in Lead. My high school football coach used to show us films of our previous game every Monday after practice, and whenever he liked a particular play, he would run it over and over again. If I had a film of SuAnne at Lead (as far as I know, no such film or video exists), I would study it in slow motion frame by frame. There's a magic in what she did, along with the promise that public acts of courage are still alive out there somewhere. Mostly, I would run the film of SuAnne again and again for my own braveheart song. I refer to her, as I do to Crazy Horse, for proof that it's a public service to be brave.

PART V

Sexuality and Sport

Part V builds upon previous sections' explorations of the physical and emotional passions that inspire athletes by taking a closer look at the complex relationship between sexuality and sport. Why would sexuality be any more relevant or important in sports than in other cultural pursuits like playing chess or singing in a choir? The physicality of sport, its associations with the revealed body (especially in sports like track, volleyball, and swimming where uniforms leave most of the body exposed), and the images of unleashed, raw or primal passion stirred by "naked competition" mirror qualities we associate with sexuality. Moreover, in sport we also value the intimacy forged among teammates, encouraging forms of intimate touch (like hugging, or patting the butt of another player) that would otherwise be seen as inappropriate displays of public affection, especially between two men or two women. Finally, notions of male physical prowess permeate both masculine sport and male heterosexuality, so that ideals of masculine sexual/physical skill in sport reinforce and are reinforced by the broader culture of American sexuality.

This connection between sport and sexuality, coupled with the dominant heterosexual culture in which most athletic activities occur, has created a climate of homophobia that pervades sports in the United States. Initially, a belief that sport unleashed physical passion and erotic feelings made some observers fear that female athleticism was sexually dangerous and would initiate a downward slide toward loose morals and loss of libidinal control in heterosexual relations. The perceived masculine nature of sports would, in this view, translate into a more masculine female eroticism—more aggressive, passionate, and imbued with a desire for dominance. These same concerns took a different course when observers feared that women athletes might gain masculine sexual attributes of another sort: they might become like (heterosexual) men in their strong attraction to and desire for other women. The underlying logic holds that if sports are masculine, and lesbianism is a form of masculinized female sexuality, then sport might appeal to—or even produce—women with same-sex attractions and a masculine eroticism. In "Changing the Game," Pat Griffin explores the many ways in which homophobia is perpetuated in women's sports and outlines ways in which sportswomen can confront homophobic attitudes and lessen their impact. Jim Buzinski's report on a University of Florida softball coach's alleged discrimination against her lesbian players reminds us that the issues Griffin raises are still very much with us. (Since the report's publication, the University of Florida settled the case out of court, admitting no wrongdoing but agreeing to provide all its coaches with diversity training dealing with homophobia. In 2005, Florida did not renew its head softball coach's contract.) In an arena in which homosexuality is so feared, accusations of lesbianism can be and are used to discredit particular athletes or entire sports.

Sport and sexuality have other connections as well, especially the shared importance of both physical pleasure and power. Selections in Part V explore these dynamics as they have contributed both positively and negatively to athletic experience. In "Less Ugly," Lesléa Newman lets the reader experience the joy of a lesbian sportswoman coming to enjoy her body, fall in love, and understand her sexual desires through participation in sport. Cynthia Hanson presents the dark side of sexuality and sport, exploring the ways in which sexuality can become a weapon in sports through sexual harassment and inappropriate sexual relations between male coaches and female players.

Part V ends with a recent controversy that blurs the line between erotic pleasure and exploitation. At the turn of the 21st century, some female athletes renowned for their strong, sexually appealing bodies have taken advantage of opportunities to earn money, fame, or notoriety by posing nude or nearly nude in advertisements, calendars, or magazine feature stories. There is widespread disagreement among sports fans, women athletes themselves, and feminist sports advocates about how to interpret this turn of events. Critics such as Penny Hastings argue that valuing athletes on the basis of their sexual appeal is degrading. Overtly sexual posing sends a message that it is not enough to be a talented athlete; one must also be sexy and beautiful (by conventional standards) to gain the public's full appreciation. In this view, any arrangement in which sportsmen are appreciated primarily for their athletic prowess, not their looks, and sportswomen are valued more if their athleticism combines with beauty and sexual appeal perpetuates gender inequality. On the other hand, advocates like Tom Maloney argue that women have worked hard to develop their bodies and find pleasure in the lean muscularity they cultivate to excel in their sports. Given this, why not celebrate it publicly? Why not take advantage of economic opportunities in a culture of sport that is thoroughly commercialized and in which women, in the financial reward system of sports, have always received the short end of the stick? This debate highlights the complexity of the connections among the body, sexuality, and sport as well as the contradictory ways in which our culture first sexualizes women and then morally condemns them for becoming too sexual in a consumer society in which sex sells.

CHANGING THE GAME

Homophobia, Sexism, and Lesbians in Sport

Pat Griffin

Throughout the history of Western culture, restrictions have been placed on women's sport participation. These restrictions are enforced through sanctions that evolved to match each successive social climate. Women caught merely observing the male athletes competing in the early Greek Olympic Games were put to death. When Baron DeCoubertin revived the Olympic tradition in 1896, women were invited as spectators but barred from participation. Even in the present-day Olympic Games, women may compete in only one third of the events.

Although the death penalty for female spectators was too extreme for the late 19th and early 20th centuries, an increasingly influential medical establishment warned white upper-class women about the debilitating physiological effects of vigorous athleticism, particularly on the reproductive system. Women were cautioned about other "masculinizing effects" as well, such as deeper voices, facial hair, and overdeveloped arms and legs. The intent of these warnings was to temper and control women's sport participation and to keep women focused on their "natural" and "patriotic" roles as wives and mothers (Lenskyj, 1986).

During the 1920s and 1930s, as the predicted dire physical consequences proved untrue, strong social taboos restricting female athleticism evolved. Instead of warnings about facial hair and displaced uteruses, women in sport were intimidated by fears of losing social approval. Close female friendships, accepted and even idealized in the 19th century, became suspect when male sexologists like Freud "discovered" female sexuality in the early 20th century (Faderman, 1981, 1991; Katz, 1976). In the 1930s, as psychology and psychiatry became respected subfields in medicine, these doctors warned of a new menace. An entire typology was created to diagnose the "mannish lesbian," whose depraved sexual appetite and preference for masculine dress and activity were identified as symptoms of psychological disturbance (Newton, 1989). Social commentators in the popular press warned parents about the dangers of allowing impressionable daughters to spend time in all-female environments (Faderman, 1991; Smith-Rosenberg, 1989).

From *Quest* 44 (1992): 251–265.

As a result, women's colleges and sports teams were assumed to be places where mannish lesbians lurked. Women in sport and physical education especially fit the profile of women to watch out for: they were in groups without men, they were not engaged in activities thought to enhance their abilities to be good wives and mothers, and they were being physically active in sport, a male activity. Because lesbians were assumed to be masculine creatures who rejected their female identity and roles as wives and mothers, athletic women became highly suspect.

The image of the sick, masculine lesbian sexual predator and her associations with athleticism persists in the late 20th century. The power of this image to control and intimidate women is as strong today as it was 60 years ago. What accounts for the staying power of a stereotype that is so extreme it should be laughable except that so many people believe it to be accurate? Whose interests are served by stigmatizing lesbians and accusing women in sport of being lesbian? Why does sport participation by women in the late 20th century continue to be so threatening to the social order? How have women in sport responded to associations with lesbians? How effective have these responses been in defusing concern about lesbians in sport?

The purpose of this article is to discuss the issue of lesbians in sport from a feminist perspective that analyzes the function of socially constructed gender roles and sexual identities in maintaining male dominance in North American society. I share the perspective taken by other sport feminists that lesbian and feminist sport participation is a threat to male domination (Bennett, Whitaker, Smith, and Sablove 1986; Birrell and Richter, 1987; Hall, 1986, Lenskyj, 1986; Messner and Sabo, 1990). In a sexist and heterosexist society (in which heterosexuality is reified as the only normal, natural, and acceptable sexual orientation), women who defy the accepted feminine role or reject a heterosexual identity threaten to upset the imbalance of power enjoyed by white heterosexual men in a patriarchal society (Bryson, 1987). The creation of the mannish lesbian as a pathological condition by early 20th-century male medical doctors provided an effective means to control all women and neutralize challenges to the sexist status quo.

To understand the social stigma associated with lesbian participation in sport, the function of homophobia in maintaining the sexist and heterosexist status quo must be examined (Lenskyj, 1991). Greendorfer (1991) challenged the traditional definition of homophobia as an irrational fear and intolerance of lesbians and gay men. In questioning how irrational homophobia really is, Greendorfer highlighted the systematic and pervasive cultural nature of homophobia. Fear and hatred of lesbians and gay men is more than individual prejudice (Kitzinger, 1987). Homophobia is a powerful political weapon of sexism (Pharr, 1988). The lesbian label is used to define the boundaries of acceptable female behavior in a patriarchal culture: When a woman is called a lesbian, she knows she is out of bounds. Because lesbian identity carries the extreme negative social stigma created by early 20th-century sexologists, most women are loathe to be associated with it. Because women's sport has been labeled a lesbian activity, women in sport are particularly sensitive and vulnerable to the use of the lesbian label to intimidate.

How Is Homophobia Manifested in Women's Sport?

Manifestations of homophobia in women's sport can be divided into six categories: (1) silence, (b) denial, (c) apology, (d) promotion of a heterosexy image, (e) attacks on lesbians, and (f) preference for male coaches. An exploration of these manifestations illuminates the pervasive nature of prejudice against lesbians in sport and the power of the lesbian stigma to control and marginalize women's sport.

Silence
Silence is the most consistent and enduring manifestation of homophobia in women's sport. From Billie Jean King's revelation of a lesbian relationship in 1981 to the publicity surrounding Penn State women's basketball coach Rene Portland's no-lesbian policy (Lederman, 1991; Longman, 1991), the professional and college sports establishment responds with silence to eruptions of public attention to lesbians in sport. Reporters who attempt to discuss lesbians in sport with sport organizations, athletic directors, coaches, and athletes are typically rebuffed (Lipsyte, 1991), and women in sport wait, hoping the scrutiny will disappear as quickly as possible. Women live in fear that whatever meager gains we have made in sport are always one lesbian scandal away from being wiped out.

Even without the provocation of public scrutiny or threat of scandal, silent avoidance is the strategy of choice. Organizers of coaches' or athletic administrators' conferences rarely schedule programs on homophobia in sport, and when they do, it is always a controversial decision made with fear and concern about the consequences of public dialogue (Krebs, 1984; Lenskyj, 1990). Lesbians in sport are treated like nasty secrets that must be kept locked tightly in the closet. Lesbians, of course, are expected to maintain deep cover at all times. Not surprisingly, most lesbians in sport choose to remain hidden rather than face potential public condemnation. Friends of lesbians protect this secret from outsiders, and the unspoken pact of silence is maintained and passed on to each new generation of women in sport.

Silence has provided some protection. Keeping the closet door locked is an understandable strategy when women in sport are trying to gain social approval in a sexist society and there is no sense that change is possible. Maintaining silence is a survival strategy in a society hostile to women in general and lesbians in particular. How effectively silence enhances sport opportunities for women or defuses homophobia, however, is open to serious question.

Denial

If forced to break silence, many coaches, athletic directors, and athletes resort to denial. High school athletes and their parents often ask college coaches if there are lesbians in their programs. In response, many coaches deny that there are lesbians in sport, at least among athletes or coaches at *their* schools (Fields, 1983). These denials only serve to intensify curiosity and determination to find out who and where these mysterious women are. The closet, it turns out, is made of glass: People know lesbians are in sport despite these denials.

In some cases, parents and athletes who suspect that a respected and loved coach is a lesbian either deny or overlook her sexual identity because they cannot make sense of the apparent contradiction: a lesbian who is competent, loved, and respected. In other instances, a respected lesbian coach is seen as an exception because she does not fit the unflattering lesbian stereotype most people accept as accurate. The end result in any case is to deny the presence of lesbians in sport.

Apology

The third manifestation of homophobia in sport is apology (Felshin, 1974). In an attempt to compensate for an unsavory reputation, women in sport try to promote a feminine image and focus public attention on those who meet white heterosexual standards of beauty. Women in sport have a tradition of assuring ourselves and others that sport participation is consistent with traditional notions of femininity and that women are not masculinized by sport experiences (Gornick, 1971; Hicks, 1979; Locke and Jensen, 1970). To this end, athletes are encouraged, or required in some cases, to engage in the protective camouflage of feminine drag. Professional athletes and college teams are told to wear dresses or attend seminars to learn how to apply makeup, style hair, and select clothes ("Image Lady," 1987). Athletes are encouraged to be seen with boyfriends and reminded to act like ladies when away from the gym (DePaul University's 1984 women's basketball brochure).

The Women's Sports Foundation (WSF) annual dinner, attended by many well-known professional and amateur female athletes, is preceded by an opportunity for the athletes to get free hairstyling and makeup applications before they sit down to eat with the male corporate sponsors, whose money supports many WSF programs. The men attending the dinner are not offered similar help with their appearance. The message is that female athletes in their natural state are not acceptable or attractive and therefore must be fixed and "femmed up" to compensate for their athleticism.

Femininity, however, is a code word for heterosexuality. The underlying fear is not that a female athlete or coach will appear too plain or out of style, the real fear is that she will look like a dyke or, even worse, is one. This intense blend of homophobic and sexist standards of feminine attractiveness remind women in sport that to be acceptable, we must monitor our behavior and appearance at all times.

Silence, denial, and apology are defensive reactions that reflect the power of the lesbian label to intimidate women. These responses ensure that women's sport will be held hostage to the *L* word. As long as questions about lesbians in sport are met with silence, denial, and apology, women can be sent scurrying back to our places on the margins of sport, grateful for the modicum of public approval we have achieved and fearful of losing it.

New Manifestations of Homophobia in Women's Sport

In the last 10 years, three more responses have developed in reaction to the persistence of the association of sport with lesbians. These manifestations have developed at the same time that women's sport has become more visible, potentially marketable, and increasingly under the control of men and men's sport organizations. Representing an intensified effort to purge the lesbian image, these new strategies reflect a new low in mean-spirited intimidation.

Promotion of a Heterosexy Image
Where presenting a feminine image previously sufficed, corporate sponsors, professional women's sport organizations, some women's college teams, and individual athletes have moved beyond presenting a feminine image to adopting a more explicit display of heterosex appeal. The Ladies Professional Golf Associations' 1989 promotional material featured photographs of its pro golfers posing pin-up style in swimsuits (Diaz, 1989). College sport promotional literature has employed double entendres and sexual innuendo to sell women's teams. The women's basketball promotional brochure from Northwestern State University of Louisiana included a photograph of the women's team dressed in Playboy bunny outfits. The copy crowed "These girls can play, boy!" and invited basketball

fans to watch games in the "Pleasure Palace" (Solomon, 1991). Popular magazines have featured young, professional female athletes, like Monica Seles or Steffi Graf, in cleavage-revealing heterosexual glamour drag (Kiersh, 1990).

In a more muted attempt to project a heterosexual image, stories about married female athletes and coaches routinely include husbands and children in ways rarely seen when male coaches and athletes are profiled. A recent nationally televised basketball game between the women's teams from the University of Texas and the University of Tennessee featured a half-time profile of the coaches as wives and mothers. The popular press also brings us testimonials from female athletes who have had children claiming that their athletic performance has improved since becoming mothers. All of this to reassure the public, and perhaps ourselves as women in sport, that we are normal despite our athletic interests.

Attacks on Lesbians in Sport
Women in sport endure intense scrutiny of our collective and individual femininity and sexual identities. Innuendo, concern, and prurient curiosity about the sexual identity of female coaches and athletes come from coaches, athletic directors, sports reporters, parents of female athletes, teammates, fans, and the general public (South, Glynn, Rodack, and Capettini, 1990). This manifestation of homophobia is familiar to most people associated with women's sport. Over the last 10 to 12 years, however, concern about lesbians in sport has taken a nasty turn.

Though lesbians in sport have always felt pressure to stay closeted, coaches and athletic directors now openly prohibit lesbian coaches and athletes (Brownworth, 1991; Figel, 1986; Longman, 1991). In a style reminiscent of 1950s McCarthyism, some coaches proclaim their antilesbian policies as an introduction to their programs. Athletes thought to be lesbians are dropped from teams, find themselves benched, or are suddenly ostracized by coaches and teammates (Brownworth, 1991). At some schools, a new coach's heterosexual credentials are scrutinized as carefully as her professional qualifications (Fields, 1983). Coaches thought to be lesbians are fired or intimidated into resigning. These dismissals are not the result of any unethical behavior on the part of the women accused but simply because of assumptions made about their sexual identity.

Collegiate and high school female athletes endure lesbian-baiting (name-calling, taunting, and other forms of harassment) from male athletes, heterosexual teammates, opposing teams, spectators, classmates, and sometimes their own coaches (Brownworth, 1991; Fields, 1983; Spander, 1991; Thomas, 1990). Female coaches thought to be lesbians endure harassing phone calls and antilesbian graffiti slipped under their doors. During a recent National Collegiate Athletic Association (NCAA) women's basketball championship, it was rumored that a group of male coaches went to the local lesbian bar to spy on lesbian coaches who might be there. Another rumor circulated about a list categorizing Division I women's basketball coaches by their sexual identity so that parents of prospective athletes could use this information to avoid schools where lesbians coach. Whether or not these rumors are true doesn't matter: The rumor itself is intimidating enough to remind women in sport that we are being watched and that if we step out of line, we will be punished.

Negative recruiting is perhaps the most self-serving of all the attacks on lesbians in sport. Negative recruiting occurs when college coaches or athletic department personnel reassure prospective athletes and their parents not only that there are no lesbians in this program but also that there *are* lesbians in a rival school's program (Fields, 1983). By playing on parents' and athletes' fear and ignorance, these coaches imply that young women will be safe in their programs but not at a rival school where bull dykes stalk the locker room in search of fresh young conquests.

Fears about lesbian stereotypes are fueled by a high-profile Christian presence at many national championships and coaches' conferences. The Fellowship of Christian Athletes, which regularly sponsors meal functions for coaches at these events, distributes a free antihomosexual booklet to coaches and athletes. Entitled *Emotional Dependency: A Threat to Close Friendships*, this booklet plays into all of the stereotypes of lesbians (Rentzel, 1987). A drawing of a sad young woman and an older woman on the cover hints at the dangers of close female friendships. Unencumbered by any reasonable factual knowledge about homosexuality, the booklet identifies the symptoms of emotional dependency and how this "leads" to homosexual relationships. Finally, the path out of this "counterfeit" intimacy through prayer and discipline is described. The booklet is published by Exodus, a fundamentalist Christian organization devoted to the "redemption" of homosexuals from their "disorder."

By allowing the active participation of antigay organizations in coaches' meetings and championship events, sport governing bodies like the NCAA and the Women's Basketball Coaches' Association are taking an active role in the perpetuation of discrimination against lesbians in sport and the stigmatization of all friendships among women in sport. In this intimidating climate, all women in sport must deal with the double burden of maintaining high-profile heterosexual images and living in terror of being called lesbians.

Preference for Male Coaches
Many parents, athletes, and athletic administrators prefer that men coach women's teams. This preference reflects a lethal mix of sexism and

homophobia. Some people believe, based on gender and lesbian stereotypes, that men are better coaches than women. Although a recent NCAA survey of female athletes (NCAA, 1991) indicated that 61% of the respondents did not have a gender preference for their coaches, respondents were concerned about the images they thought male and female coaches had among their friends and family: 65% believed that female coaches were looked upon favorably by family and friends whereas 84% believed that male coaches were looked on favorably by family and friends.

Recent studies have documented the increase in the number of men coaching women's teams (Acosta and Carpenter, 1988). At least part of this increase can be attributed to homophobia. Thorngren (1991), in a study of female coaches, asked respondents how homophobia affected them. These coaches identified hiring and job retention as problems. They cited examples where men were hired to coach women's teams specifically to change a tarnished or negative (read *lesbian*) team image. Thorngren described this as a "cloaking" phenomenon, in which a team's lesbian image is hidden or countered by the presence of a male coach. Consistent with this perception, anecdotal reports from other female head coaches reveal that some believe it essential to hire a male assistant coach to lend a heterosexual persona to a women's team. The coaches in Thorngren's study also reported that women (married and single) leave coaching because of the pressure and stress of constantly having to deal with lesbian labels and stereotypes. Looking at the increase in the number of men coaching women's teams over the last 10 years, it is clear how male coaches have benefited from sexism and homophobia in women's sport.

Suspicion, Collusion, and Betrayal among Women in Sport

The few research studies addressing homophobia or lesbians in sport, as well as informal anecdotal information, have revealed that many women have internalized sexist and homophobic values and beliefs (Blinde, 1990; Griffin, 1987; Guthrie, 1982; Morgan, 1990; Thorngren, 1990, 1991; Woods, 1990). Blinde interviewed women athletes about the pressures and stress they experienced. Many talked about the lesbian image women's sport has and the shame they felt about being female athletes because of that image. Their discomfort with the topic was illustrated by their inability to even say the word *lesbian*. Instead, they made indirect references to *it* as a problem. Athletes talked in ways that clearly indicated they had bought into the negative images of lesbians, even as they denied that there were lesbians on their teams. These athletes also subscribed to the importance of projecting a feminine image and were discomforted by female athletes who didn't look or act feminine.

Quotes selected to accompany the NCAA survey and the Blinde study illustrate the degree to which many female athletes and coaches accept both the negative stigma attached to lesbian identity and the desirability of projecting a traditionally feminine image:

The negative image of women in intercollegiate sport scares me. I've met too many lesbians in my college career. I don't want to have that image. (NCAA)

Well, if you come and look at our team, I mean, if you saw Jane Doe, she's very pretty. If she walks down the street, everybody screams, you know, screams other things at her. But because she's on the field, it's dykes on spikes. If that isn't a stereotype, then who knows what is. (Blinde, p. 12)

Homosexual females in this profession (coaching) definitely provide models and guidance in its worst for female athletes. I'd rather see a straight male coach females than a gay woman. Homosexual coaches are killing us. (NCAA)

I don't fit the stereotype. I mean the stereotype based around women that are very masculine and strong and athletic. I wouldn't say I'm pretty in pink, but I am feminine and I appear very feminine and I act that way. (Blinde, p. 12)

These attempts to distance oneself from the lesbian image and to embrace traditional standards of femininity set up a division among women in sport that can devastate friendships among teammates, poison coach–athlete relationships, and taint feelings about one's identity as an athlete and a woman. Some women restrict close friendships with other women to avoid the possibility that someone might think they are lesbians. Other women consciously cultivate high-profile heterosexual images by talking about their relationships with men and being seen with men as often as possible. As long as our energy is devoted to trying to fit into models of athleticism, gender, and sexuality that support a sexist and heterosexist culture, women in sport can be controlled by anyone who chooses to use our fears and insecurities against us.

Underlying Beliefs That Keep Women in Sport from Challenging Homophobia

The ability to understand the staying power of the lesbian stigma in sport is limited by several interconnected beliefs. An examination of these beliefs can reveal how past responses in dealing with lesbians in sport have reinforced the power of the lesbian label to intimidate and control.

A Woman's Sexual Identity Is Personal

This belief is perhaps the biggest obstacle to understanding women's oppression in a patriarchal culture (Kitzinger, 1987). As long as women's sexual identity is seen as solely a private issue, how the lesbian label is used to intimidate all women and to weaken women's challenges to male-dominated institutions will never be understood. The lesbian label is a political weapon that can be used against any woman who steps out of line. Any woman who defies traditional gender roles is called a lesbian. Any woman who chooses a male-identified career is called a lesbian. Any woman who chooses not to have a sexual relationship with a man is called a lesbian. Any woman who speaks out against sexism is called a lesbian. As long as women are afraid to be called lesbians, this label is an effective tool to control all women and limit women's challenges to sexism. Although lesbians are the targets of attack in women's sport, all women in sport are victimized by the use of the lesbian label to intimidate and control.

When a woman's lesbian identity is assumed to be a private matter, homophobia and heterosexism are dismissed. The implication is that these matters are not appropriate topics for professional discussion. As a result, the fear, prejudice, and outright discrimination that thrive in silence are never addressed. A double standard operates, however, for lesbians and heterosexual women in sport. Although open acknowledgment of lesbians in sport is perceived as an inappropriate flaunting of personal life (what you do in the privacy of your home is none of my business), heterosexual women are encouraged to talk about their relationships with men, their children, and their roles as mothers.

Magazine articles about such heterosexual athletes as Chris Evert Mill, Florence Griffiths Joyner, Jackie Joyner-Kersey, Joan Benoit, Nancy Lopez, and Mary Decker Slaney have often focused on their weddings, their husbands, or their children. Heterosexual professional athletes are routinely seen celebrating victories by hugging or kissing their husbands, but when Martina Navratilova went into the stands to hug *her* partner after winning the 1990 Wimbledon Championship, she was called a bad role model by former champion Margaret Court. Although heterosexual athletes and coaches are encouraged to display their personal lives to counteract the lesbian image in sport, lesbians are intimidated into invisibility for the same reason.

Claiming to Be Feminist Is Tantamount to Claiming to Be Lesbian
Claiming to be feminist is far too political for many women in sport. To successfully address the sexism and heterosexism in sport, however, women must begin to understand the necessity of seeing homophobia as a political issue and claim feminism as the unifying force needed to bring about change in a patriarchal culture. Part of the reluctance to embrace the feminist label is that feminists have been called lesbians in the same way that female athletes have and for the same reason: to intimidate

women and prevent them from challenging the sexist status quo. Women in sport are already intimidated by the lesbian label. For many women, living with the athlete, lesbian, and feminist labels is stigma overload.

By accepting the negative stereotypes associated with these labels, women in sport collude in our own oppression. Rather than seeking social approval as a marginal part of sport in a sexist and heterosexist society, we need to be working for social change and control over our sport destinies. The image of an unrepentant lesbian feminist athlete is a patriarchal nightmare. She is a woman who has discovered her physical and political strength and who refuses to be intimidated by labels. Unfortunately, this image scares women in sport as much as it does those who benefit from the maintenance of the sexist and heterosexist status quo.

The Problem Is Lesbians in Sport Who Call Attention to Themselves

People who believe this assume that as long as lesbians are invisible, our presence will be tolerated and women's sport will progress. The issue for these people is not that there are lesbians in sport but how visible we are. Buying into silence this way has never worked. Other than Martina Navratilova, lesbians in sport are already deeply closeted (Bull, 1991; Muscatine, 1991). This careful camouflage of lesbians has not made women's sport less suspect or less vulnerable to intimidation. Despite efforts to keep the focus on the pretty ones or the ones with husbands and children, women in sport still carry the lesbian stigma into every gym and onto every playing field.

Women in sport must begin to understand that it wouldn't matter if there were no lesbians in sport. The lesbian label would still be used to intimidate and control women's athletics. The energy expended in making lesbians invisible and projecting a happy heterosexual image keeps women in sport fighting among ourselves rather than confronting the heterosexism and sexism that our responses unintentionally serve.

Lesbians Are Bad Role Models and Sexual Predators

This belief buys into all the unsavory lesbian stereotypes left over from the late 19th-century medical doctors who made homosexuality pathological and the early 20th-century sexologists who made female friendships morbid. In reality, there are already numerous closeted lesbians in sport who are highly admired role models. It is the perversity of prejudice that merely knowing about the sexual identity of these admired women instantly turns them into unfit role models.

The sexual-predator stereotype is a particularly pernicious slander on lesbians in sport (South et al., 1990). There is no evidence that lesbians are sexual predators. In fact, statistics on sexual harassment, rape, sexual abuse, and other forms of violence and intimidation show that these offenses are overwhelmingly heterosexual male assaults against women and girls. If we need to be concerned about sexual offenses among coaches or athletes, a better case could be made that it is heterosexual men who should be watched carefully. Blinde (1989) reported that many female athletes, like their male counterparts, are subjected to academic, physical, social, and emotional exploitation by their coaches. When men coach women in a heterosexist and sexist culture, there is the additional potential for sexual and gender-based exploitation when the unequal gender dynamics in the larger society are played out in the coach–athlete relationship.

It is difficult to imagine anyone in women's sport, regardless of sexual identity, condoning coercive sexual relationships of any kind. Even consensual sexual relationships between coaches and athletes involve inherent power differences that make such relationships questionable and can have a negative impact on the athlete as well as on the rest of the team. This kind of behavior should be addressed regardless of the gender or sexual identity of the coaches and athletes involved instead of assuming that lesbian athletes or coaches present a greater problem than others.

Being Called Lesbian or Being Associated with Lesbians Is the Worst Thing That Can Happen in Women's Sport

As long as women in sport buy into the power of the lesbian label to intimidate us, we will never control our sport experience. Blaming lesbians for women's sports' bad image and failure to gain more popularity divides women and keeps us fighting among ourselves. In this way, we collude in maintaining our marginal status by keeping alive the power of the lesbian label to intimidate women into silence, betrayal, and denial. This keeps our energies directed inward rather than outward at the sexism that homophobia serves. Blaming lesbians keeps all women in their place, scurrying to present an image that is acceptable in a sexist and heterosexist society. This keeps our attention diverted from asking other questions: Why are strong female athletes and coaches so threatening to a patriarchal society? Whose interests are served by trivializing and stigmatizing women in sport?

Women in sport need to redefine the problem. Instead of naming and blaming lesbians in sport as the problem, we need to focus our attention on sexism, heterosexism, and homophobia. As part of this renaming process, we need to take the sting out of the lesbian label. Women in sport must stop jumping to the back of the closet and slamming the door every time someone calls us dykes. We need to challenge the use of the lesbian label to intimidate all women in sport.

Women's Sport Can Progress without Dealing with Homophobia
If progress is measured by the extent to which we, as women in sport, control our sporting destinies, take pride in our athletic identities, and tolerate diversity among ourselves, then we are no better off now than we ever have been. We have responded to questions about lesbians in sport with silence, denial, and apology. When these responses fail to divert attention away from the lesbian issue, we have promoted a heterosexy image, attacked lesbians, and hired male coaches. All of these responses call on women to accommodate, assimilate, and collude with the values of a sexist and heterosexist society. All require compromise and deception. The bargain struck is that in return for our silence and our complicity, we are allowed a small piece of the action in a sports world that has been defined by men to serve male-identified values.

We have never considered any alternatives to this cycle of silence, denial, and apology to the outside world while policing the ranks inside. We have never looked inside ourselves to understand our fear and confront it. We have never tried to analyze the political meaning of our fear. We have never stood up to the accusations and threats that keep us in our place.

What do we have to pass on to the next generation of young girls who love to run and throw and catch? What is the value of nicer uniforms, a few extra tournaments, and occasional pictures in the back of the sports section if we can't pass on a sport experience with less silence and fear?

Strategies for Confronting Homophobia in Women's Sport

What, then, are the alternatives to silence, apology, denial, promoting a heterosexy image, attacking lesbians, and hiring male coaches? How can women in sport begin confronting homophobia rather than perpetuating it? If our goal is to defuse the lesbian label and to strip it of its power to intimidate women in sport, then we must break the silence, not to condemn lesbians but to condemn those who use the lesbian label to intimidate. Our failure to speak out against homophobia signals our consent to the fear, ignorance, and discrimination that flourish in that silence. If our goal is to create a vision of sport in which all women have an opportunity to proudly claim their athletic identity and control their athletic experience, then we must begin to build that future now.

Institutional Policy
Sport governing organizations and school athletic departments need to enact explicit nondiscrimination and antiharassment policies that include

sexual orientation as a protected category. This is a first step in establishing an organizational climate in which discrimination against lesbians (or gay men) is not tolerated. Most sport governing organizations have not instituted such policies and, when asked by reporters if they are planning to, avoid taking a stand (Brownworth, 1991; Longman, 1991). In addition to nondiscrimination policies, professional standards of conduct for coaches must be developed that outline behavioral expectations regardless of gender or sexual orientation. Sexual harassment policies and the procedures for filing such complaints must be made clear to coaches, athletes, and administrators. As with standards of professional conduct, these policies should apply to everyone.

Education

Everyone associated with physical education and athletics must learn more about homophobia, sexism, and heterosexism. Conferences for coaches, teachers, and administrators should include educational programs focused on understanding homophobia and developing strategies for addressing homophobia in sport.

Athletic departments must sponsor educational programs for athletes that focus not only on homophobia but on other issues of social diversity as well. Because prejudice and fear affect the quality of athletes' sport experience and their relationships with teammates and coaches, educational programs focused on these issues are appropriate for athletic department sponsorship and should be an integral part of the college athletic experience.

Visibility

One of the most effective tools in counteracting homophobia is increased lesbian and gay visibility. Stereotypes and the fear and hatred they perpetuate will lose their power as more lesbian and gay people in sport disclose their identities. Although some people will never accept diversity of sexual identity in sport or in the general population, research indicates that, for most people, contact with "out" lesbian and gay people who embrace their sexual identities reduces prejudice (Herek, 1985).

The athletic world desperately needs more lesbian and gay coaches and athletes to step out of the closet. So far only a handful of athletes or coaches, most notably Martina Navratilova, have had the courage to publicly affirm their lesbian or gay identity (Brown, 1991; Brownworth, 1991; Bull, 1991; Burke, 1991; Muscatine, 1991). The generally accepting, if not warm, reaction of tennis fans to Martina's courage and honesty should be encouraging to the many closeted lesbian and gay people in sport. Unfortunately, the fear that keeps most lesbian and gay sportspeople in the closet is not ungrounded. Coming out as a lesbian or gay athlete or coach is a risk in a heterosexist and sexist society (Brown 1991; Brownworth 1991; Burton-Nelson, 1991; Hicks, 1979; Muscatine, 1991). The paradox is that more lesbian and gay people need to risk coming out if homosexuality is to be demystified in North American society.

Another aspect of visibility is the willingness of heterosexual athletes and coaches, as allies of lesbian and gay people, to speak out against homophobia and heterosexism. In the same way that it is important for white people to speak out against racism and for men to speak out against sexism, it is important for heterosexual people to object to anti-gay harassment, discrimination, and prejudice. It isn't enough to provide silent, private support for lesbian friends. To remain silent signals consent. Speaking out against homophobia is a challenge for heterosexual women in sport that requires them to understand how homophobia is used against them as well as against lesbians. Speaking out against homophobia also requires that heterosexual women confront their own discomfort with being associated with lesbians or being called lesbian because that is what will happen when they speak out. The lesbian label will be used to try and intimidate them back into silence.

Solidarity
Heterosexual and lesbian women must understand that the only way to overcome homophobia, heterosexism, and sexism in sport is to work in coalition with each other. As long as fear and blame prevent women in sport from finding common ground, we will always be controlled by people whose interests are served by our division. Our energy will be focused on social approval rather than on social change, and on keeping what little we have rather than on getting what we deserve.

Pressure Tactics
Unfortunately, meaningful social change never happens without tension and resistance. Every civil and human rights struggle in the United States has required the mobilization of political pressure exerted on people with power to force them to confront injustice. Addressing sexism, heterosexism, and homophobia in women's sport will be no different. Taking a stand will mean being prepared to use the media, college petitions, lobby officials, picket, write letters, file official complaints, and take advantage of other pressure tactics.

Conclusion

Eliminating the insidious trio of sexism, heterosexism, and homophobia in women's sport will take a sustained commitment to social justice that will challenge much of what has been accepted as natural about gender and sexuality. Addressing sexism, heterosexism, and homophobia in women's sport requires that past conceptions of gender and sexuality be recognized as social constructions that confer privilege and normalcy on particular social groups: men and heterosexuals. Other social groups (women, lesbians, and gay men) are defined as inferior or deviant and are denied access to the social resources and status conferred on heterosexual men.

Sport in the late 20th century is, perhaps, the last arena in which men can hope to differentiate themselves from women. In sport, men learn to value a traditional heterosexual masculinity that embraces male domination and denigrates women's values (Messner and Sabo, 1990). If sport is to maintain its meaning as a masculine ritual in a patriarchal society, women must be made to feel like trespassers. Women's sport participation must be trivialized and controlled (Bennett et al., 1987). The lesbian label, with its unsavory stigma, is an effective tool to achieve these goals.

If women in sport in the 21st century are to have a sport experience free of intimidation, fear, shame, and betrayal; then, as citizens of the 20th century, we must begin to reevaluate our beliefs, prejudices, and practices. We must begin to challenge the sexist, heterosexist, and homophobic status quo as it lives in our heads, on our teams, and in our schools. A generation of young girls; our daughters, nieces, younger sisters, and students; is depending on us.

REFERENCES

Acosta, V., and Carpenter, L. (1988). Status of women in athletics: Causes and changes. *Journal of Health, Physical Education, Recreation and Dance,* 56(6), 35–37.
Bennett, R., Whitaker, G., Smith, N., and Sablove, A. (1987). Changing the rules of the game: Reflections toward a feminist analysis of sport. *Women's Studies International Forum,* 10(4), 369–380.
Birrell, S., and Richter, D. (1987). Is a diamond forever? Feminist transformations of sport. *Women's Studies International Forum,* 10(4), 395–410.
Blinde, E. (1989). Unequal Exchange and exploitation in college sport: The case of the female athlete. *Arena Review,* 13(2), 110–123.
Blinde, E. (1990, March). *Pressure and stress in women's college sports: Views from Athletes.* Paper presented at the annual convention of the American Alliance for Health, Physical Education, Recreation and Dance, New Orleans.
Brown, K. (1991). Homophobia in women's sports. *Deneuve,* 1(2), 4–6, 29.
Brownworth, V. (1991, June 4). Bigotry on the home team: Lesbians face harsh penalties in the sports world. *The Advocate: The National Gay and Lesbian Newsmagazine,* pp. 34–39.
Bryson, L. (1987). Sport and the maintenance of male hegemony. *Women's Studies International Forum,* 10(4), 349–360.

Bull, C. (1991, December 31). The magic of Martina. *The Advocate: The National Gay and Lesbian Newsmagazine,* pp. 38–40.

Burke, G. (1991, September 18). Dodgers wanted me to get married. *USA Today,* p. 10C.

Burton-Nelson, M. (1991). *Are we winning yet?* New York: Random House.

Diaz, J. (1989, February 13). Find the golf here? *Sports Illustrated,* pp. 58–64.

Faderman, L. (1981). *Surpassing the love of men: Romantic friendship and love between women from the Renaissance to the present.* New York: Morrow.

Faderman, L. (1991). *Odd girls and twilight lovers: A history of lesbian life in twentieth-century America.* New York: Columbia University Press.

Felshin, J. (1974). The triple option . . . for women in sport. *Quest,* 21, 36–40.

Fields, C. (1983, October 26). Allegations of lesbianism being used to intimidate, female academics say. *Chronicle of Higher Education,* pp. 1, 18–19.

Figel, B. (1986, June 16). Lesbians in the world of athletics. *Chicago Sun-Times,* p. 119.

Gornick, V. (1981, May 18). Ladies of the links. *Look,* pp. 69–76.

Greendorfer, S. (1991, April). *Analyzing homophobia: Its weapons and impacts.* Paper presented at the annual convention of the American Alliance for Health, Physical Education, Recreation and Dance, San Francisco.

Griffin, P. (1987, August). *Lesbians, homophobia, and women's sport: An exploratory analysis.* Paper presented at the annual meeting of the American Psychological Association, New York.

Guthrie, S. (1982). *Homophobia: Its impact on women in sport and physical education.* Unpublished master's thesis, California State University, Long Beach.

Hall, A. (Ed.) (1987). The gendering of sport, leisure, and physical education [Special issue]. *Women's Studies International Forum,* 10(4).

Herek, G. (1985). Beyond 'homophobia': A social psychological perspective on attitudes toward lesbians and gay men. In J. DeCecco (Ed.), *Bashers, baiters, and bigots: Homophobia in American society* (pp. 1–22). New York: Harrington Park Press.

Hicks, B. (1979, October/November). Lesbian athletes, *Christopher Street,* pp. 42–50.

Image lady. (1987, July). *Golf Illustrated,* p. 9.

Katz, J. (1976). *Gay American History,* New York: Avon.

Kiersh, E. (1990, April). Graf's dash. *Vogue,* pp. 348–353, 420.

Kitzinger, C. (1987). *The social construction of lesbianism.* Newbury Park, CA: Sage.

Krebs, P. (1984). At the starting blocks: Women's athletes' new agenda. *Off our backs,* 14(1), 1–3.

Lederman, D. (1991, June 5). Penn State's coach's comments about lesbian athletes may be used to test university's new policy on bias. *Chronicle of Higher Education,* pp. A27–28.

Lenskyj, H. (1986). *Out of bounds: Women, sport, and sexuality.* Toronto: Women's Press.

Lenskyj, H. (1990). Combatting homophobia in sports. *Off our backs,* 20(6), 2–3.

Lenskyj, H. (1991). Combatting homophobia in sport and physical education. *Sociology of Sport Journal* 8(1), 61–69.

Lipsyte, R. (1991, May 24). Gay bias moves off the sidelines. *New York Times,* p. B1.

Locke, L., Y Jensen, M. (1970, Fall). Heterosexuality of women in physical education. *The Foil,* pp 30–34.

Longman, J. (1991, March 10). Lions women's basketball coach is used to fighting and winning. *Philadelphia Inquirer,* pp. 1G, 6G.

Messner, M., and Sabo, D. (Eds.) (1990). *Sport, men, and the gender order: Critical feminist perspectives.* Champaign, IL: Human Kinetics.

Morgan, E. (1990). *Lesbianism and feminism in women's athletics: Intersection, bridge, or gap?* Unpublished manuscript, Brown University, Providence.

Muscatine, A. (1991, November/December). To tell the truth, Navratilova takes consequences. *Women's SportsPages,* pp. 8–9. (Available from Women's SportsPages, P.O. Box 15134, Chevy Chase, MD 20825)

National Collegiate Athletic Association. (1991). *NCAA study on women's intercollegiate athletics: Perceived barriers of women in intercollegiate athletic careers.* Overland Park, KS: Author.

Newton, E. (1989). The mannish lesbian: Radclyffe Hall and the new woman. In M. Duberman, M. Vicinus, and G. Chauncey (Eds.), *Hidden from history: Reclaiming the gay and lesbian past* (pp. 281–293). New York: New American Library.

Pharr, S. (1988). *Homophobia: A weapon of sexism.* Inverness, CA: Chardon Press.

Rentzel, L. (1987). *Emotional dependency: A threat to close friendships.* San Rafael, CA: Exodus International.

Smith-Rosenberg, C. (1989). Discourses of sexuality and subjectivity: The new woman, 1870–1936. In M. Duberman, M. Vicinus, and G. Chauncey (Eds.). *Hidden from history: Reclaiming the gay and lesbian past* (pp. 261–280). New York: New American Library.

Solomon, A. (1991, March 20). Passing game. *Village Voice,* p. 92.

South, J., Glynn, M., Rodack, J., and Capettini, R. (1990, July 31). Explosive gay scandal rocks women's tennis. *National Enquirer,* pp. 20–21.

Spander, D. (1991, September 1). It's a question of acceptability. *Sacramento Bee,* pp. D1, D14–15.

Thomas, R. (1990, December 12). Two women at Brooklyn College file rights complaint. *New York Times,* p. 22.

Thorngren, C. (1990, April). *Pressure and stress in women's college sport: Views from coaches.* Paper presented at the annual convention of the American Alliance for Health, Physical Education, Recreation and Dance, New Orleans.

Thorngren, C. (1991, April). *Homophobia and women coaches: Controls and constraints.* Paper presented at the annual convention of the American Alliance for Health, Physical Education, Recreation and Dance, San Francisco.

Woods, S. (1990). The contextual realities of being a lesbian physical education teacher: Living in two worlds (Doctoral dissertation, University of Massachusetts, Amherst, 1989). *Dissertation Abstracts International, 51*(3), 788.

◆▮◆

HOMOPHOBIA ALLEGED IN UNIVERSITY OF FLORIDA SOFTBALL

Jim Buzinski

This should have been a happy time for Andrea Zimbardi. Her University of Florida softball team was in the NCAA playoffs and she had been hoping to play a key role as the team's catcher. Instead, Zimbardi was forced to sit in the stands in Gainesville and watch, wondering what might have been, and what went wrong.

Zimbardi, an SEC honor roll student and a senior captain on the team, was kicked off the Gators' squad in March. Her coach told her it was because Zimbardi had spread lies and misconceptions about an assistant coach and about the program. Zimbardi, though, suspects the real reason is that she's a lesbian.

"I was kicked off because I wanted to take a stand against everything that happened to me," said Zimbardi, 23. "I believe I was discriminated against because of my sexual orientation."

Zimbardi graduated this month with a degree in industrial engineering, and was, according to current and former teammates, a popular and talented player who came into the program as a walk-on and overcame two knee surgeries to earn a starting role. How she went from being hailed as a role model by her coach to being kicked off the team is unclear.

Zimbardi alleges that head coach Karen Johns created an atmosphere of alienation for anyone not sharing her Christian beliefs, outed other coaches and players as lesbians, and reneged on an agreement not to retaliate against Zimbardi when she took her concerns to the university's athletic administration. She further alleges that assistant coach Heather Compton-Butler made inappropriate and leading comments to her about lesbianism and lesbian relationships. Zimbardi says she was not informed about team practices, and gradually saw her playing time shrink until she was finally released on March 6.

"[Johns'] discrimination is very subtle," says Karen Doering, an attorney with the National Center for Lesbian Rights (NCLR), which is investigating Zimbardi's allegations. "Based on her deep intrusion into [players'] personal lives, outing other coaches and players, and her [religious moralizing],

From Outsports.com, 21 May 2003, http://www.outsports.com/campus/20030521andrea zimbardi.htm. An update on this case is available at http://www.outsports.com/jocktalk /index.cfm?JMonth=6&JYear=2005#6.21.2005.

she sends a clear message to the lesbian players that [homosexuality] is not acceptable. She's not doing the 'no-gay-people-can-play-for-me' thing. But she's creating an environment where lesbian athletes feel uncomfortable." The University of Florida does not include sexual orientation in its non-discrimination policy.

Similar Allegations

Zimbardi isn't the only player kicked off the team since Johns took over the program in June 2000. Outsports interviewed two former players, each of whom, like Zimbardi, had had relationships with women. These former players tell of Johns delving into what they say was inappropriate personal territory, trying to discern which players might be lesbians. Both players tell stories similar to Zimbardi's, of seeing their playing time suddenly and dramatically shrink, ending in their release for unspecified reasons. Both former players were interviewed with the promise of anonymity. In addition, e-mails and team itineraries obtained by Outsports show that Johns was vocal about her religious beliefs, confirming what the players have alleged.

"Our ongoing investigation is a result of some corroborated statements from players and coaches that could suggest a pattern of anti-lesbian comments toward team members and even other outstanding NCAA fast-pitch softball coaches around the country," says Helen Carroll, coordinator of the Homophobia in Sports program for NCLR, and herself a former coach and athletic director.

Outsports tried to speak with head coach Johns and Compton-Butler, the assistant coach. Johns, in a statement released by the school, would only say: "We acknowledge that Andrea Zimbardi is no longer on the team and we wish her the best of luck in the future." Compton-Butler was not made available for an interview.

Athletic Director Jeremy N. Foley also would not comment except to issue a statement through the school's Sports Information office:

"I've reviewed this matter and I'm very comfortable with how it was handled," Foley's statement said. "I have the utmost confidence in our coaches. The [federal] Buckley Amendment prevents us from talking about the particulars of this matter. I do understand though, how disappointed a student-athlete can get when things do not work out how they planned.

"Our coaches are totally committed to the development of all of our student-athletes. Andrea finished her degree at UF in May. We supported Andrea's applications this spring for post-graduate scholarship awards. We are proud of Andrea as well as our other graduates. The education of our student-athletes is our most important mission."

Problems with a Coach

Zimbardi has been out to her mother and step-father since her senior year in high school, and says they have been very supportive. She says her teammates knew she had a girlfriend, but that it was simply accepted and never commented on. "I know my teammates won't judge me. I love them to death. They looked at me not as gay Andrea but as a great catcher," she says.

As someone whose name appears in the Gator record books for having among the best fielding percentage for catchers in school history, Zimbardi figured her place on the team was secure for her senior season. In 2002, she caught the third most runners stealing (15) in school history and was only two away from the school record, the school's Web site says. She had a good relationship with Johns, who wrote a letter of recommendation for Zimbardi for a scholarship. But things began to change, she says, with the hiring of a new pitching coach, Compton-Butler (she was Heather Compton at the time and married in January), in the fall. Compton-Butler had been pitching coach for Florida State.

When the two went for a run together last fall, Zimbardi says, Compton-Butler began asking leading personal questions about her relationships.

"She was trying to make a comment based on what my sexuality is," Zimbardi says. She says Compton-Butler "volunteered" information on which Olympic and pro softball players were lesbians. The coach told Zimbardi she knew "how bad the lesbian relationships were with these players." She specifically told Zimbardi about how badly one player had treated her female partner.

"I kind of spoke up for female relationships," said Zimbardi, who adds that the whole conversation made her uneasy. She believes such a conversation was not appropriate between a coach and a player. "I don't want to be defined by that, especially by someone who doesn't know my personal life."

From then on, Zimbardi says, she tried to limit her contact with Compton-Butler as much as possible. But an incident in November further bothered her.

The player says she was speaking with a secretary in the softball athletic office about getting a haircut from the secretary's stylist when Compton-Butler walked by. Overhearing the conversation, Compton-Butler, according to Zimbardi, said: "I hope you don't get one of those 'butch' haircuts."

"I just stood there shocked," Zimbardi says, as she interpreted "butch" to mean lesbian. "I don't believe [the secretary] knew about me. Basically, [Compton-Butler] outed me in front of another employee of the university. I was embarrassed about it. I don't want to be defined by [being a lesbian], especially by someone who doesn't know my personal life. I felt that was an intrusion."

As the spring softball season began, Zimbardi says, she began to be frozen out of team activities. She was not receiving calls from Compton-Butler about the team's twice-a-day practices, and says that the coach got defensive when challenged. She also was the only player not invited to a pitchers-catchers dinner at Compton-Butler's house, something the coach attributed to an oversight as she made a belated invitation just hours prior to the get-together, according to Zimbardi. "I didn't want to be the only person not there that night," Zimbardi wrote in her diary of the season. "However, I still felt a much excluded feeling because everyone else knew about the dinner but me."

Christian Beliefs Prominent

Zimbardi says she had no choice but to turn to coach Johns to discuss her concerns about her treatment by Compton-Butler. Based on past comments by the head coach, the player was unsure about how she would be received.

From the moment Johns arrived as coach in Gainesville, she touted her strong Christian beliefs, Zimbardi and the other players interviewed say. They recall Johns leading the team in the Lord's Prayer on the field and occasionally inserting Biblical and religious passages in the team's printed itinerary. She would also tell the team about recruits who were "good Christians." An assistant coach under Johns—who has since left the program—held Bible study classes, and would ask the players if they were attending. "You felt guilty if you said no," Zimbardi says.

The head coach also regularly contrasted her Christian lifestyle with others, including those of gays and lesbians, Zimbardi and the two former players say. "The decision she made [to be a Christian] was the one we needed to make to be good people," one of the former players recalls Johns having said more than once.

Johns, a two-time All-American catcher at South Carolina who was hired by Florida after a successful stint as pitching coach at the University of Alabama, also committed her faith to print. In an October 2000 e-mail to Zimbardi, then recovering from knee surgery, Johns wrote: "To show His love, Jesus died for us; to show our love, we must live for Him. Hope your rehab is going good . . . let me know if I can do anything for you. GOD BLESS! GO GATORS!"

The coach also forwarded an e-mail to the entire team from an organization called Competitive Edge International, that was seeking softball players for a tour. "CEI is looking for Christian athletes (and coaches) who desire to promote and develop softball worldwide AND share their personal faith," the e-mail read. Another team-wide e-mail was simply titled "Joshua 1:9," and read: "Remember that I have commanded you to be determined and confident! Do not be afraid or discouraged, for I, the Lord your God, am with you wherever you go." In addition, the team was once given a handout by Johns titled "The Lord's Softball Team," that discussed faith and devotion to God in the context of a softball game.

The University of Florida does not have a policy regarding the promotion of religion. However, any student who felt undue pressure could file a complaint with the student grievance committee, according to Paula Rausch of the university's office of News and Public Affairs.

Athletic Director Foley, in a statement said, "In my 12 years as athletic director, I've not heard one complaint from anyone about the expression of faith." He added that it's up to each team to decide how and if they want to express their faith.

"Made Me Uncomfortable"

Religion aside, what especially troubled Zimbardi, she says, was Johns' frequent discussions of which players and coaches in the sport were gay. "She outed a lot of people," Zimbardi says. She recalls one trip to California, where Florida was playing against a school coached by one of Johns' former teammates. Zimbardi claims that at one point, Johns said that the only difference between herself and the other coach was "that she's gay and I'm not."

"These types of comments made me uncomfortable," Zimbardi says. "I wasn't sure I could then approach her about certain things."

The two former players who had also been released—both in prior seasons—say their troubles began when Johns started getting more personal than they were comfortable with. One says Johns had asked her on a team flight about which players were dating other girls, and had volunteered that a pitching coach on another team was sleeping with one of her players.

"This was not a position a head coach should be taking," the player says. "She overstepped her boundaries. I was very upset." This was not the only time Johns had asked her about other players' relationships. "She was trying to be my friend and get information about the other girls, but I was very guarded around her." This player, who says she had started the season as one of Johns' favorites, saw her playing time decrease and was soon released. "I was shocked," the player says, adding that she was never given a reason for her dismissal.

The second player released says Johns constantly intruded into her personal life. When this player was dating a baseball player, she says, Johns regularly "called his apartment and asked if I stayed there with him. I confronted her and asked her to stop." But Johns persisted in asking questions, even after the two broke up. The softball player then began dating a woman, and this also upset Johns. "If you're dating her, that's not right. It's a wrong lifestyle to choose," this player recalls Johns saying. She adds that the coach regularly made negative references to homosexual "lifestyles" and said she knew of lesbians who had committed suicide.

This second player says that by midseason her playing time was greatly reduced, even though her statistics were good. Johns put her on a leave of absence, the player says, "because she perceived a conflict between me and the other girl [she had been dating]. I was dumbfounded."

The player says she then agreed to see a school counselor as a condition of keeping her place on the team, but that she was eventually released. Johns gave her no specific reason for the decision except to say "it was for the best." The player then contacted an attorney, who said Johns could dismiss her only for insubordination, bad grades or for committing a felony. The player insists none of these criteria applied to her. "The only reason I can give [for my dismissal] was what she had gathered about my personal life."

A Pivotal Meeting

It was against this backdrop that Zimbardi approached Johns to discuss her treatment by Compton-Butler. The head coach said that Zimbardi "was doing nothing wrong" and that Compton-Butler had no issues with her. But as Zimbardi saw her playing time greatly reduced, "I wondered if it had something to do with Heather."

The issue came to a head when Zimbardi attended a Feb. 22 meeting that included her mother and step-father, coaches Johns and Compton-Butler, Athletic Director Foley and Assistant Athletic Director Ann Marie Rogers. "My parents felt it would be safe if the higher-ups were there," Zimbardi says.

The meeting seemed to go well from Zimbardi's standpoint. She says that after hearing her side, Foley told her "your perception is your reality." [Foley confirmed that he did say this.] He promised to work to resolve any problems, according to Zimbardi.

But Johns denied that any of the incidents Zimbardi described had happened, the player claims, and said "this was just my way to complain about my lack of playing time."

"I told [Johns] this was not about playing time and said 'I feel I've been discriminated against by you and Heather and this whole program.'"

The meeting then took a conciliatory turn, according to Zimbardi and her mother, Candace Carlson-Bolin. "Coach Johns stood up, hugged me and my husband and turned to Andrea, looked into her face with her arms on Andrea's and said 'I'm so sorry,'" Carlson-Bolin wrote in a letter to Foley dated April 9. Though Foley had left the meeting early, Zimbardi and her parents say they were assured by Roberts, Johns and Compton-Butler that Zimbardi would not face retaliation for speaking up.

Zimbardi was stunned when two days later she met with Johns, Compton-Butler and assistant coach Dave Majeski, and was told she had been suspended for a week. The head coach accused her of having told lies and misconceptions at the meeting with Foley, and said, "whenever you attack one of my assistants you attack me," the player recalls. "She then suggested I see a psychologist and gave me the number of one," Zimbardi says. The player refused to recant and left the meeting, telling her coach she would be ready to return behind the plate when needed.

A major source of contention occurred while Zimbardi was serving her suspension. She alleges that Compton-Butler told members of the team that Zimbardi had filed a complaint against her with a gay rights group on campus. Zimbardi says she had not done this and was upset that Compton-Butler had violated her agreement to keep details of the meeting with Foley confidential. When Zimbardi reported this to Rogers, the assistant AD said that Compton-Butler denied ever making such an allegation. However, a current player interviewed by Outsports quotes a teammate (who was also her roommate) as claiming that Compton-Butler had in fact made such a statement. Doering, the NCLR attorney, spoke with another player who said a rumor was rife among the team that Zimbardi had "filed a lawsuit" with a gay rights group.

Off the Team

Zimbardi would never make it back on the field. In a follow-up meeting with Johns on March 6, the player was told she was being released from the team "because you did nothing to clear up the misconceptions." She was allowed to keep her scholarship, but her collegiate sports career was over.

The decision infuriated Zimbardi's mother. In her three-page April 9 letter to Foley, she charged that "lies have been told by your coaching staff. . . . I only hope and pray that this injustice will be met and the truth prevail." She added that, "My daughter has been 'outed' by Coach Heather Compton-Butler subsequent to our meeting. My daughter . . . has not discussed our meeting with one other person in Gainesville that was not present at the meeting. She, on the other hand, has been slandered, lied to and [lied] about."

Doering and NCLR Homophobia in Sports coordinator Carroll were unsuccessful in getting Zimbardi reinstated for the remainder of the season. Doering is especially dismayed by the university's insistence that nothing wrong had occurred, and by the fact that Zimbardi had been retaliated against for raising her concerns.

"This is the poster child for how not to respond to allegations," Doering says. "They eliminated the problem by eliminating the victim."

The currently active player interviewed by Outsports, who spoke on the promise of anonymity, claims the team was never told why Zimbardi was released. She says the team speculated that it might have had something to do with Zimbardi's sexuality. But this player also says she didn't think Johns "was discriminatory based on someone's sexual preference." This player adds that she was not taking sides and had a good relationship with both Johns and Zimbardi. She adds that the coach praised Zimbardi even after her release, saying at one point, "Andrea reminds me so much of me."

"I believe Andrea feels the way she does for a reason," this player says. "I don't think she would make things up. It's unfortunate this could not be resolved and our team has suffered. We lost a great player and a huge asset. . . . I hope [this story] gets to the bottom of what really happened."

Zimbardi continued to attend games and root for her teammates, who made it as far as the NCAA regional finals before bowing out. Now that her playing career is over, she hopes her going public will "prevent other athletes from going through this." She still bleeds Gator Blue.

"The University of Florida always wants the best," she says. "I hope that by me doing this will make them better than they already are. If they want the best [for the softball program] they better keep looking. All I care about is the program."

◆💠◆   ·

LESS UGLY

Lesléa Newman

Chocolate pudding had just been passed out and the Minnows at the next table were busy flinging it at each other when Sam stood up and Marlene stopped breathing. Marlene was in love with Sam, with his stringy blond

From *Sportsdykes*, Susan Fox Rogers, ed. New York: St. Martin's, 1994.

hair and wire-rimmed glasses, with his long slender fingers and the way he'd wrap them around the neck of his Martin guitar, with his twangy voice which Marlene insisted was fifty times better than Bob Dylan's any day. But Sam didn't know Marlene was alive, he being a senior counselor and all, and she, like me, being a lowly Trout, which wasn't as bad as being a Minnow. But still it would be two years until we were Dolphins, and some of the Dolphins went out with counselors on the sly even though they weren't supposed to, especially since three years ago a girl got pregnant under a canoe and her parents sued Camp Wildwood for almost a million dollars. At least that's what Tina Jacobs said and she was a wealth of such vital information. She's the one who informed me that anything over a mouthful's a waste anyway the first time she saw me in a bathing suit. But Marlene said she was just jealous because Tina was as flat as the postcards our counselors handed out every Friday so we could write to our parents and tell them what a great time we were having or something to that effect if we wanted to help ourselves to a make-your-own-sundae at nine o'clock in the canteen.

Anyway, like I said, Sam stood up, cleared his throat and held up a plastic baggy full of cigarette butts. The usual roar of the dining room fell to a hushed din as Sam dramatically turned the baggy upside down and dumped its contents onto the wooden floor. "I don't smoke," he said, and for one second the room was silent except for Marlene's sigh of utter ecstasy. Then Sam sat down and the general chaos of two hundred campers and counselors started up again.

"Oh Marlene." I lowered my glasses to the tip of my nose and looked over their tortoise-shell rims at her in mock dismay. She was still staring at Sam, her eyes huge and all liquidy, like two pools of chocolate pudding about to ooze down her face. Sam was now biting into an organic Macintosh apple he had fished out of his Save-A-Tree canvas backpack and Marlene pushed her pudding aside. "What?" she asked, turning to me. "I can dream, can't I?"

"Sure," I said, sliding my glasses back up my nose, the-better-to-see-you-with, my-dear. I was doing plenty of dreaming myself that summer, but not about Sam or Larry or Wayne or Roger or even Claude, the swimming counselor who had given his whistle to Tina Jacobs to wear around her neck. No, I had it bad, and I mean B-A-D for Barney.

Barney. First of all she had straight brown hair all the way down to the bottom of her shorts. Sometimes she wore it loose and sometimes she wore it in one braid down her back, swinging like the rope to the dinner bell we all took turns pulling on to see who could make it ring the loudest. Second of all, she had light blue eyes, the color of a husky dog's. And third of all, her skin was the color of a marshmallow toasted to perfection over a Saturday night campfire when I was lucky enough to be sitting on a log right next to her, so who cared if some stupid Flying Fish got half his some'more stuck in my hair? Barney was absolute perfection in her white shorts that frayed at the bottom just right, and her blue T-shirt that matched her eyes, and her cotton socks, one hugging the tight muscles of her calf, the other rolled down twice to meet the rim of her black high-top sneaker. God, I wanted to be just like her. But how could I be? Try as I might, my hair would frizz up thirty seconds after I unrolled it from the coffee can I set it around every night. Not to mention the fact that unless I drenched myself in Coppertone my skin turned an early shade of ketchup after two minutes in the sun. And then of course there were my ugly, ugly, ugly, ugly glasses which hopefully would be replaced by contact lenses next summer, if not before.

Anyway, Barney didn't seem to worry about what she looked like. I mean, after all she was perfect, so there was nothing much to worry about anyway, but still, she didn't spend too much time hanging out with the other girl counselors who were always painting their mails and pouring peroxide into their hair to streak it. Barney didn't have time for that stuff. She was too busy tossing around a Frisbee or oiling her mitt or fixing the volleyball net. That's another reason I liked her so much. She was like one of the guys. So much so, they let her play in the annual Wildwood versus White Birch Counselor Softball Game, which was *the* event of the summer.

The Saturday of the game, me and Marlene walked down to the softball field right after lunch to get a good seat. We plopped down on the grass right behind and a little to the left of home plate, as far from Tina Jacobs and her crowd as possible. Our team was warming up; Barney had all her hair tucked up inside a NY Yankees baseball cap and Sam had a black elastic band attached to the ear pieces of his glasses, anchoring them to his head. Soon two yellow school buses full of White Birth campers and counselors arrived. After the campers got settled and the counselors warmed up, it was time to start the game.

Barney of course was spectacular. She played first base and every time the ball came her way she'd just lift her hand up in the air as easy as you please, just like she was waving hello to me, and the ball would smack into her glove and the ump would yell, "Out!" jerking his thumb over his shoulder. Once Barney caught a ball at first base and quick as a flash threw it to Sam, who tagged the runner out at second, and Marlene and I jumped up hugging each other tight and screaming so loud we practically busted each other's eardrums.

Then all of a sudden it was the bottom of the last inning. The score was tied eleven–eleven, bases loaded, two outs and it was Barney's turn to bat. Oh please God, please God, don't let her strike out, I prayed, closing my eyes for the briefest of seconds.

Barney dusted off home plate, shifted her hips from side to side, and swung her bat up to her shoulder. The pitcher let the ball fly. Barney watched it, but didn't move.

"Strike one."

Oh Barney, Barney, Barney, don't fail me now. Sam was standing behind the third base line, giving Barney encouragement. "That's it, Barney. Don't swing at anything. You pick it now. You're a hitter. You're a hitter." The Wildwoodians were screaming, "We want a pitcher, not a glass of water," as the ball beelined to Barney, who again didn't move.

"Strike two."

I clutched Marlene's arms with both hands, almost cutting off her circulation between her elbow and her wrist. What was Barney doing? She had to swing at this one. The pitcher pitched, the ball zoomed at Barney, she swung and smack! That ball was gone—over the pitcher's head, over second base, and way past the outfielder, who leaped up in the air with his glove extended anyway, before turning around and making a dash for it.

Meanwhile, Barney tossed her bat aside and loped around the bases as gracefully as the deer we had seen last week on an overnight in the backwoods. The outfielder finally caught up with the ball and threw it to second. By this time, everyone had come home except for Barney, who was rounding third. The second baseman threw the ball wildly at the catcher. It made a wide arc in the sky, then hung suspended in the air for a second, completely blocking the sun like an eclipse before hurling itself downward, straight for me.

"Heads up, heads up," someone yelled at the same time I said to Marlene, "That ball's gonna hit me in the face." And sure enough, one second later that softball, which was anything but soft, caught me right between the eyes and cracked my glasses in two, clean as a twig someone snapped in half before tossing it into the campfire. And thus I was glasses-free and just a tiny bit less ugly for the rest of that summer, so who cared that the only thing I could see clearly from then on until I went home was Barney's face, two inches from mine, her hair spilling out of her cap and brushing against my cheek, her blue eyes filled with delicious concern as she asked me over and over, "Are you all right? Are you all right?

SEX, LIES, AND VOLLEYBALL

Cynthia Hanson

When she was 15, Julie Bremner already had the long, lean muscles of an athlete and the competitive fire of a champion. As a freshman at St. Francis High School in Wheaton, her most urgent dream was to make the St. Francis varsity volleyball team. To better her chances, she followed in the snea-kerprints of many a champion before her: She tried out for Sports Performance Volleyball, a West Chicago amateur athletics club widely regarded as the best in the nation.

That was 1984. Bremner made the team, and inside of a year was well on her way to stardom. Still touted as one of the finest athletes ever to play in the program, she was named Reebok National High School Co-Player of the Year for 1987, and took a full ride to Notre Dame. She left after just a semester for a two-year stint with the women's national team, then transferred to UCLA, where she led the Bruins to the 1991 NCAA championship. But throughout her volleyball career, Bremner says, she harbored a humiliating secret: For a year and a half, beginning when she was 17, she had slept with Sports Performance coach and founder Rick Butler.

For 15 years now, 41-year-old Rick Butler has enjoyed unmatched success as a girls' volleyball coach. His program, which is primarily geared to teaching teenagers the fundamentals of competitive volleyball, has produced more winning teams and more college scholarships for its participants than almost any other women's sports program in the United States. Since Sports Performance's inception in 1980, its girls' teams have won 28 national titles, and Butler has even sent a handful of players to the women's national team and the pro beach circuit. His methods—which center on militaristic regimen and the notion that girls can and should compete as seriously as boys—have gained him more fans than detractors.

"Rick has developed the premier junior program in the country," says Doug Beal of the U.S. Volleyball Association, the sport's national governing body.

Beal, who coached the gold-medal men's team at the Los Angeles Olympics, is organizing a U.S. pro men's league. Butler, who was an assistant to

From *Chicago* 45:2 (February 1996): 56–63.

the men's Olympic team in Barcelona in 1992, was asked to coach the Chicago franchise, and, Beal says, is perpetually on the short list for the Olympic staff.

But in 1994, when Bremner blurted her secret to a therapist in Los Angeles, Butler's high-flying career began a downward arc. Within a few months of her revelation, two more former players came forward and made similar allegations before the Illinois Department of Children and Family Services (DCFS) and the volleyball association. All three women described a "coaching couch" process in which he identified them as stars, invited them to private training sessions, and eventually pushed them into sex. In remarkably similar language, each accused Butler of having abused his power and exploited her dreams. Each said that she had submitted to Butler because she believed he controlled her future, and eventually, because she thought he loved her. As one of the women said at the hearings that would follow, "I truly believed that I needed him, that I would have nothing but a wasted life without him. I feared he would take everything away if I didn't do what he wanted."

By last July, Rick Butler and his coaching program were at the center of a maelstrom, and by the end of the month, the U.S. Volleyball Association had revoked Butler's membership—a necessity for any coach who wants to compete seriously on a national level. Butler lost an administrative appeal, but on January second, filed a lawsuit against the association seeking damages in excess of $1 million. He says he "dated" all three of his accusers—but only after they had turned 18 (the age of sexual consent in Illinois when one party is in a position of trust, authority, or supervision over the other) and left the program. He blames the entire mess on a grudge match with his former business partner, Kay Rogness, who helped the women find each other and present their case.

Dozens of parents have rallied to support Butler. Pat Kennedy of Barrington Hills, whose husband owns the Chicago franchise for the pro men's league and whose 17-year-old daughter began her fourth season at Sports Performance in December, swears that Butler saved her child. "My daughter was 40 pounds overweight and a terrible student before she joined Sports Performance," Kennedy says. "Today, she has a 3.25 grade-point average, and there are 75 colleges recruiting her."

"We've never had a problem that Rick dated women who had been in the program," says Paul Stettin of Burr Ridge, one of 75 parents and players who waited outside July's hearings to root for Butler. "What he has done for my daughters goes way beyond volleyball. He's introduced them to a lifestyle that teaches discipline, hard work, and achievement."

Nevertheless, Butler's case underscores a problem that has increasingly affected other female-dominated sports in recent years. Though Butler is the first coach to be booted by the volleyball association for sexual misconduct, the national gymnastics association has expelled 11 coaches on such grounds since 1989; seven of them subsequently were convicted of criminal offenses ranging from indecent exposure to rape.

To complicate matters, policing the world of competitive sports is difficult—and often discouraged, even by those who should be the most vigilant. "Parents see scholarships dangling in front of them and they want to believe everything's OK," says one volleyball insider. "For years, rumors have circulated about Rick Butler screwing his players. But until [the women] came forward, what could anyone do about it?"

After she left Sports Performance, Bremner slowly began to disclose her involvement with Butler to former teammates. She even told her parents, who confronted Butler but took no further action. Not until after she got engaged in 1993, however, did Bremner decide to see a counselor to discuss the lingering effects. "I kept thinking it was my fault," says the 26-year-old, now a second-year medical student at UCLA. "I worried that unless I worked through my feelings, I'd end up having problems in my marriage."

Bremner says their sexual involvement began in 1987, her junior year. The previous year, Butler had invited her to train with his top team, most of whose members were seniors. Soon Bremner was spending long hours in the gym, in part to practice and in part to escape the turmoil from her parents' collapsing marriage, which ended in 1988.

"He said I had a chance to get college scholarships and play in the Olympics, if I would do what he told me to do and not question him," Bremner says. "He said, 'You may not always understand everything, but I expect 100 percent loyalty.' So I started coming to practice a couple of hours early and staying until 11:30 at night."

Joy Dooley, Bremner's mother, says she should have "detected the red flags in such an intense schedule," but at the time she believed Butler's intentions were honorable. "Rick said he'd make Julie a star, and Julie wanted to be a star," says Dooley.

In 1987, Butler, then 32, took his top team to Japan to compete. Bremner, then 17, says he invited her to his hotel room one evening to talk about the team but that when she arrived, she found him sitting on the floor wearing only a bathrobe. "He asked me to sit down next to him," Bremner recalls, "and the next thing I knew, he kissed me and stuck his hand up my shirt. I pushed him away and said, 'Why did you do that?' He said, 'I knew somebody would come to the room soon, and I knew it would be now or never.'" Bremner left abruptly, and then lay awake all night, she says, crying and shaking with anger and fear. "I'd trusted Rick more than I trusted anybody on earth," she says. "I didn't know what to do."

Two weeks later, back at home, Bremner says, Butler told her they needed to talk—but not at the gym, because he feared other players would gossip about them. Bremner says she suggested meeting in a restaurant, but that Butler declined, insisting they needed privacy. He suggested a hotel. "I believed I was going there to talk about volleyball," says Bremner, who played setter, the sport's equivalent of quarterback. "I know how dumb that sounds now." She went to the hotel, and within seconds of entering the room, she says, Butler started coming on to her. "I said, 'I don't believe in premarital sex,'" she says. "Then I started shouting, 'No! No!' but he kept saying, 'Trust me.' I tried pushing him away but I couldn't stop him. Somehow he got my jeans off and had intercourse with me."

For the next 18 months, according to Bremner, Butler pressured her into performing oral sex and intercourse in a variety of venues, including the empty gym after practice. She says he rented pornographic movies and masturbated in front of her. "I felt totally disgusted," she says. "I thought I'd done or said something to lead him on. In a sick, twisted way, I tried to pretend what he was doing to me was OK. I tried to make myself like it, and I pretended he wanted to marry me. I even thought I was in love with him, because he said sex equaled love."

In 1993, after her therapist told her that California law required mental health professionals to report incidents of child sexual abuse if the alleged perpetrator still had contact with minors, Bremner decided to take action on her own. She called the Illinois Department of Children and Family Services. The "witch hunt," as Butler calls it, had begun.

"Sports are so sexist," Rick Butler says. "The attitude has always been, 'Boys play to win, and girls play for fun.' We said, 'We can do better.'" He is wedged into the corner of his beige sofa in his modest Warrenville townhouse, where he lives with Cheryl, his wife of two years, and Kyle, the baby boy they are trying to adopt. Butler's waxy, angular face briefly breaks into a smile just once during our three-hour interview—when told that he has been described as "stoic." "I'm no-nonsense and goal-oriented," he says. "As I tell our players, 'You can be the best or you can be one of the rest.'"

It's an overcast, humid morning in early August, less than 24 hours after Butler has been suspended from the U.S. Volleyball Association. He is a tall, sinewy man with a receding hairline, and today he wears faded blue jeans and sandals—the uniform of relaxation. He is anything but relaxed, however, as he discusses his coaching career and the allegations that threaten to destroy it. "The process has been corrupt from day one," he says. "I would like this process to be governed by common sense. I would like [the volleyball association] to look at the whole picture, the histories. It's never been about sex. It's always been about power and revenge."

He says he had "a very good relationship" with Julie Bremner—after she left the program—and calls her accusations "crazy." Though he doesn't remember the accommodations on the trip to Japan, he says that as a rule, the team didn't stay in hotels, and suggests that Bremner is jealous of his wife.

Butler came to volleyball relatively late. He grew up on a farm in rural Oregon, where he "lived for" football, basketball, and baseball. At the University of Redlands, in Redlands, California, he played defensive back and studied history, planning to teach and coach football after graduation. But through his college girlfriend, a Chicago native, Butler met Bob Gajda, a Glen Ellyn physical trainer who was working with the U.S. Men's Volleyball Team, and his career path soon took an unexpected turn. He accepted a job as a fitness consultant at Gajda's Sports Fitness Institute. "I didn't know what volleyball was when I came here," says Butler, who was 24 at the time. "But I saw the U.S. men versus the Russians, and I fell in love with the dynamics of the game."

In 1980, at Gajda's suggestion, Butler, fellow Chicago fitness consultant Kay Rogness, and then-Northwestern University women's coach Jerry Angle organized a girls' volleyball team to compete in the national championships of the Amateur Athletic Union. The ten-girl team won, prompting Butler and his colleagues to form more teams the following year. The partners eventually named the program Sports Performance Volleyball, Inc., and in 1982, when Angle left, Butler took over as head coach. In 1995, 220 girls and boys competed for Sports Performance, but the emphasis remains on the girls' game, where there are more college scholarships to be harvested.

From the beginning, Butler was the most relentless kind of coach. He spent weeks observing teams in Japan, which dominated women's volleyball in the early 1980s. Back at Sports Performance, he drilled the girls in passing, digging, and spiking, effectively shaping them into what one former player dubs "little robots."

Butler is unabashed about his methods. "Regimentation is the only way to train a group," he says. "To play at a high level, you can't say, 'Do your own thing and develop your own style.' I believe, firmly, that most breakdowns in team sports come from individual breakdowns. . . . That's especially true for girls, because they aren't supposed to work very long and very hard. It comes back to the attitude 'I'm not afraid to go to the gym for three or four hours.'"

He unquestionably gets results, and his services do not come cheap: The elite players pay about $3,000 a year to compete at Butler's Great

Lakes Center, the sprawling, full-service training facility he opened in 1991. To play on the top team at Sports Performance, athletes must commit to training five or six days a week, seven months a year. Parents are banned from practices, which Butler regularly schedules on Friday night—and he benches anyone who skips to attend high-school dances. Players who criticize Butler or Sports Performance are immediately expelled from the program. And makeup is completely forbidden. "We ran extra sprints if someone wore nail polish," says Jeane Erlenborn, now 25 and a graduate student in public health at UCLA.

The girls also are required to weigh in before every practice. "Weight was a big issue," recalls a former player who is now an elementary school teacher and traces her persistent eating disorder back to Butler's stringent requirements. "No one talked about how they were making weight. Some girls threw up before practice. I tried not to eat during the week; I'd gorge on Friday, and then I'd take laxatives."

But for those who advance to Butler's senior girls' team, Sports Performance offers great rewards. The girls travel throughout the country and sometimes overseas, and 165 have received a total of more than $10 million in college scholarships. The players who excel do so by accepting the game as their religion—and Butler as their guru. The 1986 team bought him a T-shirt that read GOD.

With some distance on the program, however, some of its alumnae have begun to question their faith. "It was like being in a cult," one 26-year-old former player says. "Rick made the rules, and if you stepped out of line, he'd humiliate you verbally or punish you physically. He'd throw balls at you until you couldn't [return them] anymore."

"It was almost a status symbol to play injured," says Emily Peterson, 25, who suffers from chronic back pain from volleyball injuries. "Rick was a no-pain, no-gain coach."

Butler professes bafflement at such remarks. "The girls always talked back," he says. "They didn't have to be there. They could have left at any time. As we tell our parents, this program is not for everyone. It's for a select few."

The most select of these select few, Butler himself readily admits, became the objects of his romantic attentions. The first of the three accusers to have been involved with him, who asked that *Chicago* not use her name, says she tried out for Sports Performance because she wanted to become "the best volleyball player in the world." After three years as an outside hitter for Sports Performance in the early eighties, she won a scholarship to a Division I school. She even played for the Chicago Breeze, the short-lived professional team Butler coached for its début season in 1987.

The woman says Butler first made advances in the summer of 1981, when she was 16 and Butler was 26, on an overnight stay at Syracuse University en route to a tournament in Montreal. The day before, on a practice stop at Western Michigan University, Butler had berated her in front of the team for disobeying him at practice and threatened to send her home. Humiliated and terrified, she was exiled to the equipment van, where she sobbed all the way to New York. "When Rick called me to an upstairs lounge in the dorm, I thought, Oh, no. What's next?" recalls the woman, who is now married and lives in another state. "He said 'I'm sorry I had to do that to you. You have to obey my coaching and trust me.'" Then, she says, Butler kissed her on the lips. She was frightened, she says, but didn't know what to do.

A few weeks later, he invited her to his house in Glen Ellyn to eat Chinese food and discuss her athletic progress. While she was there, the woman says, Butler pressed her into having sex and, she notes, did not use a condom. "I had no control at all," she says. "I did not want to do it, and I didn't know how to do it." When he continued to initiate sex with her in numerous places, including the bathroom of a train in Germany, she submitted. "I was too afraid to tell anyone about the abuse," the woman says. "What if I came forward and no one [in the volleyball community] believed me? What if they believed me, but did nothing about it? What if my teammates ostracized me? I didn't want to be shunned."

She left for college in 1983, but continued to associate with Butler, even after graduation. "When I was drafted by the Chicago Breeze, it was either play for [Butler] or end my volleyball career," she says. "I'd never forgotten what happened. I'd just calloused over all the hurt Rick had caused me." The woman bristles at Butler's contention that their relationship was fully consensual. "Did I say no? Of course I did," she says. "I would say, 'No, please. No. Not now. Not here. No.'"

The next of the accusers, who also agreed to be interviewed on condition she not be named, grew up in the western suburbs, the daughter of a wrestler and a speed skater. She joined Sports Performance in 1982, and, like Bremner, she quickly warranted private coaching and a spot on the elite team. "I wanted to be the best," she says. "I was willing to do anything to be the best." A reedy woman, she looks years younger than 28, especially when her voice trembles and her eyes puddle with tears as she talks about Butler. "It's hard to imagine being so serious about something at such a young age," she says. "I was an easy target for Rick."

The first time she had sex with Butler, she says, was in the fall of 1983, when she was 16. She says she accepted his offer to help her write a paper at Kay Rogness's townhouse, where he was renting a room. "I assumed, as did my parents, that his roommate would be home, too," she wrote in the statement to the volleyball association. "But when I got to his house,

I found that it was just the two of us." After a pizza break, she claims, Butler backed her against a wall and kissed and fondled her. Then, she says, against her will, they had sex. "I was scared to death," she says. "Scared to tell him no, scared I'd get pregnant, scared my parents would find out and what they would think of me."

The woman says the sexual relations continued until she won a scholarship and escaped to a Western university. She remembers one particularly awful incident on the way to a national tournament in Rhode Island: On the bus, she says, Butler asked her to sit next to him in the front seat. She thought they were going to talk strategy, she says, but instead he placed a pillow over her lap and began fondling her genitals. "I was completely trapped and humiliated," she wrote in the statement. "I felt dirty, ashamed, powerless." Still she did not report the incident.

Today, she says, the trauma caused by the intimacy lingers. "There are days when I don't want to be touched," she says. "Even a little kiss on the cheek from my husband triggers bad memories. I feel dirty."

Butler says he never did anything wrong. "Did I ever have sex with them?" he asks. "Yes, but not when they say I did." He insists that each of the three was 18 and out of the program when romance blossomed, and that all sexual relations were consensual. He doesn't remember much about the first woman—their relationship was less serious, he says. But in the case of the second woman, he says, there was even discussion of marriage. "I went out with [her] in the summer of 1986," he says, "and sat down and picked out six names for our kids. Three boys and three girls—one of the names was Charley."

Butler recalls celebrating Thanksgiving with the woman's family in 1986, and claims that she worked for him every summer while she was in college. "She told numerous people at [school] she wanted a family, she wanted to marry me," he says. "In 1986, she came to me to borrow $725 to rent her apartment. In 1990, she called and asked me out to dinner. We went to the Chili's in Naperville. . . . If you do something that makes me repulsed and sick, I don't keep coming back and talking to you, I don't borrow money from you, I don't work for you, I don't call you, I don't go out to dinner with you. It doesn't make sense."

On occasion, Butler's outrage renders him almost incoherent. "You're telling me I have to answer to charges that we didn't have any rules for, and also, how can I answer charges that are 8 to 14 years old?" he blusters. "How can I prove where I was on this day, or this day or this day? . . .

"In 1987, the criminal statute in Illinois said the age of consent was 16. So now I'm answering charges about sex with a minor, but I'm not answering to charges that I violated any laws. But the U.S. Volleyball Association says we're not talking about breaking any laws. We're not talking about breaking any laws, not talking about violating . . . any rules, but we're talking about making a judgment on somebody and his liveli-hood. . . . Public embarrassment to USA Volleyball, that's what I'm charged with."

But a series of letters Butler wrote to the second woman undercut his assertions about her age at the time of involvement: "It seems like no matter how much we are separated I can't ever get you out of my mind . . . ," he wrote to her in January 1985, when she was 17 and he was on leave from Sports Performance to work as an assistant coach at Western Michigan University. "I think I've loved you from that first day at Burger King when I asked for your heart and soul and you gave it to me. Your [sic] such a special person in my life. I'll love you forever."

Another letter, dated May 1985, concludes: "I've seen you go from someone who was totally dependent on me to someone who I could sit and talk with for hours and never think about you only being 17. You went from someone I loved to someone I fell in love with."

In April 1994, after Julie Bremner called DCFS with her allegations against Butler, she telephoned Kay Rogness. For nearly a decade, Rogness had been Butler's colleague, friend, and landlord. But by the time Bremner contacted her, their relations had been acrimonious for years. Butler says the tension began over disparate business goals in the mid-1980s. "I wanted to coach at the Olympic level, so I had to develop a business that would enable me to take off work if the national team said, 'Can you come out for three or five weeks?'" he says. "The organization wasn't going in that direction." After Rogness left, he says, Sports Perfor-mance really took off. "She thinks she should have part of this," he said.

Rogness, who is 54 now, insists that their dispute centered strictly on her disapproval of Butler's intensive, intrusive coaching methods, and above all on his sexual relations with adolescent athletes. By 1986, Rog-ness says, Butler confirmed her suspicions by admitting to her that he'd slept with players. "I was absolutely astounded," Rogness says today. "And I was scared [by the legal implications]." Butler says no such con-versation took place.

Rogness says she went to the DuPage County state's attorney's office with the information, but was told nothing could be done unless one of the girls came forward. She then began a lengthy process of disentangle-ment from Sports Performance.

Three years later, Butler offered her about $40,000 for her half of the company. After further negotiation, they settled on a buyout for an undis-closed sum. (Sports Performance, Inc., is a not-for-profit enterprise, but its sister organization, Training and Publications, which runs volleyball camps and coaching seminars and produces videos, isn't.) By 1990, when

Rogness resigned all affiliation with Sports Performance, she was attending law school in Denver, Colorado. She says she does not harbor any grudge against Butler. He disagrees: "Kay has made it absolutely clear that she hates me."

Rogness says today that she had been ready to help Bremner for years. "Julie and I had breakfast in 1990, and I said, 'I'm pretty much aware of what the situation was between you and Rick,'" said Rogness. "I told her to call me if she ever needed any support." When the call finally came, Rogness was comfortably ensconced as an attorney in Denver, and as the director of that city's Front Range Volleyball Club. When Bremner asked her if she knew of other players who had slept with Butler (she wanted to direct them to DCFS investigators), Rogness immediately turned her attentions to the case.

Rogness says she had long known of at least two other women with whom Butler had had sexual relations. On Bremner's behalf, she called them, and the three former players began a long series of telephone calls that evolved into informal therapy sessions. They discovered that they had had much in common as teenagers: natural athletic ability, galloping ambition, flat chests, freckled faces, and brown hair, which they wore in ponytails. (The three also bear an uncanny resemblance to Butler's 33-year-old wife, a coach at Sports Performance.) For each, Butler was her first sexual partner. Over several weeks, the women came to realize that Butler had used identical tactics to cultivate their trust, isolate them from teammates, and persuade them not to talk: None of the women had gone to an authority during their relations with Butler.

Experts who treat sexual predators and their victims say delayed complaints are typical, especially when the perpetrator is well respected and holds power over the victim. Few relationships fit that pattern so well as that of coach to star athlete. "Coaches hold a revered place in the mythology of American sports," writes Joan Ryan in her 1995 book *Little Girls in Pretty Boxes: The Making and Breaking of Elite Gymnasts and Figure Skaters*. "Coaches of elite children's sports, by spending the bulk of every day with their athletes, can influence these children more than their parents or their teachers at school."

"[Butler] may have had some wonderful qualities that attracted these girls to him and made them willing to put up with [the sexual relations]," says Sharon Lamb, an assistant professor of psychiatry at Bryn Mawr college and author of the forthcoming *Blameworthy: Victims and Perpetrators of Abuse and the Problems of Responsibility*. "On some level, the girls may have felt flattered, but also abused. It's likely [Butler] had a distorted view of adolescent girls, picturing them as older and more able to make choices. I can see why an adolescent girl would have terribly mixed feelings about turning him in."

Judith Herman, assistant professor of psychiatry at Harvard Medical School and author of *Trauma and Recovery* (1992), says victims often put off making accusations against an abuser until years after the relations have ended, and even then, it often takes another forthcoming victim to inspire them to do so.

When Julie Bremner began making phone calls, that's what she found out. "I really wanted to forget the whole thing," admits the second woman Butler slept with, who refuses even to look at a volleyball today. "But when Julie called, I was seven months pregnant. I said to my husband, 'What happens if we enroll our child in a sports program, thinking it's the best and it's safe, and our child ends up getting molested?' I decided to speak out because if someone had information about a program our child was in, I'd want them to come forward. And I also didn't think Julie would be believed."

"Victims will do for others what they wish they could have done for themselves," Herman explains.

In May 1994, after interviewing Butler's accusers, questioning Butler in the gym, and evaluating a blistering five-page report from Kay Rogness, DCFS investigators classified the case against Butler as "indicated for risk of harm." This means authorities believe the evidence supports the allegations, and that the information will be kept on file for five years. Butler has appealed the classification.

Because the statute of limitations for pressing charges or filing suit has expired for all three accusers, their only remaining avenue of retribution was through the sport's governing association. In June, volleyball officials and coaches, including Rogness, convened in Tulsa for the U.S. Volleyball Association's annual meeting. Rumors about Butler's sexual misconduct spread like wildfire. Later, Rogness began a letter-writing campaign to lobby for his disqualification.

"The facts indicate [Butler] is not fit, ethically or morally, to be a coach," Rogness wrote to Rebecca Howard, chair of the U.S. Volleyball Association's Ethics and Eligibility Committee. "Therefore, at a minimum [the association] should refuse to endorse him by canceling his membership in the organization."

Thirteen months later, after investigations at the regional and national levels, and two sets of investigatory hearings, Rick Butler became the first volleyball coach in history to be expelled from the association for sexual misconduct. Under the ruling, he can reapply for membership in five years, but is prohibited from coaching girls under 18 for the rest of his life. "The act by a coach of having sexual intercourse with a junior volleyball player entrusted to his care," read the ethics committee's verdict, "constitutes such immorality, lack of judgment and unacceptable behavior as to cause USA Volleyball, at minimum, public embarrassment and ridicule by its merely having taken place."

Butler appealed the decision in October. But the volleyball association's executive committee upheld it. At press time, in addition to filing suit, Butler had asked the Cook County Circuit Court for a temporary restraining order to nullify the expulsion until the case is settled.

Butler is also under criminal investigation by the DuPage County state's attorney's office. Though it's too late for Bremner and company, if a more recent accuser comes forward, Butler could be indicted for aggravated criminal sexual abuse, a charge that carries a minimum jail sentence of four years.

Meanwhile, the volleyball association's ruling means that Butler cannot register as head coach or sit on the bench during tournaments it sponsors (which dominate the junior volleyball arena), and that he will almost certainly not coach in the 1996 Olympics. But it has not noticeably reduced the volume of business at Sports Performance, or Butler's interaction with underage girls.

Even Julie Bremner's mother, Joy Dooley, still has a daughter at Sports Performance. Bonnie Bremner, who lives with her father, plays on Butler's elite team. "Bonnie is right where Julie was, in terms of not understanding the power she is under," Dooley says. "She knows I don't want her in the program, but she is going to be there whether I like it or not. The minute she gets to college and gets some space from the program, I hope she'll see the big picture."

But the "big picture" at Sports Performance may never become clear. For many of its players, being coached by Rick Butler has altered the course of their lives positively and permanently. For others, it has been devastating. But for all the girls, the experience is unforgettable. "When Rick paid attention to you, it made your day," recalls one of Butler's former players who used to defend Julie Bremner against rumors that she was sleeping with him. She pauses and takes a deep breath. "Since I heard the truth about Julie and Rick," she continues, "I've thought a lot about what I would have done in her situation. I can't say with any certainty that I would have said no."

◀▦▶

IN THE BUFF

Female Athletes Take It All Off

Penny Hastings

The soccer player did it to copy the guys. A swimmer did it to show off her muscles. An entire team did it for money.

All are women. All are Olympic athletes. And all of them, plus an increasing number of other elite sportswomen, have recently bared their buffed bodies for public viewing and sparked a heated debate in the sports community. Nude is rude, say critics. Not so, others retort. One young woman described the criticism as ". . . a bunch of bull. We're fit. We're healthy. We do good things with our bodies and they are functional. Why not show them off?"

The furor started with Brandi Chastain, member of the USA women's soccer team, when she ripped off her soccer jersey after scoring the winning goal in the 1999 Women's World Cup.

The media went wild, and the shot seen round the world was not of the kick nor the laces on Chastain's gifted boot . . . but on her shirtless torso and black Nike sports bra. Her action was given as much ink and tube time as the game itself and a hot debate ensued over whether what she did was a spontaneous reaction to the moment or a calculated move to gain personal notoriety. Chastain claimed "temporary insanity," while her celebrity status soared.

Today, Chastain's move seems tame compared to the more recent spate of nudity among female athletes.

Take USA Olympic swimmer, Jenny Thompson, for instance. Before leaving for Sydney, she posed for *Sports Illustrated* wearing red boots, a red-white-and-blue swimsuit bottom and nothing covering her bare breasts but her fists. She said she did it to display a muscular, athletic form.

To that, Mary Jo Kane, director of the Tucker Center for Research on Girls and Women in Sport at the University of Minnesota, retorted, "It's not clear to me which muscle group naked breasts belong to."

Entire teams have dived into the nudity pool. Olympic high jumper Amy Acuff got 11 other female track and field athletes to pose in the buff for a calendar that sold for $19.95.

From Knight Ridder/Tribune, 24 September 2000. © McClatchy-Tribune Information Services. All rights reserved. Reprinted with permission.

Not to be overlooked, the Canadian women's cross-country ski team produced its "Nordic Nudes" calendar. Team member Sara Renner told *The Calgary Herald* they did it to raise money and awareness: ". . . this is a way to get cross-country skiing as a household sport, even if we have to take our clothes off to do it."

But it's the Australia's women's soccer team, the Matildas, who win the "Full Monty" award. They produced their own calendar featuring full frontal nudity.

With this new game called, "Can You Top This?" there's no telling where the notion to take it off will end . . . or even, if it will end.

What's happening here? Perhaps it's an unconscious wish to go back to 776 B.C. and the first Olympic Games, when all athletes competed in the nude? All male athletes, that is. Women were not allowed to participate in athletic events. The truth is that they were forbidden to even watch the competition and the punishment for peeking was death! Women certainly don't want to go back there.

Maybe they are merely mimicking their male counterparts. That's what Chastain said, when criticized for doffing her top. The men do it. Yes, and some men do the chicken dance after touchdowns and talk trash and get arrested.

Maybe female athletes who bare it all are doing it for publicity and the money that comes from endorsements and notoriety. Frustration at being largely ignored by the media and sponsors can make people do desperate things—like box a kangaroo, take a koala bear to lunch, or pose for a nude calendar.

Maybe it's exhibitionism—pure and simple—having nothing whatsoever to do with gender. Isn't it possible that some women—just like some men—enjoying showing off their bodies?

Critics say it's another way to sexualize female athletes, something that's been around for as long as women have been involved with sports. But, what's different now is that in this generation of athletes, a small percentage of women are not only condoning being sexualized, but even helping the process along. "As if they were saying," Kane remarks, "'Hey, we've arrived. We can be soft-porn icons, too.'"

But the Olympians who dressed down, or didn't dress at all, for their calendar and magazine photos, don't believe that what they did was wrong, much less pornographic. They say they're proud of the hard, lean, muscular bodies they've worked diligently to develop. And they should be proud. Watch Jenny Thompson, who has won more gold medals than any other American swimmer, as she prepares to dive into the pool. Who could fail to notice her strong, powerful, beautifully contoured body? A body honed to perfection by years of training and hard work. A body that performs exquisitely among the best athletes in the world.

Thompson doesn't need to take anything off for us to marvel at her athletic body. Neither do the track and field calendar girls or the Matildas. Nudity is not only inappropriate in women's sports, nude is rude.

◆◆◆

A NEW IMAGE EXPOSED

Tom Maloney

Are female athletes being exploited by showing off their muscular bodies in photos? No way says Canadian swimmer Marianne Limpert, and she's willing to show off hers.

OK, so I'm not really naked either. But it would certainly be a delight to be so, alongside Jenny Thompson, Brandi Chastain, or any of the four synchro swimmers photographed wearing a single towel. Or all four, maybe. Hmmm. There's a thought.

Or Marianne Limpert. She's beautiful too, and blessed with a toned, athletic body. Only difference is, her nationality being Canadian, the likes of *Sports Illustrated, Gear Magazine,* and *Women's Sports and Fitness* haven't asked her to do pre-Olympic, semi-nude pictorials.

Could she, would she?

"I have to say, if someone approached me, and it was going to be tastefully done, I wouldn't have a problem," says Limpert, scheduled to swim the 100 freestyle, 200 individual medley, and two relays in Sydney. "You spend four or five hours a day working out, and now, you've got a great body. I don't see what's wrong with that. If you're athletic and proud of your body, and you believe, in agreeing to do this, that it is not being exploiting, then why not? If you don't want to do it, you don't have to do it."

Limpert, confident and proud and independent, is comfortable discussing this subject seriously and lightly at the same time.

"Hey, you've got my wheels churning," the Fredericton native says with a laugh, from her current home in Vancouver, "I've got a Maclean's shoot in a couple of days. Maybe I can go topless and become the first Canadian athlete to do it!"

Thompson has already done it, sort of, by standing on a beach wearing only a stars-and-stripes bathing suit bottom for *SI.* The two-time

From *National Post* 2:263 (26 August 2000): A17. Material reprinted with the express permission of: "National Post Company", a CanWest Partnership.

Olympian is facing the camera with her fists placed strategically over her breasts.

Meantime, Chastain was covered by only a soccer ball in *Gear*. She then became famous for ripping her shirt off following the U.S. World Cup soccer victory in 1999.

Then, there are the perfectly toned, and yet nubile women from the Australian soccer team, topless in a fundraising calendar that sold in the thousands worldwide via the Web.

Last year, Nike ads showed nudes, in silhouette. This summer, *Esquire*'s Olympic spread focuses on athletic beauty, or is that, beautiful athletes?

The trend is putting some knickers in a serious twist. These elite female athletes have it, know how to use it, and aren't afraid of showing it. Gasp.

See, the feminists at the Women's Sports Foundation in New York have built careers—no, lawsuits and industries—by snooping for evidence of disrespect. They're kind of like the archaic affirmative-action specialists still employed full-time by Canadian governments, except their activities are restricted to the wide world of sports.

Their creed is: women equal to men, without qualification. Ergo, in their minds, Thompson becomes a glorified *Playboy* model, totally counter to their raison d'etre.

Like Limpert, Thompson is 27. She is tied with Bonnie Blair for most Olympic medals by an American female athlete. Like Limpert, she was cheated out of glory in Atlanta by Chinese swimmers apparently propelled by performance-enhancing substances. Heading for a medical degree at an Ivy League school, Thompson doesn't give a doodle about fuddy-duddy feminist reaction to her decisions. In fact, she wonders, why doesn't *SI* use female athletes for its infamous bathing-suit issue, rather than supermodels? Whoa.

"Exactly," Limpert agrees. "I think we present a healthier body image than some of those rake-thin models."

Women should forgive us men folk once in a while. They must agree, it is certainly adding up to a perplexing chapter in women's history. Consider the contradiction: Women from the bra-burning era now get enraged because Chastain peels her shirt to expose a sports bra.

"Are these people repressed, or what?" Limpert asks, about societal reaction in general to Chastain's (calculated? paid? spontaneous?) striptease. "I mean, what is going on here? Go jogging through a park in Vancouver and you'll see women in sports bras sitting on public benches."

Maybe this debate is just a North American thing. In Sydney, Thompson, Chastain, Limpert and all the other female Olympians can use a break from competition to go topless at fabulous Bondi Beach. In fact, by sunbathing with their tops on, they would be distinguishing themselves prudishly from the rest of the women on the beach.

Thompson's pose, and Limpert's attitude, at least to this Cro-Magnon, seem to represent evolutionary development from the women's movement on this continent.

Thompson didn't pose as a sexual object. She is showing off a muscular, hyper-fit female body that would have been regarded as freakish in 1960. Limpert argues that such photos repair the notion that the ideal female athlete should resemble a lithe figure skater.

Lost in all the women's-lib, hysterical reaction to the photos is the fact that some 40% of Olympians in Sydney will be female. Among them are big, strong women's water polo players, granted admission to the Summer Games for the first time.

"When we start exposing more elite female Olympic athletes to the general public, I think we get a little more used to the idea that it's OK to play tough, physical sports like water polo," says Heather Kaulback, operations director for the Canadian team. "I think we're still educating the general public that it's OK to be female and a good athlete, and getting away from that age-old tomboy [stigma]."

At the same time, the posing athletes are staying honest about it. It's a commercial world, and we'd be naive to believe these media-aware, Internet-generation athletes aren't fully cognizant of the effect they're having. This particularly evolutionary trend happens to please the male eye.

"Sex sells," Limpert says.

PART VI

The Feminine Image in Sports and Sports Media

Part VI takes as its subjects the representation of women athletes in sports media and in the fictional world of feature films, as well as the embattled history of women journalists covering men's sports. Media matters because of the commercial nature of big-time sports. Women's professional sports, especially embryonic professional soccer, basketball, softball, and volleyball leagues, face a conundrum. To gain popularity a sport must be visible, which in our society means gaining television and print media attention. But for networks to assume the cost of televising a sport, they must be confident that advertisers will pay to promote their products during telecasts. Marketers base their decisions on the perceived popularity of the particular sport or league as they try to gauge market size and potential profits and losses. This becomes a vicious circle for promoters of women's sports: sports promoters need adequate media coverage to attract an audience for a sport, yet promoters cannot interest the media in covering a sport unless it is already deemed popular.

Although the question of whether a sport receives media coverage is an important one, this section concentrates primarily on *how* women's sports are covered by the various media. The section begins with Michael Messner, Margaret Carlisle Duncan, and Kerry Jensen's key article on television coverage of women's sports. "Separating the Men from the Girls" uncovers some of the ways in which television sportscasters consciously or unconsciously adopt different styles for the coverage of men's and women's events, perpetuating the gender bias that pervades women's sports, as explored in Parts IV and V. A shorter item, the transcript of Richard C. Crepeau's Sport and Society radio broadcast, discusses how NBC adopted a new style of television coverage for the 1996 Olympic Games in hopes of capturing a larger female audience, turning the Games into a sporty soap opera. Crepeau is not the only sports scholar to have made that connection.

Movies are another site of cultural representation. Women's sports films, of which there were comparatively few until the 1990s, have enjoyed a rise in popularity in the last fifteen years with films such as *A League of their Own*, *Blue Crush*, and *Million Dollar Baby*. Taken as a group, these presumably modern stories about female athletes and the manner in which they are filmed tell us much about the dominant cultural attitudes toward sportswomen. In an industry that typically spends a lot to make a lot, every film has to perform well at the box office and in the film rental industry to generate a profit. So, what sorts of stories "sell" when the protagonist is a woman athlete? In "The Women's Sports Film as the New Melodrama," Jean O'Reilly uncovers some disturbing messages embedded in films that purport to celebrate the modern sportswoman.

Similarly, in reporting on sporting events, which actions or events do journalists consider newsworthy and which ones are ignored or dismissed? For instance, when a long-distance runner started menstruating and bled through her uniform in a televised race, should broadcasters have discussed or politely ignored the story? Lorie Conway argues for frank discussion of normal biological processes in "It's Time to Tell the Bloody Truth." If a female athlete's husband or boyfriend sits in the stands, television cameras are likely to turn in his direction while announcers identify him and comment on his admirable support. The same can be said for male athletes' wives and girlfriends. Yet there is seldom any visual or spoken acknowledgement of an athlete's same-sex partner who sits in the stands, rooting just as ardently. Media coverage, which does much to influence the popularity of certain sports and sports figures, also dictates which sports-related stories are newsworthy, which are insignificant, and which are simply taboo.

The absence of information and accurate representation can influence athletic experience, also. In the case of boxing, the media often treat women's events as a spectacle, freak show, or sidelight to the main event rather than a legitimate activity. When matches are sold to the public as spectacle rather than as evenly matched competitions, boxers do not always receive adequate preparation. Moreover, no competent organizational body regulates the sport. In at least one case this dangerous situation led to a tragic outcome in which a novice boxer with insufficient training sustained a serious, permanent brain injury. Joe Posnanski tells the tale in "Bloodsport: Woman's First Pro Fight Is Her Last." As the calamitous outcome, rather than the boxing match, becomes news it can encourage the belief that women are not tough enough for the sport, reinforcing the "truth" that boxing is a hyper-masculine sport even as most women boxers refute that claim with their skill and moxie. The media, then, not only report the news but shape the culture of sport, influencing the news they then report.

When women journalists cover men's sporting events, the shoe is on the other foot. Sexual harassment, especially of female reporters in men's locker rooms, has on occasion become a news story itself, as Sherry Ricchiardi demonstrates in "Offensive Interference." Women reporters have often been singled out and sexualized in a context that is supposed to be purely professional, creating a dynamic that influences both the culture and coverage of men's sport. That dynamic also shapes the broader athletic culture in which women compete by marking some women as sexual objects instead of serious, competent professionals. And so the discriminatory media treatment of women athletes in the United States has, to a certain extent, been reenacted within the machinery of the very sports media that women journalists represent.

◄◆►

SEPARATING THE MEN FROM THE GIRLS

The Gendered Language of Televised Sports

Michael A. Messner, Margaret Carlisle Duncan, and Kerry Jensen

Introduction

Feminist scholars have argued that in the twentieth century, the institution of sport has provided men with a homosocial sphere of life through which they have bolstered a sagging ideology of male superiority.[1] Through the exclusion of women, and the association of males with physical competence, strength, power, and even violence, sport has provided a basis through which men have sought to reconstitute an otherwise challenged masculine hegemony (Bryson, 1987; Hall, 1988; Kidd, 1987; Messner, 1988; Theberge, 1981; Whitson, 1990).

But starting with the 1972 passage of Title IX in the U.S., athletic participation of school-age girls increased dramatically. In 1971, only 294,015 girls participated in high school sports, compared with 3,666,917 boys. By the 1989–90 academic year, there were 1,858,659 girls participating in high school sports, compared with 3,398,192 boys.[2] Increased numerical participation in sports by girls and women has been accompanied by changing attitudes as well. A nationwide survey found large majorities of parents and children agreeing that "sports are no longer for boys only" (Wilson and Women's Sports Foundation, 1988). With increases in opportunities for female athletes, including expanded youth programs, better and earlier coaching, and increases in scholarships for college women athletes, some dramatic improvements in female athletic performance have resulted. In fact, the "muscle gap"—the degree of difference between male and female athletic performance in measurable

From Michael Messner, Margaret Carlisle Duncan, and Kerry Jensen, *Gender and Society* (7) pp. 121–137, copyright 1993. Reprinted by Permission of Sage Publications, Inc.

sports like swimming and track and field—has closed considerably in the past fifteen years (Crittenden, 1979; Dyer, 1982; Kidd, 1990). In short, the dramatic increase in female athleticism has begun to challenge the assumption that sport is and should be a "male world." Organized sports, though still dominated by men at nearly all levels, has in the past two decades become a "contested terrain" of gender relations (Birrell, 1987/ 1988; Messner, 1988).

Much of the continued salience of sport as an institutional site for the construction and legitimation of masculine power lies in its role as a mass-mediated spectacle (Clarke and Clarke, 1982; Hargreaves, 1986; Willis, 1982). There *has* been a boom in female athletic participation, but the sports media has been very slow to reflect it. Bryant's (1980) two-year content analysis of two newspapers revealed that only 4.4% of total column inches devoted to sports focused on women's sports. Graydon (1983) observed that in the early 1980's, over 90% of sports reporting covered men's sports. Rintala and Birrell's (1984) analysis of *Young Athlete* magazine, and Duncan and Sayaovong's (1990) examination of *Sports Illustrated for Kids* magazine revealed that visual images of male athletes in these magazines tend to outnumber those of female athletes by a roughly two-to-one ratio. Moreover, text and visual images tend to frame female and male athletes "as fundamentally and essentially different," and thus to support stereotypical notions of natural differences between the sexes (Duncan and Sayaovong, 1990:91). In part of our study (not dealt with in this paper), we examined four major metropolitan daily newspapers and found that over a three-month period in 1990, 81% of all sports column inches were devoted exclusively to men's sports, 3.5% covered women's sports, and 15.5% covered both men's and women's sports, or gender-neutral topics. We also examined six weeks of a leading television newscast, and found that 92% of sports news time was devoted exclusively to men's sports, 5% covered women's sports, and 3% covered gender-neutral topics. This sort of ignoring or underreporting of existing women's events contributes to the continuation of what Gerbner (1978) called "the symbolic annihilation" of women's sports.

Despite the paucity of coverage of women's sports by the media, there are some recent signs of increased coverage, especially on cable television (Eastman and Meyer, 1989). If there is indeed a "window of opportunity" for increased coverage of women's sports on television, the question of *how* women's and men's sports are covered becomes crucial. To date, very few analyses of the quality of live, televised, play-by-play coverage of women's sports have been conducted. Studies of 1970's and 1980's, revealed that women athletes (when they were reported on television at all) were likely to be overly trivialized, infantilized, and sexualized (Boutilier and San Giovanni, 1983; Duncan, 1990; Dyer, 1987; Felshin, 1974). Even excellent performances by women athletes were likely to be framed "ambivalently" by sports commentators (Duncan and Hasbrook, 1988).

We were interested in comparing how live, play-by-play television sports commentators talk about women's sports and women athletes with how they talk about men's sports and men athletes. We constructed our research design, in part, from the now-vast feminist literature on gender and language. In short, this literature demonstrates that the ways men and women talk—and the ways we are talked about—are deeply gendered. For instance, a woman secretary would likely use the formal "Mr.," along with the last name, when speaking to her male boss, while he would probably feel free to refer to her by her first name. This kind of language convention tends to (often subtly) mark gender difference (and, in the above example, social class difference as well) in ways that support and reinforce the power and privilege of "dominants" over "subordinates." The micropolitical realm of face-to-face interaction and language both reflects and constructs the micropolitical realm of unequal power relations between groups (Henley, 1977, 1987; Lakoff, 1975; Miller and Swift, 1977; Thorne, Kramarae and Henley, 1985; Schultz, 1975; Spender, 1980).

Description of Research

Our aim was to utilize feminist insights on gendered language to examine the ways that television commentators talk about women's and men's sports. We chose to examine two sports where televised coverage of women's and men's contests could be compared: basketball and tennis. For a number of years, women's tennis has been highly visible on television, but women's college basketball is only recently beginning to be televised (albeit mostly on cable TV, and often on late-night tape delay). We reasoned that a comparison of the more "established" television sport of tennis with the relative "newcomer" of women's basketball might be revealing.

Live televised coverage of the 1989 women's and men's NCAA final four basketball tournaments were compared and analyzed. (It should be noted that we chose the "final four," rather than regular-season games because there are so few women's regular season games actually broadcast on television.) This amounted to three women's games and three men's games, including introductions/lead-ins and halftime shows. We also examined the four final days of televised coverage of the 1989 U.S. Open tennis tournament. Televised coverage consisted of four men's singles matches (two quarterfinals, one semifinal, and the final), three women's singles matches (two semis and the final), one men's doubles match (the final), two women's doubles matches (a semi and the final), and one mixed doubles match (the final).

Three general questions guided our analysis: First, do commentators overtly trivialize and/or sexualize women's sports and individual women athletes in the ways that previous analysts have identified? Second, do sports commentators speak about women's and men's athletic contests differently? In particular, to what extent (if any) are women's and men's events verbally "gender marked" (e.g., "the *women's* national championship")? Third, do commentators speak of individual women and men athletes differently? For instance, are women athletes referred to as "girls" or as "women"? Are men athletes referred to as "boys" or as "men"?

First, we recorded the basketball games and tennis matches on videotape, and conducted a pilot study of the tapes. The pilot study had two outcomes: First, the research design was fine-tuned. In particular, a preliminary list of specific qualitative and quantitative questions was constructed. Next, we developed standardized ways of analyzing the verbal commentary. Then, the research assistant viewed all of the tapes and compiled a detailed record of her observations. Next, all of the tapes were independently viewed and analyzed by one of the investigators, who then added her written analysis to that of the research assistant. Finally, the data was compiled and analyzed by the two investigators, using both sets of written descriptions of the tapes, and by viewing portions of the tapes once again.

Our data revealed very little of the overtly sexist commentary that has been observed in past research. Women's sports and women athletes were not overtly trivialized in tennis or in basketball commentary. And though camera angles at times may have subtly framed women athletes (especially in tennis) as sexual objects in ways that were not symmetrical with the ways men were framed, the verbal commentary did not frame women in this way. However, we did find two categories of differences in the verbal commentary: (1) Gender marking; (2) A "hierarchy of naming" by gender, and to a certain extent by race.

Women Marked as Other

In women's basketball, gender was constantly marked, both verbally and through the use of graphics. We were continually reminded that we were watching the "*Women's* final four," the NCAA *Women's* National Championship Game," that these were some of the best *women's* college basketball teams," that coach Pat Summit "is a legend in *women's* basketball," that "this NCAA *women's* semifinal is brought to you by. . . ."

Gender was also marked through the use of graphics in the women's games which CBS broadcast, but not in the ESPN game. The CBS logo marked the women's championship game: "NCAA Women's National Championship," as did their graphics above game scores. ESPN's graphic did not mark gender: "NCAA Semifinal." As Table 1 indicates, over the course of the three women's games, there were 28 instances of graphic, and 49 cases of verbal gender marking, for a total of 77 instances of gender marking. This meant that gender was being marked an average of 25.6 times per women's game.

During the women's games, when commentators were discussing the next day's men's games, the men's games were sometimes gender marked (e.g.: "the *men*'s championship game will be played tomorrow.") But during the men's basketball games, we observed no instances of gender marking, either verbal or graphic. Men's games were always referred to as universal, both verbally and in on-screen graphic logos (e.g., "The NCAA National Championship Game," "The Final Four," etc.).

Women's and men's tennis matches were verbally gender-marked in a roughly equitable manner (e.g., "Men's doubles finals," "Women's singles semifinals," etc.). Verbal descriptions of athletes, though, revealed a tendency to gender mark women, not men. For instance, in the mixed doubles match, the commentators stated several times that Rick Leach is "one of the best doubles players in the world," while Robyn White was referred to as one of "the most animated girls on the circuit." An instance of graphic gender marking in tennis which we found notable was the tendency by CBS to display a pink on-screen graphic for the women's matches, and a blue on-screen graphic for the men's matches.

How might we interpret these observations? Stanley (1977) suggests that although *asymmetrical* gender marking tends to mark women as "other," *symmetrical* gender marking is not necessarily oppressive. In fact, she argues that the move toward a totally gender-neutral language may serve to further render women invisible. This would probably be the case if the language of sports reporting and commentary became gender neutral. In fact, in certain cases (in the daily television program, for instance) gender marking is probably necessary to clarify what the viewer will be tuning in to watch. We observed this sort of gender-marking in

Table 1
Gender Marking in Basketball (three women's games, three men's games)

	Women	Men
Verbal	49	o
Graphic	28	o
Total	77 (25.6)	o

tennis, where women's and men's matches (though not always women and men *athletes*) were verbally gender-marked in a roughly symmetrical manner. The rough symmetry of gender-marking in tennis might be explained by the fact that the women's and men's tennis tournaments were being played in the same venue, with coverage often cutting back and forth to women's, men's, and mixed-doubles matches. In this context, symmetrical gender-marking probably provides a necessary sense of clarity for the viewers, though the pink (for women) and blue (for men) graphic onscreen logos tended to mark gender in a manner which reinforced conventional gender stereotypes.

By contrast, the women's and men's basketball games were played in different cities, on different nights. And our data revealed a dramatic asymmetry in the commentary: Women's games were verbally and graphically gender marked an average of 25.6 times per game, while men's games were never gender marked. We did not include gender-marked team names (e.g., "Lady Techsters, Lady Tigers, Lady Volunteers") in these tabulations because we reasoned that team names are the responsibility of their respective universities, not the networks or commentators. Nevertheless, gender-marked team names have recently been criticized as "contributing to the maintenance of dominance within college athletics by defining women athletes and women's athletic programs as second class and trivial" (Eitzen and Baca Zinn 1989:362). In several colleges and universities in recent years, faculty and students have attempted to change gender-marked women's team names (Eitzen and Baca Zinn, 1990). In the three women's basketball games which we examine, team names were gender marked 53 times graphically, 49 times verbally (a total of 102 times). As Table 2 reveals, when we add these numbers to our original tabulations, we see that the combination of on-screen graphics, verbal commentary, and team names and logos amounted to a constant barrage of gender marking in the women's games: gender was marked in some fashion an average of 59.7 times per women's game. By contrast, the men's games were always simply referred to as "the national championship games," etc. As a result, the men's games and tournament

Table 2

Gender Marking in Basketball (three women's games, three men's games, including gender-marked team names)

	Women	Men
Verbal	98	0
Graphic	81	0
Total	179 (59.7)	0

were presented as the norm, the universal, while the women's were continually marked as the other, derivative (and by implication, inferior) to the men's.

A Gendered Hierarchy of Naming

There were stark contrasts between how men athletes and women athletes were referred to by commentators. This was true both in tennis and in basketball. First, and as we had expected, women were commonly referred to as "girls" as "young ladies," and as "women." (Often the naming of women athletes was ambivalent. For instance, Steffi Graf was referred to as "the wonder girl of women's tennis.") By contrast, the male athletes, *never* referred to as "boys," were referred to as "men," "young men," or "young fellas." Second, when athletes were named, commentators used the first name only of the women far more commonly than for the men. This difference was most stark in tennis commentary, as revealed in Table 3.

In basketball, the degree of difference in the use of first names of women and men players was not as dramatic, but the pattern was similar. In the three women's basketball games, we counted 31 incidents of women athletes being referred to by their first name only. This occurred 19 times in the men's games.

How do we interpret these differences in how commentators talk about male and female athletes? After these research findings were released at a national press conference, Diana Nyad, one of the USA Network tennis commentators, stated that the difference in first and last name use in women's and men's tennis commentary is not due to "sexism," but is simply a result of the fact that the women tennis players are more likely to be "teen-aged girls," while the men players are likely to be older (Herbert, 1990). This was an interesting response, given that in the tennis matches we examined in our study, the range of ages for the male players was 19–29, with the mean age 22.8, and the range of ages for female players was 19–32, with the mean age 24.0. In the NCAA basketball tournaments, all of the female and male players were college students, and

Table 3
First and Last Name Use in Tennis Commentary (totals [percentages], by sex)

	First Only	Last Only	First & Last
Women	304 (52.7)	166 (28.8)	107 (18.5)
Men	44 (7.8)	395 (69.8)	127 (22.4)

roughly the same age. Clearly, actual age differences do not explain commentators' tendency to refer to women athletes as "girls," "young ladies," and by first name only.

Research has demonstrated that "dominants" (either by social class, age, occupational position, race, or gender) are more commonly referred to by their last names (often prefaced by titles such as "Mr."). "Dominants" generally have license to refer to "subordinates" (younger people, employees, lower class people, ethnic minorities, women, etc.) by their first names (Henley, 1977; McConnell-Ginet, 1978; Rubin, 1981; Wolfson and Manes, 1980). The practice of referring more "formally" to dominants, and more "informally" (or "endearingly") to subordinates linguistically grants the former adult status, while marking the latter in an infantilizing way. And research suggests that these linguistic differences both reflect and (re)construct inequality. For instance, Brannon (1978) had 462 college students read a story describing a female's application for a high-level executive position, in which she was referred to either as a "girl" or as a "woman." Students' ratings of personality traits described the "woman" as more tough, brilliant, mature, and dignified, more qualified to be hired, and more deserving of a higher salary than the "girl." Similarly the term "lady" tends to "evoke a standard of propriety, correct behavior, and elegance" (Miller and Swift, 1977), and "carries overtones recalling the age of chivalry, implying that women are helpless and cannot do things for themselves," all of which are characteristics which are "decidedly unathletic" (Eitzen and Baca Zinn, 1990: 5–6). It can be concluded that tennis commentators' tendency to call women athletes "girls" and "young ladies," and their utilization of the first name only of women athletes (52.7% of the time) far more commonly than men athletes (7.8% of the time) reflects the lower status of women athletes. Moreover, it is reasonable to speculate that this language is likely to be received by viewers in such a way that it reinforces any already-existing negative attitudes or ambivalences about women's sports and women athletes.

We can speculate as to why the contrast in gendered patterns of naming was not as stark in basketball as it was in tennis. Perhaps since female tennis players have traditionally been stereotyped in more conventionally "feminine" ways than other female athletes, there is more of a (probably unconscious) tendency for commentators to view them (and talk about them) in an infantilizing manner. Moreover, women tennis players are often participating in the same venue as the men (and in the case of mixed doubles, in the very same *matches* with the men), and perhaps this contributes to an unconscious tendency to verbally separate them from the men by naming them differently. By contrast, female basketball players are participating in a traditionally defined "male" sport that requires a good deal of physically aggressive body-contact. Perhaps as a result, commentators are less likely to (again, probably unconsciously) view them and talk about them using conventionally "feminine" and infantilizing language. And since the women's basketball games are being constantly and thoroughly gender-marked, both graphically and verbally, there is little chance that their games will be confused with those of the men. There may therefore be less of an unconscious tendency on the part of commentators to verbally differentiate them from the men in terms of how they are named.

In addition to the tendency to linguistically infantilize women, while granting men athletes adult status, the quality of commentators' verbal attributions of strength and weakness, success and failure, for women's and men's events also tended to differ. In basketball, verbal attributions of strength to women were often stated in ambivalent language which undermined or neutralized the words conveying power and strength: "big girl," "she's tiny, she's small, but so effective under the boards," "her little jump hook," etc. A difference in descriptions of basketball coaches was also noted. Joe Ciampi (male) "yells" at his team, while Pat Summit (female) was described twice in the Auburn vs. Tennessee game as "screaming" off the bench. Men coaches were not described as "screaming," a term which often implies lack of control, powerlessness, even hysteria.

In tennis, "confidence" was very frequently used to describe strength for women, but not so often for men. We speculated that confidence is considered a "given" for men, but an attribute for which women players must constantly strive. Even very strong descriptors, for women, were often framed ambivalently: "That young lady Graf is relentless," or sexualized: "Sabatini has put together this first set with such naked aggression." And whereas for women, spectacular shots were sometimes referred to as "lucky," for the men, there were constant references to the imposition of their wills on the games (and on opponents). In men's doubles, for example, "You can feel McEnroe imposing his will all over this court. I mean not just with Woodford but Flach and Seguso. He's just giving them messages by the way he's standing at the net, the way he kind of swaggers between points."

There was little ambivalence in the descriptions of men: There are "big" guys with "big" forehands, who play "big games." There was a constant suggestion of male power and agency in the commentary. Even descriptions of men's weaknesses were commonly framed in a language of agency: "He created his own error. . . ." Discussion of men's "nervousness" was often qualified to make it sound like strength and heroism. For instance, early in the Becker/Krickstein match, the two commentators had this exchange: "They're both pretty nervous, and that's pretty normal." "Something would be wrong if they weren't." "It means you care." "Like Marines going into Iwo Jima saying they weren't nervous, something's a little fishy."

In both basketball and tennis, there were also qualitative differences in the ways that success and failure were discussed for women and men athletes. In fact, two formulae for success appeared to exist, one for men, the other for women. Men appeared to succeed through a combination of talent, instinct, intelligence, size, strength, quickness, hard work, and risk-taking. Women also appeared to succeed through talent, enterprise, hard work, and intelligence. But commonly cited along with these attributes were emotion, luck, togetherness, and family. Women were also more likely to be framed as failures due to some combination of nervousness, lack of confidence, lack of being "comfortable," lack of aggression, and lack of stamina. Men were far less often framed as failures—men appeared to miss shots and lose matches not so much because of their own individual shortcomings (nervousness, losing control, etc.), but because of the power, strength, and intelligence of their (male) *opponents*. This framing of failure suggests that it is the thoughts and actions of the male victor that win games, rather than suggesting that the loser's lack of intelligence or ability is responsible for losing games. Men were framed as active agents in control of their destinies, women as reactive objects.

A Hierarchy of Naming by Gender and Race

It was not simply women athletes who were linguistically infantilized and framed ambivalently. Our research suggests that black male basketball players shared some of this infantilization. Previous research revealed racial bias in televised commentary in men's sports. For instance, Rainville and McCormick (1977) found that white players received more praise and less criticism from football commentators than comparable black players. And Jackson (1989) reported that white male football and basketball players were much more likely to be credited with "intelligence and hard work," while the successes of their black male counterparts were more likely to be attributed to "natural athleticism." Our examinations of basketball commentary occurred in the wake of widespread public discussion of Jackson's (1989) research. We observed what appeared to be a conscious effort on the part of commentators to cite both physical ability *and* intelligence when discussing successful black and white male and female players. However, this often appeared to be an afterthought. For instance, a commentator would note of a star white player that "He has so much court intelligence . . . AND so much natural ability!" And a typical comment about a black star player was "What a great athlete . . . AND he really plays the game intelligently!"

Though it appeared that television commentators were consciously attempting to do away with the "hard work/intelligence" (white) vs. "natural athlete" (black) dichotomy, we did find an indication of racial difference in naming of male basketball players. In the three men's basketball games, in each of the cases in which men were referred to by their first names only, the commentators were referring to men of color (e.g. Rumeal [Robinson], Ramon [Ramos]). Though there were several "star" white male basketball players (e.g., Danny Ferry and Andrew Gaze) in these games, they were *never* referred to by their first names only.

These findings suggest that T.V. sports commentators are (again, probably unconsciously) utilizing a "hierarchy of naming": At the top of the linguistic hierarchy sit the always last-named white "men," followed by (sometimes) first-named black "men," followed by (frequently) first-named "girls" and "young ladies." We found no racial differences in the ways that women athletes were named. We speculate that (at least within televised sports commentary) gender is the dominant defining feature of women athletes' shared subordinate status. By contrast, sports commentary tends to weave a taken-for-granted superordinate, adult masculine status around male athletes. Yet in the case of male athletes of color, the commentary tends to (subtly and partially) undermine their superordinate masculine status. This suggests, following the theory of gender stratification developed by Connell (1987) and applied to sport by Messner (1989), Messner and Sabo (1990) and Kidd (1987), that sports media reinforce the overall tendency of sport to be an institution which simultaneously (1) constructs and legitimizes men's overall power and privilege over women; and (2) constructs and legitimizes heterosexual, white, middle class men's power and privilege over subordinated and marginalized groups of men.

Conclusion

An individual who watches an athletic event constructs and derives various meanings from the activity. These meanings result from a process of interaction between the meanings that are built into the game itself (the formal rules and structure, as well as the history and accumulated mythology of the game), with the values, ideologies and presuppositions that the viewer brings to the activity of watching. But viewing an athletic contest on television is not the same as watching a contest "live." Televised sport is an event which is mediated by the "framing" of the contest by commentators and technical people (Clarke and Clarke, 1982; Duncan and Brummett, 1987; Gitlin, 1982; Gruneau, 1989; Jhally, 1989; Morse, 1983; Wenner, 1989). Thus, any meanings that a television viewer constructs from the contest are likely to be profoundly affected by the framing of the contest (Atheide and Snow, 1979; Antin, 1982; Conrad, 1982;

Duncan and Hasbrook, 1988; Fiske and Hartley, 1979; Innis, 1951; McLuhan, 1964; Morse, 1983).

Televised sports are live and largely unscripted, but the language which commentators use to frame the events tends to conform to certain linguistic conventions which are themselves a result of "a complex articulation of technical, organizational, economic, cultural, political, and social factors" (Jhally, 1989: 84). And as Gruneau (1989) has argued, though commentators are often aware of themselves as "storytellers," they are not necessarily aware of the political and ideological ramifications of the linguistic conventions to which they—apparently unconsciously—conform.

Language is never neutral. An analysis of language reveals imbedded social meanings, including overt and covert social biases, stereotypes, and inequities. There is an extensive body of literature which documents how language both reflects and reinforces gender inequalities (Baron, 1986; Henley, 1977, 1987; Lakoff, 1975; Miller and Swift, 1977, 1980; Schultz, 1975; Spender, 1980; Thorne, Kramarae and Henley, 1985; Van Den Bergh, 1987). In a recent study of the gendered language of sport, sociologists D. Stanley Eitzen and Maxine Baca Zinn (1989: 364) argue that

[Gendered] language places women and men within a system of differentiation and stratification. Language suggests how women and men are to be evaluated. Language embodies negative and positive value stances and valuations related to how certain groups within society are appraised. Language in general is filled with biases about women and men. Specific linguistic conventions are sexist when they isolate or stereotype some aspect of an individual's nature or the nature of a group of individuals based on their sex.

The media—and sports media in particular—tend to reflect the social conventions of gender-biased language. In so doing, they reinforce the biased meanings built into language, and thus contribute to the reconstruction of social inequities.

Newspaper editors and television programmers often argue that they are simply "giving the public what it wants." Programming decisions are clearly circumscribed by market realities, and research does indicate that with few exceptions, men's athletic events draw more spectators than women's. But one question that arises concerns the reciprocal effect of, on the one hand, public attitudes, values and tastes, and on the other hand, the quantity and quality of coverage of certain kinds of athletic events. What comes first: public "disinterest" in televised women's athletics, or lack of quality coverage? Perhaps a more timely question now that women's sports are getting at least incrementally more coverage is: How do the ways that women and men's sports are covered on television affect the "interest" of the public in these events?

Our research on women's and men's tennis and basketball coverage indicated that commentators today are less likely than their predecessors to overtly sexualize or trivialize women athletes. However, the language used by commentators tends to mark women's sports and women athletes as "other," infantilize women athletes, and frame their accomplishments negatively or ambivalently. Our research also suggests that black male athletes share in some of the linguistic infantilization that is commonly used to describe women athletes. As a result, the language of sports commentary tends to (often subtly) reconstruct gender and racial hierarchies.

Though subtle bias is no less dangerous than overt sexism, the decline of overtly sexist language suggests that some commentators are becoming more committed to presenting women's athletics fairly. For instance, women's basketball commentator Steve Physioc re-named "man-to-man defense" as "player-to-player" defense. This is an example of a conscious decision to replace an androcentric language with language which is not gendered. Though Physioc did not do this consistently, the fact that he did it at all was an indication of his awareness of the gender biases built into the conventional language of sports. Critics might argue that changing language subverts the history or the "purity" of the game. But in fact, terminology used to describe sports is constantly changing. For instance, in basketball, the part of the court nearest the basket that used to be called "the key" through the 1950's was re-named "the lane" in the 1960's, and is more recently referred to as "the paint" or "the block." These changes have come about as a result of changes in the rules of the game, changes in the sizes and styles of players, and general changes in social values and mores. But language does not simply change as a "reflection" of social reality. Language also helps to construct social reality (Shute, 1981; Van Den Bergh, 1987). Thus the choice to use non-sexist language is a choice to linguistically affirm the right of women athletes to fair and equal treatment.

Viewed in this context, Physioc's use of "player-to-player defense" can be viewed as a linguistic recognition that something significant has happened to basketball: It is no longer simply a men's game. There are women players out there, and the language used to report their games should reflect and endorse this fact.

NOTES

1. This research is based on a larger study of gender and sports media which was commissioned by the Amateur Athletic Foundation of Los Angeles. The authors gratefully acknowledge the assistance of Wayne Wilson of the AAF, and of Barrie Thorne, who commented on an earlier version of this paper.

2. These statistics are compiled yearly by the National Federation of State High School Associations in Kansas City, MO. The 1989–90 statistics were received via a phone interview with the NFSHSA. For a discussion of the implications of this continuing trend of increasing high school athletic participation by girls, see D. Sabo (1988) "Title IX and Athletics: Sex Equity in Schools," in *Updating School Board Policies* 19 (10), November.

REFERENCES

Altheide, D. L., and Snow, R. P. (1979) *Media Logic*. Beverly Hills, CA: Sage.
Antin, D. (1982) "Video: The Distinctive Features of the Medium," pp. 455–477 in H. Newcomb (Ed.), *Television: The Critical View* (3rd ed.). New York: Oxford University Press.
Baron, D. (1986) *Grammar and Gender*. New Haven: Yale University Press.
Birrell, S. (1987–1988) "The Woman Athlete's College Experience: Knowns and Unknowns," *Journal of Sport and Social Issues* 11: 82–96.
Brannon, R. (1978) "The Consequences of Sexist Language." Paper presented at the American Psychological Association Meetings, Toronto.
Bryant, J. (1980) "A Two-year Investigation of the Female in Sport as Reported in the Paper Media," *Arena Review* 4: 32–44.
Bryson, L. (1987) "Sport and the Maintenance of Masculine Hegemony," *Women's Studies International Forum* 10: 349–360.
Boutillier, M. A., and SanGiovanni, L. (1983) *The Sporting Woman*. Champaign, IL: Human Kinetics.
Clarke, A., and Clarke, J. (1982) "Highlights and Action Replays: Ideology, Sport, and the Media," pp. 62–87 in J. Hargreaves (Ed.) *Sport, Culture, and Ideology*. London: Routledge and Kegan-Paul.
Connell, R. W. (1987) *Gender and Power*. Stanford, CA: Stanford University Press.
Conrad, P. (1982) *Television: The Medium and Its Manners*. Boston: Routledge and Kegan-Paul.
Crittenden, A. (1979) "Closing the Muscle Gap," pp. 5–10 in S. Twin (Ed.), *Out of the Bleachers: Writings on Women and Sport*. Old Westbury, NY: The Feminist Press.
Duncan, M. C. (1990) "Sports Photographs and Sexual Differences: Images of Women and Men in the 1984 and 1988 Olympic Games," *Sociology of Sport Journal* 7: 22–43.
Duncan, M. C., and Brummet, B. (1988) "The Mediation of Spectator Sport," *Research Quarterly for Exercise and Sport* 58: 168–177.
Duncan, M. C., and Hasbrook, C. A. (1988) "Denial of Power in Televised Women's Sports," *Sociology of Sport Journal* 5: 1–21.
Duncan, M. C., and Sayaovong, A. (1990) "Photographic Images and Gender in *Sports Illustrated for Kids*," *Play and Culture* 3: 91–116.
Dyer, G. (1987) "Women and Television: an Overview," pp. 6–16 in H. Baeher and C. Dyer (Eds.), *Boxed In: Women and Television*. New York: Pandora Press.
Dyer, K. (1983) *Challenging the Men: The Social Biology of Female Sport Achievement*. St. Lucia: University of Queensland.

Eastman, S. T., and Meyter, T. P. (1989) "Sports Programming: Scheduling, Costs, and Competition," pp. 97–119 in L. A. Wenner (Ed.), *Media, Sports, and Society*. Newbury Park, CA: Sage Publications.

Eitzen, D. S., and Baca Zinn, M. (1989) "The De-athleticization of Women: The Naming and Gender Marking of Collegiate Sport Teams," *Sociology of Sport Journal* 6: 362–370.

Felshin, J. (1974) "The Social View," pp. 179–279 in E. W. Gerber, J. Felshin, P. Berlin, and W. Wyrick (Eds.), *The American Woman in Sport*. Reading, MA: Addison-Wesley.

Fiske, J., and Hartley, J. (1978) *Reading Television*. New York: Methuen.

Gitlin, T. (1982) "Prime Time Ideology: The Hegemonic Process in Television Entertainment," pp. 426–454 in H. Newcomb (Ed.), *Television: The Critical View* (3rd ed.). New York: Oxford University Press.

Gruneau, R. (1989) "Making Spectacle: A Case Study in Television Sports Production," pp. 134–154 in L. A. Wenner (Ed.), *Media, Sports and Society*. Newbury Park, CA: Sage Publications.

Hall, M. A. (1988) "The Discourse on Gender and Sport: From Femininity to Feminism," *Sociology of Sport Journal* 5: 330–340.

Hargreaves, J. (1986) "Where's the Virtue? Where's the Grace? A Discussion of the Social Production of Gender Through Sport," *Theory, Culture and Society* 3: 109–121.

Henley, N. M. (1977) *Body Politics: Power, Sex and Nonverbal Communication*. Englewood Cliffs, NJ: Prentice Hall.

Henley, N. M. (1987) "This New Species that Seeks New Language: On Sexism in Language and Language Change," pp. 3–27 in J. Penfield (Ed.), *Women and Language in Transition*. Albany: State University of New York Press.

Herbert, S. (1990) "Study Charges Sexism in Women's Sports Coverage," *Los Angeles Times*, Thursday, August 30, 1990, p. F-2.

Innis, H. A. (1951) *The Bias of Communication*. Toronto: University of Toronto Press.

Jackson, D. Z. (1989) "Sports Broadcasting: Calling the Plays in Black and White," *The Boston Globe* (Sunday, January 22).

Jhally, S. (1989) "Cultural Studies and the Sports/Media Complex," pp. 70–93 in L. A. Wenner (Ed.), *Media, Sports, and Society*. Newbury Park, CA: Sage Publications.

Kidd, B. (1987) "Sports and Masculinity," in M. Kaufman (Ed.), *Beyond Patriarchy: Essays by Men on Pleasure, Power, and Change*. Toronto and New York: Oxford University Press.

Kidd, B. (1990) "The Men's Cultural Centre: Sports and the Dynamic of Women's Oppression/Men's Repression," pp. 31–44 in M. A. Messner and D. F. Sabo (Eds.), *Sport, Men and the Gender Order: Critical Feminist Perspectives*. Champaign, IL: Human Kinetics Publishers.

Lakoff, R. (1975) *Language and Woman's Place*. New York: Harper and Row.

McConnell-Ginet, S. (1978) "Address Forms in Sexual Politics," pp. 23–35 in D. Butturff and E. L. Epstein (Eds.), *Women's Language and Style*. Akron, Ohio: L and S Books.

McLuhan, M. (1964) *Understanding Media: The Extensions of Man*. New York: Signet Books.

Messner, M. A. (1988) "Sports and Male Domination: The Female Athlete as Contested Ideological Terrain," *Sociology of Sport Journal* 5: 197–211.

Messner, M. A. (1989) "Masculinities and Athletic Careers," *Gender and Society* 3: 71–88.

Messner, M. A., and Sabo, D. F. (1990) "Toward a Critical Feminist Reappraisal of Sport, Men and the Gender Order," pp. 1–16 in M. A. Messner and D. F. Sabo (Eds.), *Sport, Men and the Gender Order: Critical Feminist Perspectives.* Champaign, IL: Human Kinetics Publishers.

Miller, C., and Swift, K. (1977) *Words and Women: New Language in New Times.* Garden City, NY: Doubleday/Anchor.

Miller, C., and Swift, K. (1980) *The Handbook of Nonsexist Writing.* New York: Lippincott and Crowell.

Morse, M. (1983) "Sport on Television: Replay and Display," pp. 44–66 in E. A. Kaplan (Ed.), *Regarding Television.* Los Angeles: American Film Institute/University Publications of America.

Rainville, R. E., and McCormick, E. (1977) "Extent of Covert Prejudice in Pro Football Announcers' Speech," *Journalism Quarterly* 54: 20–26.

Rintala, J., and Birrell, S. (1984) "Fair Treatment for the Active Female: A Content Analysis of *Young Athlete* Magazine," *Sociology of Sport Journal* 3: 195–203.

Rubin, R. (1981) "Ideal Traits and Terms of Address for Male and Female College Professors." *Journal of Personality and Social Psychology* 41: 966–974.

Sabo, D. (1988) "Title IX and Athletics: Sex Equity in Schools," *Updating School Board Policies* 19 (10), November.

Schultz, M. (1975) "The Semantic Derogation of Women," pp. 64–75 in B. Thorne and N. Henley (Eds.), *Language and Sex: Difference and Dominance.* Rowley, MA: Newbury House.

Shute, S. (1981) "Sexist Language and Sexism," pp. 23–33 in M. Vetterling-Braggin (Ed.), *Sexist Language: A Modern Philosophical Analysis.* Totowa, NJ: Littlefield, Adams.

Spender, D. (1980) *Man Made Language.* London: Routledge and Kegan-Paul.

Stanley, J. P. (1977) "Gender Marking in American English: Usage and Reference," pp. 43–74 in A. P. Nilsen et al. (Eds.), *Sexism and Language.* Urbana, IL: National Council of Teachers of English.

Theberge, N. (1981) "A Critique of Critiques: Radical and Feminist Writings on Sport." *Social Forces* 60: 387–394.

Theberge, N., and Cronk, A. (1987) "Work Routines in Newspaper Sports Departments and the Coverage of Women's Sports," *Sociology of Sport Journal* 3: 195–203.

Thorne, B., Kramarae, C., and Henley, N. (1985) "Language, Gender and Society: Opening a Second Decade of Research," pp. 7–24 in B. Thorne and N. Henley (Eds.), *Language, Gender and Society.* Rowley, MA: Newbury House.

Van Den Bergh, N. (1987) "Renaming: Vehicle for Empowerment," pp. 130–136 N. J. Penfield (Ed.), *Women and Language in Transition.* Albany: State University of New York Press.

Whitson, D. (1990) "Sport in the Social Construction of Masculinity," pp. 19–30 in M. A. Messner and D. F. Sabo (Eds.), *Sport, Men and The Gender Order: Critical Feminist Perspectives.* Champaign, IL: Human Kinetics Publishers.

Wenner, L. A. (1989) "Media, Sports and Society: The Research Agenda," pp. 13–48 in L. A. Wenner (Ed.), *Media, Sports and Society.* Newbury Park, CA: Sage Publications.

Willis, P. (1982) "Women in Sport in Ideology," pp. 117–135 in J. Hargreaves (Ed.), *Sport, Culture, and Ideology.* London: Routledge and Kegan-Paul.

Wilson Sporting Goods Co. and the Women's Sports Foundation (1988) "The Wilson Report: Moms, Dads, Daughters and Sports" (June).

Wolfson, N., and J. Manes (1980) "Don't 'Dear' Me!" pp. 79–92 in S. McConnell-Ginet, R. Borker, and N. Furman (Eds.), *Women and Language in Literature and Society.* New York: Praeger.

◀▓▶

SPORT AND SOCIETY BROADCAST FOR FRIDAY, AUGUST 16, 1996

Richard C. Crepeau

It was being touted as the Women's Olympics even before it started. As the games proceeded and especially as the U.S. Women turned in excellent performances the claim that this was the Year of the Woman at the Olympics was reinforced. But what did that mean?

Commentators cited the performance of the U.S. women as evidence of the impact of Title IX. They talked about how the image of the female athlete had changed. How women are competing as children and adolescents in larger numbers than ever before, and in all kinds of sports, not just those that had been traditionally acceptable for women. Others talked about how women in African countries came of age in this Olympics. In fact women worldwide seem to be competing athletically in societies where previously competitive sport had been tabu for women.

For those who viewed the Olympics largely through the prism of the NBC television coverage, the year of the woman had a very different meaning. Dick Ebersol's feminization of the Olympics was not exactly the result of Title IX or the result of any great advance in social attitudes toward women and sport. In fact the Ebersol–NBC Olympics, seemed to be driven by many of the traditional visions of women and sport.

Prior to the games NBC spent countless hours in market research trying to determine what version of the Olympics women wanted to see, and then did their best to provide it. Ebersol told David Remnick of *The New Yorker* that NBC's ratings success was achieved by bringing a feminine sensibility to the games. Empathy with the athlete and their struggles, both on and off the field of competition, caused women to flock to television coverage.

Broadcast on Dick Crepeau's Sport and Society Broadcast, 16 August 1996.

It was really a simple matter confirmed by ten thousand NBC marketing surveys. Men come to sport "from the outside in" while women come "from the inside out." Men view the event and then might make a connection to the athletes, while women must connect to the athlete before they have an interest in the event. For women the story is the thing, while winning and losing are secondary concerns.

David Remnick suggests that as a result NBC took a soap opera approach to its presentation of the games creating a "seventeen-day-long, multi-character, open-ended narrative." In doing so they created a television show of enormous appeal to women, or so say the ratings.

Somehow I don't think that this is what people were talking about when they spoke about the Year of the Woman in the Olympics.

In developing their feminine Olympics NBC decided that women's team sport was of little interest. While 65,000 people, some of whom were women, jammed into Sanford Stadium in Athens to watch the U.S. Women win the soccer gold medal, NBC provided thirty seconds of highlights. While the U.S. women played before packed houses in Columbus at the softball venue, NBC offered a few minutes of highlights. Even the U.S. women's basketball team failed to get much notice from those sensitive to the sensibilities of women. General Mills followed the NBC lead when they ignored women from team sports for the Wheaties box.

To see the U.S. women marching to gold medals in three team sports, and to watch NBC ignore them, was an astounding sight and one that women and men will not soon forget. To see superb performances by unknown women from around the world, is indicative of a tremendous growth of women's sport worldwide. Instead what NBC presented was hour upon hour of swimming and gymnastics, two traditional women's sports displaying women in swim suits and little women in tights.

Then there was the Michael Johnson story. His great achievement in doubling in the 400 and 200 meter events was worthy of the coverage it got. But did you notice that Marie-Jose Perec of France did the same thing in the women's 400 and 200? Was this a less significant achievement than Michael Johnson's? What did NBC's market research indicate about feminine interest in this achievement? Was it a lesser achievement in the eyes of NBC because Perec is French or because Perec is a woman?

So who is right in their reading of the Atlanta games as the year of the Woman in the Olympics? Although television ratings and market research may tell us one thing, I suspect that event results and the large crowds that were attracted to women's venues tell us something quite different.

There is a market for and interest in women's sport, including women's team sport and women athletes over four-feet six–inches tall. In the future it will include your daughters and granddaughters.

And that is the significance of these Olympics; an excellent storyline—better even than a soap opera.

On Sport and Society this is Dick Crepeau reminding you that you don't have to be a good sport to be a bad loser.

◄❖►

THE WOMEN'S SPORTS FILM AS THE NEW MELODRAMA

Jean O'Reilly

The 1984 film *Just the Way You Are*[1] presents a love triangle at an upscale European ski resort among three talented, successful, independent professionals: elite skier Bobbie (Alexandra Paul), photographer Peter Nichols (Michael Ontkean) and physically disabled flautist Susan Berlanger (Kristy McNichol). Bobbie and her boyfriend Peter are working hard, Bobbie competing in her sport and Peter photographing the ski competition. Susan, unlucky in love and ever wondering if it's only the brace on her leg or something else about her that turns men off, has impulsively canceled the rest of her European concert tour, booked two weeks at the ski resort, and replaced her brace with a plaster cast. If she can pass as an injured skier, perhaps she'll experience how unimpaired people flirt and score.

Bobbie, an aggressive, attention-seeking, impatient woman who might soon want to forgo sex to preserve her competitive energies, is too busy skiing and too moody off the course to hold Peter's attention once he meets the charming, sexually eager, and enticingly evasive Susan. With her career temporarily on hold, Susan also has plenty of free time to devote to Peter. Unsurprisingly, the demanding sportswoman eventually loses her man to the less career-oriented flautist who is more interested in her ailing love life than her prestigious tour.

It's a bit disingenuous to highlight this particular narrative line from a film more concerned to explore attitudes toward physical disability than toward women and sports. Nevertheless, both the fate of Bobbie's relationship and the tension the film establishes between being a successful woman (i.e, attracting men) and having a successful career are issues that appear often in feature films that focus on sportswomen.

The rise of the women's sports film, a boom that began in the early 1990s and includes such films as *A League of Their Own, Love and Basketball, Blue Crush,* and *Million Dollar Baby,* has generally been regarded as an encouraging correction to the historically meager media coverage of female athletes. But a closer look at what appears to be a group of forward-thinking films about strong women reveals a disturbing return to the stifling conventions of a much older, well-established Hollywood genre, the melodrama. Far from heralding the rightful place of women in sports, several of these films convey surprisingly subversive messages about the place of women in the sports arena, and in the world at large.

Melodrama, a term Hollywood pirated from an older critical lexicon and reoriented to publicity use, is known as "The Women's Film" as well. It dates back to the silent era with films such as *True Heart Susie*[2] and *The Big Parade*.[3] The genre came into its own in the Depression era films of the 1930s and the war films of the 1940s, and flourished with the lush, elegant women's weepies of the 1950s. Classic melodramas always feature a female protagonist torn between, and ultimately choosing between, mutually exclusive desires. The eponymous main character in *Stella Dallas*,[4] hopelessly low-class, wants to be part of her daughter's life but also wants her daughter to enjoy, unfettered, the upper-class life to which she is suited. In *All That Heaven Allows*,[5] middle-class Cary Scott (Jane Wyman) loves and is loved by her younger, working-class gardener Ron Kirby (Rock Hudson), but she cannot marry him without embarrassing the children she loves and becoming the subject of hurtful small-town gossip. Melodramas are also known by their use of repression and excess. Characters, often female, are prevented by social and family pressure, often patriarchal, from pursuing what they truly desire, which leads to emotional outbursts and outbreaks of transgressive behavior. In melodrama, these transgressions are always punished; this contributes to the moral weightiness and the usually unambiguous distinctions between right and wrong that typify this film genre.

Once highly popular, the melodrama lost much of its appeal somewhere in the middle of the women's rights movement. Film scholars such as Brian Henderson have questioned the staying power of older film genres such as melodrama and screwball comedy that to modern sensibilities seem old-fashioned.[6] But film genres are surprisingly adaptable. Just as the western and the musical keep returning from the dead, so too the melodrama has continued long beyond its heyday, sometimes showing its face in historical dramas, where heavy-handed social and familial repression of women may seem more credible (*Fried Green Tomatoes*,[7] *Vera Drake*[8]), sometimes in remakes of old melodramas (*A Star Is Born*,[9] *Far from Heaven*[10]), and sometimes by fashioning a hybrid of melodrama and comedy, which allows a denouement in which the protagonist reconciles her conflicting desires and gets everything she wants (*Baby Boom*,[11] *Working Girl*[12]). But melodrama's most potent modern incarnation is the women's sports film, which takes as its subject women's infiltration of one of the few remaining aggressively patriarchal arenas in the modern Western world.

Men's sports films, in contrast, constitute a much larger and more diverse group of films that collectively foreground hard work and individual achievement. In the words of sports film scholar Aaron Baker, men's sports films typically feature a "heroic individual who overcomes obstacles and achieves success through determination, self-reliance, and hard work [. . .] [T]he male protagonist defines and proves himself through free and fair competition modeled on American society, which claims that rewards go to the most deserving individuals."[13] In addition to their focus on individuality and success, men's sports films are also numerous enough to have developed, over time, distinct plotlines that are associated with different types of sports. In *Sports in the Movies*, Ronald Bergen explains that football films often follow the formula of "boy meets ball, boy loses ball, boy gets ball—co-existing with the usual boy meets girl theme,"[14] while films about male boxers often feature an athlete who represents an entire race.[15] The boxer's power of representation reaches the level of nationhood in *Rocky IV*,[16] in which American Rocky Balboa (Sylvester Stallone) fights and defeats Soviet boxer Ivan Drago, and Bergen and other film critics have observed that films about male Olympic athletes often do the same. Baseball films, according to Wes D. Gehring, are "about reconnecting with father figures,"[17] and Howard Good adds that "[b]aseball films often deal with the struggle for psychological independence and moral maturity. [. . .] In film after film, a character or team emerges from danger, disgrace, or ineptness to demonstrate unsuspected powers."[18] Rather than transgressing the rules of a society that is structured and controlled by the other gender, the male sports film protagonist operates in a man's world, where father-son relationships and issues of race and class (not gender) offer the most likely obstacles to achievement. Male protagonists may be challenged about the *type* of sport they play, but they are not often challenged about the basic activity of playing sport.

Women in men's sports films typically appear as supportive wives and girlfriends (*Rocky*,[19] *Bull Durham*[20]) and ineffective obstacles to sporting achievement, such as the unscrupulous female owner/coach/agent (*Major League*[21]) or the unsupportive love interest who must be won over or discarded (*Damn Yankees*[22]). Any notion of gender conflict in the sports arena is thereby greatly reduced by the presence of loyal, largely unquestioning women and weak, easily thwarted antagonists. As Bergen puts it, "[i]n sports movies, if women did not exist, there would be no need to invent them."[23]

In the women's sports film, however, gender conflict is the biggest issue, and female protagonists must often struggle simply to defend their desire to play sports, to be "mannish," in the dominant male society. The very fact of playing sports thus provides the main social and sexual transgression in the melodramatic plot structure that many of these films adopt.

In "The Position of Women in Hollywood Melodramas," Barbara Creed usefully outlines the basic structure of the classic Hollywood melodrama of the late 30s and early 40s, which I summarize here:

1. **Sexual transgression:** The heroine transgresses the socially acceptable female role, usually through some aspect of her sexuality: refusal to marry, an affair with a married man, loose behavior. She is often confronted by another character who demands that she reform her ways, and she is usually contrasted with a conventional female.
2. **The redeeming power of love:** The heroine falls in love with a man and is then separated from him. The love affair makes the heroine change her previous ideas/appearance/lifestyle, moving her toward socially acceptable behavior.
3. **Sacrifice and tears:** The heroine offers some form of self-sacrifice to atone for her social sins, leading to a denouement that is never unconditionally happy.[24]

A brief look at some of the most popular women's sports film narratives of the past thirty years reveals a striking correspondence to those historical characteristics. Consider *A League of Their Own*,[25] the 1992 summer hit about the 1943 formation of the All-American Girls Professional Baseball League. The film establishes the heroine's love interest early on: Dottie Hinson (Geena Davis) is a happily married woman whose husband Bob (Bill Pullman) is away, fighting in World War II. In early scenes in which she is heavily recruited to play ball, she several times resists joining the AAGPBL, citing the unseemliness of a married woman leaving home to play baseball. She only changes her mind so that her little sister Kit (Lori Petty) can also try out for the league, Dottie's desire to be a good wife conflicting with her desire to be a good sister.

As the film progresses, Dottie engages in two forms of sexual transgression. First, by joining the AAGPBL she (temporarily) turns her back on her marriage in favor of sport. Second, as the baseball season develops, so does a low-key, somewhat too-friendly relationship with her coach, Jimmy Dugan (Tom Hanks). While she transgresses her role as wartime wife, Dottie also begins to enjoy playing baseball at such a high level, and she becomes known as one of the best and most competitive players in the league.

The redeeming power of love exerts its influence over Dottie when her husband returns from the war toward the end of the baseball season. Dottie immediately quits the team, sacrificing a lifestyle she's grown to love, friendship with a man who appreciates her baseball skills, and possibly her relationship with her sister, from whom she separates badly. Dottie does return to play in the championship match, but it is her last professional game and she has already lost her competitive edge, flubbing the last play to lose the game. It is only many years later, after the death of her husband releases her from her wifely duties, that Dottie reconnects with her old teammates and finally makes peace with her sister, both of them claiming their rightful place in sports history.

It could be argued that *League*'s historical setting and subject matter encourage its melodramatic structure, but we can see the same sort of pattern at work in a powerful and complex film about women's track in the post–Title IX era, *Personal Best*.[26] As film scholar Linda Williams suggests, *Personal Best* can be seen on one level as a cautionary tale of the dangers of homosexuality among sportswomen.[27] Chris Cahill (Mariel Hemingway), a young, talented, poorly trained hurdler of indeterminate sexual orientation, is noticed and nurtured by older, homosexual track star Tory Skinner (Patrice Donnelly). Tory gets her coach, Terry Tingloff (Scott Glenn), to take on Chris's training, and Tory and Chris become teammates, competitors, and lovers as they prepare with several other women for the 1980 Olympic trials. The confrontation about Chris's sexual transgression comes from Coach Tingloff. After Chris becomes seriously injured in a way she suspects may have been engineered by Tory, Tingloff reads Chris the riot act, both for being a lesbian and for dating a teammate. He berates her—and all sportswomen—for being emotionally needy. He then makes a pass at her.

Although Chris fends him off, the lesson takes hold: she soon begins dating male ex-Olympic swimmer Denny Stites (Kenny Moore), and when her injury has healed she rejoins her team, "too old, too hurt, and too tired" to put up with Tingloff's worries that she will fall under Tory's spell again. Chris's shift to heterosexuality has a transformative effect upon her as an athlete. Although she falters early on in the Olympic trials, Denny gives her the pep talks she needs to perform well at her weak events, and she ends up in a good position to make the Olympic team with one event to go. ·

Tory, at this point, ends up in the injury tent, weeping and unconfident about her athletic skills and ready to quit. The camera shot of her physical position on a cot with an ice bag on her knee links her visually to earlier images of the injured Chris before her transformation.

As with Dottie in *League*, Chris's self-sacrifice takes the form of denying her sporting talent. Wanting to win a place on the Olympic team yet wanting to help her ex-lover and teammate, Chris sacrifices her lock on an Olympic berth by running her last race badly so that Tory can win the race and make the Olympic team. As Williams explains,

By the end of the film Chris, who began as a whiny little girl in terror first of her father then of her male coach, finds the strength to oppose her coach's order not to associate with Tory. [. . .] Chris's maturity is then proven [. . .] when she defies her coach to befriend the now weakened and childlike Tory. Although Chris's support of Tory prepares the "happy end" of both women's mutual triumph in the final meet, the moral is clear: Chris's strength and maturity derive not from Tory, who mothered her, but from Denny whose laid-back fathering has finally made her a woman.[28]

In a satisfyingly complex ending, Tory wins the race and Chris manages to hold onto third place to qualify for the Olympics—but this is 1980, the year the United States boycotted the Moscow Games, so both women's victories are empty ones. Once again there is no unconditionally happy ending.

There is more to the melodrama formula, however, than transgression, transformative love, self-sacrifice, and unhappy endings. As Elizabeth Dalton explores in "Women at Work: Warners in the 1930s," there is a subgenre of the melodrama that deals specifically with women infiltrating the traditionally male social arena of employment. Warner Brothers in the 1930s tended to produce melodramas whose heroines were working women. In most cases, the women were shown to be out of place in the working world, and only tolerated (or in some cases only tolerating it themselves) until marriage relieved them of the burden of employment. As Dalton explains, "[i]n the conceptions of women that they put forth, and in the plot resolutions they offered, they revealed a traditional male bias: a woman is made for love, not work."[29] Or, as actress Rosalind Russell put it, "My wardrobe [in those films] had a set pattern: a tan suit, a grey suit, a beige suit, and then a negligee for the seventh reel, near the end, when I would admit to my best friend that what I really wanted was to become a dear little housewife."[30] This subgenre follows the general pattern outlined by Creed with the addition of a plot that involves the heroine's foray into the working world, which in most cases she abandons to become a wife or girlfriend. According to Dalton, a heroine who refused to leave the working man's world did so at her own peril, for "a woman may not *really* be a passive, exploitable, 'feminine' creature, but she damn well had better be if she expects to be happy."[31]

Some modern sports films use the sporting world as a male bastion to which unwelcome women gain entrance, adapting the pattern of those 1930s working-girl melodramas. That pattern plays out with predictable unhappiness in the 2000 film *Girlfight*,[32] in which Diana Guzman (Michelle Rodriguez) yearns to be a boxer. In her one-parent household, Diana's father Sandro (Paul Calderon) pressures her little brother Tiny (Ray Santiago) to take boxing lessons, which he hates, while both Sandro and Tiny repeatedly exhort Diana to be more of a lady. After Diana persuades Tiny's trainer Hector (Jaime Tirelli) to take her on as a pupil and Tiny offers her his place at the gym, Diana finds herself responding well to the discipline of training and develops some skills. She learns to stop apologizing when she hits competitors, and she learns to control her temper. Boxing is something she grows to love, and her trainer sees and nurtures her talent.

Diana falls in love with Adrian (Santiago Douglas), a fellow boxer who dreams of going pro. They train together peaceably until they enter the same local competition and find themselves pitted against each other in the championship fight. Before the fight, Diana goads the reluctant Adrian to take her seriously as a competitor, telling him he shouldn't be a boxer if he doesn't have the stomach for fighting her. On the night itself she's the better performer, landing more effective punches than he does and winning the championship. After a brief moment of celebration, we see Diana alone in the locker room, weeping.

The final moments of the film are filled with uncertainty about Diana and Adrian's future as a couple. Adrian seems to have given up boxing in favor of full-time work for his father, a job he was hoping to escape. An anxious Diana watches him at work but doesn't approach. Adrian finally confronts Diana at the gym, where they praise each other's boxing skills but dance around the subject of their relationship. In their last soft exchange, Adrian asks Diana, "So, you gonna dump me now?" to which Diana answers "Probably." She then kisses him until he smiles. That ambiguity, and the fact that Diana feels she has a choice, is an opening to a new, positive ending for the melodrama, one in which, without the help of comedy, the heroine has a chance of holding onto both work and love.

Two other post-millennium sports films, *Blue Crush*[33] and *Bring It On*,[34] combine the conventional melodramatic formula with a glimmer of hope at the end. *Blue Crush* contains the classic melodramatic conflict of work versus love: Anne Marie (Kate Bosworth), a talented young Hawaiian surfer training for the Pipe Master Competition, starts a relationship with NFL quarterback Matt Tollman (Matthew Davis) one week before the surfing competition and begins to neglect her training. In a twist from the usual melodramatic structure, she is compared with and confronted by not a conventional woman who follows traditional social guidelines and encourages her to do the same, but by two fellow athletes, her friend and fellow amateur surfer Eden (Michelle Rodriguez, who played Diana in *Girlfight*) and professional surfer Keala Kennelly, playing herself. Both urge Anne Marie, through word and action, to ignore conventional ideas of how a woman should act and instead be the world-class surfer she was born to be, even if it means losing her boyfriend. And Matt himself chimes in with similar advice, urging her to be the sort of woman who wouldn't ask a man what she should do.

Anne Marie's crisis of confidence echoes that of sportswoman Pat Pemberton (Katharine Hepburn) in the classic 1952 sports film, *Pat and Mike*.[35] Pat, a skilled golfer and tennis player, falls apart every time her criticizing fiancé watches her perform, her natural ability melting away as soon as she feels his eagle eye upon her. She must ultimately get rid of him and marry her supporting and admiring manager, Mike Conovan (Spencer Tracey), to come into her own as a sportswoman. Like Pat, Anne Marie fits the role of the melodramatic heroine not so much out of social pressure to conform (although the film contains its share of men berating women for trying to surf pipe) but out of her own personal fears: because of a prior surfing accident, Anne Marie is afraid to surf pipe and is eager to find an excuse to pull out of the competition. Romance offers her a traditional escape from competing in a man's world, but her boyfriend, friends, and fellow competitors won't let her get away with it. Anne Marie, in other words, is a melodramatic heroine trapped in a film that tries not to be a melodrama, or that perhaps is a reverse melodrama, pushing its heroine away from rather than towards social conformity. Matt, rather than encouraging Anne Marie to be more ladylike, transforms her through his love from a timid surfer into a risk-taking sportswoman. The effect seems somehow more optimistic because Anne Marie is held back by internal demons rather than the suffocating weight of social expectation. The dominant society portrayed in the film gives her the chance to compete in the man's world of sports and encourages her to take it.

Blue Crush's ending is as up-in-the-air as *Girlfight*'s. Anne Marie gets a little bit of everything she wants: she doesn't win the competition, but she does get in one good run and get a sponsorship contract, and although her relationship with Matt may or may not continue, that seems less important to her. Having resolved her personal conflict, Anne Marie will presumably continue surfing and enjoy a successful love life, with Matt or not.

Bring It On offers a similarly optimistic view of sportswomen, although unlike *Blue Crush* the move away from traditional melodrama here is helped enormously by the use of comedy, which sets up the expectation that all conflicts will find resolution in the final scene. As with *Blue Crush*, the heroine of *Bring It On* wrestles not with social pressure to act as a woman ought, but with internal pressure: Torrance Shipman (Kirsten Dunst) isn't sure if she has what it takes to lead her team to a cheerleading championship. Taking over from Big Red (Lindsey Sloane), an angry, ambitious cheerleader (reminiscent of Bobbie in *Just the Way You Are*) who led the Rancho Carne High School Toros to several consecutive championships, Torrance finds that as the new team captain she doesn't have the heart to steal routines from other squads as Big Red did to keep them on top. In the ruthless world of high school cheerleading, Torrance fears she's too nice. Like *Blue Crush*'s Anne Marie and *Pat and Mike*'s Pat, Torrance needs to toughen up and trust her own skills before she can fulfill her potential as both sportswoman and squad leader. Like *Blue Crush, Bring It On* ends with partial victory, as Torrance's team settles for second place in the national competition. And like *Pat and Mike, Bring It On* entails a shift in romantic allegiances as Torrance, at the turning point in her story, dumps her cheating, inattentive college boy-friend for the loyal and supportive Jesse Bradford (Cliff Pantone).

Both *Blue Crush* and *Bring It On* are a far cry from the much earlier WWII-era sports film, *National Velvet*,[36] in which heroine Velvet Brown (Elizabeth Taylor) must pretend to be a man in order even to compete in her sport. Velvet, who dresses as a man to ride her beloved horse Pie to victory in the Grand National steeplechase in England, faints at the end of the race, is discovered to be a girl, and has her win struck from the record. Although she and Pie are the best competitors in the field, the rac-ing rules stipulate that no woman may ride in the Grand National, and so her performance is simply ignored. Although in *National Velvet* no char-acter ever questions that a woman is barred from a sporting event (even Velvet doesn't question her disqualification), in *Blue Crush* and *Bring It On* there is no doubt that women can compete and perform well. Such open-mindedness is not restricted to post-millennium films. Traces of it surfaced not only in *Personal Best*, but in the 1980 British film *Gregory's Girl*[37] in which the schoolboys on a particularly poor soccer team put up little resistance when new girl Dorothy (Dee Hepburn) replaces one of their own as striker and outplays them all.

Another more recent film takes these optimistic developments a step farther. In *Wimbledon*,[38] tennis ace Lizzie Bradbury (Kirsten Dunst again) sees no problem with mixing tennis and pleasure as long as she continues to win her matches. Against her overprotective father's wishes, she em-barks upon a fling with fellow tennis player Peter Colt (Paul Bettany) dur-ing her bid for the women's singles title at Wimbledon. Lizzie gets knocked out of the tournament and, in a scene reminiscent of *Just the Way You Are*, blames her energy-robbing sexual activities with Peter for her loss, breaking off their relationship: "Love means nothing in tennis! Zero! It only means you lose." Peter, meanwhile, goes on to win the men's singles title, and wins back Lizzie's love in the process.

What sounds at first like a familiar story—overly aggressive sports-woman finds love and loses competitive edge—develops at the last mo-ment a surprising twist. At the close of the film, we see Lizzie playing an informal game of tennis in New York City with a little girl while Peter looks on, holding an infant. These are their children, and Peter, in voice-over, describes the job he's taken in New York to be with Lizzie. The viewer might be led to assume that both of them have dropped out of the elite tennis circuit to marry and start a family. But, almost as an after-thought, Peter informs us that Lizzie's loss at Wimbledon was just a blip in her career: in the intervening years, she's won that tournament twice, plus the U.S. Open. The offhand, last-minute manner in which Peter de-livers this information conveys the strong feeling that Lizzie's achieve-ments are almost literally unremarkable. It's obvious to Peter, and should be to us, that a woman of her talents would manage successfully to com-bine love, family, and sport. Of course she's won Wimbledon: what did you think?

So it would seem that at least in some recent sports films, women's mel-odramatic conflicts remain the same while the heavy-handed social repres-sion that melodrama ought to forecast has been reduced significantly. There is, however, one instrument of social repression specific to melo-drama that still figures importantly in today's sports films: The Family.

Family melodrama takes all of the social repression of traditional melodrama and concentrates it in those closest to the heroine. In other words, the pressure to conform, to act like a proper lady, comes not from society at large but rather from mothers and fathers, aunts and uncles, grandparents and siblings. We get a taste of the family melodrama in *Girlfight* as Diana, the only woman in her family, faces both her father's disgust with her fighting at school and her brother Tiny's embarrassment when she slugs his sparring partner at the gym after he takes a cheap shot at Tiny. It appears in *Wimbledon* when Lizzie's father (Sam Neill) tries several times to break up her relationship with Peter. But we can also see it in much greater force in three other recent sports films, the British film *Bend It Like Beckham* and the US films *Love and Basketball* and *Million Dollar Baby.*

Bend It Like Beckham[39] tells the story of Jess Bhamra (Parminder Nagra), a second-generation immigrant Indian girl living in London. Jess plays soccer in the park with the neighborhood boys and is eventually en-ticed by her new friend, Jules Paxton (Keira Knightley), to play for the local women's team, the Hounslow Harriers. Both girls know that Ameri-can scouts sometimes come to their games, and each hopes to earn a soc-cer scholarship to a university in the United States and a professional ca-reer with the Women's United Soccer Association (WUSA). Both girls also face enormous pressure from their families to behave like conven-tional women and daughters. Jules's mother (Juliet Stevenson) chastises her constantly for her boyish behavior, lives in terror that her daughter is a latent lesbian, and eventually becomes terrified that Jules and Jess are lovers, going so far as to attack Jess verbally in front of her own family for leading her daughter astray. Jess faces even stronger pressure at home:

not only is she forbidden by her Sikh parents (Anupam Kher and Shaheen Khan) to play soccer, where she would show too much skin and behave in an unladylike manner, but her older sister Pinky's (Archie Panjabi) up-coming wedding also keeps forcing Jess into a role she doesn't want: the family's wedding activities require her to wear traditional Indian cloth-ing, dance and serve food at family parties, learn to cook, and miss soccer practices and games. The constant refrain she hears is that soccer was fine when she was young, but now she must give up the play of her childhood and become a woman. Pinky is the conventional, socially acceptable woman with whom Jess is unfavorably compared, and Pinky's wedding ceremony, scheduled for the same date as the Hounslow Harriers' cham-pionship game, becomes the focus of Jess's self-sacrifice.

Like *Beckham*, *Love and Basketball*[40] focuses on two families and the sports-based friendship and rivalry that develop between the children. Quincy McCall (Omar Epps) is the only child in a two-parent family. His on-again-off-again girlfriend, Monica Wright (Sanaa Lathan), lives next door with her parents and older sister. Quincy and Monica are skilled basketball players who win four-year scholarships to the same university. The sport they share holds their relationship together, but it also becomes a source of tension in their college years: Monica resents the attention and celebrity Quincy enjoys as a male basketball player, especially from other women, while Quincy resents the time Monica devotes to her sport when there are so many more attentive women he could date. Quincy and Monica also encounter a great deal of family pressure. Quincy wants to become an NBA basketball player like his father Zeke (Dennis Haysbert), whom he adores, but Zeke exhorts him to consider other professions and use basketball solely to get a good bachelor's degree. Monica's family pressure is more generalized: as a devoted sportswoman living with her ultra-feminine mother and sister (Monica's father is largely unseen and unheard), Monica is told repeatedly by both to be more feminine, look after her hair, wear dresses, and stop being so aggressive. While Quincy's father attends all of his games, Monica's mother rarely attends hers.

Quincy's family troubles come to a head during his freshman year of college, when he discovers his father has been cheating on his mother. Quincy breaks all ties with his father, then turns to Monica for comfort, expecting her to stay with him beyond her coach's curfew. Forced to choose between her boyfriend and her sport, Monica keeps her curfew and loses Quincy. As reviewer Cynthia Fuchs explains,

Monica refuses to lose her newly assigned starting position on the USC women's team, and of course, Q can't realize that he's asking her to perform the same long-suffering, self-abnegating role he's seen his mother play, because he's a freshman facing his first real emotional crisis.[41]

Ironically, Monica's refusal to support Quincy in the same way his mother does sets up an eventual confrontation with her own mother concerning (among other topics) Monica's failure to hold onto Quincy—her failure as a woman. Throughout the film, Monica and Quincy are affected by family pressures and alliances, which in turn cause them to put pressure on each other to behave "appropriately."

Both *Beckham* and *Love and Basketball* offer happy, rather last-minute resolutions to their main characters' conflicts. Jess and Jules get their college scholarships and leave for California with their parents' blessings. (As a side note, any sequel to *Beckham* will likely have to address the shutdown of the WUSA in 2003: presumably, Jess and Jules will be back with the Hounslow Harriers in four years.) For their part, Monica and Quincy make peace with their parents and, through Quincy's convenient career-ending injury and the timely introduction of the WNBA, Monica ultimately finds a way to combine love and basketball.

Million Dollar Baby[42] offers the viewer another twist on the family melodrama theme. Much like Diana in *Girlfight*, Maggie Fitzgerald infiltrates a men's gym and convinces has-been Frankie Dunn (Clint Eastwood) to train her as a boxer. But *Baby* is a far darker film than *Girlfight*, *Beckham*, or *Love and Basketball* could ever be.

Maggie is played by Hilary Swank, who starred in *The Next Karate Kid*[43] and *Boys Don't Cry*,[44] and who earlier appeared as a conventional Valley girl against whom cheerleader/vampire-battling kickboxer Buffy Summers (Kristy Swanson) is contrasted in *Buffy the Vampire Slayer*.[45] In *Million Dollar Baby*, Maggie wants to become a professional boxer, but she also wants to please her white-trash family, especially her mother. She succeeds at the first goal but a scene with her family makes it clear she will never please her mother or siblings. When Maggie visits home to show her mother the house she bought her out of her fight earnings, her mother complains that owning a house will ruin her welfare status. And in general, Maggie's family is unhappy to see her and finds her boxing career a joke.

Although her family's attitude distresses her, it never prompts Maggie to abandon her career or conform to her mother's template. The viewer's main worry is that Maggie, who misses her dead father and feels a duty to look after the remaining family, will waste too much of her time and money trying to please her kin. Indeed this becomes the focus of one of the film's tensest scenes, in which the now severely injured Maggie is asked by her family to sign over to them all of her assets. Although the boxing association is paying for Maggie's medical care, it's clear that her mother and siblings are worried her medical and eventual funeral expenses will eat up what funds Maggie has, leaving them with nothing. Still craving her mother's love and affection (Maggie has spent days waiting for a visit from her family), the emotionally-tortured Maggie appears determined to make the wrong decision. Like Jess in *Beckham,* Maggie's conflict revolves around how to please those she loves, although in this script the conflicts are posed not only as family versus sport, but in choices that are truly deadly.

A second layer of family melodrama is superimposed in this film upon Maggie's struggles with mother and siblings. In agreeing to train Maggie, Frankie uses her as a replacement for his own daughter: Frankie and Maggie form a second family with its own conflicts. As film scholar Tania Modleski explains,

The maternal melodrama asks its audience to recognize the goodness of the self-sacrificing mother, of whom the working-class Stella Dallas, who gives up her beloved daughter to the daughter's upper-class, well-to-do father, is perhaps the paradigmatic example. Now and again a "paternal melodrama" comes along to challenge the primacy of women in the parenting and self-sacrificing departments—*Kramer vs. Kramer* is one example of such a film; *Million Dollar Baby* is another. True to the dictates of the genre, Frankie sacrifices his surrogate daughter who wants to be freed from life-support machines; whereas, what he really wants is to keep her with him always.[46]

But Maggie's death isn't simply the sacrifice Frankie makes in his role as melodramatic father figure. It is also Maggie's punishment for transgressing gender boundaries.

The conventions of melodrama will at some point in the film require of the heroine some form of self-sacrifice to atone for her sin of social nonconformity. In many cases, this takes the form of giving up something she loves that either prevents her from acting in an acceptable manner or that symbolizes an unacceptable lifestyle: an illegitimate child, a lover, a career . . . or a sport. In the darkest melodramas, however, the heroine's self-sacrifice takes the form of her death. This adds to the film another dimension, perhaps essentially external to the film itself, because it fulfills three societal needs in ways that a film's plot doesn't necessarily demand. It cleanses society of a potentially evil element, it elevates the heroine's self-sacrifice to the highest possible ("uplifting") level, and it punishes in no uncertain terms her bad behavior. We can see such extreme sacrifices in classic and modern melodramas such as *Camille,*[47] *Dark Victory,*[48] and even *Love Story,*[49] where it can be said that working class girl Jennifer Cavalleri's (Ali McGraw) illness and death allow her husband Oliver Barrett IV (Ryan O'Neal) to make amends with his father and return to the lifestyle to which he is most suited.

In *Million Dollar Baby,* Maggie's fate underscores the heroine's appallingly poor luck, and, in the manner of her death, it also highlights her determination to control her own destiny. But it also raises the disturbing idea that, in the fictional world of the film (and what does art do at its best but reflect reality?), there is no place for a tough, honest, highly skilled, exuberant, woman boxer. At the height of her powers, on the verge of winning her biggest fight yet, Maggie is sucker-punched by another woman, robbed of her physical powers, made a quadriplegic dependent for her most basic bodily functions upon machines, and sent on the long road toward death. What does it mean that the agent of this social expulsion is another sportswoman? Or that the sportswoman/villain acts with the tacit approval of her male trainer? Or that society appears to impose no punishment for the deed? *Million Dollar Baby* poses a number of uncomfortable questions about society's attitude toward sportswomen, and about sportswomen's attitudes toward each other.

The conventions of melodrama that pervade women's sports films suggest at best an ambiguity about the choices strong women may wish to make. And it is not a stretch to assert that most major commercial women's sports films of the past three decades—by male and female directors alike—have been developed explicitly within the conventions of that genre. Modern films that appear to celebrate female athletes don't necessarily convey the impressions, or the encouragement of young women, that many think they do. So what does it mean, ultimately, that women's sports films of the past thirty years have been plotted according to the templates of the weepies of the thirties, forties, and fifties?

The bad news is that the very structure of melodrama, and the fact that so many of the most popular women's sports films follow that structure, strongly suggests that sportswomen are unwelcome in the male-dominated sporting world. At the very least, their choices are meant to prompt ambiguous reaction. The lesson these films offer to their viewers is that the woman who wants to find a place of her own in sports must be willing to sacrifice things that are dear to her, such as romance, the love and acceptance of her family, and even life itself.

The good news is that some of the films noted above offer evidence that things may be changing. The structure of melodrama may be adapting to new realities in ways that suggest women are making headway toward acceptance in the sporting world, and as themselves in the wider world. The film industry, which typically invests a lot to make a lot, is most interested in making films that people will want to watch. Films that are not predicted to sell don't get made. This is an especially cheering thought when reflecting upon the handful of recent, well-made, often high-budget sports films that do not feature heavy-handed repression of sportswomen, such as *Blue Crush, Bring It On,* and *Wimbledon.* Even *Girlfight* and *Love and Basketball,* which deviate little from the classic melodramatic formula, put their heroines in an unusual position of control at the end of the film. Given that art reflects life and that most Hollywood films don't show their viewers too much of what they don't want to see, this new form of melodrama currently emerging from women's sports films may signal a basic change in the way our society, male and female, views sportswomen.

NOTES

1. Directed by Edouard Molinaro for MGM and released in 1984.

2. D. W. Griffith, Artcraft Pictures Corp., 1919.

3. King Vidor, MGM, 1925.

4. King Vidor, Samuel Goldwyn, Inc., 1937.

5. Douglas Sirk, Universal, 1955.

6. Brian Henderson, "Romantic Comedy Today: Semi-Tough or Impossible?," *Film Quarterly* 31:4 (1978) 11–12.

7. Jon Avnet, Fried Green Tomatoes Prod./Act III/Electric Shadow, 1991.

8. Mike Leigh, Untitled 03/Thin Man Films, 2004.

9. Frank Pierson, Berwood/First Artists, 1976.

10. Todd Haynes, Vulcan/Focus Features/TFI International, 2002.

11. Charles Shyer, MGM/UA, 1987.

12. Mike Nichols, 20th Century-Fox, 1988.

13. Aaron Baker, *Contesting Identities* (Chicago, U. Illinois Press, 2003) 3, and repeated on 49.

14. Ronald Bergen, *Sports in the Movies* (London, Proteus Books, 1982) 45.

15. Bergen, *Sports,* 14.

16. Sylvester Stallone, United Artists, 1985.

17. Wes D. Gehring, *Mr. Deeds Goes to Yankee Stadium: Baseball Films in the Capra Tradition* (London, McFarlane and Co., 2004) 13.

18. Howard Good, *Diamonds in the Dark: America, Baseball, and the Movies* (Lanham MD, Scarecrow Press, 1997) 11.

19. John G. Avildsen, United Artists, 1976.

20. Ron Shelton, The Mount Company, 1988.

21. David S. Ward, Morgan Creek, 1989.

22. George Abbott, Warner Bros., 1958.

23. Bergen, *Sports,* 9.

24. Summarized from Barbara Creed, "The Position of Women in Hollywood Melodramas," *Australian Journal of Screen Theory* 4 (1978) 27–8.

25. Penny Marshall, Columbia/Longbow/Parkway, 1992.

26. Robert Towne, Geffen Co./Warner Bros., 1982.

27. Linda Williams, "*Personal Best:* Women in Love," *Jump Cut* 27 (1982) 1, 11–12.

28. Williams, 12.

29. Elizabeth Dalton, "Women at Work: Warner's in the 1930s," *The Velvet Light Trap* 6 (1972) 15.

30. David Shipman, *The Great Movie Stars* (New York, Crown Publishers, 1971), 483. Quoted in Dalton, 17.

31. Dalton, 19.

32. Karyn Kusama, Independent Film Channel/Green/Renzi, 2000.

33. John Stockwell, Mikona/Universal/Imagine, 2002.

34. Peyton Reed, Beacon/Universal, 2000.

35. George Cukor, MGM, 1952.

36. Clarence Brown, MGM, 1944.

37. Bill Forsyth, Lake Film/National Film Trustee/National Film Finance/Scottish TV, 1980.

38. Richard Loncraine, Working Title/Universal/StudioCanal, 2004.

39. Gurinder Chadha, Kintop/Bend It Films/Road Movies Filmproduktion GmbH/Roc Media, 2002.

40. Gina Prince-Blythewood, New Line/40 Acres and a Mule, 2000.

41. Cynthia Fuchs, "Make You Do Right," review of *Love and Basketball*, PopMatters.com, 2000, PopMatters Magazine, 8 February 2006 <http://www.popmatters.com/film/reviews/1/loveandbasketball.shtml>.

42. Clint Eastwood, Warner Bros./Malpaso/Ruddy/Morgan Productions, 2004.

43. Christopher Cain, Jerry Weintraub Productions, 1994.

44. Kimberly Pierce, 20th Century Fox/Fox Searchlight/Independent Film Channel/Killer Films, 1999.

45. Fran Rubel Kuzui, Sandollar/Kuzui/20th Century Fox, 1992.

46. Robert Sklar and Tania Modleski, "*Million Dollar Baby:* A Split Decision," *Cineaste* 30:3 (2005) 10.

47. George Cukor, MGM, 1936.

48. Edmund Goulding, Warner Bros./First National, 1939.

49. Arthur Hiller, Paramount, 1970.

❖

IT'S TIME TO TELL THE BLOODY TRUTH

Lorie Conway

Only 24 years ago the Boston Athletic Association allowed the first woman to run officially in the Boston Marathon. Until then, women were either thrown off the course or elbowed out of the way by male runners. On April 15 of this year, during the running of the 100th Marathon, Uta Pippig, the first woman to cross the finish line, had menstrual blood and diarrhea running down her legs.

While the crowd gathered in Copley Square roared their support, male commentators on radio and TV were, uncharacteristically, tongue-tied. Ironically, the only person to graphically describe what was happening on live TV was commentator Katherine Switzer. "Look, there's been a history of diarrhea in marathons, for any world class competitor knows it happens," Switzer said. "You just don't worry about it. You've got a race to run." There was no mention of bleeding. It was "diarrhea" that surprised

From *Nieman Reports* 50:2 (Summer 1996): 30–32.

people and that announcers picked up on. During the 1967 Marathon, it was Switzer who had registered to run as K. Switzer but had her number ripped off her chest while running past a BAA official who discovered she was a woman.

During the 100th Marathon, it was apparent to hundreds of thousands of spectators, watching the race on TV and in person, that Pippig, the winner of the last two Boston Marathons, was in trouble. Gone was the playful demeanor she was known for; replacing it was a face wrenched in pain and legs covered with blood. "Physical problems and diarrhea," said some commentators. Others stopped at the phrase "physical problems," not wanting to utter the word diarrhea on live television. Meanwhile, at water stops, Pippig had to worry not only about overtaking Kenyan Tegla Loroupe, but also about maintaining her dignity. She explained at the post-race news conference, "I used a lot of water around me so that I look better and also for my legs that I could clean up a bit." At one point, she shooed the cameraman in the truck ahead of her away and told him to stop filming her.

So, how was Pippig's victorious battle of mind over body, at "that time of the month," covered in the press the day after? Well, as can be expected of certain sophomoric radio talk show hosts, it was open season for bad taste. For others, even male sportswriters who couldn't get beyond the description "female problems," it was the beginning of a discussion on a topic that was long overdue.

The *Boston Globe*'s Dan Shaughnessy wrote: "There is no delicate way to put this. Pippig had female issues at the worst possible time. She was in pain. She was a mess. And she thought about dropping out of the race." He left it to Pippig to say the real reason, which she stated shyly but openly at the post-race press conference. "I had some problems with my period." Period. A word she could say but few others could. Another *Globe* sportswriter, Joe Burris, almost got it right. He wrote, "Pippig, who had nearly been forced out of the race by menstrual cramps and diarrhea, stormed past Loroupe at the marker and opened a lead of 200 yards en route to a stunning triumph."

The *Boston Herald* captioned a frontpage finish-line photo with ". . . overcoming cramps," while articles inside got a bit more detailed. Michael Gee wrote, "There were few smiles from Pippig. She ran the course in visible pain and disarray, her body going dysfunctional when she needed it most." Then he goes on to describe the scene at the water stops. "Pippig was stopping at water stations not to drink, but to freshen up. Distance running, like childbirth, isn't exactly a dainty process." Another *Herald* writer, Stephanie Tunnera, wrote that Pippig was "battling stomach pain," in an article that had "Cramps End Strong Run," as the headline.

It was the next day, however, in a *Boston Globe* column written by Eileen McNamara (Nieman Fellow 1988), that it all came together. Titled "Uta's victory a female thing," McNamara got up close and personal about the issue that was on display for all to see but had yet to be truly discussed. McNamara said it was the boorish behavior of talk radio hosts that motivated her to bring the discussion out of the ladies room and into the newspaper. "The talk radio was misogynistic and disgusting. I felt it was about time." She wrote: "When Pippig grabbed that water bottle to clean her legs, there were all of our private female moments made starkly public. That time you picked the wrong day to wear a white skirt. That time you had to back out of the dining room." McNamara went on, "Her victory was sweet as it was messy. Many men just saw the mess. . . . They like their women athletes pretty, perky and photogenic. Uta Pippig has always been that. On Monday, though, those men had to confront the fact that this extraordinary athlete is no Marathon Barbie; she's a real flesh and blood woman."

The roar of reaction to Eileen McNamara's column was almost as loud as when Uta crossed the finish line. Across breakfast tables, computers and water coolers, an ensuing discussion raged. This time, it was not split by gender. "How dare you?" wrote one grandmother. "It was unnecessary and I'm deeply offended by it."

Another woman complained in a letter to the editor: "I am always interested in reading about blood over breakfast." Perhaps for that reader the usual stories of murder and mayhem are acceptable but not the taboo of menstrual blood. McNamara was flooded with calls, letters and E-mail. "The response was huge, overwhelming," she said. "Mostly from women who felt at long last someone was saying what they were thinking. One woman posted the article on line on a bulletin board." And then there were the responses from men. One response still has McNamara shaking her head. "John Doe," wrote, "I hope your son grows up to hate you as much as you hate me and my son." Or the one caller who wanted to know, "What's your problem, you feminazi?"

On the television side, most sports anchors sidestepped the issue with phrases like "menstrual cramps and severe diarrhea." Except David Robichaud of WBZ, who was assigned to report a story on "Pippig as role model." But by the time he had completed several random man-on-the-street interviews, the real issue people wanted to talk about was how Pippig overcame both the pain and stigma of her period. And McNamara's column in support of her. When it came time to write his script, Robichaud asked his female executive producer "how to put it." "She told me to say what it really was, menstrual bleeding. So I did, live on the 6 o'clock news. I'm a hero to all the women in the newsroom. Not bad for a reporter who just started reporting in January!"

For Switzer the major point of Pippig's ordeal was this: "She's overcome incredible adversity. This is wonderful for women to show that women can go through considerable distress and anguish like this and emerge as heroes."

Next year, I've been asked to do live commentating from the lead women's truck during the 101st Boston Marathon. Having just completed my ninth marathon during the 100th, I accepted the opportunity without a moment's hesitation. I'm more than happy to ride the next one out. But what if someone in the pack happens to suffer the same indignities that befell Pippig? Will I be able to talk about it on live television? Yes, although I think I will be armed with research about the effects of running on women's periods and be ready to put some facts behind the graphic video. Facts such as those found in one recent study that showed one in every five serious runners is amenorrheic—they don't menstruate. And in another study, on elite runners like Pippig, half were found to be "period free."

Although the direct cause is still unknown, many doctors link intense training, low body fat, and subsequent loss of estrogen to losing periods. So why did an elite runner like Uta Pippig, with very little body fat, end up bleeding so profusely? According to her coach, the pressure of winning the 100th intensified the usual pre-race stress and may have contributed to her difficulties. Medical tests done on Pippig after the race were inconclusive. But whatever the reasons, her victory over severe cramps and bleeding challenged the stigma of periods and performance.

The ensuing coverage, while uncomfortable for some, is about a fact of life for all women, those who wear a laurel wreath and those who don't. And it's time we start reporting it as such.

◄█►

BLOODSPORT

Woman's First Pro Fight Is Her Last

Joe Posnanski

KANSAS CITY, MO.—No woman in the United States has ever died boxing. Only one has ever come close. This is the story of Katie Dallam. She almost died shortly after her first fight. This is the story of Sumya Anani. She was the woman who punched relentlessly.

They met briefly before their fight on a Wednesday in December at the Firefighter's Union Hall in St. Joseph, Mo. Anani talked about her days as a yoga instructor and massage therapist. Dallam talked about her days as a drug-and-alcohol counselor for the state of Missouri. They spoke nervously, like two women sitting in a dentist's waiting room. Then they walked into the hall, into the roar and the haze, and struck each other for seven minutes.

The two women tapped gloves.

The crowd screeched at the sight of blood.

Dallam collected $300. Anani made $400.

Few saw the ambulance leave the building.

Everybody remembers the details differently, but that's not unusual on nights of tragedy. One remembers shrieks where another recalls silence. One sees fury where another senses calm. Danny Campbell, the boxing promoter, remembers Dallam talking freely when the fight ended. Stephanie Dallam, Katie's sister, remembers only silence and a deadness to her eyes. Katie Dallam herself remembers nothing. She only sees the fight in her painting, with red strokes blushing against canvas.

Then, nobody sees women's boxing itself quite the same way.

Women's boxing yanks a million emotions out of people. It is violence and blood and sex and gimmick and sport blended together so intensely, so furiously that no one can feel one part without tasting another. In a few weeks boxing's biggest promoter, Don King, will put on the first ever pay-per-view card with all women fighters. Some people laugh. Some are sickened. Some cheer. Some plunk down their money.

In England and other European countries, women's boxing is banned. In the United States, it swims toward mainstream.

From *Kansas City Star*, 8 June 1997. All rights reserved. Reprinted with permission.

"You have to understand, this is not powder-puff stuff," boxing promoter Danny Campbell says. "These girls really fight. That's one of the reasons it is becoming so popular. And it is becoming popular, I tell you.

"Women are not educated boxers, understand? They're still learning the sport. They don't know how to slip punches or block punches. They just stand in front of each other, punch away and the toughest girl wins. Blood flows, you might see a nose broke. They're exciting fights."

Campbell promoted the Anani-Dallam fight of Dec. 11. He says everybody wants to see women's boxing these days, and he gives the same reason every boxing promoter gives. Christy Martin. She fought Ireland's Deirdre Gogarty on the under card of a Mike Tyson fight, and they stole the night with a six-round spectacle. Martin won the fight, though blood covered her face and body. Soon afterward she glared from the cover of *Sports Illustrated*. Women's boxing had its first legitimate star. Martin now demands a six-figure purse for her fights.

Martin is one extreme. Another is Kansas City's Mary Ortega, who just turned 17, wears braces and says she has her mother's permission to become a professional boxer. She spars with men, hungrily hits the heavy bag and hopes to have her first pro fight in August.

"There are just no opportunities for women in amateur boxing," she says.

Another is Julie Ardwin, who lives in Kansas City, gives physical examinations by day and then throws stiff left jabs under smoky lights. She began fighting a year ago to get in shape. They told her she could make money in this gig. She has won five of six fights. She is tall, intelligent, athletic and stunning.

"A beautiful girl," trainer Joe Gallegos says. "Believe me, that sells."

"Promoters come up to me and say, 'I'm going to make you a star,'" Ardwin says. "And I say, 'How are you going to do that?' They just smile. We're a sideshow. There's not a lot of legitimacy in women's boxing."

Last week Julie Ardwin fought two fights. She won Monday in Kansas City. She was knocked out Thursday in Baton Rouge, La.

"I guess that's pretty stupid, huh?" she says.

The first view of the Anani-Dallam fight comes from ringside. Danny Campbell did not know much about Katie Dallam. In the program the fight was listed this way: Female welterweights, featuring Sumya Anani.

Reporters were told that Dallam was a 26-year-old fighter from Jefferson City, Mo. Actually, she was 37, had a master's degree from the University of Missouri and had lived in Columbia, Mo., her entire life except for the four years she spent in the Air Force. This was her first pro fight. She had been training for six weeks with Gallegos. She had trained as a kick boxer for a while but had never stepped in the ring. Her entire ring experience consisted of one round in the women's portion of a Tough Man contest. She lost.

"(Gallegos) called me and said he was looking for a fight for his girl," says Campbell, who was more interested in Anani, the fighter he promotes still. Anani had been fighting for only six months, but she won all three of her fights. She was 24. She grew up in Kansas City but had briefly been a massage therapist and a blackjack dealer in Jamaica. Campbell called her the Island Girl and the Jamaican Sensation. It was tough narrowing down from there.

Dallam outweighed Anani by 35 pounds. The Missouri State Boxing commission does not allow boxers to fight out of their weight class unless special permission is granted. It was granted for this fight.

"There are not many women's fighters," Campbell says. "They're pretty lenient about weight differences."

The day before the fight, Dallam received her boxing license. That night, Dallam was in a car wreck serious enough to send her trainer into the hospital.

"She was driving and seemed OK," Gallegos says. "I was covered in blood from head to toe. But then, I'm a bleeder."

Campbell says he was never told about the accident, nor was the Missouri Office of Athletics. After a routine pre-fight physical, the fight went on as planned.

"It was the kind of physical a 90-year-old man could pass," Dallam's sister, Stephanie, says.

"This is absolutely sickening to me," says Tom Moraetes, an amateur boxing trainer in Augusta, Ga., for 24 years and the tournament director for the first-ever amateur women's boxing championships this July. "I can't even believe this fight was sanctioned. She's 37. She's never fought before. She's trained for six weeks. She's in a car wreck. This is the worst of boxing, right here."

The fight began at 9:41 p.m.

Anani wore a yellow sports bra and shorts.

Dallam wore a black, oversized tank top.

Anani began landing punches almost immediately.

"It was an incredible fight," Campbell says. "It was a lot better than I expected it to be. Sumya decided to go toe to toe with the girl. She would just throw so many punches. The other girl was just not in the kind of condition to survive all that later in the fight. She wouldn't go down, though—showed a lot of heart."

Dallam's nose began bleeding less than a minute into the fight. Anani was simply too quick for her. In the cloud of memory from the fight, Dallam would only vaguely recall the first punch, and it seemed like four gloves coming at once. Anani flailed away. In the second round, Anani landed blows time after time to the head, including a four-punch combination to the face. In the third round, people in the crowd screamed for

Anani to finish her off. It was a 12-punch flurry to the head in the fourth round that prompted the referee to pause the fight for the first time and give Dallam a standing-eight count. Gallegos threw in the towel.

Dallam remained on her feet the entire fight.

She never stopped trying to fight back.

The videotape shows Anani landed 119 punches to the head. Dallam landed fewer than 40. Because it was a professional bout, neither fighter wore headgear.

When the fight ended, Dallam slumped to her corner. Many things happen at the end of a fight, so many it is hard to keep track. The ringside doctor, C. Daniel Smith, says he briefly checked Dallam, found her responsive and let her go. Katie's sister says the doctor never got up from his seat. Anani says she tried to speak to Dallam but got no response. Stephanie Dallam says her sister's arms were ice cold.

"She didn't even recognize me," she says.

Gallegos says Dallam didn't feel faint until she reached the dressing room. She asked for an aspirin. She couldn't swallow it. She collapsed.

By the time Dallam reached Heartland Regional Medical Center, her brain bled profusely.

Stephanie Dallam's life revolves around her sister. Entirely. She spends her mornings in Olathe, Mo., taking Katie to speech therapy, then they visit a psychologist and then there's physical therapy. Stephanie reminds her sister to eat. She drives her around town. She tells her several times a day what is next on the schedule. Katie can't remember for herself.

"In a way I'm lucky," Katie says. "I don't remember any of it. It's like my short-term memory is gone. I see stuff on television, and it's almost like the whole thing happened to somebody else. Stephanie remembers everything for me."

The memory haunts Stephanie Dallam. Not just the aftermath, when Katie Dallam lurched in and out of coherence following a one-day coma, when her eyes sunk deep into the sockets, her face was black, her body clung to a respirator, a blood clot weighed on her brain. Doctors said she might not survive. "That night," Stephanie Dallam says, "I kept waiting for the phone to ring (and for someone) to ask me if we wanted to donate the organs."

No, it goes beyond the coma, beyond the 3½-hour surgery to repair a vein that had been torn at the top of the brain, beyond the broken nose and the hollow eyes, beyond the terrible moments at the bedside when she thought Katie was dead, beyond the terrible moments when she understood that Katie might survive but would never be the same.

It goes beyond the weeks in the hospital, beyond the brief time when Katie wanted to kill herself, beyond the daily grind of telling her sister the same stories again and again. Stephanie Dallam had been a critical-care nurse in Columbia. She had seen pain before. "I've seen hundreds of people die," she says. "It was agonizing watching Katie in pain."

No. The fight itself is what haunts Stephanie Dallam.

"A women's boxing match in rural Missouri is one step up from a dog-fight," she says. "I'm not even sure it's one step up.

"Everybody knew they were supposed to be rooting for the other girl. She came in wearing the shorts; she was cuter, and so everybody screamed for blood. Katie was just an opponent. They just threw her in and let her get beat up. And they wouldn't stop it. It just kept going on and on, and the people were screaming, 'Kill her,' and nobody stopped it."

Stephanie Dallam is angry. Katie can't return to her job as a counselor. She can't drive because she forgets where she's going. Small changes frighten her. She can't read, because it hurts her eyes. She can't jog, because it jars the brain. And often by the end of sentences, she forgets what she was saying. Doctors say it will take six more months to determine whether all the damage is permanent. They are not optimistic.

"We don't ever talk about the future," Stephanie says. "It upsets Katie too much. She had a master's degree. She was an athlete. She ran half-marathons. Now we have to deal with the fact that this might be Katie's life, and it's just too hard. We look one day ahead. We can't look beyond that."

Stephanie and Katie have hired an attorney, Sly James, and they are contemplating a lawsuit. James won't specify against whom. Meanwhile, Stephanie Dallam fights insurance companies. She fights with Social Security people. She takes care of her sister. The fight has changed Stephanie's life completely, too.

"These people . . . they threw her in the ring and didn't protect her," she says. "I used to be naive. I used to believe that people would do the things they promised. They promised my sister everything would be all right."

Campbell explained, however, that both fighters had signed a customary disclaimer acknowledging the danger. No one, he added, promises safety in the ring.

"I hate what happened to Katie," Campbell says. "But there is risk in boxing like there is in all sports. You get hit in the head. Everybody who steps in the ring knows that."

Since Katie Dallam has left the hospital, she has longed to see a video of the fight. She wants to know what happened. She wants to see where everything went wrong. Stephanie vows to never see the tape.

"I saw the fight once," she says. "That was too much."

Sumya Anani is a contender. She has six victories and zero defeats now. She has knocked out two opponents since that night in December. Christy Martin's people have called for a fight. Others shy away. "Women are scared of her," her trainer, Barry Becker, says.

"I don't want to hear that tough-guy, male-dominated garbage," Anani says. "Nobody is afraid of me. That's the kind of stupid stuff you hear in male boxing. 'Oh, he's afraid.' That's so stupid. It makes me mad. I want women's boxing to be different than that."

Anani says she fights only to spread the word of the healing touch. She studies holistic healing. "I know that sounds kind of weird," Anani says. "But I know that's why I'm here. People always say, 'Why am I here?' I know. I'm here to tell people that life is in their health. People make themselves sick. I'm here to spread the word that they don't have to live with the pain."

Anani did not hear about Katie Dallam's injury the night of the fight. When she heard the next day, she went to the hospital and held a candlelight vigil in the waiting room. She asked to give Dallam a healing message in the intensive-care unit. She wrote a long letter to Dallam and asked her to move in. "We'll climb trees together and sing songs," she wrote.

"I'm sure they thought I was a quack," Anani says. "But I was a wreck. I kept writing and writing, and I'm no writer. I had my book on the healing touch with me. I just wanted to do something to help her."

The two have not seen each other since the fight. Katie Dallam says she does not blame Anani. These are the things that happen in the ring. But she has no desire to see her. Anani has not tried to make contact since that day in the hospital.

"I asked them to call me, and they never did," Anani says. "I feel bad. I considered quitting boxing. But I don't believe things just happen by accident. I think there's a reason this happened. I think someday we will connect again. I believe that."

For now, Anani works out three times a day. She says she's ready to fight anytime. She might have a fight sometime next month, though things change quickly in this game. She says the publicity after the Dallam fight has given her an opportunity to tell more people about the healing touch.

"Ironic, isn't it?" she says.

One day Katie Dallam painted the fight. She does not remember the fight. She does not remember the weeks leading up to the fight. She does not remember the weeks afterward. All of it is a blur, a nightmare forgotten. She knows only that she is not the same anymore. And that there was a fight.

"Sometimes, I think I remember things," she says. "But then, it's gone. I guess it's good I don't remember too much."

Talk comes hard. Before the fight, Dallam spoke breathlessly, crashing words together, but now she squints and pauses, struggling to find the simplest words. Each day she works with a speech therapist. Progress is slow.

So, without the words, she painted the fight. Details still hide behind her memory. She often painted before the accident—she was an art major at Missouri—though she usually concentrated on things like cactuses and people in her portraits. She painted for love in those days. This time she painted for anger.

"Sometimes, I think it's hard for Katie to express the rage of what happened to her," her sister says. "Sometimes, she still doesn't understand what happened to her."

Dallam painted an angry crowd that gazes down, a man with horns, deformed faces, faraway eyes. She painted a cage, and inside the cage is a big fighter throwing a hard jab. Inside the cage there is a little fighter, trying to cover up, only she cannot cover up, and a dark red spills from her head; it spills out into the cage, into the ring, and off the canvas.

Funny, she still likes boxing. She watches it when she can. She hopes the doctors let her work out again someday, though she never wants to step in the ring. No, she would just like to hit the heavy bag for a while.

"Boxing made me feel strong," Dallam says. "I had never felt strong before. I had always been afraid. I didn't want to be afraid anymore. I wanted to be strong. It made me feel so good.

"If I knew everything beforehand, I would not have fought. I thought it would be, like, a sport. I didn't think anybody would get hurt. I had seen women box before, and nobody got hurt. No woman had ever gotten hurt like me, I guess. I don't know what happened. I guess I'm bitter about it, but I don't know."

Katie Dallam looked down at her painting, the cage, the red, the howling faces. Stephanie asked her sister what she thought about when she painted it. Katie stared blankly.

"I don't remember," she said.

◀◆▶

OFFENSIVE INTERFERENCE

Sherry Ricchiardi

Her adrenaline was pumping as sportswriter Paola Boivin, 25, rushed into the St. Louis Cardinal clubhouse in pursuit of postgame coverage. As she maneuvered through the mass of bodies, a Cardinal player menacingly

From *American Journalism Review*, December/January 2005. Reprinted with permission by American Journalism Review.

blocked her way. In a voice dripping with vitriol, he asked whether she was there to interview someone or to look at a bunch of guys' penises.

Before the stunned reporter uttered a word, a sweat-soaked jock strap sailed through the air, smacking Boivin in the head and falling to the floor. She remembers looking down and thinking, "Oh my God!" as she turned and fled her tormentors.

"That incident came close to ending my career," recalls Boivin, who was covering sports for a small newspaper in California. The game with the Los Angeles Dodgers was one of her first big assignments. The year was 1985.

The bullying of Boivin in the locker room was indicative of the times.

As greater numbers of women invaded the temples of male supremacy—the press box, the sidelines and, most sacrosanct of all, the locker room—a testosterone frenzy erupted in sports venues across the country, igniting the worst rash of sexism ever witnessed against a group of reporters. Being called a bitch was the least of the indignities, according to pioneers who began forging a new frontier in American journalism in the mid-1970s.

Battle lines quickly formed as women inched their way into terrain where no precedents existed for a female presence. By 1978, women sportswriters had acquired a powerful weapon: A lawsuit was filed when Major League Baseball Commissioner Bowie Kuhn prevented *Sports Illustrated* reporter Melissa Ludtke from interviewing players in the locker room during the 1977 World Series. A year later, a federal court judge ordered equal access for female reporters, as coaches, players and some male sportswriters howled in protest. Finally the doors were open.

Twenty-six years later, the life of a woman sportswriter has changed dramatically. Today, there appears to have been a steady erosion of the blatant sexism that plagued women into the 1990s. The benchmarks of progress most often mentioned include significant changes in the sports department culture over the years resulting in more opportunities for high-profile assignments and promotions. While the forerunners operated in a vacuum, without mentors or role models, the Association of Women in Sports Media, with 450 members, offers a supportive network.

But despite the inroads, the playing field still is far from level.

Women complain that their numbers are paltry on three fronts: Not enough have been tapped for top management positions, or for the coveted role of sports columnist. They often feel overlooked for glitzy assignments like the Super Bowl or the World Series. Many struggle to balance travel and work with marriage and family. Prejudice still appears unexpectedly.

Tracy Dodds, a groundbreaker in women's sports reporting, recalls early male stereotypes of female sportswriters as "sluts and groupies."

Has that changed today? "Very much so, but there still is a long way to go," says Dodds, a sports enterprise writer for the *Indianapolis Star* and a former president of the Associated Press Sports Editors.

Joanne Gerstner, 33, president of AWSM, the women sports journalists organization, talks about the sacrifices made by those who came before her. "These women went through hell, through utter degradation, to do their jobs," she says. "I am walking on a road paved by many who gave up their souls, their psyches to get us where we are today."

Early in the struggle, women sportswriters rarely went public about the mistreatment by coaches, players and, sometimes, even their male co-workers. They focused on their jobs, keeping a low profile, hoping the friction would subside.

Women sportswriters tell of facing a gauntlet of intimidation. At times, a fraternity-prank mentality took hold. A slap on the rump with a wet towel as they waded through a sea of male athletes or catcalls as a player mischievously urinated in front of them. Disapproval came from a myriad of sources, including players' wives and girlfriends who took umbrage at the notion of strange women seeing their men in the buff.

Some of the more outrageous episodes have become legendary among the ranks of female sportswriters. Susan Fornoff was on assignment for the *Sacramento Bee* the night she accepted a delivery from an usher during a Kansas City Royals–Oakland Athletics game. As male colleagues watched, she opened a pink box to discover a live rat with a note attached that read, "My name is Sue."

The sender, she learned, was an Oakland A's player who felt "a lady should be a lady. He just doesn't think I belong in the locker room," said Fornoff at the time of the incident in June 1986. She left sports for the first time in 1992 because, "I was, frankly, beaten down by the maleness of the locker room," says Fornoff, who writes for the home and garden section of the *San Francisco Chronicle*. She later did a two-year stint covering golf, but "this time the schizoid hours and travel got to me," she says. "I am very excited about the change."

Rookie reporter Joan Ryan was conducting a locker-room interview for the *Orlando Sentinel* when she found herself surrounded by players from the now-defunct United States Football League. First, they hurled derogatory remarks, then a player who had been cutting tape off his ankle began to slide the blade of a long-handled razor up and down her leg.

Ryan later described the scene in a column: "I happened to be the first reporter down to the dressing room. I pushed open the door, knots in my stomach, and walked smack into a path of naked men, trudging from the showers back to their lockers. They stopped in their tracks, then shouted and laughed, barking obscenities and closing in on me like bullies in an alley."

After 13 years, Ryan, one of the country's first female sports columnists and a founder of AWSM—also known as "awesome"—switched beats. After a stint on the op-ed page, she now writes a metro column for the *San Francisco Chronicle*. "The older you get, the less patience you have with 22-year-olds blowing you off in the locker room. It's been a great transition; I don't miss it at all," she says.

One case of locker-room brutality stands out above all other.

Lisa Olson's September 17, 1990, mugging by a group of New England Patriot players is considered a watershed moment for women in sports journalism. The sheer rawness of the players' taunts and the investigation, firing and fines that followed set clear parameters for intolerable behavior backed by the NFL's hierarchy.

Olson, who was 26 and working for the *Boston Herald,* described being accosted by naked football players who made vulgar comments and lewd gestures as she conducted a practice-day locker-room interview. The NFL's investigation, which resulted in a 108-page report, noted that one player, Zeke Mowatt, was seen fondling himself at an arm's length from Olson and asking her: "Is this what you want?" Others gyrated their hips behind the reporter, echoing Mowatt's comments. The reporter told how the players "positioned themselves inches away from my face and dared me to touch their private parts." She depicted the incident as "mind rape."

Olson reported receiving 100 obscene phone calls and 250 pieces of hate mail from Patriot fans after the news broke. When the tires on her car were slashed, the perpetrator left a message that threatened, "The next time it will be your neck." When her apartment was burglarized, a note ordered her to "leave Boston or die." Patriots Owner Victor Kiam publicly labeled Olson "a classic bitch."

The sportswriter fled to Australia and took a job with the *Sydney Daily Telegraph Mirror.* She settled a civil harassment suit against the Patriots, reportedly for $250,000, and eventually returned to the United States. Olson, who writes about sports for New York's *Daily News,* did not return phone calls requesting an interview.

"She went through hell and she's chosen not to dwell on it anymore," explains Joanne Gerstner, who, like many others, is protective of Olson. In 1993, the reporter made a rare public appearance at an AWSM convention. Asked how it felt to be the focus of such intense media attention, she replied, "When I see my name like that, it doesn't seem like me anymore. It's like I stop being Lisa Olson."

. . .

While some men were hell-bent on running women sportswriters out, others offered a lifeline of support and cooperation. Women interviewed for this story stressed that most of the men they dealt with on assignment and in the sports department were not insufferable chauvinists. Many male editors helped boost their careers. Some, like Vince Doria, vice president and director of news at ESPN, made diversifying staff a priority.

Doria brags that ESPN was the first network to hire women as sports anchors and to make them part of reporting teams for high-profile events. Gayle Gardner, an early role model in the field, was a prominent presence from 1983 to 1988, during ESPN's formative years.

Once Doria joined ESPN in 1992, he continued the effort to bring more women into sports journalism. "I have hired a lot of women. It always seemed to me to be the right thing to do," says Doria. He was one of nine male sports editors to contribute $100 each to help jump-start AWSM in 1987, when he was with the *Boston Globe*.

"Today female sportswriters are all over the place. No one gives it a second thought," says Doria, who believes that women can have an edge over men in the field. He has been quoted as saying that men are bombarded by clichés from an early age and look for the conventional angle. Women might be more likely to offer a fresh view.

Diversity also is a top priority for Roy Hewitt, sports editor at Cleveland's *Plain Dealer*. "You're limiting yourself when you don't do it. Diversity is good for any department at the newspaper, including sports," says Hewitt, who had a run-in with Penn State University's legendary football coach, Joe Paterno, over locker-room access for a female reporter in the mid-1980s. Hewitt was then deputy sports editor at the *Philadelphia Inquirer*.

Rather than allow her in, a stubborn Paterno closed the locker room to everybody. Instead, the coach selected players to come into an interview room for post-game chats. "The male reporters hated it," recalls Hewitt. "The reporter got a lot of under-the-breath comments. They blamed her for being shut out."

The editor appealed to the Penn State sports information director, noting that if modesty was the issue, the newspaper would purchase robes for the players. "They never took [the paper] up on it," says Hewitt, who did not see the situation resolved during his time at the *Inquirer*.

Tracy Dodds was associate sports editor under Hewitt at the *Plain Dealer*. In a column she wrote after leaving the paper, she credited him with "going beyond a token hire, to continue to recruit, promote, and, most important, support women in sports. He is not the only one. There are a handful of others."

Welcoming women into the mix should have been a no-brainer, especially since sports fans cross all race and gender lines, says Jerry Micco, president of the Associated Press Sports Editors. "The more people in the department that reflect that, the better. I can't imagine that a sports editor at any paper of any size with a brain of any size would say anything different."

By the mid-1980s, the four major professional leagues—the NFL, NHL, NBA and Major League Baseball—hammered out policies that complied with the federal court's equal-access ruling.

Some, like Micco, credit female sports reporters with adding a richer mix to overall coverage. "Maybe [women] do bring a little more to the party when it comes to working sources, getting inside people's heads better. They might approach a story from a more human standpoint than men do," says Micco, assistant managing editor of sports at the *Pittsburgh Post-Gazette*.

Karen Crouse was reporting for the *Daily News* of Los Angeles in May 2001 when she walked past the locker of Lakers player Horace Grant and noticed a picture of his mother. That led to a poignant story of Grady Mae Grant's influence on her son as he grew up in Sparta, Georgia. "It clearly never occurred to any men covering the team to write that story," says Crouse, now a sports columnist for the *Palm Beach Post*.

Also, noted sports journalist Christine Brennan has turned the spotlight on Olympic figure skating, and she triggered a national debate when she wrote about the Augusta National Golf Club's ban on female members in her column in *USA Today* (see "Howell Much is Too Much?" March 2003).

The progress for women sportswriters has been monumental. Yet, many say they are still butting against a glass ceiling, a hierarchical system that prefers men for the top jobs.

There are exceptions, such as Brennan, who works on contract for ESPN as well as *USA Today*; Michelle Tafoya, reporting from the sidelines for ABC's "Monday Night Football"; and Sally Jenkins, prize-winning sports columnist for the *Washington Post*. Still, many work in low- to mid-level positions where they are likely to be pigeonholed, covering women's sporting events or low-profile competition like college water polo.

No one seems to have a handle on the number of women who function as department heads, columnists or sports beat writers. APSE's Micco says that women make up about 6 percent of the 682 members of his organization. When it comes to women sports editors, "There's not a whole heck of a lot of them around," he says.

Dodds, a former sports editor at the *Austin American-Statesman*, notes that "in the early 1970s, you could name all the women in the business because there were so few. Today, you can name all the female sports editors and columnists."

Although 1,000 media credentials were issued for the Ryder Cup golf tournament held in Detroit earlier this year, only a handful of women were among the press corps, says Gerstner, a sportswriter for the *Detroit News*. "I can name you almost every single woman who was there," says Gerstner, who counted nine. She admits she might have missed a few, but "the numbers were slim." A few years ago, AWSM put the number of women working in some phase of sports journalism at about 500.

Prejudice still comes unexpectedly and leaves a sting. It can happen at work when Gerstner answers the sports department phone. "The caller will say, 'Can I please speak to a sports reporter?' I say, 'I am.' Then the caller says, 'I want to speak to a man.' It reminds you that you are different, that you stick out," she says.

The obstacles women face often vary according to the stage of their careers. It might be juggling a travel-intensive beat and a marriage/family relationship. For others, it could be the barriers to becoming a columnist or sports editor. It might be the pressure to look good on TV when one isn't the 20-something ingénue anymore, says Gerstner. "We joke at [AWSM] conventions that we all need cabana boys to help at home. Men often have women to take care of the kids. They don't have to make that choice."

Female sports journalists who cover high-profile teams say their jobs tend to demand long road trips, with more night and weekend schedules than many other newsroom positions. Premier sportscaster Lesley Visser, a trailblazer with ESPN and CBS Sports, notes, "I have worked every weekend for 30 years" when the beats she covers, like football, are in season. Many female sports reporters spent up to a month in Athens last summer to cover the Olympics.

Sometimes, the rigors of the job clash with responsibilities at home, forcing a career change. Claire Smith, one of the first women to cover Major League Baseball, broke through the editing ranks to become assistant sports editor at the *Philadelphia Inquirer,* a job that, she says, better accommodates her role as the single parent of a 17-year-old son and caretaker for elderly parents. Her hours are more predictable; there is less stress and less time out of town.

"It definitely was time for me to get off the road," says Smith, who began covering baseball in 1982 and left the beat in 1998 to be a sports columnist. She became an editor in 2001. "This job doesn't require me to get in an airplane or try to raise my son by telephone."

Smith cites another reason why women make the switch. "A lot of us go to the news side because you get tired of being the only girl in the traveling boys' band. It wears on you after awhile."

Michele Himmelberg opted out of sports nine years ago, despite being a founder of AWSM and a trailblazer who fought—and won—a legal battle for equal access against the NFL's Tampa Bay Buccaneers in 1979. She was writing for Fort Myers' *News-Press* at the time. "I left the business because I had two children and my lifestyle was chaotic. I somehow managed in the early years . . . I felt tugged and pulled," says Himmelberg, now a business writer with the *Orange County Register.*

Is she sorry she left sports? "I am glad I [covered sports]; it was interesting, fun, exciting. That was a good chapter in my life. Now I have another chapter."

Some make the juggling act work through strong support from a spouse or relatives. Ann Killion, a sports columnist for the *San Jose Mercury News,* spent three weeks in Athens covering the summer Olympics. She got home the day after school started. While she was away, her children, 13 and 9, were in the care of her husband, a school administrator, who has a set schedule and predictable hours.

"You have to have a spouse who totally supports you," says Killion, who has another safety net—her father-in-law and mother live nearby.

Still, there can be an emotional toll. Killion talks about bursting into tears at times when being out of town forces her to miss her children's soccer games or other important school activities.

It is a reality, she says, that having a family limits career options. "It's pretty well known in the sports world that I have two kids, own a house and live near relatives. It's like, 'She's never going to leave.' I don't get a lot of calls for jobs in Chicago."

For some women, like Karen Crouse of the *Palm Beach Post,* parenting just isn't part of the mix. "With my hectic schedule, I don't see how I could do the job the way I do it now and give full energy to raising children," says Crouse, who has been married for 10 years. Her husband is a copyeditor at the *Post.*

During an interview, Crouse broaches another common issue. As the lone female covering sports at the *Post,* she sometimes feels isolated and frets over whom she would turn to if a problem, such as being harassed or not taken seriously on the job, cropped up.

"I could tell a male sportswriter and he would look at me like I'm from Mars because these experiences are uniquely ours in this business," the columnist says. "I have a great relationship with my editor, but he doesn't know what it is like to walk in our shoes. He tries to be empathetic, but it only goes so far."

Crouse turned to a psychologist for advice on handling job stress, including feedback from readers laced with sexual slurs. "You take it personally and it eats at you," she says. "I have had people call me the 'c-word.' None of the men gets called the equivalent of that."

In response to one of her columns, a caller left a voice mail message that said, "You have no talent for this shit. You need to go into the entertainment business, lady." On the same day, she received this one: "What the fuck do you know about the Lakers? You don't know anything about the NBA, female." Some have suggested she write recipes instead of covering sports.

"That's the thing about being a woman in this business," says Crouse. "It's never just about yourself. For better or worse, you're representing the entire gender."

That reality, among others, hangs heavy over women in the field, according to sports sociologist Mary Jo Kane, who poses theories about the highly personal and sexually charged responses hurled at these professionals over the years.

Female sportswriters often have been targets, says Kane, because they have "backstage access" to one of the most powerful and revered symbols of male superiority in American culture, coupled with a public voice, through the media, to criticize men. That, she concludes, places them in a unique position regarding the power relationship between the sexes.

"For men to regain control, women have to be reassigned to the role of sex object. The gender order is upset when women enter a locker room," the researcher says.

"If your baseline is where female reporters were in the Phyllis George era, we are light-years ahead of that," Kane adds. "But if the baseline is where women are in the 21st century compared to their male counterparts, we are still literally and figuratively limited to the sidelines in men's major sporting events. It's a tougher nut to crack."

(Phyllis George, crowned Miss America in 1971, has been billed as the first woman sportscaster in America, coanchoring "The NFL Today" show with Brent Musburger from 1975 to 1984.)

Younger women entering sports journalism "often don't know the history and they take it for granted. There is little appreciation for the blood that was spilled to get them where they are today," says Kane.

In that case, Paola Boivin has important lessons to teach. When her editor filed a complaint with the St. Louis Cardinals management after the jock strap incident in 1985, a curt reply noted that an investigation had found no truth to the allegation, despite a room full of witnesses. Boivin recalls a bright spot on that dreadful day. As she fled the locker room, a male sportswriter chased after her. "I saw that; it was horrible. You didn't deserve it. Is there anything I can do?" he asked. Boivin didn't recognize him and was too flustered to ask his name. "I wish I did because I would like to thank him," she says.

"It's funny," she adds. "For all the male reporters who made you feel like you were intruding in their domain, so many others have gone out of their way to be supportive. I look back now and realize how much that mattered."

At 44, Boivin is a past president of AWSM and an award-winning sports columnist for the *Arizona Republic*. Why did she decide not to quit? Boivin answers: "There was a pull towards not giving up and letting them win."

PART VII

Law and Equity: Title IX and Its Aftermath

This section includes historical documents that span from the passage of Title IX to the most recent conflicts over its intent and application. Some selections present information on Title IX's interpretation and impact while others highlight competing views for and against Title IX. Part VII begins with a reprint of Title IX of the Education Amendments of 1972, followed quickly by the Women's Sports Foundation's "Title IX Media Helper," which explains what Title IX is and how compliance with the law is determined. When Congress passed Title IX, which nowhere even contains the word *athletics* or *sport*, few people anticipated the enormous impact it would have on all levels of sports. For this reason, commentators often treat it as a singular turning point, suggesting that nothing that came before Title IX was ever again the same, and everything that came after its passage was entirely new. This approach makes it hard to understand why the amendments were passed and their subsequent history.

Title IX represents a true watershed moment. But we can point to feminist sentiments burgeoning inside the world of sport and exploding beyond it in the late 1960s and early 1970s to understand why a law demanding gender equity in education struck legislators as reasonable and uncontroversial. The Equal Rights Amendment (ERA), which would have extended the requirement of equality between women and men throughout the entire legal system, was passed the same year and received immediate support from most politicians on state and national levels. But the ERA's eventual failure to win state ratification provides clues to the history of Title IX. Instituting changes unimaginable ten or fifteen years before its passage, during its thirty-five year history Title IX has met with and continues to meet resistance from athletic departments, in Congress, and within enforcement agencies. Part VII contains a description of one of the more famous legal actions involving Title IX, that of *Cohen v. Brown University*, as well as "Title IX at 30," an overview of changes in gender equity in sports during the thirty-year history of Title IX.

Title IX can serve as a lens through which to analyze the tremendous growth of women's sport and the persistent opposition it has provoked. Initially, Congress and most male athletic administrators found it hard to believe that the law would even apply to sports, hoping to establish a legal exemption for athletics. Strong initial resistance explains why it took seven years for the federal government to finalize regulations for the law's application and standards for judging compliance. Once these regulations went into effect in 1979 the battle moved to the courts, where an initial reversal, followed by a Congressional Act restoring the intended meaning (inclusive of sports) of Title IX, then two decades of litigation have produced a body of case law that has consistently upheld the principle of gender equity and clarified the steps schools must take to achieve it.

Themes from previous sections resurface in the controversies surrounding the law. Opponents argue that natural differences between men and women should be taken into account, claiming that the mandate for equity distorts reality by ignoring men's naturally greater interest and women's lesser interest in sports. Arguments about nature versus nurture, whether differences of ability and interest are a result of biology or culture, have been a constant reference point as supporters and opponents weigh the merits of Title IX. We see as well the recurrent theme of competition between the sexes, although nothing in Title IX requires girls and boys to compete on the same teams or against each other. The struggle over athletic resources—money, scholarships, gym time, coaches' salaries, and the type and number of sports a school offers—has for opponents become a struggle to defend men's athletic opportunities against the encroachments of women. George F. Will raises some of these points in "A Train Wreck Called Title IX," while Emily Badger's article about the University of Maryland's plan to make cheerleading a varsity sport in order to help with Title IX compliance makes one wonder about the wisdom of compliance for compliance's sake—especially given statistics (see Part III) about the rise in catastrophic injuries in cheerleading.

The battle over resources could be interpreted in other ways, for instance as a disagreement over how much money should be spent on major sports like men's basketball and football and minor sports like wrestling, gymnastics, hockey, and track for either women or men. But when men's teams get cut or reduced, Title IX critics blame the growth of women's sport rather than the fantastically high costs of sports like football that limit the resources available to other athletes, regardless of gender. And even as these battles continue, some have raised a quieter complaint, wondering if women should follow the path of men's sport, marred by chronically low graduation rates, academic and sexual scandal, serious injuries, and financial corruption.

This section ends with a look at the most recent attempt by the federal government to take the teeth out of Title IX. "Title IX—The Good News, the Bad News" functions as an update to the article "Title IX at 30," informing the reader of the Bush Administration's latest tinkering with this law. Given the arguments for and against Title IX's continued existence, readers might ask themselves as they progress through Part VII whether Title IX might suffer the same slow collapse that has occurred with Affirmative Action in employment and educational settings. They might question, too, whether Title IX's model of mandated equity is the best solution to gender hierarchy in sports, even as we applaud the tremendous increase in athletic opportunity Title IX has afforded girls and women who, as "entitled" athletes, will continue to push against unjust constraints, in sports and in life.

◆◗

TITLE IX, EDUCATION AMENDMENTS OF 1972

Title 20 U.S.C. Sections 1681–1688

U.S. Department of Labor

Section 1681. Sex

(a) **Prohibition against discrimination; exceptions.** No person in the United States shall, on the basis of sex, be excluded from participation in, be denied the benefits of, or be subjected to discrimination under any education program or activity receiving Federal financial assistance, except that:

(1) **Classes of educational institutions subject to prohibition**
in regard to admissions to educational institutions, this section shall apply only to institutions of vocational education, professional education, and graduate higher education, and to public institutions of undergraduate higher education:

(2) **Educational institutions commencing planned change in admissions**
in regard to admissions to educational institutions, this section shall not apply (A) for one year from June 23, 1972, nor for six years after June 23, 1972, in the case of an educational institution which has begun the process of changing from being an institution which admits only students of one sex to being an institution which

From the U.S. Department of Labor, http://www.dol.gov/oasam/regs/statutes/titleix.htm.

admits students of both sexes, but only if it is carrying out a plan for such a change which is approved by the Secretary of Education or (B) for seven years from the date an educational institution begins the process of changing from being an institution which admits only students of one sex to being an institution which admits students of both sexes, but only if it is carrying out a plan for such a change which is approved by the Secretary of Education, whichever is the later;

(3) Educational institutions of religious organizations with contrary religious tenets
this section shall not apply to any educational institution which is controlled by a religious organization if the application of this subsection would not be consistent with the religious tenets of such organization;

(4) Educational institutions training individuals for military services or merchant marine
this section shall not apply to an educational institution whose primary purpose is the training of individuals for the military services of the United States, or the merchant marine;

(5) Public educational institutions with traditional and continuing admissions policy
in regard to admissions this section shall not apply to any public institution of undergraduate higher education which is an institution that traditionally and continually from its establishment has had a policy of admitting only students of one sex;

(6) Social fraternities or sororities; voluntary youth service organizations
this section shall not apply to membership practices—
(A) of a social fraternity or social sorority which is exempt from taxation under section 501(a) of Title 26, the active membership of which consists primarily of students in attendance at an institution of higher education, or
(B) of the Young Men's Christian Association, Young Women's Christian Association; Girl Scouts, Boy Scouts, Camp Fire Girls, and voluntary youth service organizations which are so exempt, the membership of which has traditionally been limited to persons of one sex and principally to persons of less than nineteen years of age;

(7) **Boy or Girl conferences**
this section shall not apply to—
   (A) any program or activity of the American Legion undertaken in connection with the organization or operation of any Boys State conference, Boys Nation conference, Girls State conference, or Girls Nation conference; or
   (B) any program or activity of any secondary school or educational institution specifically for—
      (i) the promotion of any Boys State conference, Boys Nation conference, Girls State conference, or Girls Nation conference; or
      (ii) the selection of students to attend any such conference;

(8) **Father-son or mother-daughter activities at educational institutions**
this section shall not preclude father-son or mother-daughter activities at an educational institution, but if such activities are provided for students of one sex, opportunities for reasonably comparable activities shall be provided for students of the other sex; and

(9) **Institutions of higher education scholarship awards in "beauty" pageants**
this section shall not apply with respect to any scholarship or other financial assistance awarded by an institution of higher education to any individual because such individual has received such award in any pageant in which the attainment of such award is based upon a combination of factors related to the personal appearance, poise, and talent of such individual and in which participation is limited to individuals of one sex only, so long as such pageant is in compliance with other nondiscrimination provisions of Federal law.

(b) **Preferential or disparate treatment because of imbalance in participation or receipt of Federal benefits; statistical evidence of imbalance.**
Nothing contained in subsection (a) of this section shall be interpreted to require any educational institution to grant preferential or disparate treatment to the members of one sex on account of an imbalance which may exist with respect to the total number or percentage of persons of that sex participating in or receiving the benefits of any federally supported program or activity, in comparison with the total number or percentage of persons of that sex in any community, State, section, or other area; *Provided,* that this subsection shall not

be construed to prevent the consideration in any hearing or proceeding under this chapter of statistical evidence tending to show that such an imbalance exists with respect to the participation in, or receipt of the benefits of, any such program or activity by the members of one sex.

(c) **Educational institution defined.** For the purposes of this chapter an educational institution means any public or private preschool, elementary, or secondary school, or any institution of vocational, professional, or higher education, except that in the case of an educational institution composed of more than one school, college, or department which are administratively separate units, such term means each such school, college, or department.

Section 1682. Federal Administrative Enforcement; Report to Congressional Committees

Each Federal department and agency which is empowered to extend Federal financial assistance to any education program or activity, by way of grant, loan, or contract other than a contract of insurance or guaranty, is authorized and directed to effectuate the provisions of section 1681 of this title with respect to such program or activity by issuing rules, regulations, or orders of general applicability which shall be consistent with achievement of the objectives of the statute authorizing the financial assistance in connection with which the action is taken. No such rule, regulation, or order shall become effective unless and until approved by the President. Compliance with any requirement adopted pursuant to this section may be effected (1) by the termination of or refusal to grant or to continue assistance under such program or activity to any recipient as to whom there has been an express finding on the record, after opportunity for hearing, of a failure to comply with such requirement, but such termination or refusal shall be limited to the particular political entity, or part thereof, or other recipient as to whom such a finding has been made, and shall be limited in its effect to the particular program, or part thereof, in which such noncompliance has been so found, or (2) by any other means authorized by law: *Provided, however,* that no such action shall be taken until the department or agency concerned has advised the appropriate person or persons of the failure to comply with the requirement and has determined that compliance cannot be secured by voluntary means. In the case of any action terminating, or refusing to grant or continue, assistance because of failure to comply with a requirement imposed pursuant to this section, the head of the Federal department or agency shall file with the committees of the House and Senate having legislative jurisdiction over the program or activity involved a full written report of the circumstances and the grounds for such action. No such action shall become effective until thirty days have elapsed after the filing of such report.

Section 1683. Judicial Review

Any department or agency action taken pursuant to section 1682 of this title shall be subject to such judicial review as may otherwise be provided by law for similar action taken by such department or agency on other grounds. In the case of action, not otherwise subject to judicial review, terminating or refusing to grant or to continue financial assistance upon a finding of failure to comply with any requirement imposed pursuant to section 1682 of this title, any person aggrieved (including any State or political subdivision thereof and any agency of either) may obtain judicial review of such action in accordance with chapter 7 of title 5, United States Code, and such action shall not be deemed committed to unreviewable agency discretion within the meaning of section 701 of that title.

Section 1684. Blindness or Visual Impairment; Prohibition Against Discrimination

No person in the United States shall, on the ground of blindness or severely impaired vision, be denied admission in any course of study by a recipient of Federal financial assistance for any education program or activity; but nothing herein shall be construed to require any such institution to provide any special services to such person because of his blindness or visual impairment.

Section 1685. Authority Under Other Laws Unaffected

Nothing in this chapter shall add to or detract from any existing authority with respect to any program or activity under which Federal financial assistance is extended by way of a contract of insurance or guaranty.

Section 1686. Interpretation with Respect to Living Facilities

Notwithstanding anything to the contrary contained in this chapter, nothing contained herein shall be construed to prohibit any educational institution receiving funds under this Act, from maintaining separate living facilities for the different sexes.

Section 1687. Interpretation of "Program or Activity"

For the purposes of this title, the term "program or activity" and "program" mean all of the operations of—

(1)(A) a department, agency, special purpose district, or other instrumentality of a State or of a local government; or

  (B) the entity of such State or local government that distributed such assistance and each such department or agency (and each other State or local government entity) to which the assistance is extended, in the case of assistance to a State or local government;

(2)(A) a college, university, or other postsecondary institution, or a public system of higher education; or

  (B) a local educational agency (as defined in section 2854(a)(10) of this title, system of vocational education, or other school system;

(3)(A) an entire corporation, partnership, or other private organization, of an entire sole proprietorship—

   (i) if assistance is extended to such corporation, partnership, private organization, or sole proprietorship as a whole; or

   (ii) which is principally engaged in the business of providing education, health care, housing, social services, or parks and recreation; or

  (B) the entire plant or other comparable, geographically separate facility to which Federal financial assistance is extended, in the case of any other corporation, partnership, private organization, or sole proprietorship; or

(4) any other entity which is established by two or more of the entities described in paragraph (1), (2) or (3);
any part of which is extended Federal financial assistance, except that such term does not include any operation of an entity which is controlled by a religious organization if the application of section 1681 if this title to such operation would not be consistent with the religious tenets of such organization.

Section 1688. Neutrality with Respect to Abortion

Nothing in this chapter shall be construed to require or prohibit any person, or public or private entity, to provide or pay for any benefit or service, including the use of facilities, related to an abortion. Nothing in this section shall be construed to permit a penalty to be imposed on any person or individual because such person or individual is seeking or has received any benefit or service related to a legal abortion.

◀▣▶

TITLE IX MEDIA HELPER

Women's Sports Foundation

1. What Is Title IX?

- Title IX of the Education Amendments of 1972 is a federal law that prohibits sex discrimination in any educational program or activity at any educational institution that is a recipient of federal funds.
- Athletics, drama, band and other extracurricular student activities are considered to be educational programs under this law.
- Title IX also prohibits all forms of sex discrimination in federally funded educational institutions, including sexual harassment, discrimination in admissions and counseling, discrimination against married or pregnant students, etc.

2. Which Schools Must Comply with Title IX?

- Title IX applies to educational institutions that receive any federal funds—whether public or private. (There are very few private colleges but many private elementary and secondary schools that do not receive federal money.)
- Almost all private colleges are covered because they receive federal funding through federal financial aid programs used by their students.

From the Women's Sports Foundation, www.WomensSportsFoundation.org, 1999, revised January 2002.

Many private elementary and secondary schools receive federal funding through various programs as well.

3. How Is Title IX Applied to Athletics?

There are three basic parts of Title IX as it applies to athletics:

- Participation: requires that women be provided an equitable opportunity to participate in sports as men (not necessarily the identical sports but an equal opportunity to play).
- Scholarships: require that female athletes receive athletic scholarship dollars proportional to their participation (e.g., if there are 100 male athletes/100 female athletes and a $200,000 scholarship budget, then the budget must be split $100,000 to men/$100,000 to women).
- Other Benefits: requires equal treatment in the provision of (1) equipment and supplies, (2) scheduling of games and practice times, (3) travel and daily allowance, (4) access to tutoring, (5) coaching, (6) locker rooms, (7) practice and competitive facilities, (8) medical and training facilities and services, (9) publicity and promotions (10) recruitment of student athletes, and (11) support services.

4. Does Title IX Require that Equal Dollars Be Spent on Men's and Women's Sports?

- No. The only provision that requires that the same dollars be spent (proportional to participation) is "scholarships." Otherwise, female athletes must receive equal "treatment" and "benefits."
- The standard is one of "quality" rather than dollars spent. For example, if a school spends $700 outfitting a male football player, it does not have to spend $700 outfitting a female lacrosse player. However, male and female athletes must be provided with the same quality uniforms, and they must be replaced under the same circumstances.
- Unequal budgets can also affect the number of athletes on a team. Insufficient funds may not permit a coach to supply the necessary equipment, uniforms, and travel costs to a large number of players. Such disparities may violate Title IX.

5. Does Title IX Require Identical Athletic Programs for Males and Females?

- No. Males and females can participate in different sports. Rather, Title IX requires that the athletic programs meet the interests and abilities of each gender.
- Under Title IX, one team is not compared to the same team in each sport. The Office for Civil Rights examines the total program afforded to male athletes and the total program afforded to female athletes and whether each program meets the standard of equal treatment.
- Title IX does not require that each team get exactly the same services and supplies. Rather, it requires that the men's program and the women's program receive the same level of service, facilities and supplies. Variations within the men's program and within the women's program are allowed.

6. Are Most Schools and Colleges in Compliance with Title IX?

- No. Current estimates are that 80% or more of all colleges and universities are not in compliance.
- At the high school level, financial data are unavailable. Participation data reveal that while females comprise 54% of the general student population, they receive only 41% of athletic program opportunities (1999–2000 Gender-Equity Study). [See table 1]
- Male athletes at the college level receive 133 million dollars more than female athletes in college athletics scholarships *each year* (1999 NCAA Gender-Equity Study)!

7. Does Title IX Apply to Booster Clubs and Other Types of (Similar) Support for Athletic Teams?

Yes, if the school permits an individual or group to donate funds for the benefit of a specific gender or sport, it must also make sure that benefits and services are equivalent for both sexes.

8. Is Any Sport Excluded from Title IX?

- No. All sports at an institution are included under Title IX.
- During the 1970s, there were four efforts to amend Title IX to exclude football, and each effort failed.

Table 1
1999–2000 Gender-Equity Study

	Division I—Overall		Division I-A		Division I-AA	
	Male	Female	Male	Female	Male	Female
Undergraduates	47%	53%	49%	51%	46%	54%
Athletes	59%	41%	61%	39%	60%	40%
Operating Expenses	64%	36%	67%	33%	62%	38%
Recruiting Expenses	68%	32%	71%	29%	66%	34%
Scholarships	57%	43%	60%	40%	57%	43%
Head Coach Salaries	59%	41%	62%	38%	57%	43%
Assistant Coach Salaries	72%	28%	74%	26%	72%	28%

	Division I-AAA		Division II		Division III	
	Male	Female	Male	Female	Male	Female
Undergraduates	42.5%	57.5%	43.5%	56.5%	44.3%	55.7%
Athletes	52%	48%	62%	38%	62%	38%
Operating Expenses	55%	45%	66%	34%	59%	41%
Recruiting Expenses	55%	45%	65%	35%	65%	35%
Scholarships	48%	52%	59%	41%	N/A	N/A
Head Coach Salaries	55%	45%	54%	46%	55%	45%
Assistant Coach Salaries	55%	45%	72%	28%	69%	31%

9. Should Football Be Excluded from Title IX Coverage?

- No. No sport should be excluded from Title IX compliance. Males are entitled to participate in the sports in which they have an interest and females are entitled to participate in the sports in which they have an interest.
- The point is that if male athletes prefer to use 100 participation opportunities playing football, that's fine. If female athletes prefer to use their 100 participation opportunities playing soccer, softball and field hockey, that's fine too.

10. Does Title IX Enforcement Hurt Football Programs?

- No. Football programs already receive protection under Title IX as mandated by the Javits Amendment which allows increased expenditures based on "the nature of a sport" (i.e., football uniforms and protective equipment cost more than uniforms in other sports).
- Some have argued for the exclusion of football from Title IX because it not only costs more to fund a football program, but it earns more money, which funds other sports. This is a myth. Among NCAA football programs in all competitive divisions, 81% spend more than they bring in and contribute nothing to other sport budgets. Even among Division 1-A football programs, more than a third are running deficits in excess of $1 million per year.
- Affording special consideration to football would permit an economic justification for discrimination. This would allow an institution to say, "We're sorry we can't afford to give your daughter the same opportunity to play sports as your son because football needs more money."

11. Does Title IX Mandate Decreases in Opportunities for Male Athletes in Order to Provide Increased Opportunities for Females to Participate?

- No. Title IX's purpose is to create the same opportunity and quality of treatment for female athletes as is afforded male athletes. The law does not require reductions in opportunities for male athletes.
- Some educational institutions have chosen to cut men's non-revenue sports and maintained that this was necessary in order to comply with Title IX, thereby making women's programs the easy scapegoat to blame for the loss of these men's programs. However, it is the school's choice to cut back in this unfortunate manner.

- Title IX is not to blame for school priorities that short-change men's minor sports. During the 1980s, when few schools were expanding opportunities for women to play sports, men's minor sports were being eliminated in order to spend more money on football and other men's revenue-producing sports.
- Cutting men's sports is not the intent of Title IX. The intent of Title IX is to bring treatment of the disadvantaged gender up to the level of the advantaged group.

12. Does Title IX Require Institutions to Meet "Quotas"?

- No. Every institution has three options to meet the participation standard of Title IX, only one of which is to provide athletic participation opportunities in substantial proportion to each gender enrollment. They only need to meet one of the following:
- Option 1: Compare the ratio of male and female athletes to male and female undergraduates. If the resulting ratios are close, the school is probably in compliance with the participation standard.
- Option 2: Demonstrate that the institution has a history and continuing practice of program expansion for the underrepresented gender.
- Option 3: Demonstrate that the institution has already effectively accommodated the interests and abilities of the underrepresented gender.

13. Has Title IX Increased Female Participation over the Last 25 Years?

- In 1970, only 1 out of every 27 high school girls played varsity sports. Today, that figure is 1 in 2.5. Female high school participation increased from 294,015 in 1971 to 2,784,154 in 2000. College participation has more than quadrupled, from 31,000 to 150,916.

14. Are Females Less Interested in Sports than Males?

- No. There is no evidence suggesting girls are inherently less interested in sports than boys. We do know that at an early age (six to nine years old), they are equally as interested. However, participation opportunities decline sharply as girls get older.
- The participation rate of boys (twice that of girls) reflects the opportunities that are offered to them—not lack of interest on the part of girls.

15. How Do I Know if My School Is in Compliance with Title IX?

- Ask. Every school by law has to have a Title IX Coordinator. Find out who this person is and ask them about the school's compliance. Title IX covers many areas, from participation numbers to quality of available coaching. If the school doesn't have a Title IX Coordinator, report it to the Office for Civil Rights (OCR) at the U.S. Department of Education.
- At the high school level, find out if the school is accommodating the sports interests of both boys and girls. Are there programs not being offered for girls where there's substantial interest to field a program? Compare the number of participation opportunities available to boys (not the number of teams but the actual number of players) to the number of opportunities for girls.
- At the college level, it's become a little easier for anyone to find out if an institution is in compliance. In 1994, Congress passed the Equity in Athletics Disclosure Act (EADA) which requires all institutions of higher education to report each year on athletic participation numbers, scholarships, program budgets and expenditures, and coaching salaries by gender. This information is to be made available to anyone in a timely fashion (1–2 weeks) upon request. Simply call the institution's athletic department and request it. As it is broken down by gender, it's easy to see whether an institution is being equitable.
- Grade your school at www.GeenaTakesAim.com.

16. Who Is Responsible for Enforcing Title IX?

- Schools and colleges are responsible for complying with federal law.
- The OCR is specifically charged with enforcing the law. Anyone can file an OCR complaint and the identity of the complaining party will be kept confidential.
- Courts—affected parties have the individual right to sue (courts may award damages).

17. What Is the Penalty for Non-Compliance with Title IX?

- The ultimate penalty for non-compliance is withdrawal of federal funds from the offending institution. Institutions may also be required by court or the OCR to make changes in their programs and to pay damages to the students for their lost opportunities.

- Although most institutions are not in compliance with Title IX, no institution has lost any federal funds as a result of non-compliance with Title IX. Office for Civil Rights states that it does not have sufficient staff/budget to fully enforce Title IX. Institutions have had to pay substantial damages and attorneys' fees in cases brought to court.

18. Are Institutions Prohibited from Retaliation against Persons who File Title IX Complaints or Lawsuits?

- Yes. Retribution is prohibited.
- However there are many coaches of women's teams who have complained about Title IX violations and who have not had their contracts renewed, ostensibly for other reasons.

19. The boys' teams receive letter jackets from the booster club at the end of the year while the girls' teams receive certifictes from the school. Is this a Title IX violation?

- Yes. If permission is given by the athletic director for an action or expenditure that benefits the boys' programs, a similar benefit must be provided to the girls' programs.

20. Is it a violation of Title IX when cheerleaders, pep squads and/or bands are provided for men's athletic events but not for women's athletics events?

- Yes. Cheerleaders, pep squads and bands are considered publicity services. If they are provided for the men's program, they must be provided for the women's program.

21. Does Title IX require an equal number of teams for male and female athletes?

- No. Title IX deals with participation opportunities or number of individual participation slots for males and females to play—not numbers of teams.

22. Our high school girls play at 4:00 pm on Fridays, and the boys play at 7:00 pm on Fridays. Is this a violation of Title IX?

- Yes. Later times for games are more valued because parents, friends and spectators can attend.
- In order to comply with Title IX, many schools flip-flop early and late starting times for men's and women's teams.

23. Can "cheerleading" be considered a varsity sport?

- Generally, no. However, if they have a coach, practice as frequently as a regular varsity team and compete against other cheerleading teams on a regular basis and more frequently than they appear to cheer for other teams, they may meet the definition of a varsity team.

◆❖◆

BROWN UNIVERSITY AGREES TO GUARANTEE PARTICIPATION RATES FOR WOMEN ATHLETES AND FUNDING FOR CONTESTED WOMEN'S TEAMS

Trial Lawyers for Public Justice

Trial Lawyers for Public Justice (TLPJ) announced today that Brown University had agreed to guarantee intercollegiate athletic participation rates for women athletes and funding for four contested women's teams to resolve TLPJ's landmark Title IX class action against the school. The proposed settlement of the outstanding claims against Brown's program in *Cohen v. Brown University* was presented to and preliminarily approved by United States District Judge Ernest Torres in Providence, Rhode Island, today.

"This is a tremendous victory for women athletes and potential athletes at Brown, as well as everyone in the nation who cares about equality," said TLPJ Executive Director Arthur H. Bryant, who personally negotiated the

From press release, Trial Lawyers for Public Justice and the TLPF Foundation, www.tlpj .org, 23 June 1998.

settlement. "We are delighted that women at Brown are finally going to get the intercollegiate athletic opportunities and treatment that they deserve."

Under the terms of the agreement, as long as Brown continues to offer the full array of women's university-funded and donor-funded sports currently in its intercollegiate athletic program and does not change the balance between men and women by adding or upgrading men's teams, Brown must ensure that women's intercollegiate athletic participation rate is within 3.5 percentage points of women's undergraduate enrollment rate at the school. If Brown eliminates or downgrades a current women's team, or adds or upgrades a men's team without adding or upgrading a corresponding women's team, then Brown must ensure that women's intercollegiate athletic participation rate is within 2.25 percentage points of women's undergraduate enrollment rate at the school.

In addition, Brown agreed to upgrade women's water polo from club to donor-funded varsity status and to guarantee funding for the four women's teams that now-retired U.S. District Court Judge Raymond S. Pettine found Brown had not adequately supported—gymnastics, fencing, skiing, and water polo. While calling the teams "donor-funded," Brown will fund the teams at significantly increased levels for the next three (or, in gymnastics' case, four) years, whether or not sufficient funds can be raised from donors. For the next four years, Brown will also provide gymnastics with the same benefits and treatment it received last year, when it was treated as a "university-funded" team under Court order.

"We are especially pleased that we obtained increased opportunities and funding for women without sacrificing opportunities or funding for men," said TLPJ lead counsel Lynette Labinger of Providence's Roney and Labinger. "That was one of our goals from the start. We applaud all of the parties and newly-appointed Brown President E. Gordon Gee for finding a constructive way to resolve this litigation and enhance women's opportunities at Brown."

The *Cohen* class action lawsuit was filed in April 1992, after Brown terminated funding for its women's gymnastics and volleyball teams. The suit charged Brown with violating Title IX of the Education Amendments of 1972, the federal law that prohibits sex discrimination by all educational institutions receiving federal funds.

In December 1992, TLPJ won a preliminary injunction requiring Brown to reinstate the women's teams. In April 1993, the U.S. Court of Appeals for the First Circuit unanimously affirmed the preliminary injunction pending trial. In March 1995, after a three-month trial, Judge Pettine found Brown in violation of Title IX and ordered it to submit a proposed plan to come into compliance. In July 1995, Judge Pettine found Brown's proposal unacceptable and ordered it to upgrade four women's teams— gymnastics, fencing, water polo, and skiing—to university-funded varsity status. In November 1996, the First Circuit affirmed the decision finding Brown in violation of Title IX, but said that the school should be given another chance to develop its own plan for compliance. On April 21, 1996, the U.S. Supreme Court denied Brown's petition for review.

Brown subsequently proposed a new compliance plan and plaintiffs objected that it, too, was insufficient. An evidentiary hearing on whether Brown's proposal would, in fact, bring the school into compliance with Title IX was scheduled to begin before Judge Torres on Monday, June 22, but the settlement eliminated the need for the hearing.

Brown University originally announced that it was eliminating funding for women's volleyball and gymnastics in 1991 in order to save $64,000 annually. The school reinstated women's volleyball on the eve of trial in 1994. Under the settlement agreement preliminarily approved today, Brown will spend $64,400 on women's gymnastics in 1998–99.

Formal notice of the settlement will be distributed to the class members in September, shortly after classes start. A final hearing on the proposed settlement is scheduled for October 8 before Judge Torres. If the settlement is approved, all issues in the case will be resolved, except for costs and attorneys' fees.

In addition to Labinger and Bryant, TLPJ's litigation team in *Cohen* includes Amato DeLuca of DeLuca and Weizenbaum and Ray Marcaccio of Blish and Cavanaugh, both of Providence, Sandra Duggan of Philadelphia, and TLPJ's Leslie Brueckner.

◆▶

TITLE IX AT 30

Report Card on Gender Equity—Athletics, C+

National Coalition for Women and Girls in Education

For many people, Title IX is synonymous with expanded opportunities in athletics. Women's and girls' increased participation in sports, the impressive achievements of the nation's female athletes, their stunning advances in summer and winter Olympic Games, and the creation of nationally televised

Excerpted from The National Coalition of Women and Girls in Education, *Title IX at 30: Report Card on Gender Equity*. Washington, D.C.: NCWGE, June 2002. Full text downloadable from www.ncwge.org. Reprinted with permission from National Coalition for Women and Girls in Education (www.ncwge.org).

professional women's basketball and soccer leagues demonstrate Title IX's success. It takes a large and vibrant base of general sports participants and 15 to 20 years of elite athlete support to create an Olympic gold medalist or professional athlete—years in which an athlete is given access to quality coaching, sports facilities, weight rooms, athletic scholarships, and competition. Before Title IX, women and girls were precluded from taking advantage of most athletic opportunities in school, but the outcome of equal opportunity on the playing fields is becoming more apparent.

Still, Olympic medals and professional sports contracts are not what Title IX is all about. Rather, the quest for equal opportunity in sports has always been about the physiological, sociological, and psychological benefits of sports and physical activity participation. Research studies commissioned by the Women's Sports Foundation in 1998 and 2000 found that girls who play sports enjoy greater physical and emotional health and are less likely to engage in a host of risky health behaviors (i.e., drug use, smoking and drinking) than nonparticipants. Other studies have linked sports participation to reduced incidences of beast cancer and osteoporosis later in life. Yet compared to boys, girls enjoy 30 percent fewer opportunities to participate in high school and college sports and are twice as likely to be inactive. Much distance remains between the current status of women and girls in sports and the ultimate goal of gender equity.

Participation Rates and Resource Allocation

Prior to 1972, women and girls looking for opportunities for athletic competition were more likely to try out for cheerleading or secure places in the bleachers as spectators. In 1971 fewer than 295,000 girls participated in high school varsity athletics, accounting for just 7 percent of all high school varsity athletes. The outlook for college women was equally grim. Fewer than 30,000 females competed in intercollegiate athletics. Low participation rates reflected the lack of institutional commitment to providing athletics programming for women. Before Title IX, female college athletes received only 2 percent of overall athletic budgets, and athletic scholarships for women were virtually nonexistent.

Title IX has changed the playing field significantly. By 2001 nearly 2.8 million girls participated in athletics, representing 41.5 percent of varsity athletes in U.S. high schools—an increase of more than 847 percent from 1971. Progress on college campuses also has been impressive. Today, 150,916 women compete in intercollegiate sports, accounting for 43 percent of college varsity athletes—an increase of more than 403 percent from 1971. Contrary to media reports, men's participation levels at both the high school and college level have been increased. See Figure 1, Figure 2, and Table 1.

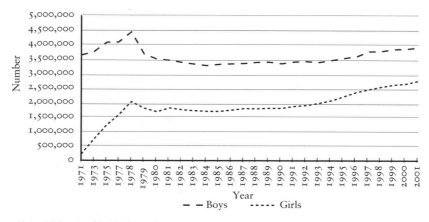

National Federation of State High School Associations, 2001

Figure 1

While significant, these gains still stop short of providing girls and women with their fair share of opportunities to compete. In 1999–2000 female students represented about 54 percent of the student body at four-year colleges, yet only 23 percent of all NCAA Division I colleges provided women with athletic opportunities within five percentage points of

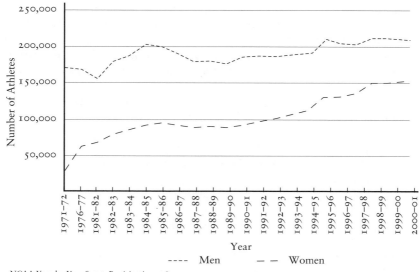

NCAA Year-by-Year Sports Participation 1982–2001
Sports and Recreation Programs of Universities and Colleges 1957–1982 (NCAA)

Figure 2

Table 1
Female High School and Collegiate Participation

Year	1971–72	2000–01	Increase
High School Varsity Athletes			
Female	294,015	2,784,154	847%
Male	3,666,917	3,921,069	6.9%
Collegiate Varsity Athletes			
Female	29,972	150,916	403%
Male	170,384	208,866	23%

NCAA Year-By-Year Sports Participation 1982–2001; Sports and Recreation Programs of Universities and Colleges 1957–82 (NCAA), National Federation of State High School Associations in 2001

female student enrollment. The percentage increased from 9 percent in 1995–96.

Although the resources and benefits allocated to female athletes also have improved significantly since Title IX's passage, they also fall short of what equity requires. After 30 years the gap is still significant and closing much too slowly. Institutions are not exercising restraint on men's sports expenditures while women's sports catch up. See Table 2.

- In the past four years, for every new dollar going into athletics at the Division I and Division II levels, male sports received 58 cents while female sports received 42 cents.
- Each year male athletes receive $133 million or 36 percent more than female athletes in college athletic scholarships at NCAA member institutions.
- In Division I, colleges spent an average of $2,983 per female athlete compared to $3,786 for male athletes.

No national data on expenditures exist for girls' and boys' interscholastic sports, but anecdotal evidence suggests that similar financial disparities also exist at the elementary and secondary levels.

Coaches, Administrators, and Other Athletic Personnel

Women in coaching, athletic administration, and other sports positions lack the improved opportunities enjoyed by female students and athletes since Title IX's enactment. In the early 1970s women head coaches led 90 percent of women's collegiate teams. By the 2001–02 school year, female head coaches led only 44 percent of women's intercollegiate athletic teams, the lowest total since the passage of Title IX. This number is down from 47.7 percent in 1995–96. Since 2000, 90 percent of the available head coaching positions in women's athletics have gone to men. A similar decline in the percentage of women coaching girls' teams can be witnessed at the high school level.

To make matters worse, the loss of coaching opportunities in women's sports has not been offset by a corresponding increase in opportunities for women to coach men's teams. To the contrary, women are virtually shut out of these jobs, holding only 2 percent of the coaching positions in men's collegiate sports, a percentage that has remained constant over the last 30 years. No signs indicate a slowing in the downward trend.

Women's college basketball, considered by most to be the greatest economic success among all women's collegiate sports, is one of the few exceptions to diminishing coaching opportunities for women. The number of women intercollegiate basketball coaches has remained relatively constant over the past 10 years with women currently holding 62.8 percent of these head coaching jobs. Among 24 women's NCAA championship sports, however, female coaches rank in the majority in only seven. See Table 3.

The impact of such sex discrimination on coaching opportunities for women is exacerbated by the striking disparity in the salaries paid to coaches of men's and women's teams. At the Division I level, men's basketball head coaches average $149,700. By contrast, women's basketball head coaches average just $91,300: 61 cents to every dollar paid to men. This trend continues at the assistant coach level, where men's basketball assistant coaches average $44,000 while women's basketball assistant coaches average $34,000. Only in fencing, volleyball, and tennis, the sports paying the lowest salaries to coaches of male teams, do coaches of women's sports receive equal or greater pay than coaches of the equivalent male sports.

Table 2
Disparities in Funding Intercollegiate Athletics for 1999

	Division I		Division II		Division III	
	Men	Women	Men	Women	Men	Women
Scholarships	$1,411,400	$1,055,500	$392,100	$268,000	N/A	N/A
Recruiting	184,200	85,900	18,900	20,100	13,200	7,100
Head Coach Salaries	484,900	330,500	136,700	114,500	127,000	102,600
Operating Expense	882,100	486,200	225,600	115,100	137,000	94,700

NCAA 1999–2000 Gender-Equity Report

Table 3

Coaches of Women's Sports by Gender for 2002

Sport	Female	Male	Sport	Female	Male
Archery	33.3%	66.7%	Riflery	27.3%	72.7%
Basketball	62.8%	37.2%	Sailing	11.1%	88.9%
Bowling	33.3%	66.7%	Skiing	6.9%	93.1%
Crew/Rowing	37.9%	62.1%	Soccer	30.7%	69.3%
Cross Country	21.3%	78.3%	Softball	65.1%	34.9%
Fencing	26.5%	73.5%	Squash	33.3%	66.7%
Field Hockey	96.8%	3.2%	Swimming/Diving	23.0%	77.0%
Golf	39.2%	60.8%	Synchronized Swimming	100.0%	0.0%
Gymnastics	44.3%	55.7%	Tennis	34.5%	65.5%
Ice Hockey	40.0%	60.0%	Track	19.0%	81.0%
Lacrosse	85.9%	14.1%	Volleyball	57.3%	42.7%
Ride/Equestrian	81.0%	19.0%	Water Polo	25.7%	74.3%

Acosta and Carpenter, *Women in Intercollegiate Sport,* 2002

Athletic directors at the college level are also predominantly male (83.1 percent). As the status and salary of these positions increase, female representation decreases (8.4 percent in Division I versus 25.5 percent in Division III). Males also dominate the positions of sports information director (87.7 percent) and athletic trainer (72.2 percent). As the competitiveness of a division and average salary increases, women's representation in these athletics positions also decreases. This trend remains true for every position except for head coaching jobs, for which gender representation in Division I and Division III is equal, although average salaries are not. See Table 4.

Title IX Enforcement

The record of Title IX enforcement in interscholastic and intercollegiate athletics over the past 30 years is fair at best, as evidenced by the persistent disparities highlighted above. In 1975 the then Department of Health, Education, and Welfare (HEW) issued federal Title IX regulations, which included sweeping requirements for equal athletic participation opportunities, proportional athletic scholarship funding, and equality in the treatment of and benefits provided to male and female athletes. The regulations allowed colleges and high schools a three-year phase-in period and elementary schools a one-year phase-in period. HEW explained the regulations in greater detail through a Policy Interpretation issued in 1979.

Enforcement in intercollegiate athletics, however, was largely nonexistent throughout the 1980s, in part because of the Supreme Court's 1984 decision in *Grove City College v. Bell*. In that case, the court limited Title IX's application to the specific programs within colleges and universities that actually received federal funds (usually not the case for athletic programs), rather than applying Title IX to entire institutions should any of their programs receive federal funds. Congress overturned this decision in 1988 through the passage of the Civil Rights Restoration Act.

Even with the full scope of Title IX restored, few enforcement actions were brought by OCR. When colleges responded to budget constraints by cutting already beleaguered women's teams, parents and female athletes responded by taking their Title IX complaints to court. Numerous lawsuits in the 1990s resulted in the creation of a uniform body of law protecting the right to equal athletic opportunity regardless of sex, despite defendants' strenuous objections that men purportedly are more interested in playing sports than women and therefore deserve disproportionate participation opportunities. Progress has been made largely on a case-by-case basis, with gains gradual and piecemeal. Most notably, in the case of *Cohen v. Brown University*, the First Circuit rejected the university's argument that women are less interested than men in playing sports because the argument rests on stereotypical notions about women and only perpetuates the discrimination that women face in athletics.

Other cases have helped root out discrimination by athletic associations, which control college and high school athletic programs but claim they have no responsibilities to comply with civil rights laws. The Supreme Court decided otherwise in *Brentwood Academy v. Tennessee Secondary School Athletic Association*. The court held that the high school athletic association is subject to the Constitution, which governs the conduct of government entities only, because the association is essentially an arm of the state. In *National Collegiate Athletic Association v. Smith*, the Supreme Court held that the NCAA is not subject to Title IX just because it receives dues from its federally funded member schools, but the court specifically left open other legal arguments for coverage of athletic associations. The court adopted one of these arguments in *Communities for Equity v. Michigan High School Athletic Association*, in which a federal district court in Michigan held that the association is subject to Title IX, the Constitution, and Michigan state law. Accordingly, the court found that the association discriminated against girls by scheduling six girls' sports, but no boys' sports, in nontraditional or disadvantageous seasons.

Women's progress, albeit limited, has sparked a backlash by Title IX opponents who claim that Title IX has gone "too far" and has "hurt" men's sports. After holding hearings on this issue in May 1995, some members of Congress asked OCR to revisit its 1979 Policy Interpretation and consider weakening its enforcement standards, particularly the equal participation requirement. In response, OCR strongly affirmed its long-standing interpretation through a 1996 Policy Clarification, which explains how institutions can and must comply with the equal participation opportunities requirements. Courts have also rejected suits brought by male athletes claiming schools have discriminated against them by either cutting or capping men's teams, holding that Title IX does not require these actions but gives schools flexibility in structuring their athletics programs as long as they treat men and women equally. Nonetheless, the challenges continue. In January 2002 the National Wrestling Coaches Association and other Title IX opponents filed a federal lawsuit against the Department of Education challenging the Title IX regulations and policy guidance regarding athletics opportunities. The government's response fails to indicate whether it will vigorously defend the longstanding athletics policies.

Given the absence of equal opportunity after 30 years, OCR is not providing adequate leadership in enforcement efforts. In 2001 OCR initiated only two Title IX athletics reviews of institutions. Since Title IX's inception, not one institution has had its federal funding withdrawn because it is in violation of Title IX. OCR's lack of enforcement coupled with an increase in Title IX lawsuits suggests aggrieved parties are required to seek relief through the court system. Parties filing lawsuits incur considerable costs and risk retribution. In light of the number of schools still not in compliance, OCR needs to step up its enforcement activities.

Recommendations

- Congress should mandate data collection on the participation of high school students in physical education and high school athletics programs as part of the administration's proposal for the reauthorization of the Office for Educational Research and Improvement.
- The Department of Education should support the continuation of existing strong compliance standards and increase OCR enforcement of these standards.
- To encourage the filing of actionable complaints, OCR should develop a standard complaint form with a checklist of alleged Title IX violations.
- School athletic administrations should use the Equal Employment Opportunity Commission guidelines (www.eeoc.gov/regs/index.html) to make sure coaches of male and female sports receive equal treatment.

REFERENCES

Athletics
Acosta, R. V., and L. J. Carpenter, *Women in Intercollegiate Sport: A Longitudinal Study—Twenty-Five Year Update, 1977-2002.*
American Association of University Women Legal Advocacy Fund, *A License for Bias: Sex Discrimination, Schools, and Title IX* (2000).
Chronicle of Higher Education data available at http://chronicle.com/stats/gender equity/.
Medicine and Science in Sports and Exercise 28: 105-133 (1996).
National Collegiate Athletic Association, *1995-1996 Gender-Equity Report.*
National Collegiate Athletic Association, *1999-2000 Gender-Equity Report* (available at http://www.ncaa.org/).
National Collegiate Athletic Association, *Participation Statistics Report: 1982-2001* (available at http://www.ncaa.org/).
National Collegiate Athletic Association, *Sports and Recreation Programs of Universities and Colleges, 1957-82.*
National Federation of State High School Associations, *Athletics Participation Totals,* Fact Sheet (2001).
Title IX of the Education Amendments of 1972: A Policy Interpretation; Title IX and Intercollegiate Athletics, 44 Fed. Reg. 71,413 (1979).
Women's Sports Foundation, *Health Risks and the Teen Athlete* (2000).
Women's Sports Foundation, *Sport and Teen Pregnancy* (1998).
Wyshak, G., and R. E. Frisch, "Breast Cancer Among Former College Athletes Compared to Non-athletes: A 15-Year Followup," 82 *British Journal of Cancer* 726-731 (2000).

◀▓▶

A TRAIN WRECK CALLED TITLE TITLE IX

George F. Will

On this 30th anniversary of the enactment of Title IX, the law prohibiting sexual discrimination in education, consider this: has even more nonsense been written about Title IX than has been committed in its name?

Title IX, as adumbrated by ideology-besotted Education Department regulation writers has produced this lunacy:

Colleges have killed more than 400 men's athletic teams in order to produce precise proportionality between men's and women's enrollments and men's and women's rates of participation in athletics. And Title IX

From *Newsweek*, 27 May 2002. © 2002, The Washington Post Writers Group. Reprinted with permission.

has given rise to a huge "gender equity" industry of lawyers, sensitivity-trainers and consciousness-raisers.

The industry prefers the word "gender" to "sex" because "sex" suggests immutable differences, while "gender" suggests differences that are "socially constructed" and can be erased by sufficiently determined social engineers. The story of the policy train wreck that Title IX has become in the hands of such engineers, and of further misadventures that may be coming, is told in a timely book, "Tilting the Playing Field: Schools, Sports, Sex, and Title IX" by Jessica Gavora, a senior policy adviser at the Justice Department.

The U.S. soccer players who won the 1999 Women's World Cup were called "daughters of Title IX," and when the WNBA began playing in 1997, arenas displayed THANKS TITLE IX! banners. This propaganda pleased people who believe all progress comes from government. But throughout the 1970s, the years of the most rapid growth of participation of girls in high-school sports, which presaged the growth of women's college sports, Title IX was, Gavora says, unenforced and unenforceable because no athletics regulations had been written.

The first Title IX implementing regulations for athletics were written in 1979, and through most of the 1980s athletics were exempted from Title IX coverage. By which time, the women of the 1999 soccer triumph and of the WNBA were already excelling in their sports. By 1979, one in four high-school girls was participating. Since then, the Title IX "revolution" has made the number one in three. Clearly, autonomous cultural change, not Congress, produced the increase in female participation, which carried over into college athletics, where the real Title IX revolution has been perverse.

Gavora says the "ever-mutating" Title IX has been construed on the basis of a non sequitur: if there is unequal participation when there is discrimination, there must be discrimination when there is unequal participation. Title IX fanatics start from the dogma—they ignore all that pesky evidence about different male and female patterns of cognitive abilities, and brain structure and function—that men and women are identical in abilities and inclinations.

Confronted with evidence of what Gavora calls "the sportsmania gap"—men care more about playing sports—the fanatics say: This is the result of historical conditioning, which colleges must combat. Colleges must not just satisfy women's demands for sports, they must create demands. Until it is created, statistical proportionality often can be achieved only by cutting men's teams. Leo Kocher, University of Chicago wrestling coach, explains the Alice in Wonderland logic:

"Say there's a school that has equal numbers of boys and girls and it decides to offer 200 athletic opportunities. If they have 100 girls who want to play sports and they have 1,000 boys who want to play sports, the law says you must give 100 opportunities to those 100 girls and you must give 100 opportunities to those 1,000 boys. In the end, 100 percent of the girls are fully accommodated but only 10 percent of the boys are taken care of."

Between 1992 and 1997, 3.4 men's positions on college teams were cut for every woman's spot created. UCLA's swimming and diving team, which has produced winners of 22 Olympic medals? Gone. University of Miami's? Going. As are hundreds of men's gymnastics, wrestling, base-ball, track and other teams.

Under what Gavora calls Title IX's "affirmative androgyny," it is illegal to accept the fact that men and women have different interests, abilities and zeal regarding competition, or that young men have distinctive needs for hierarchy and organized team activities. As Gavora says, Title IX fem-inists seem to think "young girls aren't worthy of respect and admiration unless and until they act like young boys." And until women have their consciousnesses "raised" by social engineering, they need not be thought of as individuals, but merely as malleable raw material.

And now some Title IX imperialists want to extend it from locker rooms to classrooms: If participation in sports must mirror the sexual composition of the student body, why not participation in the engineering department? And why not in extracurricular activities other than sports—debating, orchestra, choir, cheerleading?

Title IX has become, Gavora says, the "codification of feminism," and "the story of this law is in many ways the story of the women's move-ment." A depressing story.

◀◆▶

IN THE SPIRIT OF TITLE IX

Emily Badger

Emily Pieplow spent every Saturday last fall on the sidelines of the Univer-sity of Maryland football games, she spent New Year's Eve at the Peach Bowl in Atlanta and late March at the NCAA basketball tournament in

From *The Washington Post*, 26 September 2003. © 2003, *The Washington Post*. Reprinted with permission.
Researcher Julie Tate contributed to this report.

San Antonio, cheering for the Terrapins in the one pair of Nike gym shoes that the athletic department gave her every year.

This year Pieplow won't get a free ticket or a ride in the back of the bus to any of those games. In fact, she won't lead a single "Go Terps!" cheer. But she'll travel to 10 cheerleading competitions and in exchange get her little piece of an athletic scholarship to help pay for her final semester of school.

Along with women's water polo, Maryland promoted part of its cheerleading squad to varsity status this year to create more scholarships and playing opportunities for female athletes on campus. The move was designed to keep Maryland in compliance with Title IX while returning some scholarships to the school's eight underfunded men's programs.

But Maryland is charting new territory with an activity that many— including the NCAA—aren't even sure is a sport. And whether it succeeds in silencing its critics may determine if Maryland has found a new model for approaching the contentious gender-equity legislation.

Cheerleading isn't recognized as a sport by the NCAA, and since 1975, the Department of Education's Office for Civil Rights, which enforces Title IX, has advised schools that "drill teams, cheerleaders and the like" cannot be considered athletic programs for the purpose of complying with Title IX.

Some colleges offer partial financial aid to their cheerleaders, but both Maryland and the OCR say this is the first instance of a school seeking to use cheerleading scholarships toward Title IX compliance. Susan Aspey, a spokeswoman for the Department of Education, said no other college has requested help from the OCR in applying any sport not recognized by the NCAA toward its compliance.

"Our expectation is that we're the first, but the first of many," said Michael Lipitz, Maryland's associate athletics director for administration. "At Maryland we always try to be on the cutting edge with what we're doing, and this is just another example of that. We try to think not only creatively, but innovatively."

Sincerity Questioned

Critics see Maryland's plan as a way to skirt the original intent of Title IX, and even Pieplow is under no illusions as to why Maryland recently offered to help foot her tuition bill.

"We knew that when we got this it was because the boys needed more scholarships as well," she said, sitting in the bleachers of Comcast Center's auxiliary gym during the team's fall tryouts. "But if they want to fund us, that's fantastic."

On a recent September evening, the gym was a jumble of red lipstick and black jogging shorts—the women who make up one half of this latest Title IX balancing act. The 1972 legislation mandated equal opportunity for women in all federally funded education programs, although it has become shorthand for gender equity in college sports.

Schools must offer women the same athletic opportunities as men in the form of scholarship dollars, pure participation numbers and program funding, relative to the makeup of the student-body enrollment.

According to Charles Wellford, the chairman of Maryland's Athletic Council, the Terrapins have been in compliance since the early '90s, in part at the expense of their men's programs. Now that it has evened the playing field, Maryland is in position to give back to the men by beefing up the women's rosters even more.

The plan is that by creating 12 cheerleading scholarships—four this year as the program is phased in over three seasons—and eight water polo scholarships, the men's programs will be given 20 as well, as the funding becomes available.

Maryland's plan would seem to satisfy everyone at a time when many are wailing that Title IX has cost men just as many opportunities as it has granted women.

But still some women's sports advocates are questioning the school's sincerity.

"With other conferences obviously not engaging in bona fide competition in cheerleading—that's not to say one school can't—but it seems like they're looking for the easiest way out, that their intent is to conform to the letter of the law, but not necessarily the spirit," said Donna Lopiano, the CEO of the Women's Sports Foundation. "If they had club teams that wanted varsity status, why go and manufacture one out of cheerleaders?"

Lipitz said water polo and cheerleading were the only teams that presented themselves to the Athletic Council this past year in a bid for promotion. But the women's ice hockey, crew and equestrian clubs have all sought the status in the past.

"When I read it the first time, I couldn't believe they were considering [cheerleading] as an actual sport," said Erika Hyrowski, the president of Maryland's ice hockey club team. "I thought that they could probably have picked another team. I always thought that ice hockey should become one. But our day will come."

Is It or Isn't It?

At the heart of the debate is a simple question that has flaunted easy answers: "What is a sport?"

It sounds like a silly barroom debate—is the answer measured in miles, minutes or pounds bench-pressed?—but for the purpose of Title IX, it is a serious exercise with scholarship dollars and lawyer hours in the balance.

The OCR has created a list of 10 criteria to evaluate whether an activity is a sport, questioning the participants' athletic ability, the length of the season and the governing body that determines competition rules.

One criterion reads as if it were drafted with an eyebrow raised specifically toward cheerleading: whether the primary purpose of the activity is athletic competition and not the support or promotion of other athletes.

That stipulation helps explain why the OCR sent a letter in September 1975 to the country's high school superintendents and college presidents informing them that cheerleading could not be considered "part of the institution's 'athletic programs' within the meaning of the [Title IX] regulation."

The OCR, however, evaluates each school on a case-by-case basis. It offers guidelines to aid schools in making their own decisions and then returns to the case only if a complaint is filed against the institution, meaning Maryland's decision will not be evaluated unless someone outside the school challenges it.

"There's been no change in policy," said Aspey, the Department of Education spokeswoman. "The University of Maryland requested assistance, and it's nothing more, nothing less."

The OCR's last communication with Maryland was in a May 8 letter to Director of Athletics Deborah Yow responding to the school's proposal. The letter suggested that the team would satisfy many of the factors but raised questions about one: Who would govern the practice and competition season?

Cheerleading has no such organization, and this has been Maryland's biggest stumbling block, one that the school's cheerleading coach Lura Fleece believed would prevent the squad from ever becoming varsity.

Competitions are produced by the National Cheerleaders Association, but even that organization considers itself more of a company—the competitions and camps are the products—than an oversight body.

The NCAA, on the other hand, provides instant legitimacy to a sport simply by recognizing it, as it does with bowling, equestrian and synchronized swimming.

Like the OCR, the NCAA offers no final pronouncements on what is a sport and who can play it but instead reacts to the concerns of individual institutions.

"Who's making the definition?" said Laronica Conway, a spokeswoman for the NCAA. "If you ask anybody is cheerleading a sport, you don't know if the answer is yes or no. It's not our decision. It's the membership's decision, and we're doing what the membership wants."

A Split Decision

In seeking to clearly differentiate competitive cheer from its sideline counterpart—a distinction likely necessary to satisfy the OCR—Maryland divided its cheerleading squad in two. Starting on Oct. 15 one will cheer at games, and the other will only attend competitions in which gymnastics are emphasized and cheering eliminated.

The latter will receive the scholarships, new uniforms and priority registration for classes; the former will continue riding around in the back of other teams' buses, with each woman carrying her one pair of shoes in tow.

Prior to this school year, Maryland offered each of its 30 cheerleaders the choice to join either the competitive cheer team or spirit squad, and the decision divided the group almost equally.

"They're splitting us only so they can convince whoever the head of Title IX is that cheerleading can be considered a sport," said senior Erin Valenti, who opted to stay with the spirit squad. "To make it a sport, you're taking out the whole reason to do cheering to begin with."

In the past, the single cheerleading unit went to football and basketball games while simultaneously preparing for one competition, the NCA's national championship. That model made sense at the time—it led to a championship in 1999—and the spirit squad will continue to follow it.

That group will send a small contingent to the championships this year to compete in the coed division, but unlike the competitive cheer team, the spirit squad will have to fundraise to cover much of the $17,000 cost.

The disparity between the two groups may be at its greatest then, but Fleece—who has been coaching Maryland's cheerleaders, and lobbying for varsity status, since 1991—maintains the perks of cheering at games nearly equal the more tangible benefits of varsity status.

"This is what I've been dying for so long, and now that I've got it, it's like wow, I'm not going to be at the football games anymore," said Fleece, who said she received an increase in salary to $22,000 annually to work only with the competitive team.

"It has been very hard for them. It's been hard to decide if I even want to coach. There's a part of you that says I love what goes along with the games, being a part of that win, the smell of the football field—I'm really going to miss those things."

Lopiano, on the other hand, looks at the situation and wonders if it wouldn't have made more sense to promote another intact club team from outside the department, like crew—as opposed to going through all the contortions and uncertainty of being "the first of many."

Fleece doesn't see the notion of cheerleaders as varsity athletes as such a stretch.

"People are going to follow suit," she said. "This will happen just because it makes sense."

◆❖◆

TITLE IX—THE GOOD NEWS, THE BAD NEWS

California Women's Law Center

Title IX of the Education Amendments of 1972 is a federal law prohibiting gender discrimination in any school receiving federal funds.[1] Although the law prohibits sex discrimination of any kind, it is best known for its role in promoting athletic opportunities for women. While female athletic programs have made great strides since 1972, there is still much to be done to level the playing fields. Here is the latest news on Title IX:

The Good News

In March 2005, the Supreme Court of the United States decided a landmark case involving Title IX, *Jackson v. Birmingham Board of Education*.[2] Roderick Jackson, head coach of the girls' basketball team at Ensley High School in Birmingham, Alabama, knew that it was unfair that the girls' basketball team had to practice in an old, unheated gymnasium, travel to games by carpool, and give up revenue from ticket sales while the boys' team practiced in a new, regulation sized gym, rode to games in school buses, and kept their ticket proceeds.[3] Jackson notified school administrators that this discrimination against girls violated Title IX.[4] Instead of responding to his concerns, the school board punished him by giving him negative work evaluations and eventually dismissing him from his position as head coach.[5] Jackson sued the Birmingham school board, alleging that the board had retaliated against him because he had complained about sex discrimination in the high school's athletic program, and that such retaliation violated Title IX. The Supreme Court agreed.

From the Web site of The California Women's Law Center, www.cslc.org, 2005.

- The court held that retaliation against a person for complaining about sex discrimination was a form of *intentional discrimination* encompassed by Title IX's private right of action.[6]
- The court interpreted Title IX broadly, to protect not only those who are personally the victims of gender bias (in this case, the girls' basketball team), but also those who seek to vindicate the rights of girls. Without this protection, Title IX would be meaningless because schools could retaliate against adults who stand up for minors' rights.

The Bad News

Although the Jackson case is a victory for Title IX, the Bush Administration has stealthily attempted to undermine more than thirty years of progress. In 2003, the Department of Education promised to "respect and enforce the long-standing policies mandating equal opportunity in athletics"[7] and not to make any changes to Title IX without opportunity for public comment.[8] However, in March 2005 the Department of Education issued a new "policy clarification" on its website, without any notice or public input. Previous Title IX policies established a three-part test for schools to prove they provided equal opportunities to play sports.[9] The new policy substantially modifies the third prong of the test, making it easier for schools to continue to offer fewer athletic opportunities for female athletes. Specifically, the "clarification" allows schools to determine female students' athletic interests and abilities solely from the results of an email survey.

- **Under the new policy, schools may show they are in "compliance" with the law based solely on the results of an email survey sent to female students.**[10] Previously, surveys were only one of the many factors in a school's determination of unmet athletic interest or ability; other factors included requests to add new teams, existence of club or intramural teams on campus, and looking to feeder schools or community athletic programs to determine what sports were being played in the area. Now, the government says a survey alone is enough.
- **A non-response may be counted as lack of interest.** Under the new policy, non-responses to the survey may be counted as lack of interest or ability to play sports. This method is flawed because the non-response rate is extremely high for email surveys; students may delete the survey, not realize its significance, or be too busy to respond.
- **The survey depends on girls' self-assessment of ability.** The survey requires girls to determine whether they have the ability to compete on a varsity team. Because many girls may significantly underestimate their

own ability, they may falsely indicate that they do not have the skill to compete on a varsity team. Furthermore, if the school does not currently offer a varsity team, girls may never have had the chance to compete and therefore do not know whether they have the requisite ability.

- **The new policy shifts the burden to female athletes to prove discrimination.** Under long-standing policies, schools have had the burden of proof to show that they are not in violation of Title IX, but the new law requires students to prove that the school does not provide equal opportunities. Furthermore, only "direct and very persuasive evidence of unmet interest to sustain a varsity team" can overcome a strong "presumption of compliance."[11]
- **Unless there are already enough girls to form a varsity team for a particular sport, a school is under no obligation to add any further female teams.** Essentially the new policy creates a huge loophole for schools to avoid the equal opportunities component of Title IX. Unless there are enough *enrolled* girls who are interested and able to form a varsity team, the school does not have to add any more female teams, ever. Since it is unlikely that girls who are skilled at a particular sport would attend a school that does not offer that sport, the policy allows the situation to remain at status quo or even move backwards if any further female teams are cut. Interest cannot be judged apart from opportunity, yet this new policy would discourage the creation of further opportunities.[12]

The NCAA Executive Committee has adopted a resolution that urges the U.S. Department of Education to rescind its March 17 "Additional Clarification" and has also urged NCAA members to follow the long-standing policies of Title IX instead of the new procedures set forth in the clarification.[13]

NOTES

1. 20 U.S.C. § et. seq.
2. *Jackson v. Birmingham Board of Education* __U.S.__, __ [125 S. Ct. 1497, 161 L. Ed.2d 361] (2005).
3. Lipka, *U.S. Supreme Court Hears Arguments on Interpretation of Title IX* (Dec. 1, 2004) The Chronicle for Higher Education.
4. *Jackson, supra.* 125 S. Ct. 1497, 1502.
5. *Id.*
6. *Id.*
7. National Women's Law Center, E-Update, "Bush Administration Covertly Attacks Title IX by Weakening Athletic Policies." 5 April 2005. 29 July 2005. http://www.nwlc.org/details.cfm?id=2211&section=infocenter.

8. Hosick, Michelle Brutlag. "Title IX Clarification Again Reveals Fault Line." *The NCAA News Online*. 11 April 2005. http://www2ncaa.org/media_and_events /association_news_online/2005/04_11_05/front_page_news/4208no1.html

9. United States Department of Education. "Clarification of Intercollegiate Athletics Policy Guidance: The Three-Part Test." 16 January 1996. 3 August 2005. http://www.ed.gov/about/offices/list/ocr/docs/clarific.html

10. United States Department of Education. "Additional Clarification of Inter-collegiate Athletics Policy: Three-Part Test—Part Three." 17 March 2005. 29 July 2005. http://www.ed.gov/about/offices/list/ocr/docs/title9guidanceadditional.html

11. *Id.*

12. National Women's Law Center, E-Update, "Bush Administration Covertly Attacks Title IX by Weakening Athletic Policies." 5 April 2005. 29 July 2005. http://www.nwlc.org/details.cfm?id=2211&section=infocenter.

13. Brown, Gary. T. "Executive Committee Urges Against Title IX Compli-ance Option." *The NCAA News*. 9 May 2005. 2 August 2005. http://www2ncaa .org/media_and_events/association_news/ncaa_news_online/2005/05_09_05/ association_wide/4210no8.html

INDEX